WHAT IF?

Writing Exercises
for Fiction Writers

Other Books by the Authors

ANNE BERNAYS

Novels
Professor Romeo
The Address Book

The School Book
Growing up Rich

The First to Know
Prudence, Indeed
The New York Ride
Short Pleasures
Nonfiction
Back Then; Two Lives in 1950's New York (with Justin Kaplan)
The Language of Names (with Justin Kaplan)

PAMELA PAINTER

Getting to Know the Weather
The Long and Short of It

WHAT IF?

Writing Exercises
for Fiction Writers

COLLEGE EDITION

SECOND EDITION

Anne Bernays
Nieman Foundation, Harvard University

Pamela Painter
Emerson College
Vermont College

PEARSON
Longman

New York San Francisco Boston
London Toronto Sydney Tokyo Singapore Madrid
Mexico City Munich Paris Cape Town Hong Kong Montreal

Vice President and Editor-in-Chief: Joe Terry
Managing Editor: Erika Berg
Associate Editor: Barbara Santoro
Senior Marketing Manager: Melanie Craig
Production Manager: Ellen MacElree
Project Coordination, Text Design, and Electronic Page Makeup: Electronic
Publishing Services Inc., NYC
Cover Design Manager: Nancy Donahy
Cover Designer: Keithley and Associates, Inc.
Manufacturing Buyer: Roy Pickering
Printer and Binder: R. R. Donnelly & Sons, Inc.
Cover Printer: Lehigh Press

For permission to use copyrighted material, grateful acknowledgment is made to
the copyright holders on pp. 485–486, which are hereby made part of this copyright page.

Library of Congress Cataloging-in-Publication Data

Bernays, Anne.
    What If? : writing exercises for fiction writers / Anne Bernays,
Pamela Painter.— College ed., 2nd ed.
        p. cm
Includes bibliographical references and index.
ISBN 0-321-10717-9
    1. English language—Rhetoric—Problems, exercises, etc. 2.
Fiction—Technique—Problems, exercises, etc. 3. Creative writing—Problems,
    exercises, etc.
I. Painter, Pamela. II. Title.

PE1413.B47 2004
808.3—dc22

                                                                2003053694

Please visit our website at http://www.ablongman.com

ISBN 0-321-10717-9

4 5 6 7 8 9 10—DOC—06 05

To Our Students

Contents

PART THREE
Characterization   59

PART FOUR
Perspective, Distance, and Point of View   87

PART FIVE
Dialogue 101

PART SIX
The Interior Landscape of
Your Characters 119

PART SEVEN
Plot 139

PART EIGHT
The Elements of Style 161

PART NINE
A Writer's Tools 173

PART TEN
Invention and Transformation 201

PART ELEVEN
Revision: Rewriting Is Writing   221

PART TWELVE
Games   243

PART SIXTEEN
A Collection of Short Stories   301

Preface

What If? was designed to introduce the beginning writer to an assortment of tools used by short-story writers and novelists by means of exercises that spotlight a particular skill, such as dialogue, characterization, and point of view. You can find many examples—in literary anecdotes, writers' letters, and journals—of ideas for novels that began as unacknowledged writing exercises. For instance, the germ of the novel *Frankenstein* found a fertile host in nineteen-year-old Mary Shelley, wife of the Romantic poet, Percy Bysshe Shelley, one night in 1816, when the Shelleys and several guests listened to ghost stories read aloud to them by Lord Byron. When he had finished reading, he suggested that each of those present write a gothic story of their own. Mary, who had never written a book, took the suggestion very seriously and began writing her classic novel, the uncanny *Frankenstein*. We trust that, by completing the exercises in this book, students will acquire the craft needed to write good strong fiction.

What If? was first published, in a shorter version, in 1990. Since then it has been enthusiastically received by teachers, students, and others interested in learning how to write better fiction because it puts the process of writing ahead of any theoretical, abstract, or emotional consideration. Students learn to write not by thinking about writing or negotiating with their feelings but by sitting down and actually writing.

Approach and Organization

Conventional wisdom urges beginning writers to get in touch with their feelings. We're convinced that these feelings are like children raised in the wild; our job, as writers, is to tame and guide them. Out of this conviction grew another: that structure helps, rather than hinders, those starting out in a craft new to them. Absolute freedom, as in "go home and write a story," leads the student to make the same mistakes over and over. By breaking down the elements needed to create effective fiction, we give students the opportunity to master one tool at a time. Thus was born the original *What If?*

The format of this edition stays the same. The book is organized around the following fourteen topics: Beginnings; Notebooks, Journals and Memory; Characterization; Perspective, Distance and Point of View; Dialogue; The Interior Landscape of Your Characters; Plot; The Elements of Style; A Writer's Tools; Invention and Transformation; Revision: Rewriting is Writing; Games; Learning from the Greats; and Sudden, Flash, and Microfiction: Writing the Short Short Story. *What If?* also includes a selection of short short stories and another of contemporary, longer stories.

As before, each section offers exercises related to that section's topic. In turn, each exercise consists of an introductory paragraph, instructions for completing the exercise, a paragraph explaining its objective, and, finally, in some, but not all cases, an example executed by a student. By breaking down the exercises into their constituent parts, we ensure that student and teacher understand both the rationale behind the task and the method by which to complete it.

Enduring Features

Like the previous edition, this edition includes numerous exercises by fiction writers who are also teachers; examples of student responses, many of which have gone on to be published stories; an anthology of short fiction so that students will not need a separate anthology; and inspiring quotations from writers' letters and journals, and interviews with writers.

Features New to This Edition

- A new section called "The Interior Landscape of Your Characters." This collection of exercises illustrates how students can use their characters' interior landscapes—as their characters hope, imagine, suspect, and explore their mixed motives—to enhance the stories and worlds they inhabit. It provides numerous examples from the masters of fiction and makes their techniques accessible to all writers of fiction.

- A new section called "Sudden, Flash, and Microfiction: Writing the Short Short Story." The short short story of under 1,000 words is more popular than ever and an increasing number of magazines are open to this form. This section grew out of a workshop we've developed over the past few years that focuses entirely on the short short story.

- Expanded sections: "Beginnings," "A Writer's Tools," and "Revision."

- New exercises from first-time contributors, among them Margot Livesey, Frederick Rieken, and Lise Haines.

- An expanded section of short short stories, including "The Custodian," a story by our then-student Brian Hinshaw, which won that year's The World's Best Short Short Story Contest.

- New stories have been added to the anthology section of the book, including the work of Ron Carlson, Margot Livesey, and Hester Kaplan.

Suggestions on How to Use *What If?*

There are many ways to use *What If?* Using the structure of our exercises as a model, some teachers ask their students to make up their own exercises, based on a writer's work. This assignment encourages students to read as a writer. Some teachers require students to turn in five first sentences each week throughout an entire semester. By the end of the term, students have fifty to seventy-five possible new stories to return to. One teacher has her students write a short paragraph every week in response to a quote from *What If?* that speaks to each of them as a writer, and to find personal signposts for their own writing process. But most of all we encourage students, teachers, and also writers working on their own to write in our book, to add their own exercises to it, and to move around at will—in short to find their own path through *What If?*

Acknowledgments

During our revisions, we have had help, encouragement, and advice from a lot of people. We want to thank all our students who have done the exercises and offered suggestions. We thank the students who contributed their examples—students from Arizona, California, Connecticut, Massachusetts, Michigan, Ohio, Tennessee, Utah, Vermont, Copenhagen, and Paris. They are too numerous to name here, but it has been gratifying to see many of these student examples enlarged to become published stories.

We want to thank the teachers of fiction who have used the trade edition of *What If?* and helped us to refine our work, and we particularly thank those who reviewed and made suggestions for this revised and expanded edition of *What If?*—Gail Galloway Adams, West Virginia University; Ann Kiernan Davis, Dalton College; Anne Greene, Wesleyan University; Karla Horner, Chattanooga State Technical Community College; Mona Houghton, California State University, Northridge; Jo-Ann Mapson, Orange Coast College; Mary O'Connor, South Dakota State University; Karen Piconi, Iowa State University; John Repp, Edinboro University of Pennsylvania; Chris Roberts, Clark State Community College; Ronald Spatz, University of Alaska Anchorage; and David Wojahn, Indiana University.

We are also especially grateful to those teachers who have contributed their own exercises to this book: Thomas Fox Averill, Tony Ardizzone, Douglas Bauer, François Camoin, Ron Carlson, Laurence Davies, George Garrett, Katherine Haake, Lise Haines, Christopher Keane, William Melvin Kelley, Thomas Kennedy, Rod Kessler, William Kittredge, Elizabeth Libbey, Margot Livesey, Alison Lurie, Robie Macauley, David Madden, Carol-Lynn Marrazzo, Alexandra Marshall, Christopher Noël, Joy Nolan, David Ray, Frederick Reiken, Ken Rivard, Lore Segal, Thalia Selz, Peter Jay Shippy, Sharon Sheehe Stark, James Thomas, and Melanie Rae Thon. We thank the students and former students who have granted us permission to print their entire stories in *What If?:* Derrick Ableman, Antonia Clark, Lee Harrington, Brian Hinshaw, Hester Kaplan, Molly Lanzarotta, Kim Leahy, Mariette Lippo, Matt Marinovich, Melissa McCracken, Sheehan McGuirk, Christine McDonnell, Tom McNeely, Josie Milliken, Judith Claire Mitchell, Terry Theumling, and Kate Wheeler.

We also thank the following people for their editorial and emotional support: Justin Kaplan, Robie Macauley, Hester Kaplan, Anne Brashler, Alice Hoffman, Laurence Davies, Rick Kot, Lisa Moore, Barbara Santoro, Tom Maeglin, Gina Maccoby, Roberta Pryor, Colleen Mohyde, and our colleagues at Emerson College, Vermont College, and the Nieman Foundation at Harvard University.

Anne Bernays

Pamela Painter

Introduction

ANNE BERNAYS: Good writers know how to do two very different things equally well—write like a writer and think like one.

Writing like a writer is about craft, and means gaining absolute control over your material and your tools. It means, for instance, knowing when to use dialogue and when to summarize discourse, learning how to use adjectives and adverbs—that is, sparingly—and concentrating on the specific rather than the vague and abstract. It means anchoring your story in a particular time and place; beginning writers often neglect to supply basic and crucial information: Who are these characters? Where are they? When is this story taking place?

Thinking like a writer is more complex, because it involves the unconscious. You can rely just so much on your five senses; after that you must call on curiosity, imagination, and skepticism—an open attitude not to be confused with cynicism. Skepticism obliges you to look beneath the obvious to get at the true meaning of, say, a smile, a crying jag, or a burst of anger. Things, in other words, are rarely what they seem. The writer must "think" his or her way past *seems* to *is*.

We have included exercises that ask you to assume the voice of the opposite gender, to search for subtext, and to supply several scenarios leading up to the same event—in other words, to enhance that intuitive quality of mind possessed by all good fiction writers.

PAMELA PAINTER: The exercises in *What If?* are also meant to set something in motion. Each exercise is designed to help you to think in new ways, to discover your own material, to enrich the texture and language of your fiction, and to move steadily toward final meaning. And coming full circle, to help you begin again. No matter how widely published a writer is, there is always the need to begin again.

We hope this book will be useful for people who have begun to publish and for those who have never written a word of fiction and are just now taking their first workshop. Our objectives for a workshop are that students will become familiar with the various techniques for writing fiction, the language used to talk about the creative writing process, and the tools to discuss and criticize each other's work in a supportive and constructive manner. When reading each other's work, it is important to make up your own mind about the effectiveness of a story's beginning, or whether there are missing scenes, or how clear the ending is, etc. The more you hone your critical skills in regard to the work of others, the more you will be able to revise your own work with a cool, discerning eye.

BERNAYS: "Can you *really* teach people how to write?" I have been asked this question more often than any other during almost two decades of teaching. Beneath the question is the implication that being able to write well is a divine gift—either you have it or you don't, so no amount of schooling is going to make a difference. Obviously I disagree. Besides, if you alter the question slightly and make it, "Can you really demystify the process of inventing stories and writing them down?" my answer is, "Absolutely."

This book separates and isolates the many elements of fiction, making them a manageable size and shape. Thus broken down and examined one by one, the components of a story or novel are rendered easier to master. This book should help you solve specific writing problems, like finding a good title, deciding on a point of view, discovering where and how to enter a story. Once you feel confident in your ability to exploit these particular skills, it's time to move on and fuse and combine what you have been learning step by step from *What If?*

At the very least you will feel more at ease with written prose and will experience the joy of saying exactly what you want to say the way you want to say it.

PAINTER: To "demystify the process" was the precise intention of *What If?* We didn't set out to write a book about how to write a short story—a write-by-numbers manual—because it can't be done. One of my students, Robert Solomon, spoke to this issue: "The book's value lies in helping me to understand fiction's components and their significance. . . . The exercises serve a preparatory function for when I begin my own true work, when I must deal with various choices and issues in accordance with my own particular vision and the demands it makes."

Writing exercises have long been a part of the learning process for new and established writers. A good many entries in the published notebooks of writers such as Chekhov, Flaubert, Hemingway, Fitzgerald, and Maugham, among others, are unlabeled writing exercises—exercises that grew out of analyzing or talking about what these authors were reading at the time. And many entries are tributes to those writers who had shown them by written example how something worked in fiction. Fitzgerald speaks of a "trick" he and Hemingway learned from Conrad (page 250). John Gardner says of writing that it is a matter of "catching on." In *The Art of Fiction,* he says of exercises, "When the beginning writer deals with some particular, small problem, such as a description of a setting, description of a character, or a brief dialogue that has some definite purpose, the quality of the work approaches the professional." And eventually, for writers who are persistent, the exercises you do here will strengthen your writing as a whole.

BERNAYS: It's possible for one person to be a marvelous storyteller—so long as he or she doesn't have to write it down. Another can form adequate sentences, even whole pages, and yet her story will just lie there, dead on the page.

The exercises in this book should help you sharpen your skills, both in the use of various tools and in the play of your mind. After completing these exercises the raconteur will be able to translate his story into writing and the competent but reticent writer will have learned to exploit her imagination.

You will notice that we make a point of distinguishing and segregating the elements of fiction rather than focusing on the novel and the short story as discrete entities. This is because we believe that the tools and processes are similar for both, as is the emphasis on precision, clarity, and freshness.

PAINTER: We also believe in practice and more practice. Just as every singer, visual artist, dancer, and composer must constantly practice his craft, the writer too must practice. Even though we use language every day in talking and in writing letters, notes to "fill up the gas tank and leave the keys in the pantry," memos for our jobs, or ad copy or newspaper articles, this does not mean that we can forego the practice required in other arts. Practice and persistence are also crucial to a writer. Learn to throw away the flawed sentence, to recast a weak character without feeling a sense of failure. You are growing by making these evaluations of your work. You are practicing the writer's craft. And when you give yourself to your work, immerse yourself in it, you will feel it giving something back to you as if it had a beneficent will and energy of its own.

BERNAYS: If the writer's engine is persistence, then the writer's fuel is the imagination; unlike real fuel, we have an endless supply of it and it costs nothing. Imagination is there in all of us, just waiting to be released.

PAINTER: I became a believer in exercises when I did one for the first time in a writing workshop taught by Tom Bracken, a cofounder of *StoryQuarterly.* Bracken gave us disparate elements to combine and weave into a story: banjo music, a penny, and an arresting photograph of two eyes peering through the grainy slats of a boarded-up window. Suddenly, for me, these things were transformed into a story about a lonely teenage girl sitting on an orange crate in a country store. She has a penny under her shoe—and knows that only the boy watching her through the boarded-up window has seen her slide it there. Even using the same details, we were amazed at how our stories were totally different from the others. Of course: because each individual imagination—and voice and vision—used these details in a unique, personal way.

Since that time, I have worked with all kinds of exercises. Some are created as a result of reading the work of another writer—I think I will always ask of a particularly effective beginning: What has been set in motion, and how? Some exercises simply appeared out of thin air: "What if?" And others grew out of class discussion, as when my student Ben Slomoff asked a question that suddenly illuminated everything. "You mean it's as if every story has its own history?" Yes, yes—that's it. And an exercise was born to convey just that to every class that followed his.

BERNAYS: A boring story is worse than one with rough edges. As a matter of course, I always start off the semester with: "I don't want to see any polite stories." In order to keep you from long-windedness, hot air, and the temptation to stray from the point, we have kept many of these exercises down to 550 words. When you don't have much space, you learn not to waste words. I've found that when a student goes much over the word limit his or her work tends to sound fuzzy and padded. Each exercise is meant, like a well-designed container, to hold the material destined for it.

Either Ms. Painter or I have assigned every one of these exercises to our students (some undergoing revision along the way) at such places as Harvard, Emerson College, Vermont College, Holy Cross, the University of Massachusetts, and numerous summer writing conferences and workshops.

PAINTER: I should say a word here about our "contributors." We've included a number of exercises from friends who are writers who also teach and use exercises in their classrooms. Exercises such as "Ways to Begin a Story," from Robie Macauley, and "Changing Your Life," from Joy Nolan, and other exercises from Richard Bausch, François Camoin, Ron Carlson, Elizabeth Libbey, William Kittredge, Alison Lurie, Sharon Sheehe Stark, James Thomas, etc. We are all writers who believe in the power of exercises to demystify writing and at the same time to instill an appreciation for the joy and magic of writing something well.

BERNAYS: The trade edition of *What If?* came out in 1990. Since then our students have published stories in numerous magazines and journals, and many students who contributed the "Student Examples" in the original edition of *What If?* went on to use that beginning or excerpt for stories they eventually published. Others have won competitions or awards. Still others have gone on to become teachers of writing, making up new exercises for their students. We hope you'll invent your own exercises for particular skills or techniques and paste them onto the white spaces in this book.

PAINTER: Yes, for example, Hemingway is known for his stripped-down dialogue, so you can imagine my delight when a student brought in a superb example of summarized dialogue from one of Hemingway's stories. I first pasted it into my book, and it is now printed in this edition.

BERNAYS: Unlike the trade edition, this textbook incorporates 28 stories by contemporary writers like Ron Carlson, Raymond Carver, Margot Livesey, and Alice Munro. They are here as examples of the art at its best and most powerful, and demonstrate a challenging diversity of subject matter, style, voice, and narrative technique.

The table of contents of this book is a more or less arbitrary arrangement of the elements and techniques of fiction. Some exercises are more difficult than others, but you won't find the easiest is the first in any one section, nor the hardest the last. Don't feel you have to do them in any particular order but complete those that seem to meet your immediate needs. We do suggest that you read the introductions to each section before starting to work.

PAINTER: We made several discoveries while shaping the table of contents. We found that both of us believed in "character-driven" stories as opposed to "plot-driven" stories when we realized that we'd left "plot" as a distinct category out of our first draft. And when asked to add a section on revision, we realized that many of the exercises scattered elsewhere in the book were actually exercises about revision.

We hope you will return again and again to various sections of *What If?*—combining and rearranging the exercises to lead you into your own limitless well of material, to explore that wonderful intersection of biography and fiction, and to realize your potential as a writer. We also hope that you will use the writers whose work we have cited in our examples as a sort of organic reading list. Buy their books and read them; highlight specific passages, write in the margins, type out their sentences. The work of the masters is for the writer the best education, the best inspiration of all.

PARIS REVIEW *INTERVIEWER: How do you describe the perfect state in which you can write from early morning into the afternoon?*

JOYCE CAROL OATES: One must be pitiless about this matter of "mood." In a sense, the writing will create the mood. If art is, as I believe it to be, a genuinely transcendental function—a means by which we rise out of limited, parochial states of mind—then it should not matter very much what states of mind or emotion we are in. Generally I've found this to be true: I have forced myself to begin writing when I've been utterly exhausted, when I've felt my soul as thin as a playing card, when nothing has seemed worth enduring for another five minutes...and somehow the activity of writing changes everything.

PART ONE

Beginnings

First sentences are doors to worlds.

—Ursula K. Le Guin

The biggest stumbling block to beginning a story is that new writers think they have to know where their story is going and how it will end—before they even begin. Not true. Flannery O'Connor says, "If you start with a real personality, a real character, then something is bound to happen; and you don't have to know what before you begin. In fact, it may be better if you don't know what before you begin. You ought to be able to discover something from your stories. If you don't, probably nobody else will."

Another stumbling block is that new writers—whether they're starting a story or a novel—take the word "beginning" too literally. They cast around for the "beginning" of a story, forgetting that the place where it all began probably showed no hint of the conflict, trouble, or complications to come.

A story can begin with dialogue, narrative summary, description, or whatever, but it must begin *in medias res*, in the middle of things. You must resist the temptation to give the reader too lengthy an explanation as to how things got to this point. Remember, you are trying to hook the reader's attention, to pull the reader into your story so that he won't wonder, *What's on television tonight?*

The following exercises are designed to encourage you to think about real characters who are involved in situations that are already under way—situations that are starting to unravel because of, or in spite of, the desires and actions of their beleaguered characters. Proceed sentence by sentence. Don't worry about middles or endings yet. Just give yourself over to setting stories in motion—you will soon know which stories capture your imagination and seem unstoppable, which stories demand to be finished. Until that time, begin and begin and begin.

Literature was not born the day when a boy crying "wolf, wolf"
came running out of the Neanderthal valley with a big gray
wolf at his heels: literature was born on the day when a boy
came crying "wolf, wolf" and there was no wolf behind him.
—VLADIMIR NABOKOV

1

First Sentences:
Beginning in the Middle

In a *Paris Review* interview, Angus Wilson says, "Plays and short stories are similar in that both start when all but the action is finished." This goes along with Horace's injunction to begin the story *in medias res*—in the middle of things.

Yet, beginners' stories often meander for three or four pages before the story begins to rear its head. One day, out of curiosity, we decided to examine the first lines of stories in big and little magazines, story collections, and anthologies. We discovered that many *first sentences* put the reader in the middle of things. That exploration became the basis for this first exercise.

All of the following examples are the first sentences of short stories. We suggest that you begin a list of first sentences from novels that illustrate *in medias res.*

The Exercise

Consider how many of the opening lines below pull you into the center of the story. What do you know about the story—situation, characters, geography, setting, class, education, potential conflict, etc.—from reading the titles and the following opening lines? What decisions has the author already made about point of view, distance, setting, tone, etc.? Notice how many of the titles are directly related to the first line of the story.

"The Lady with the Dog"   ANTON CHEKHOV
They were saying a new face had been seen on the esplanade: a lady with a pet dog.

"Lost"   ROBIE MACAULEY
Morning was desolate, with a wet wind blowing from the northeast, off the ocean, and the sky like a dirty sheet, but Uncle Gavin rose at six and made a pitcher of bloody marys, which put all the other adults, as one by one they rose from bed and wandered into the kitchen, in a philosophical mood; not so the children.

"Love is Not a Pie"   AMY BLOOM
In the middle of the eulogy at my mother's boring and heartbreaking
funeral, I began to think about calling off the wedding.

"What You Pawn I Will Redeem"   SHERMAN ALEXIE
One day you have a home and the next you don't, but I'm not going to tell
you my particular reasons for being homeless, because it's my secret story,
and Indians have to work hard to keep secrets from hungry white folks.

"Gesturing"   JOHN UPDIKE
She told him with a little gesture he had never seen her use before.

"Exchange Value"   CHARLES JOHNSON
Me and my brother Loftis came in by the old lady's window.

"Buried Lives"   BHARATI MUKHERJEE
One March midafternoon in Trincomalee, Sri Lanka, Mr. N.K.S. Venkate-
san, a forty-nine-year-old schoolteacher who should have been inside a St.
Joseph's Collegiate classroom explicating Arnold's "The Buried Life"
found himself instead at a barricaded intersection, axe in hand and shouting rude slogans at a truckload of soldiers.

"Everywhere My Father"   ANNE BRASHLER
Gramma said an eight-year-old girl shouldn't sleep with her own father,
but my father said that a rolled-up rug down the middle made a double
bed the same as two beds.

"The Remission"   MAVIS GALLANT
When it became clear that Alec Webb was far more ill than anyone had
cared to tell him, he tore up his English life and came down to die on
the Riviera.

"Medley"   TONI CADE BAMBARA
I could tell the minute I got in the door and dropped my bag, I wasn't
staying.

"A White Horse"   THOM JONES
Ad Magic had one of his epileptic premonitions a split second before the
collision, and managed to approximate a tuck-and-roll position just as
the truck smashed into the back of the mini tour bus.

"Funktionslust"   MELISSA PRITCHARD
Up and down the dull coastline of her desk, Amerylys ticked her fingernails, Minnie Mouse airbrushed onto each bismuth pink shield.

"A Girl Like Elsie"   KIRAN KAUR SAINI
I tell Mama I waitress in the Village so she don't have to cut me out of
her heart.

"Covering Home"   JOSEPH MAIOLO
Coach discovered Danny's arm when Danny's parents were splitting up at
the beginning of the season.

"Judgment"   KATE WHEELER
When Mayland Thompson dies he wants to be buried with the body of
a twelve-year-old girl.

"Werewolves in Their Youth"   MICHAEL CHABON
I had known him as a bulldozer, as a samurai, as an android programmed
to kill, as Plastic Man and Titanium Man and Matter-Eater Lad, as a Buick
Electra, as a Peterbilt truck, and even, for a week, as a Mackinac Bridge,
but it was as a werewolf that Timothy Stokes finally went too far.

"Sonny's Blues"   JAMES BALDWIN
I read about it in the paper, in the subway, on my way to work, I read it,
and I couldn't believe it, and I read it again.

"Nickel a Throw"   W. D. WETHERELL
These are the things Gooden sees from his perch eight feet above the
dunking tub at the Dixford Congregational Church's Charity Bazaar.

"The Water-Faucet Vision"   GISH JEN
To protect my sister Mona and me from the pains—or, as they pronounced
it, the "pins"—of life, my parents did their fighting in Shanghai dialect, which
we didn't understand; and when my father one day pitched a brass vase
through the kitchen window, my mother told us he had done it by accident.

"Freeze"   DAVID JAUSS
At first Freeze Harris thought Nam was a crazy nightmare, an upside-down
place where you were supposed to do everything that was forbidden back
in the world, but after a while it was the world that seemed unreal.

"Inventing the Abbots"   SUE MILLER
Lloyd Abbot wasn't the richest man in our town, but he had, in his
daughters, a vehicle for displaying his wealth that some of the richer men
didn't have.

"aw, babee, you so pretty"   NTOZAKE SHANGE
not only was she without a tan, but she held her purse close to her hip
like a new yorker or someone who rode the paris metro.

"Bigfoot Stole My Wife"   RON CARLSON
The problem is credibility.

"Demonology"   RICK MOODY
They came in twos and threes, dressed in the fashionable Disney costumes of the year, Lion King, Pocahontas, Beauty and the Beast, or in the

costumes of televised superheroes, protean, shape-shifting, thus arrayed, in twos and threes, complaining it was too hot with the mask on, *Hey, I'm really hot!,* lugging those orange plastic buckets, bartering, haggling with one another, *Gimme your Smarties,* please? as their parents tarried behind, grownups following after, grownups bantering about the schools, or about movies, about local sports, about their marriages, about the difficulties of long marriages, kids sprinting up the next driveway, kids decked out as demons or superheroes or dinosaurs or as advertisements of our multinational entertainment-providers, beating back the restless souls of the dead, in search of sweets.

"Sinbad's Head   PAUL WEST
In every library there is a book that kills.

"Rock Springs"   RICHARD FORD
Edna and I had started down from Kalispell, heading for Tampa-St. Pete where I still had some friends from the old glory days who wouldn't turn me in to the police.

"Saturnino el Magnifico"   ALBERTO ALVARO RIOS
The entire circus train fell in the manner of a child's toy into the ravine just outside of town, its cars folding up in the fall so that from a distance they looked like the rough-angled line of teeth on a saw.

"Last Request"   JILL McCORKLE
My mother's last words to me were, "No matter what happens, no matter how lousy your life becomes, stick to your marriage, stay there, and *make* it work."

"The Blue Men"   JOY WILLIAMS
Bomber Boyd, age thirteen, told his new acquaintances that summer that his father had been executed by the state of Florida for the murder of a Sheriff's deputy and his drug-sniffing German shepherd.

"Woman Hollering Creek"   SANDRA CISNEROS
The day Don Serafin gave Juan Pedro Martinez Sanchez permission to take Cleofilas Enriqueta DeLeon Hernandez as his bride, across her father's threshold, over several miles of dirt road and several miles of paved, over one border and beyond to a town *en el otro lado*—on the other side—already did he divine the morning his daughter would raise her hand over her eyes, look south, and dream of returning to the chores that never ended, six good-for-nothing brothers, and one old man's complaints.

"The Silver Bullet"   JAMES ALAN McPHERSON
When Willis Davis tried to join up with the Henry Street guys, they told him that first he had to knock over Slick's Bar and Grill to show them what kind of stuff he had.

"Wickedness"   RON HANSEN
At the end of the nineteenth century a girl from Delaware got on a milk train to Omaha and took a green wool seat in the second-class car.

"Jump-up Day"   BARBARA KINGSOLVER
Jericha believed herself already an orphan—her mother was in the ground
by the time she could walk on it—so the loss of her father when it came
was not an exceptional thing.

"Brownies"   Z Z PACKER
By the end of our first day at Camp Crescendo, the girls in my Brownie troop
had decided to kick the asses of each and every girl in Brownie Troop 909.

"The Handsomest Drowned Man in the World"
                                          GABRIEL GARCÍA MÁRQUEZ
The first children who saw the dark and slinky bulge approaching through
the sea let themselves think it was an enemy ship.

Now, write ten of your own opening lines for ten different stories. When
you read, look for opening lines that immediately pull you into the story.
And if you keep a journal or notebook, consider starting a new section
and adding one first sentence each day—for the rest of your life.

The Objective

To cultivate the habit of beginning your stories in the middle of things.
Because you are not obligated to finish these stories, this exercise lowers the
emotional stakes and helps to shake up and surprise the imagination.

Student Examples

She was trying to tell the joke right but it was his joke and she had to
keep checking with him.

—FRANCES LEFKOWITZ

I don't know who found me, or why I was left in a dumpster, but there was
one piece of lore about my rescue that was not forgotten and that they
made sure to hand down to me: written on my chest in navy blue Magic
Marker, my original owner had put the word "Gem," and that is my real
and only name.

—BRIGID CLARK

Jason Dyvik's heart, like all bartenders' hearts, was a needy and gluttonous
muscle.

—ERIC MECKLENBURG, "YELLOW SILK"

Nothing more to say—the storm, son walking further along the cliff than
dad, normal as you please, and the sea reached up and snicked him.

—PERRY ONION

By the time I was ten I had concluded that death was just a matter of moving furniture.

—AMANDA CLAIBORNE, "JEMMA"

My mother explained what sex was the day after I first had it.

—ROBERT SOLOMON

When the fog rolls into Portsmouth a peculiar, anonymous intimacy descends, taming difficult women and angry men.

—JIM MARSH

At Saint Boniface, on the first day of school, Mrs. Riordan found her fourth-grade class was nothing more than Sister Mary's third grade from the year before, with one exception: A quiet boy with eyes the color of water, who occupied the front row window seat the way a vacuum takes up space.

—BRIDGET MAZUR

Anecdotes don't make good stories. Generally I dig down underneath them so far that the story that finally comes out is not what people thought their anecdotes were about.
—ALICE MUNRO

2

The Story's History

In "First Sentences: Beginning in the Middle," we illustrate how most stories and novels begin in situation, in the middle of things. But, you might ask, what about the "beginning" of the story itself? Well, a few years ago, during the discussion of a flashback, a student said, "You mean it's as if every story has its own memory, its own history." Yes, that is exactly right. Each story has a history; all characters have pasts; the plots of most stories or novels are affected by something that happened before sentence one on the first page. Yet this history is woven so skillfully into the narrative of the story that most times we don't realize we are actually reading about the past of the story.

It might be helpful to think of the story as a straight line with the first sentence appearing somewhere beyond the start of the line—ideally near the middle. At some point, most stories or novels dip back into the past, to the beginning of the straight line and catch the reader up on the situation—how and why X has gotten himself into such a pickle with character Y. Tolstoy's novel *Anna Karenina* starts off with a household in a flutter over the husband's affair with the governess. Margaret Atwood's novel *Life Before Man* starts *after* someone has committed suicide. Yet these events foreshadow and affect the stories to come.

The forward movement of Flannery O'Connor's "A Good Man Is Hard to Find" is so compelling that it is easy to overlook how the grandmother's past informs the action of the story. And the past of Amy Hempel's story "Today Will Be a Quiet Day" is filled with ominous events: children's fights that led the father to say he wanted "Today will be a quiet day" written on his tombstone; the parents' divorce; the boy's friend who told the boy, "Never play Ping-Pong with a mental patient because it's all we do and we'll kill you" and who later committed suicide; the kids learning the guillotine joke; the dog that had to be put to sleep—all this before page one. That's good writing.

The Exercise

First, return to a favorite story and make a list of events that occurred before page one. Ask: How do these events affect the story after page one and move the story to resolution? Do this exercise with several stories and novels.

Then look at a draft of one of your own stories. Take notes on your story's history. Does your story have a past? A history all its own? Is the current situation grounded in the history of the story? You might discover that your stories have a case of amnesia—a lack of history that makes the current situation thin or lacking in alternatives and tension.

The Objective

To understand how stories and novels—and the characters in those stories and novels—all have a history that affects their forward movement and resolution.

This discovery of being bound to a particular society and a particular history, to particular sounds and a particular idiom, is for the writer the beginning of a recognition of himself as finite subject, limited, the beginning of a recognition that first puts his work in a real human perspective for him. It is a perspective which shows him his creaturehood.
—FLANNERY O'CONNOR

3

Ways to Begin a Story
from Robie Macauley

There are many different means a writer might use to begin a story, and the problem is to choose one that most appropriately raises the curtain on the narrative to follow. Ask yourself such questions as these: Do I want my story to open with the sound of voices as people discuss something about their lives? Or do I want to bring one important character forward into the descriptive spotlight and let the reader have a good, long look at her before action begins? Or do I want to begin with an activity—one person, or more than one, engaged in doing something that will be significant for the story to follow?

To judge these three possible openings, the writer might then ask questions of the unwritten story: Story, are you going to be about some involvement of people and their attitudes and opinions; are the ways they voice their thoughts going to be important? Or, Story, are you going to concern yourself with the traits, ideas, experiences, and emotions of one person who must seize the reader's imagination at once? Or are you going to be involved with an event—or events—in which the characters take part, and thus you want an opening that shows actions? Here are some of the possible ways of leading off.

With a Generalization

My mother believed you could be anything you wanted to be in America.

—AMY TAN, "TWO KINDS"

When people become characters, they cease to be regarded as human, they are something to be pointed out, like the orange tree that President Kruger planted, the statue in the park, or the filling station that once was the First Church hall.

—NADINE GORDIMER, "THE LAST KISS"

What really separates animal from man is the ability of one to accept the unexpected as the way things are, and the inability of the other to do anything but come up with theories.

—RITA DOUCETTE, "BULLET ADAGIO"

With a Description of a Person

He was lifting his knees high and putting his hand up, when I first saw him, as if crossing the road through that stinging rain, he were breaking through the bead curtain of a Pernambuco bar. I knew he was going to stop me.
—V. S. PRITCHETT, "THE SAILOR"

Besides the neutral expression that she wore when she was alone, Mrs. Freeman had two others, forward and reverse, that she used for all her human dealings.
—FLANNERY O'CONNOR, "GOOD COUNTRY PEOPLE"

With Narrative Summary

An unfortunate circumstance in my life has just recalled to mind a certain Dr. Crombie and the conversations I used to hold with him when I was young. He was the school doctor until the eccentricity of his ideas became generally known.
—GRAHAM GREENE, "DOCTOR CROMBIE"

The Jackman's marriage had been adulterous and violent, but in its last days they became a couple again, as they might have if one of them were slowly dying.
—ANDRE DUBUS, "THE WINTER FATHER"

Jim and Irene Westcott were the kind of people who seem to strike that satisfactory average of income, endeavor, and respectability that is reached by the statistical reports in college alumni bulletins.
—JOHN CHEEVER, "THE ENORMOUS RADIO"

With Dialogue

"Don't think about a cow," Matt Brinkley said.
—ANN BEATTIE, "IN THE WHITE NIGHT"

I'm afraid Walter Cronkite has had it, says Mom.
—JAYNE ANNE PHILLIPS, "HOME"

With Several Characters but No Dialogue

During the lunch hour, the male clerks usually went out, leaving myself and three girls behind. While they ate their sandwiches and drank their tea, they chattered away thirteen to the dozen. Half their conversation I didn't understand at all, and the other half bored me to tears.
—FRANK O'CONNOR, "MUSIC WHEN SOFT VOICES DIE"

With a Setting and Only One Character

After dinner, with its eight courses and endless conversation, Olga Mikhailovna, whose husband's birthday was being celebrated, went out into the garden. The obligation to smile and talk continuously, the stupidity of the servants, the clatter of dishes, the long intervals between courses, and the corset she had put on to conceal her pregnancy from her guests, had wearied her to the point of exhaustion.

—ANTON CHEKHOV, "THE BIRTHDAY PARTY"

With a Reminiscent Narrator

I was already formally engaged, as we used to say, to the girl I was going to marry.

—PETER TAYLOR, "THE OLD FOREST"

With a Child Narrator

Eugene Kessler was supposed to be my brother's best friend, but he and I actually had a lot more in common.

—ALICE HOFFMAN, "FLIGHT"

I don't have much work to do around the house like some girls.

—TONI CADE BAMBARA, "RAYMOND'S RUN"

When I was in the third grade I knew a boy who had to have fourteen shots in the stomach as the result of a squirrel bite.

—ELLEN GILCHRIST, "VICTORY OVER JAPAN"

By Establishing Point of View

First Person
Since Dr. Wayland was late and there were no recent newsmagazines in the waiting room, I turned to the other patient and said: "As a concerned person, and as your brother, I ask you, without meaning to offend, how did you get that scar on the side of your face?"

—JAMES ALAN MCPHERSON, "THE STORY OF A SCAR"

There was no exchange of body fluids on the first date, and that suited both of us just fine.

—T. CORAGHESSAN BOYLE, "MODERN LOVE"

I left India in 1964 with a certificate in commerce and the equivalent, in those days, of ten dollars to my name.

—JHUMPA LAHIRI, "THE THIRD AND FINAL CONTINENT"

I'm Push the bully, and what I hate are new kids and sissies, dumb kids and smart, rich kids, poor kids, kids who wear glasses, talk funny, show off, patrol boys and wise guys and kids who pass pencils and water the plants—and cripples, especially cripples.

—STANLEY ELKIN, "A POETICS FOR BULLIES"

Third Person
The August two-a-day practice sessions were sixty-seven days away, Coach calculated.

—MARY ROBISON, "COACH"

Climbing up with a handful of star decals to paste on the bathroom ceiling, Claire sees a suspect-looking shampoo bottle on the cluttered top shelf.

—Francine Prose, "Other Lives"

The Exercise

This one is in two parts. First experiment with different types of openings for different stories until you feel comfortable with the technique of each. Then see how many ways there are to open one particular story you have in mind. How does the story change when the opening changes from a generalization to a line of dialogue?

The Objective

To see how experimenting with several ways of opening your story can lead you to a better understanding of whose story it is, and what the focus of the story will be.

For me writing—the only possible writing—is just simply the conversion of nervous force into phrases.
—Joseph Conrad

4

Begin a Story with a "Given" First Line

from William Kittredge

It can be challenging to begin a story with a "given" first line—especially one that starts in the middle. You can use a line from a poem, make one up, or use the one in this exercise. Or ask a friend or fellow writer to give you a first line—this is what Doris Lessing's characters do in her novel *The Golden Notebook*. When we come to the place in the novel where Saul gives Anna the first line "The two women were alone in the London flat," we realize that Anna did write her book, and that *The Golden Notebook,* which begins with that exact line, is Anna's novel.

The Exercise

Begin a story with this line: Where were you last night?

The Objective

The objective is to once more start the story *in medias res*—in the middle of things. Notice how this question begins in the middle of a situation. For example, "last night," the subject of the question, has already happened. If one character asks another this question there are already two people "on stage." And the question will probably produce a conflict. But don't get hung up on making it a line of dialogue—it can be used many different ways.

Student Examples

Where were you last night was the one thing she couldn't ask him anymore, so they talked about the death of Huey Newton. They were in the kitchen having breakfast, Marcy was eating Special K and Tom, Shredded Wheat. As usual, he had bought two copies of the *Times* and they each came upon the story at the same time. Twenty-three years had gone by since they had met and fallen in love during the height of the demonstrations at Berkeley and now Huey Newton was as dead as their marriage.

—LYNDA STURNER

21

"Where were you last night?" Tony asked, wiping down the bar in front of me with a gray towel. He doesn't look me in the eye.

"Vegas," I said, fingering an earring, noticing how bald he is, how short. "Where do you think?" Of course, I didn't really spend the night in Vegas or in any place worth mentioning, but when you're forty-one and planted on a bar stool, it's nice to think you still have possibilities, even if you can only reach them in your head.

—BRIDGET MAZUR

Here are several other "given" first lines:

I met him on the stairs.

(Note how many different ways the characters could be moving: both up; both down; or passing each other.)

The neighbors were at it again.

"One more thing before you go."

This is a story I've been avoiding for a long time:

If I went there a second time . . .

(This is the first line of Enid Shomer's poem "First Sunset at Outler's Ranch" from her book, *Stalking the Florida Panther*.)

Sharon Sheehe Stark gives her students the following prompts:

I haven't been the same since . . .

See that house over there? Let me tell you...

I remember a sentence I opened one story with, to show you how bad I was: "Monsieur Boule inserted a delicate dagger in Mademoiselle's left side and departed with a poised immediacy." I like to think I didn't take myself seriously then, but I did.
—EUDORA WELTY

5

Person, Place, and Song

from Ron Carlson

At the outset of any writing class I always give an assignment. I don't want to see the stories that these writers have in their files—yet. I also don't want to start a class with them talking; they are without exception excellent talkers. They are experts. I want to use that expertise later. Right off, I want them to write. No fears, tears, theory, or clashing agendas. Just a little writing. I want them to take the risk of writing something new—*all of them on an equal footing.*

The assignments I've been making have changed several times, but they're all essentially *prompts,* specific ways of starting. The most recent I simply call Person, Place, and Song. It comes from the second paragraph of Leonard Michaels' story "Viva La Tropicana," which appeared in *The Best American Short Stories 1991.* The paragraph starts:

> The first time I heard mambo, I was in a Chevy Bel Aire, driving from Manhattan to Brooklyn with Zev's son, my cousin Chester. We'd just graduated from high school and were going to a party. To save me the subway ride, Chester came to pick me up. He wore alligator shoes, like Zeb's dancing shoes, and a chain bracelet of heavy silver, with a name tag, on his left wrist. It was a high school fashion, like penny loafers and bobby socks. Chester had spent time in Cuba, but mainly he lived with his mother in Brooklyn and hardly ever saw his father. Uncle Zev, I believe, didn't love Chester too much, or not enough. This accounts for an eccentric showy element in his personality, which distinguished him in high school as a charming ass, irresponsible to girls, obnoxious to boys. As we drove, he flicked on the radio. The DJ, Symphony Sid, began talking to us, his voice full of knowing, in the manner of New York. He said we could catch Tito Puente this Wednesday at the Palladium, home of Latin music, 53rd and Broadway. Then Symphony Sid played a tune by Puente called "Ran Kan Kan."

This paragraph is rich with the specific data that offers clues and sets the tone for the rest of the piece. I could talk about it—all the work it does—for half an hour.

The Exercise

Write a short piece of fiction—about a thousand words. It may be a complete short story and it may be the beginning of a longer piece. But it starts as follows:

The first time I (or Name) heard SPECIFIC SONG TITLE by SPECIFIC ARTIST OR GROUP, I (or Name) was down/up/over at PLACE and we were doing ACTION.

The Objective

To begin a story simply and specifically. Nothing grand, just close evidence that may lead somewhere. As I have said somewhere else, at greater length: solve your problems through physical detail.

Student Examples

The first time I heard the song, "Let it Be," was on Route 80 near Wheaton, Pennsylvania, three days after my divorce. I was coming cross country in a Pinto wagon with my ex-husband. It was hour number five.

I was leaving New York to be poet-in-residence at Grailville, a women's retreat in Loveland, Ohio. James was moving back to our old hometown in Findlay, to take over his father's medical practice. Pretty separate paths, huh? They should have been separate journeys too, but God must have been bored one day and needed to see a good show, because 48 hours after I said a final goodbye to James, I was saying hello to him on the phone.

He called in a panic. His car had been stolen, his job started in two days, he didn't have any money for a plane ticket because he'd spent it on legal fees for the divorce I had wanted, and he was desperate. Would I please take him with me to Ohio.

I liked the desperate part, so I said yes.

—KRISTINA M. ONDER

6

Stirring Up a Fiction Stew

from Sharon Sheehe Stark

When you don't have a story pushing to be written, it is still a good idea to write anyway, to exercise language and story. This is especially true for beginning writers who sometimes have to be shown they can "wing it" without knowing exactly where they are going.

The Exercise

Begin a story from random elements such as two characters, a place, two objects, an adjective, and an abstract word. If you are not in a class, give this list to someone and have them provide you with the words so you will be surprised by them. If you are in a class, have the class make up a random list. Then everyone must use these elements in the first two pages of a story.

The Objective

To exercise your imagination, to prove to yourself that all you need is a trigger to get you started writing. And if you care about the story you start, the finish will take care of itself.

Student Example

Below are the words students chose in a workshop and one student's story written from this list.

pyromaniac	skycap
all-night diner	tuna fish
bowling pin	gardenia
polyester	infinity

Next to the airport: Dante's Diner, open 24 hours, red neon sign blinking on and off. Red's a cheerful color.

I been night cook here at Dante's for twenty years. Dante, he died last March. House burned down; some pyromaniac lit it. Hell of a thing. Dante's kid owns the place now. Never seen her. But her lawyer came by yesterday—skinny guy, in one of those crummy polyester suits. Asking a lot of questions, sticking his pointy nose into everything. Told me she wanted to sell.

What does she care? So I'm out of a job—so what's it to her? They'll turn the goddamn place into a Lum's or a Hardee's or something. Progress. Premade frozen burgers—premeasured milk shake mix—packaged pie. Progress? Hey, this is a diner—a *diner,* with diner food: hot beef sandwiches, real mashed potatoes, rice pudding, tuna on rye with potato chips and a pickle, and my lemon meringue pie.

I like the people who come in here: skycaps, tourists, kids on dates, hippies, businessmen. Last night a bowling league came in from a tournament over at Airport Lanes. All of them in satin jackets with big bowling pins embroidered on the backs, eating and talking and looking at a couple of pretty girls in the back booth, girls with long hair, shiny pink lips and perfume like gardenias.

I like night work. It's my time. The nights stretch on forever—what's that word? Infinity. The dark outside, all blue, the red neon blinking. Jukebox going. The way I slap my spatula down on the grill, the way I flip eggs over. The way people look when they come in—hungry, tired, and when they leave, they look fed. I get so I'm almost sorry when it's morning. Especially now with that lawyer ruining my day.

—GINA LOGAN

7

What Word Comes Next?

from François Camoin

Some narratives are driven by plot, by the idea of what happens next. We visualize a character, a scene, and ask ourselves what happens next. Other narratives are driven by language, by the writer's search for the next word, the next phrase, often without conscious attention to narrative logic. This sort of writing is analogous to a sculptor following the grain of wood with her chisel, seeking what *it* wants to say, and trusting that something recognizable and perhaps interesting will emerge. Instead of asking ourselves what happens next, a writer using this method will ask *what word comes next.* Instead of choosing words to describe something already present in the mind, the writer will let the grain of the language move the narrative along.

The Exercise

Write the first sentence of a narrative. Any sentence will do. Then take two or three words from that first sentence and use them again in the second sentence. Take two or three words from those first two sentences and use them in the third sentence. Go on until the story begins to acquire a logic of its own.

The Objective

To learn to be surprised by what a story has to say, instead of deciding in advance what it must say. To get in touch with that part of ourselves that isn't always immediately available to the conscious mind. Focusing on technique, on a trick, will often allow us to write things we wouldn't otherwise write, things that frighten or disturb us.

Examples

First Sentence
Frost's lover has a job at the University Hospital; for fifty dollars an hour Cynthia lets medical students practice pelvic examinations on the body which, she tells Frost, she detaches herself from for just as long as it takes the young men to get done with their little explorations.

Second Sentence

She learned the technique of detaching herself from her body, of temporarily allowing herself to float above herself, of not being there except in spirit while she earns her fifty dollars, from Mme. Seroka, her astral flight instructor at the YWCA.

Third Sentence

Astral flight is a science and not an art, she explains to Frost; you push from the inside, against the soles of your feet, yourself sliding out of yourself through that little spiritual hole behind your own left ear.

Fourth Sentence

It's a science, because you've learned how you can do it every time, not like making love, which you can only do when you're in the mood, and which, she says, touching the most tender part of Frost, is not all that spiritual, though it is something a person can enjoy.

One of the most difficult things is the first paragraph. I have spent many months on a first paragraph and once I get it, the rest just comes out very easily. In the first paragraph you solve most of the problems with your book. The theme is defined, the style, the tone. At least in my case, the first paragraph is a kind of sample of what the rest of the book is going to be. That's why writing a book of short stories is much more difficult than writing a novel. Every time you write a short story, you have to begin all over again.

—Gabriel García Márquez

8

Ice Breaker

from Lise Haines

There's a great story by Charles Baxter, called "Snow." A teenage boy, his girlfriend, and his kid brother walk across frozen Five Oaks Lake in mid-winter. They've heard that a car went under a pressure ridge in the lake. What they find is a fully submerged, 2-door Impala, hardened in place like an object in amber. In this work of fiction, Baxter does a handsome job of rendering details from the era of his own adolescence. I highly recommend that Baxter's story "Snow" be assigned and discussed the week before this exercise is explored. Special attention can be given to the use of metaphor and symbol, which is so rich in this story.

The Exercise

Ask students to call out single words that remind them of the 1980s—words which relate to styles, social behavior, foods, music, books, movies, etc. (I used the 1980s since my students were fairly young and all of them had direct memories from this time. A volunteer from the class and I stood at the blackboard and had to write fast to keep up.) Once the board is filled, ask students to silently write down five words in their notebooks not listed on the board, words that have personal meaning to them from the 1980s, which could include names of people they knew, of course. Next, each student should choose five words from the board and add these to the five words they already have on their personal list. The final assignment is to write a two-page story using all ten of their words.

The Objective

To give students access to their frozen memories individually as well as collectively. This exercise stimulates stories, lends a confidence to the process of tapping into memory, encourages students to look at their memories in a metaphorical way, and creates a group dynamic that is playful and cooperative.

It is fun to see where objects overlap and yet it is a reminder of the fact that each of us has individual stories to tell.

9

The Newspaper Muse:
Ann Landers and the
National Enquirer

In her essay, "The Nature of Short Fiction; or, the Nature of My Short Fiction," Joyce Carol Oates says that she is "greatly interested in the newspapers and in Ann Landers' columns and in *True Confessions* and in the anecdotes told under the guise of 'gossip.' Amazing revelations!" She says she has written a great number of stories based on "the barest newspaper accounts...it is the very skeletal nature of the newspaper, I think, that attracts me to it, the need it inspires in me to give flesh to such neatly and thinly-told tales, to resurrect this event which has already become history and will never be understood unless it is re-lived, re-dramatized." One student, Tom McNeely, brought in a newspaper clipping and a very strong story beginning, and I said, "Keep going." His complete story "Sheep," which was eventually printed in *The Atlantic Monthly*, appears on page 410.

The Exercise

Collect Ann Landers columns, gossip columns, and stories from *Weekly World News* or *True Confessions* that seem to you to form—either partially or wholly—the basis for a story. Often, these newspaper accounts will be the "end" of the story and you will have to fill in the events leading up to the more dramatic event that made the news that day. Or perhaps the story leads you to ask what is going to happen to that person now.

Clip and save four or five items. Outline a story based on one of them, indicating where the story begins, who the main characters are, what the general tone (that is, the emotional timbre of the work) will be, and from whose point of view you elect to tell the story. These articles can be used for shorter, more focused exercises. For example, describe the car of the person in the article, or the contents of his wallet. Or have the person from the article write three letters.

The Objective

The objective is threefold. One is to look for an article that triggers your imagination and to understand how, when you dramatize the events, the story then becomes *your* story. The second is to increase the beginning writer's awareness of the stories all around us. And third to practice deciding how and where to enter a story and where to leave off.

Student Example

One writer used an article from *Weekly World News* about a Japanese moving company that specializes in moving people at "odd times of the day." The service was popular with debtors avoiding creditors and with girlfriends leaving boyfriends. In one case, a woman took her boyfriend to dinner, while the moving company removed her possessions from their apartment.

When I went for the job interview, I found the owner in a garage-office, seated at his desk, which wobbled on three legs and a stack of cinder blocks. He was writing in a ledger and stuffing a jelly doughnut into his mouth between calculations.

I cleared my throat and he turned to boom a "Hi there, kid" at me, then wiped his fingers on his shirt and shook my hand. We sat down on the ripped red vinyl of an old car seat and Jake lit up a Marlboro. In between drags, he tried to explain how he'd founded the business, but he kept getting interrupted by calls from potential customers. He'd put each caller on hold, telling them he'd have to check with the personnel department or ask the mechanics about the truck fleet. When I asked what all that was about, he said he wanted people to think his company was some kind of big deal outfit.

"Impresses the hell out of most of them." He glanced out the door at the company truck—the "fleet" that he'd mentioned on the phone—parked by the curb. "There's another gag I pull. Y'know what people always ask me?" When I shrugged he said, "They ask, 'Where's Darkness Falls?'"

I wanted the job so I humored him. "So what do you say?"

I tell them it's just south of Northboro. Sometimes I say just east of Westboro. I want them to think that we're a really mysterious outfit."

"What's so mysterious about moving stuff?"

His cigarette ashes fluttered down on my jeans as he leaned toward me. "It's not that simple, Kerry. Let's say you want to be moved with no questions asked, any time of night. Maybe your business wasn't cutting the mustard, so you figure you better move your equipment before the bank moves it out for you. Who do you call? The Darkness Falls Moving Company," he said, grinning. "When you want to make a sudden move, we're the move to make."

Everyone else who interviewed me had given me the look of death when I said I had to quit in September, but Jake just shrugged and said he could use me about four nights a week. "Be prepared to work anytime between dusk and dawn," he said. "I'm the Robin Hood of the moving business."

—Scott Weighart, "The Darkness Falls Moving Company"

10

Pairs of Sentences

from Alexandra Marshall

Sometimes less is more, and sometimes it is just less. But no matter what, writing with a strict economy of purpose can force useful answers to fundamental questions. Even from one sentence you can learn both who the character is and what the story is about. To provide focus, it is helpful to begin by writing sentences in arbitrary pairs with established parameters.

The Exercise

Write the first sentence of a story about a birth. Now write the first sentence about a death. Try other pairs, such as falling in love and filing for divorce. Try pairs that are not in opposition, such as spring and summer. Then invent your own pairs.

The Objective

To write a succinct beginning sentence: one that signals the essential "who" and "what" to come.

Student Example

A Birth and a Death
1. I won't be doing any bonding with either one of them for quite a while; I knew I shouldn't have gone into the delivery room.
2. "He doesn't look peaceful or tortured or saintly, and no, he doesn't look 'just like himself'; he looks like some dead thing that I never knew, and I don't know why I'm here."

Falling in Love and Filing for Divorce
1. It could have happened to him a dozen times before and with women prettier, smarter, richer, funnier, sexier, even nicer, but it didn't, did it?
2. I don't want to throw her out the window or cheat her out of the money or tell her what a shit she is; I want to thank her for every goddamn day of it.

—CHRISTOPHER LYNCH

11

Taking Risks

One of the great pleasures of writing fiction is letting your imagination and fantasies take off anywhere they want to go. Most people feel guilty when they think of doing something awful to someone they dislike; writers can invent a story and in it fling a hated character from a moving car or have him go blind. Another fantasy you can play out is doing something the very idea of which terrifies you—like parachuting from a plane or sailing across the ocean solo. As a fiction writer you're at a serious disadvantage if you can't write about an experience you're unlikely ever to know firsthand. This is not as easy as it seems, because you must sound not only plausible diving to the depths of the Aegean, you've also got to know what you're talking about—all those details about the scuba gear have to sound absolutely authentic. This is why a lot of novelists spend so much time in libraries—they're making sure they get it right.

The Exercise

Using the first person, describe an event or action you are fairly sure you will never experience firsthand. Be very specific—the more details you incorporate the more likely it is that your reader will believe you. Include your feelings and reactions.

The Objective

"Write what you know" is all very well but it certainly does restrict most of us within narrow confines. You must also be able to write what you don't know, but can imagine. This is what your imagination is for. Let it fly.

Student Example

I've been a missing person for ten days and the novelty is starting to wear off. My girlfriend's losing her patience, and my wife is on the eleven o'clock news.

"How can you just lie there and watch her cry like that?" Maura says.

"I left a note for Chrissakes. She's trying to humiliate me," I say. Every day, all over America, guys leave their wives and nothing happens. Mine calls the FBI and reports me as missing.

Joe Shortsleeve, WBZ-TV's intrepid reporter, is asking my wife if I was involved in any illegal activities.

"No," she says gloomily. Her eyes are puffy. "He's the most normal person in the world."

"You can have him back," Maura shouts at the television. She's lying next to me like a big white corpse. Naked. I wish she'd cover herself after sex. I already feel like I know her too well. She's furious that I'm getting all this attention. The camera is following a helicopter as it circles above some wooded area. I can't figure out why they're searching for me there. I hate forests.

Tomorrow I'll go home and become the biggest joke in Massachusetts.

I tell Maura I'm going to take a walk, and I put on my Celtics cap. It's one of the items I was wearing when my wife last saw me. I might as well be conspicuous, now that things have been decided.

My first stop is the Store 24, where I buy the *Boston Herald* and a scratch ticket. I let the little Pakistani guy behind the counter get a real good look at me. He points to something on the front page and smiles. That's it, I say to myself, it's all over.

"Beel Clin-Ton," he says and shakes his head in mock disgust.

I wind up at Mister Donut. There's a cute girl there who works the late shift. It's starting to snow and we're talking about skiing. She tells me she gets homesick every time it snows because she grew up in Vermont. I sip my coffee but save my jelly stick for later. I don't like eating donuts in front of good-looking women because crumbs get stuck in my moustache. I watch her as she mops between the tables. I can't be sure if she likes me or she's just a nice person, but I have the secret that might tip the scales. I want to confess.

"I'm a missing person," I say as she squeezes the water into a grimy yellow bucket on wheels.

"Listen," she says. "I know the feeling."

—MATT MARINOVICH

PART TWO

Notebooks, Journals, and Memory

In a cartoon by William Hamilton, a harassed-looking young woman is seated at a desk, holding several manuscript pages. Her typewriter has been pushed to one side, as she says into the phone, "Frances, can I get back to you? Gordon ran away with the babysitter and I'm trying to see if there's a short story in it."

Of course there's a story in it, probably more than one, but now might be a little soon to begin writing about Gordon's flight. Hamilton's young woman needs to take to heart what Wordsworth said about poetry, that it is "emotion recollected in tranquillity."

What this young woman should do, since she is determined to find a story, is jot down in a notebook or journal a few details that she doesn't want to lose. Perhaps Gordon left an odd note? Or one of the children asked if Gordon, who had recently lost his Wall Street job, was going to start a babysitting business. Or perhaps the harassed wife discovered she was secretly delighted that Gordon was gone?

When she returns to this material and her notes at a later time, she might want to tell the story from Gordon's point of view—a story about a man who leaves his wife because he knows that she will someday leave him. Or from the babysitter's point of view—a story about a babysitter who feels sorry for a husband whose wife begins typing the minute he gets home from work.

The point is, as writers we lead double lives. We live in the world as the people we are. But we also live in the world as writer/observers ready to see a story anywhere, to note a detail that simply couldn't be made up, to record an overheard line of dialogue, to borrow the stories of family and friends, to explore our enemies' points of view, and to sift through memory—did we really have a happy childhood? A writer's notebooks and journals are a testimony to this double life. As Socrates said, "The unexamined life is not worth living." For an illuminating essay on the intersection of autobiography and fiction, rendered with insight and humor, read Stephen Dunn's "Truth: A Memoir," from *Walking Light.* •

Journals and notebooks function in several ways. One writer may use them as a repository for the raw material for fiction that he will turn to for inspiration. Another writer may keep a notebook but never look at what he writes again—for him, the act of selecting and writing something down was the valuable exercise, keeping his writer's ear and eye in shape. And yet another writer may use her journal for deepening stories she's already written.

Alexandra Johnson has written eloquently on the practicality and art of keeping a journal in her book *Leaving a Trace: The Art of Transforming a Life into Stories.* Johnson talks of her own experience in keeping a journal, how a museum stub "sparked a sketch about a summer in Italy when I first met someone who lent me an apartment." She identifies patterns hidden in a journal's pages, speaks to the freedom that might come from sharing a journal with a friend or a writing group, and provides exercises for beginning a journal or using the material that has been accumulating unexamined, unused, in your journal for years. In the final pages, Johnson pays tribute to her grandmother who taught her "how to make connections. How to listen. How to observe the world. The real gift she was giving me, though, was the legacy of the imagination, of knowing how to transform stubborn facts into stories, how to recognize that the story not told is often the most interesting one. How every story—and life—is of value." *Leaving a Trace* is a book for every writer's shelf.

Our own exercises are designed to show you some of the possibilities and rewards of keeping a journal or notebook. It is the perfect place to jot down that odd name you found on a program—"Buck Gash"—a name you'll never legally be able to use, but one you want to remember. Or to make a list of all the places you've ever lived. Or to write a journal entry from the point of view of the babysitter titled "Why I'm running away tomorrow with Mr. Farnham (I call him 'Gordie')."

Fiction gives us a second chance that life denies us.
—PAUL THEROUX

12

Who Are You?
Somebody!

Richard Hugo, in an essay titled "In Defense of Creative Writing Classes," recalls the most important lesson he ever learned, "perhaps the most important lesson one can teach. You are someone and you have a right to your life." He decries the way the world tells us in so many ways that "individual differences do not exist" and that "our lives are unimportant." He says, "A creative writing class may be one of the last places you can go where your life still matters." The same thing is true for the writer who sits alone at her desk.

The Exercise

Buy a notebook to use for just this one exercise. Then, on a regular basis, perhaps at the beginning of your writing time or before you go to bed, write for ten to twenty minutes addressing each of the following subjects:

- List in detail all the places you have lived—one place per page. (This is a good way to begin because it gives the entire notebook a concrete grounding in time and place.) You might even want to get very specific, say, by recounting all the kitchens, or bedrooms.

- Next, recall if you were happy or unhappy in those places.

- Consider your parents' relationship, from their point of view.

- List important family members: brothers and sisters, grandparents, uncles and aunts, cousins. What were the dynamics of your nuclear family, your extended family? (Some of these subjects may take several twenty-minute sessions. Leave space for unfinished business.)

- List smells—indoor and outdoor—and the memories they conjure up.

- How do your clothes define you—or not?

- Do you have any recurring dreams or nightmares? Start a section for dreams.

- Ask yourself, What did I care about when I was five, ten, fifteen, twenty, twenty-five, thirty, etc.? What do I care about now?

- Did anyone ever give you advice that changed your life?
- What are the forks in your road? Imagine the road not taken.
- What is your five-year plan?

These are the kinds of questions that help you define who you are. Now make up questions of your own to answer in your notebook. In fact, making up questions to bring back the past, to explore the present, and to voice your hopes and expectations for the future is part of the fun of this exercise.

The Objective

To lead an examined life. Your notebook will become a lifetime companion and an invaluable source of material.

I always write from my own experiences whether I've had them or not.
                                                    —RON CARLSON

13

Put Your Heart
on the Page

In a letter to a Radcliffe student, F. Scott Fitzgerald wrote of the price she must pay for aspiring to be a professional writer:

> You've got to sell your heart, your strongest reactions, not the little minor things that only touch you lightly, the little experiences that you might tell at dinner. This is especially true when you begin to write, when you have not yet developed the tricks of interesting people on paper, when you have none of the technique which it takes time to learn. When, in short, you have only your emotions to sell.

Too many writers avoid their own strongest feelings because they are afraid of them, or because they are afraid of being sentimental. Yet these are the very things that will make beginning work ring true and affect us. Your stories have to matter to you the writer before they can matter to the reader; your story has to affect you, before it can affect us. William Kittredge says, "If you are not *risking* sentimentality, you are not close to your inner self."

The Exercise

Make a notebook entry on an early childhood event that made you cry or terrified you, or that made you weak with shame or triumphant with revenge. Then write a story about that event. Take us back to those traumatic times, relive them for us through your story in such a way so as to make your experience ours.

The Objective

To learn to identify events in your life that are capable of making you laugh and cry. If you can capture these emotions and put them on paper, chances are you will make your readers laugh and cry as well.

14

People from the Past: Characters of the Future

---

*You don't have anything if you don't
have the stories.*

—LESLIE MARMON SILKO, CEREMONY

Most of us have an unsettling memory of another child who loomed larger than life as we were growing up. Someone we resented, feared, hated, or envied. It might have been a sibling, a cousin, someone from the neighborhood, or someone from school. Often, that child—perhaps a little older or a little younger—had the power to make us take risks we would never have taken on our own, or had the power to make us miserable. This is the subject of Margaret Atwood's novel *Cat's Eye,* in which artist Elaine Risley is haunted by Cordelia, just such a childhood tormentor and "friend." Well, eventually these children grow up.

The Exercise

First, think about your childhood between the ages of six and twelve and try to recall someone whose memory, even now, has the power to invoke strong, often negative feelings in you. Was that person the class bully, the clown, the daredevil, the town snob, the neighborhood bore, etc? Write down details of what you remember about this person, how she looked and talked. Did you ever have any encounters with this person? Or did you just observe her from a distance?

Next, if you haven't seen this person for ten years or longer, imagine what she is doing now, where she lives, etc. Be specific.

If you had a long acquaintance with this person, or still know her, imagine where she will be ten years from now.

The Objective

To understand how our past is material for our imaginations and how writing well can be the best revenge.

Student Examples

His first name was Frank, or Frankie. We went to a small private day school in California. There were thirteen students in my eighth grade class and all of us were afraid of Frankie, who was in the ninth grade. He was the school bully, a mean person, bottom line.

Once when I walked into the locker room, Frankie threw a Japanese Ninja throwing star into the wall just next to me. "Damn, I missed," he said. He talked about how his father had hit him with a 2×4 and he'd asked him for more. He bragged that his father had shot and killed a black man. Frankie hated everyone.

I can imagine Frankie in ten years. He'll be a white supremacist living in rural Georgia and working in a factory. He'll be married with three kids. He'll keep loaded shotguns and pistols around the house and will threaten to kill the kids. Before he's 35 he'll be doing time for a murder he committed outside a bar.

—HUNTER HELLER

Darlene was two years older than me, heavyset, a great football player. She loved the Dallas Cowboys just like all the guys—although we also liked the cheerleaders. Darlene taught me to ride a bike because she was sick of riding me around on her handlebars. One day, she put me on her Sears ten-speed and pushed me into the street, where I smashed into a parked car. She got mad because I "messed up the paint" on her bike. She says I ruined her first sexual experience one night when all the neighborhood kids were playing "Ring-O-Leveo." According to her, she was under a bush, about to "make her move" on Jeremy Witkins, when I saw her and called out her name and location. We used to smoke Marlboro Reds and drink stolen Budweisers behind the local swimming pool. In the five years I knew her, she never once wore a skirt.

I'll bet Darlene went to Grattenville Trade School—she was tough and good with tools. She probably kept wearing concert-Tees, denim jackets, and eventually got into heavy metal. I wonder if her teeth got straightened and her acne went away and her breasts got even bigger. I can imagine her dropping out of school, fighting with her folks all the time, and scooping ice cream nine to five at Carvel, or selling 36-shot film out the little Fotomat window. She'll buy takeout most nights. I can see her standing in line for a couple of beers and a slice of pepperoni for her live-in boyfriend, a muffler mechanic named Al, who is too high to deal with the counter person.

—DANIEL BIGMAN

I never travel without my diary. One should always have something sensational to read on the train.
—OSCAR WILDE

15

An Image Notebook

from Melanie Rae Thon

As playwright and actor Sam Shephard traveled cross-country, he kept a notebook that later became *Motel Chronicles,* a book of poems, images, scenes, and snatches of dialogue that evoke the disorienting experience of being continually on the move. A move or arrival at college often has the same effect. It may be difficult to make sense of all that's happening while you're in the middle of it, just as Shephard couldn't make sense of his experiences. But you can render these moments vividly, as Shephard did, put them together, and see what surfaces. This is a good exercise when you're between stories, unsure of where you want to go next. It keeps you writing without pressure and provides a space where material may surface.

The Exercise

For the length of the semester, keep an "image notebook." Every day, record at least one image. (Date these entries.) Use all your senses. Ask yourself: What's the most striking thing I heard, saw, smelled, touched, tasted today? Images begin with precise sensual detail. One day you may overhear a strange bit of conversation, another you may smell something that triggers a memory of a familiar smell. Another day you might find a photograph or take one or do a drawing. You might make a collage of words and pictures from magazines. This assignment is very open. Length is variable. Some days you may write a page, another day a line. Don't get behind. Interesting juxtapositions emerge when you're not conscious of how images are colliding. If you do your week's work all at once, you'll lose this mystery.

The Objective

To learn to pay attention to detail. To gather images for later use. To find interesting juxtapositions to use in stories. To find threads of narrative that lead to stories. To become clearer about what's interesting to you.

Examples

I think of a white dog in Foot's yard. Big as a husky. White with white eyes, almost white eyes. Leaping to the end of his chain and later running free, dodging cars, but just barely.

I'm remembering the London Tube, the man looking at the punked-out girl as if he wanted to kill her, as if she were disgusting, vile—how the tears welled in my eyes, because I knew how it felt to be looked at that way—but she didn't see. She had spiked, red hair, a lime-green miniskirt, torn fishnet stockings, black—a teenager. He was middle-aged, working class? I wonder if he had a daughter of his own. It scared me, the way he looked at her, because I really thought he might leap, might pummel her, might rip her throat.

Down the street the children have made a Snow Snake. This was before the storm. Fifteen feet long, two feet high—sweet-faced serpent. Disappeared now for sure.

There's this point in the perm process where Annette smears gel along the hairline, then wraps cotton under the curlers to keep the solution off my face. It's the gel that gets me. Cool, slick. And I tell her it reminds me of women getting electroshock, how they smeared gel on the head before they applied the electrodes.

Christine tells me this story. Her friend is riding his bicycle but is completely spaced out. He crashes in Harvard Square, runs into a tree. (Where did he find a tree?) Breaks his wrist but doesn't know it. Is just embarrassed. Hops back on the bike. Peddles away. Then the shock hits him and he's down again. When he comes to, he finds himself in a fireman's arms. Christine and I howl. Make our plans for collapse. To wake that way.

It's not wise to violate the rules until you know how to observe them.
—T. S. ELIOT

16

Changing Your Life
from Joy Nolan

Art is art because it is not nature.

—GOETHE

Good fiction has a confluence of detail that real life seldom has. We've all been told "write what you know," and it's true that autobiographical material enriches fiction with vivid details. But don't sell your fiction short by sticking to the facts—what you know extends far past the specific incidents of your life. The more flexible and elastic your use of facts and feelings borrowed from life, the stronger your writing will be. Marcel Proust said, "Creative wrong memory is a source of art."

As a writer of fiction, you have to be more loyal to the fiction than to the facts that inspired it. Remembering being chased by a vicious dog as a child may give you just the right flavor of terror to vividly describe a thief's fear while fleeing the police in your story. Or you can invest a fictional event with remembered emotion, or use a real-life scene as a backdrop for your imagination, changing the feelings and consequences entirely.

The Exercise

Choose a central dramatic incident from your life.

- Write about it in first person, and then write about it in third person (or try second person!). Write separate versions from the point of view of each character in the incident.

- Have it happen to someone ten or twenty years older or younger than yourself.

- Stage it in another country or in a radically different setting.

The Objective

To become more fluent in translating emotions and facts from truth to fiction. To help you see the components of a dramatic situation as eminently elastic and capable of transformation. To allow your fiction to take on its own life, to determine what happens and why in an artful way that is organic to the story itself. As Virginia Woolf said, "There must be great freedom from reality."

I am a great believer in diaries, if only in the sense that
bar exercises are good for ballet dancers: it's often through
personal diaries (however embarrassing they are to read now)
that the novelist discovers his true bent—that he can narrate
real events and distort them to please himself, describe character,
observe other beings, hypnotize, invent, all the rest. I think that
is how I became a novelist, eventually.
　　　　　　　　　—JOHN FOWLES

17

Journal Keeping
for Writers
from William Melvin Kelley

Everybody has a day to write about, and so writing about the day makes everybody equal. Keeping a diary separates the act of writing from creating character and plot. You can write every day and learn certain fictional techniques without having to invent fiction on command.

The Exercise

Write one page a day. Concentrate on observation and description, not feeling. For example, if you receive a letter, the ordinary reaction is to write in the diary, "I received a letter that made me happy." (Or sad.) Instead, describe the size of the envelope, the quality of the paper, what the stamps looked like.

Keep your diary without using the verb *to be*. Forms of the verb *to be* don't create any vivid images. By avoiding its use, you get into the habit of choosing more interesting verbs. You'll also be more accurate. For example, some people will say "John Smith is a really funny guy," when what they really mean is "John Smith makes me laugh," or "I like John Smith's sense of humor."

Experiment with sentence length. Keep the diary for a week in sentences of ten words or less. Then try writing each day's account in a single sentence. Avoid use of "and" to connect the parts of the long sentence; try out other conjunctions.

Switch your diary to third person for a while, so that instead of writing *I,* you can write about *he* or *she*. Then, try mixing the point of view. Start the day in third person and switch into first person to comment on the action. By interspersing first- and third-person points of view, you can experiment with stream of consciousness and the interior monologue.

Try keeping your diary in an accent—first the accent of somebody who is learning how to write English, then the accent of somebody learning to speak English.

Keep it in baby talk: Baby want. Baby hurt. Baby want food. Baby want love. Baby walk.

Try making lists for a diary entry—just a record of the nouns of that day: toothbrush, coffee, subway tokens, school books, gym shoes.

The Objective

To enhance your powers of observation and description without having to juggle the demands of characterization and plot.

All really satisfying stories, I believe, can generally be described as spendthrift. . . . A spendthrift story has a strange way of seeming bigger than the sum of its parts; it is stuffed full; it gives a sense of possessing further information that could be divulged if called for. Even the sparest in style implies a torrent of additional details barely suppressed, bursting through the seams.
—ANNE TYLER, INTRODUCTION TO *BASS 1983*

18

Creative Wrong Memory

One of the dangers of writing about something that really happened is the urge to stay too close to the literal truth. Because you don't quite trust your memory of it you come up with a thin narrative with very little texture, or you add details or events the reader may find unconvincing. "It really happened that way" or "It's a true story" is no defense. Also, keep in mind that a recital of just the facts rarely adds up to a satisfying fictional truth, to the emotional truth underlying what really happened.

This is another exercise to show you how to remember what you don't know—how to combine autobiography and imagination to achieve what Proust calls "creative wrong memory."

The Exercise

1. Recall an event or dramatic situation from your childhood and describe the event in one or two sentences at the top of the page.

2. Next, using both words and phrases, make a list of all the things you remember about the event.

3. Now make a list of all the things you don't remember about that event.

4. Finally, begin a story using several details from the list you remember and several from the list you don't remember—details you have made up. One way to make this work is to link important details before you begin. For example: I remember that Uncle Cal and Aunt Marie had a fight, but not what started it.

The Objective

To enlarge and deepen your autobiographical material by making up what you don't remember and adding it to what you do.

Student Example

Italics indicate the parts that are "made up."
> Notes
> EVENT: death of a classmate (Albert Parsons)

I REMEMBER: my puzzlement about his sudden disappearance. He was dark-haired and serious. It was fall. Shortly afterwards my favorite uncle died and I went to his funeral at the cathedral and cried. I remember lying in bed, knowing my parents would not be there forever, that they would die. I remember at that moment a terrifying fear and sense of loss.

I DON'T REMEMBER: how Albert Parsons died. An illness? I don't remember how I found out. I don't remember how the others in my class reacted. Nor do I remember how my uncle died or how my aunt and parents reacted.

Beginning of Story

It was a crisp, fall afternoon *with both sides lined up on the field for soccer practice when I saw* that Albert Parsons wasn't there. *Earlier, in the classroom, I hadn't noticed that Albert was missing.* He was a solemn, dark-haired boy who sat quietly *at the back of the first row; he didn't join in any of the recess games.* But soccer was compulsory *and I was worried that our side, Ayre House, was a man shy for the scrimmage. Things weren't in order.*

"*Mister Todd," I yelled to our coach, really our fifth grade teacher.* He wore a topcoat and bowler hat, *and was eager to blow his whistle to get us started so he could get away to the sideline for a cigarette.*

"*Albert Parsons isn't here," I called. "It's not fair."*

Mr. Todd swung around, taking the whistle from his mouth. "You a coward, Campbell," he barked. He jerked his head at the other side, Harrington House, whose color was yellow. "You afraid the yellow-bellies over there are going to beat you and you won't end up on the winning side? What's not fair? That you might lose or that Albert Parsons isn't here?"

His outburst of questions startled me. We were all leery of Mr. Todd. More creepy stories were told about him than any of the other teachers; his class loomed ahead of us like a dragon's cave we would have to someday enter.

—DONALD FRASER MCNEILL

19

Family Stories, Family Myths

from Katherine Haake

What I sometimes describe as the "private enduring instinct behind the narrative impulse" is the habit of making things up as you go along. And sometimes I think that "who" I am is just a combination of all the stories I have told about myself, or those others have told about me. And "my" stories are only a fraction of the larger family stories, this enormous mythology about our history and something else as well, something like our fate, that determines who we all are in the intricate interconnectedness of our lives. All four of my grandparents met and married in a small mining town in northern California that was subsequently flooded behind Shasta Dam, which my uncle designed and helped to build. My grandmother decorously lit the wicks of candles before she put them out, while her daughter, my mother, chased neighbors with a pitchfork. My father never speaks of his own father, who died when he was very young. I have a therapist sister who makes up her own stories about my father's silence, my mother's early violence, what went on in the town under the lake, and of course I have my own version of things.

To live in a family, any family, is to participate in the making of myths, and the myths are all different, depending on who is constructing them. Writing, in large part, is a process of translating those myths into language.

The Exercise

Part One

Select a family story, any family story but especially the kind that gets told over and over again—about, say, Aunt Ethyl's one true love, or why the Brewer twins refused to dress alike anymore in high school—and assume the persona of one of the central players. Become Aunt Ethyl herself, or one of the twins, and explain in a letter to another family member (again, not yourself) the "truth" of exactly what happened. That's it. Don't think too much. Just write the way you'd write any letter to someone about whom you care a great deal and whom you suspect won't entirely believe you.

Part Two

Select a writing partner and exchange letters. Read your partner's letter, and respond by writing a letter in the persona of the addressee in your partner's original letter.

The Objective

To understand the story-making elements of family life and their relation to writing fiction. To gain some distance on our own mythologies by reading them as other people read them. To discover the unexpected character that lives in the space between letter and response. To be aware of how all written narratives contain, in addition to the narrator, who speaks, a narratee, who listens, and of how each profoundly affects both writing and reading. To see how our families, our pasts, and we ourselves are made and perpetually transformed in language.

I have lost too much by losing, or rather by not having acquired, the note-taking habit. It might be of great profit to me; and now that I am older, that I have more time, that the labor of writing is less onerous to me, and I can work more at my leisure, I ought to endeavor to keep, to a certain extent, a record of passing impressions, of all that comes, that goes, that I see, and feel, and observe. To catch and keep something of life— that's what I mean.
——HENRY JAMES, *NOTEBOOKS*, NOVEMBER 25, 1881

Let Us Write Letters

*Nine-tenths of the letters in which people speak
unreservedly of their inmost feelings are written
after ten at night.*

THOMAS HARDY

Several writers we know save copies of letters written to close friends as a sort of journal, and another writer writes a one-page letter every morning before turning to her fiction. Writing letters can be a form of limbering up. The exercise "Let Us Write Letters" isn't really an exercise but rather the suggestion that we all write more letters—to family and friends (and even to the editorial pages of magazines and newspapers). Robert Watson makes a good case for this in his poem "Please Write: don't phone."

> While there is mail there is hope.
> After we have hung up I can't recall
> Your words, and your voice sounds strange
> Whether from a distance, a bad cold, deceit
> I don't know. When you call I'm asleep
> Or bathing or my mouth is full of toast.
>
> I can't think of what to say.
> "We have rain"? "We have snow"?
>
> Let us write instead: surely our fingers spread out
> With pen and paper touch more of mind's flesh
> Than the sound waves moving from throat to lips
> To phone, through wire, to one ear.
> I can touch the paper you touch.
> I can see you undressed in your calligraphy.
> I can read you over and over.
> I can read you day after day.
> I can wait at the mailbox with my hair combed,
> In my best suit.
> I hang up. What did you say?
> What did I say? Your phone call is gone.
> I hold the envelope you addressed in my hand.
> I hold the skin that covers you.

History Lesson

There are as many ways of describing something as there are eyes and ears—all the way from a flat, physical description to an emotionally loaded portrait and history. The things your characters carry, their props, must all mean something to those characters, and, by extension, to the reader. This exercise combines description from both ends of the continuum and attempts to connect a person emotionally with his or her props. Probably the best example of props that deliver on an emotional level can be found in Tim O'Brien's novel, *The Things They Carried*.

The Exercise

Choose something on your person, e.g., a piece of jewelry, a watch, a key chain with its keys, and write, first, a short (one hundred words) description of it, one you would give to someone who can't see.

This should be as precise as you can possibly make it, and should include size, shape, feel—anything that makes it "visible" to someone who is blind. Next, connect this object to yourself, by writing a short history of the object—where you got it, how long you've had it, what it means to you, etc. Generally, this works best if there's another person involved, someone who gave it to you or who it reminds you of.

The Objective

To help the writer understand that while specific details can and should deliver on one level, giving a "prop" a history and an emotional life can deliver on another. A writer has to be able to describe physical objects in an assortment of ways, depending on what is needed by the narrative. Thus, an object in a boy's pocket can be coldly described as a key chain with three keys, two brass and one silver metal. Asked what the keys open, the boy says that one key opens his mother's house, the second his father's, and the third his bicycle lock. We now know that his parents are divorced and that they live within bicycle distance of each other.

Losing Your Mind

from Thomas E. Kennedy

Writers sometimes get trapped in their consciousness, trying to "understand" their story before it even exists, to find "meaning" in every detail,
to portray some intellectual idea, to fulfill some preconceived balance—
in short, going for an idea rather than for a story, writing from the mind
instead of from the heart. This can be a kind of writer's block. This exercise is designed to help you get out of the conscious mind and past the mind
police, to enable you to slip into the unconscious and find the source of the
imagination there.

The Exercise

Part One

If the mind is the house, the unconscious is the basement. To leave the
restricted upper rooms of thought, the writer might descend into the basement where the heat source and water supply originate. Picture the basement of your childhood home or apartment or some other house. Go to
it. Is there a door? Open it. Stairs? Descend. Place your hand on the familiar banister, feel its texture against your palm. Smell the dusty fragrance.
You see everything there: the quality of light, the texture of the floor and
walls. Perhaps you hear the grumble of the oil burner, see the water tank,
hear the tick of the gas meter, but . . . behind the tank, in the shadows, is
a door you never noticed before, an old wooden door, slightly ajar. You go
to it, take the knob in your hand, draw the door open, and the images break
free from your mind. Describe them. Write.

Part Two

The imagination can be like a person who has stayed inside too long, alone
in his or her house. The house is like a closed mind, a clenched fist; the
objective is to open the door and leave. Dusk. You sit on a back porch
behind a screen door or on cool cement steps. A breeze through the screen
carries the aroma of honeysuckle mixed with the bitter scent of weeds or

the smell of the doughnut shop on the corner mixed with the acrid scent of spilled gasoline. At the back of the yard is a weathered picket fence, a rusted barbed-wire fence, or a cement wall. And a gate. You rise and cross to the gate. Go through the gate into the dusky shadows. There are people there. What is it? Write.

The Objective

To open the doors and gates into our subconscious minds and let the images flow freely from the surprises beyond.

I got the idea of Loving *from a manservant in the Fire Service during the war. He was serving with me in the ranks, and he told me he had once asked the elderly butler who was over him what the old boy most liked in the world. The reply was: "Lying in bed on a summer morning, with the window open, listening to the church bells, eating buttered toast with cunty fingers." I saw the book in a flash.*

— HENRY GREEN

23

Total Recall

from Alison Lurie

The following exercise works best if it is done first and discussed and analyzed afterward.

The Exercise

This exercise should be done with two or more people; one to read the instructions aloud while the others concentrate on recalling the experience. Read slowly and pause between sentences and paragraphs; the whole process should take at least five minutes.

Shut your eyes. Go back in your mind to some summer or part-time job you had in the past. Look at the surroundings in which you were working. See the place in which you worked: factory, schoolroom, restaurant, hospital, store, library, whatever. Or perhaps it is an outdoor scene: beach, road, garden, construction project, ranch, café. Notice the shapes and colors of what is around you. Look at the materials with which you are working, note their shapes and colors.

Now look at the other people who are present in this scene: coworkers, boss, customers in the restaurant or shop, children at camp, or a babysitting job. Choose one person and observe her closely; notice what she is wearing and the expression on her face. What is she doing as you watch? What gestures is she making?

Now begin to hear the sounds that belong to this scene. The clank of machinery, the sizzle of hamburgers cooking on the grill, the splash of water in the pool, the ringing of phones, the thump and hum of music, whatever it may be. Listen to the voices; what are they saying? Perhaps you will hear a line or two of dialogue. What is the person you especially observed saying, and what do you or someone else say in reply?

Now allow yourself to experience the smells that belong to this scene: food cooking, fresh-cut grass, motor oil, sweat, flowers, disinfectant, whatever. If you are working in a restaurant or bar, or eating on the job, you may want to become aware of taste, too: the lukewarm bitterness of instant coffee in a plastic cup, the sugary chocolate slickness of a candy bar hidden in your desk drawer.

Look around you at this point and become aware of the climate of your surroundings. Is it winter or summer? If you are working outdoors, what is the weather like? What time of day is it? If you are indoors, is the air stuffy or fresh, smoky or clear? What can you see out the window?

Next, become aware of the sense of touch, of the textures of the things you are working with: soft or rough, smooth or fuzzy, wet or dry. Notice heat and cold: the damp, icy feel of a glass of soda, the warm silky texture of a child's hair; the hot oily parts of a broken lawnmower.

Now turn your sense of touch inward; become aware of the motions you are making and the sensations in your muscles: the strain of lifting sacks of dirt or cement, the pleasure of stirring cake batter round a big stainless-steel bowl, the weight of a tray of drinks on your shoulder.

Finally, notice your emotions. Do you like this job or hate it? Are you interested in what is going on around you or bored? Are you tired and depressed or in good spirits? Where will you go when work is over for today?

Do you like or dislike the people around you? What do you feel about the person you chose to observe? What do you think she feels about you? What would you like to say to her? If you said it, what would this person probably say or do?

When all these things are clear in your mind, but not until then, open your eyes and record them as rapidly as possible. Write in the present tense. Don't bother about legible handwriting, complete sentences, or spelling words correctly: the point is to get this material down on paper while it is still fresh and vivid in your memory. You are not composing a story, only making notes.

Notes For Discussion

Writers differ in their sensitivity to the world. Some especially notice shapes, some smells, some colors, some textures; some see gestures, others see clothes or facial expressions. James Joyce, whose eyesight was poor, perceived the world mainly in terms of words and sounds; Thomas Wolfe, a large man with an even larger appetite, was famous for his awareness of the tastes and odors of food.

As you look over your notes, ask yourself whether there are kinds of perception you are neglecting in your writing, or passing over too rapidly. Do you habitually describe scenes and people in black and white, for instance? If you are doing this exercise in a group, read your notes aloud and ask the other people present what they noticed about your strengths and weaknesses of recall. Once you are aware that you don't always remember to include colors, smells, sounds, texture, or whatever, you can make a conscious effort to do so, and your writing will become more vivid.

If this exercise worked especially well for you, perhaps it could be turned into a story. Suppose the two main characters were you and the person you observed and spoke to, what might happen between them? What change in them or in their relationship might take place?

No matter what you are writing, you can use this technique. If you like, you can concentrate on people rather than scenes; visualize them in detail, see what they are doing, hear their words, etc. Once you become really familiar with the process, it is not even necessary to go back in imagination to a real scene or a real person; you can call up an invented character or event in the same way.

The Objective

To make some experience as vivid as possible, to recall it in full sensual and emotional detail before you begin to write.

I want stories to startle and engage me within the first few sentences, and in their middle to widen or deepen or sharpen my knowledge of human activity, and to end by giving me a sensation of completed statement. The ending is where the reader discovers whether he has been reading the same story the writer thought he was writing.
—JOHN UPDIKE, INTRODUCTION TO *BASS 1984*

PART THREE

Characterization

*I live with the people I create and it has made my essential
loneliness less keen.*

—CARSON MCCULLERS

When you meet someone for the first time, you immediately begin to make
a judgment about her, an assessment partly conscious and partly instinctive.
You take in, for instance, her clothes, her haircut, the type of watch she wears.
When she talks you notice her accent and vocabulary and especially what
she says to you. You see if she smiles easily or whether she seems standoff-
ish. These are just a few of the clues you process intuitively.

As a writer, you owe it to your readers to supply your characters with
just such a host of clues. The more specific you make these attributes, the
more immediate your characters will be. Thus characterization means fleshing out the people who inhabit your fiction by providing them with physical characteristics, habits and mannerisms, speech patterns, attitudes,
beliefs and motives, desires, a past and a present, and finally, actions. This
last attribute—how your characters act in a given situation—will determine
your character's future (as she is further revealed through action) and shape
the forward movement and final resolution of your story. As Heracleitus
said, "Character is destiny."

Now, where fully realized characters come from is another story. Perhaps it is best summed up by Graham Greene when he says, "One never
knows enough about characters in real life to put them into novels. One gets
started and then, suddenly, one can not remember what toothpaste they
use; what are their views on interior decoration, and one is stuck utterly.
No, major characters emerge; minor ones may be photographed." One
place that characters can emerge from is your notebooks. For example, read

F. Scott Fitzgerald's notebooks to see how a writer's mind works. He even had classifications for notes such as *C*—Conversation and Things Overheard, *P*—Proper Names, *H*—Descriptions of Humanity, etc. Notebooks are a good place to collect names, lines of dialogue, and those details you just couldn't make up—like the guy we saw on the subway who, just before he got off, carefully tucked his wet chewing gum into his ear.

What makes me feel as though I belong here, out in this world, is not the teacher, not the mother, not the lover but what goes on in my mind when I am writing. Then I belong here, and then all of the things that are disparate and irreconcilable can be useful. I can do the traditonal things that writers always say they do, which is to make order out of chaos. Even if you are reproducing the disorder, you are sovereign at that point. Struggling through the work is extremely important—more important to me than publishing it.

If I didn't do this, then I would be a part of the chaos.
—TONI MORRISON

24

Oh!...That Sort of Person

Carefully chosen details can reveal character in fascinating and different ways. Writer and teacher Ron Carlson calls such details "evidence"—as if you were creating/gathering evidence for/against your character to bring his case (his story) to the reader. Sometimes details tell something about the character described and also something different about the character making the observation.

This is true of Anna Karenina's reaction on seeing her husband, Alexey Alexandrovitch, after a trip to Moscow, during which she patched up her brother's marriage and also met her future lover, Vronsky. Anna returns to St. Petersburg and is met at the train station by Alexey: "'Oh, mercy! Why do his ears look like that?' she thought, looking at his frigid and imposing figure, and especially the ear that struck her at that moment as propping up the brim of his round hat." We see him as stern and ludicrous and we also feel her dismay as she becomes aware of her feelings toward him for the first time.

In other cases a character reveals more about himself than he suspects. For example, there is a vivid character in *The Great Gatsby* called Meyer Wolfsheim who calls Nick Carraway's attention to his cuff buttons and then boasts, "Finest specimens of human molars." Clearly, Wolfsheim means to impress his listener, but instead of charming Nick (or the reader), this detail has the opposite effect.

In *Rabbit, Run,* John Updike uses physical characteristics to account for Rabbit's nickname. "Rabbit Angstrom, coming up the alley in a business suit, stops and watches, though he's twenty-six and six-three. So tall, he seems an unlikely rabbit, but the breadth of white face, the pallor of his blue irises, and a nervous flutter under his brief nose as he stabs a cigarette into his mouth partially explain the nickname, which was given to him when he too was a boy." And clearly, Rabbit is still appropriately called Rabbit, even though he's dressed in a suit and is no longer a boy.

In Pam Houston's story "Highwater," two women tell each other about the men in their lives. Houston writes:

> Besides drawing me a picture of Chuck's fingers, Casey told me these things: Chuck used to be a junkie but now he's clean, he had a one-bedroom basement apartment and one hundred and twenty-seven compact disks, and he used moleskin condoms which don't work as well but feel much better. This is what I told her about Richard: He put marinated

asparagus into the salad, he used the expression "laissez-faire capitalist" three times, once in a description of himself, he played a tape called "The Best of One Hundred and One Strings," and as far as I could tell, he'd never had oral sex.

The women's early descriptions of apparently dissimilar men are important because by the end of the story, they have each been abandoned by their lover, and Millie says, "I wondered how two men who at one time seemed so different could have turned out, in the end, to be exactly the same."

The first lines of Bobbie Ann Mason's "Shiloh" also bring a character immediately to life. "Leroy Moffitt's wife, Norma Jean, is working on her pectorals. She lifts three-pound dumbbells to warm up, then progresses to a twenty-pound barbell. Standing with her legs apart, she reminds Leroy of Wonder Woman." By the end of the story, Norma Jean is working just as hard at improving her mind—and at not being Leroy's wife.

The Exercise

First work with a story that you've already written, one whose characters need fleshing out. Write the character's name at the top of the page. Then fill in this sentence five or ten times:

He (or she) is the sort of person who _____.

For example: Meyer Wolfsheim is the sort of person who boasts of wearing human molars for cuff links.

Then determine which details add flesh and blood and heart to your characters. After you have selected the "telling" detail, work it into your story more felicitously than merely saying, "She is the sort of person who. . . ." Put it in dialogue, or weave it into narrative summary. But use it.

The Objective

To learn to select revealing concrete details, details that sometimes tell us more than the character would want us to know. Evidence.

Student Examples

Phillip is the sort of person for whom every transaction in life can be enacted with a Post-it Note.

—DINA JOHNSON

Mary is the sort of person who gets cast as a tree with two lines, and becomes the most interesting part of the play.

—JAMES FERGUSON

Emily was the sort of person who was practical in situations where most people were sentimental: When someone died she arrived with toilet paper, paper cups, and a three-pound can of coffee.

—BETSY CUSSLER

Will Greene is the sort of person who always has to be the better-looking one in a relationship.

—ABBY ELLIN

At fifteen, Tony was the sort of person whose heart rejected premarital sex, but whose body was already down at the corner drug store buying condoms.

—JOANNE AVALLON

She is the sort of person whose bookshelf is lined with Penguin classics but she has hundreds of Harlequins stacked behind the dresses in her closet.

—TED WEESNER, JR.

Willie is the sort of kid who'd make friends by lighting the cigarette of the bully who'd just knocked him on his ass.

—ROD SIINO

He's the kind of kid who'd make fun of your lunch.

—ERIC MAIERSON

I have always regarded fiction as an essentially rhetorical art— that is to say, the novelist or short-story writer persuades us to share a certain view of the world for the duration of the reading experience, effecting, when successful, that rapt immersion in an imagined reality that Van Gogh caught so well in his painting "The Novel Reader." Even novelists who, for their own artistic purposes, deliberately break that spell have to cast it first.
—DAVID LODGE

25

What Do You Know
about Your Characters?

*I could take a battery of MMPI and Wonderlic
personality tests for each of my people and answer
hundreds of questions with as much intimate
knowledge as if they were taking the test.*

—RICHARD PRICE

In *Death in the Afternoon,* Hemingway said, "People in a novel, not skillfully constructed characters, must be projected from the writer's assimilated experience, from his knowledge, from his head, from his heart and from all there is of him. . . . A good writer should know as near everything as possible." Yet students frequently write stories about a major event in a character's life, although they don't know some of the most elementary things about that character—evidence, information that, if known, most certainly would affect the character's motives and actions.

Hemingway again speaks to this issue of being familiar with characters:

> If a writer of prose knows enough about what he is writing about he may omit things that he knows and the reader, if the writer is writing truly enough, will have a feeling of those things as strongly as though the writer had stated them. The dignity of movement of an iceberg is due to only one-eighth of it being above water. A writer who omits things because he does not know them only makes hollow places in his writing.

The Exercise

Work with one of your completed stories that has a character who needs fleshing out. Take out a sheet of paper and number from one to thirty-four. At the top of the page, write in the title of your story and the main character's name—and start filling in the blanks.

Character's name: _____

Character's nickname: _____

Sex: _____

Age: _____

Looks: _____

Education: _____

Vocation/occupation: _____

Status and money: _____

Marital status: _____

Family, ethnicity: _____

Diction, accent, etc.: _____

Relationships: _____

Places (home, office, car, etc.): _____

Possessions: _____

Recreation, hobbies: _____

Obsessions: _____

Beliefs: _____

Politics: _____

Sexual history: _____

Ambitions: _____

Religion: _____

Superstitions: _____

Fears: _____

Attitudes: _____

Character flaws: _____

Character strengths: _____

Pets: _____

Taste in books, music, etc.: _____

Journal entries: _____

Correspondence: _____

Food preferences: _____

Handwriting: _____

Astrological sign: _____

Talents: _____

Friends: _____

Relatives: _____

Enemies: _____

As seen by others: _____

As seen by self: _____

Scars: _____

Tattoos, piercings, etc.: _____

Salary: _____

What is kept in fridge, glove compartment, medicine cabinet, junk drawer: calendar, appointment book, rolodex, etc.: _____

No doubt you will be able to add to this list.

Note: This exercise should be done *after* you have written your story. It is not a way to conceive a character, but rather a way to reconceive a character. It is designed to discover what you know about your characters *after* you have written your story—and what you don't know. For example, one writer, Samuel R. Delany, tells his students to know exactly how much money their characters make and how they make it. And why not apply this list to some of your favorite stories? Note how much is known about the unforgettable grandmother in Flannery O'Connor's story "A Good Man Is Hard to Find" or about the compelling, bewildered narrator in Peter Taylor's story "The Old Forest."

The Objective

To understand how much there is to know about a character you have created. Of course, it is possible to write a successful story about a character without knowing everything on this list—or perhaps only knowing two or three things. On the other hand, beginning writers often don't know more than a character's age or gender—and frequently neglect an essential piece of information that would have greatly informed or shaped their story. You needn't include these details in the story, but their presence in your mind will be "felt" by the reader.

I give characters more moral latitude than I give myself. And when I create characters who transgress on moral codes I possess—they startle me.
                                                                                    —EVE SHELNUTT

26

Naming Your Characters

When you name a baby you're taking a real chance, because you have no idea how the little tyke is going to turn out; we all know people whose names seem to belong to someone else. When you name a fictional character you have no excuse for getting it wrong because you should know him better than the members of your own family. The names you choose to give your characters should suggest certain traits, social and ethnic background, geography, and even things that have yet to occur in your story. Think of Vladimir Nabokov's Humbert Humbert and Henry James's Merton Densher—they just *sound* right. Charles Dickens was so adept at this subliminal skill that some of his characters' names have become generic, representing personality types—like Uriah Heep and, most notably, Ebenezer Scrooge. The names you choose have a strong and subtle influence on how your readers will respond to your characters. You may have to rename a character several times before you get it right.

The Exercise

Name the following characters, keeping in mind that you can plant, within a name, a clue to that character's role in your fiction.

- A petty, white-collar thief who robs his boss over several years
- An envious, bitter woman who makes her sister miserable by systematically trying to undercut her pleasure and self-confidence
- A sweet young man too shy to speak to an attractive woman he sees every day at work
- The owner of a fast-food restaurant who comes on to his young female employees
- A resentful mother-in-law
- The dog owned by a pretentious couple

The Objective

To recognize that the names you give your characters should not be drawn out of a hat but carefully tested to see if they "work." Sometimes you may want to choose an "appropriate" name ("Victoria" for a member of the British aristocracy) and once in a while it's a good idea to choose a name that seems "inappropriate" ("Bruce" for the child of migrant farm workers). In each case, you are sending a message to the reader about who the character is, where he came from, and where he is headed. A name can send a message as powerful as a title.

Journalism allows its readers to witness history; fiction gives its readers the opportunity to live it.
—JOHN HERSEY

27

Supplying Props

In their haste and enthusiasm to get something underway, new writers often forget to supply their characters with the props of ordinary—or extraordinary—life. Real people wear clothes, eat meals, sit on furniture, drive cars, go to the bathroom, change into sweats, shop, and on and on through the infinite number of things that impact physically on them. Remembering to use props, and using them productively, will enhance the reality of your story. I often tell my students to imagine that they are designing a set for a play or a movie. Each object they bring on the set must add on to and be consistent with the life lived by the character who will play out the scene against this backdrop.

The Exercise

Invent a character before you start writing. Then make a list of the things you would find in that character's refrigerator, car trunk, closet, and medicine chest. Do this for three or four characters. Read your lists and then remain silent while the rest of the class tries to guess from this "evidence" what sort of person your character is, whether they live alone or with someone else, about how old they are, what they do for a living, what their personalities are like, and so on.

The Objective

People do not float naked in time and space; they live in the real world in which "things" swarm. You have a wonderful opportunity to reveal what a character is like by showing his "things," rather than telling us, for instance, that she has a "well-stocked refrigerator," or a "full closet." Each time you name a thing you add luster to your character and present a gift to your readers.

28

What Do Your Characters Want?

In her superb book *Writing Fiction,* Janet Burroway stresses the importance of knowing what characters *want:*

> It is true that in fiction, in order to engage our attention and sympathy, the central character must *want* and want intensely. The thing that character wants need not be violent or spectacular; it is the intensity of the wanting that counts. She may want only to survive, but if so she must want enormously to survive, and there must be distinct cause to doubt she will succeed.

Sometimes *want* is expressed in terms of *need, wish, hope,* etc.—and it is amazing how many times these words appear in the first two pages of stories.

In the Gabriel García Márquez story "No One Writes to the Colonel," a colonel has been waiting for a certain letter for almost sixty years. As a young man, he had taken part in a successful revolution and, afterward, the government had promised him and other officers travel reimbursement and indemnities. The colonel's whole life has been a matter of marching in place and waiting ever since. Even though he has hired a lawyer, filed papers, written endlessly, and seen laws passed, nothing has happened. The lawyer notes that no official has ever taken responsibility. "In the last fifteen years, there have been seven Presidents, and each President changed his Cabinet at least ten times, and each Minister changed his staff at least a hundred times." The colonel says, "All my comrades died waiting for the mail"—but he refuses to give up, even though his life has been wasted and he has grown older, sicker, and crankier in the course of time.

The *want* that gives dynamic force to the story can take the form of a strong emotion, or an obsession, such as the colonel's determination to have his place in history recognized (probably his real motive); or it can be expressed in some specific plan or scheme.

Henry James's novel *The Wings of the Dove* is a good example of an elaborate scheme. Kate Croy, a London woman, knows that her one-time acquaintance Milly Theale, a rich and charming American, is dying of a mysterious disease. The doctors think that Milly's only chance for recovery lies in finding happiness—such as that of falling in love. Kate's scheme is to have her lover, Merton Densher, woo and marry Milly, inherit her money when she dies, and then marry Kate.

In Fitzgerald's *The Great Gatsby,* Jay Gatsby's whole ambition is to recover the past—specifically the idyllic time of his love affair with Daisy Buchanan years before.

Sometimes an ostensible *want* hides or overlays a greater one. Robert Jordan in Hemingway's *For Whom the Bell Tolls* intends to blow up a bridge to halt the advance of Franco's fascist troops. But as he waits for the strategic moment, an underlying desire to experience the life of Spain and identify with the Spanish people emerges as his real *want.*

Leslie Epstein's *King of the Jews* offers the reader an enigmatic mixture of purposes. I.C. Trumpelman, the Jewish puppet-leader whom the Nazis install as head of the ghetto, wishes to preserve his people from the Holocaust—but he also has a drive to rule, dictate to, and punish them.

Wants in fiction aren't always simple and straightforward things, just as peoples' motives are seldom unmixed. The more complicated and unsuspected—both to her and to us—are a protagonist's aims, the more interesting that character will be and the more interesting will be the unfolding of her story.

The Exercise

Look at the stories you've already written and ask

- What does the central character want?

- What are her motives for wanting this?

- Where in the story is this made clear to the reader?

- How do we learn what the central character wants? Dialogue? Actions? Interior thinking?

- What or who stands in the way of her achieving it?

- What does that desire set in motion?

If you don't know the answers to these questions, you don't know your character and her desires as well as you should. Aristotle said, "Man is his desire." What your central characters desire will inform the situations and ultimately the elements of the plots in which they are involved.

The Objective

To understand how your central character's desires shape her life. To see characterization as more than description and voice and mannerisms.

No man consciously chooses evil because it is evil; he only mistakes it for the happiness that he seeks.
—MARY WOLLSTONECRAFT SHELLEY

29

Making Heroes Flawed

from Douglas Bauer

In *Aspects of the Novel*, E.M. Forster wrote that "all actors in a story are, or pretend to be, human beings. Since the [fiction writer] is also a human being, there is an affinity between him and his subject matter which is absent in many other forms of art." If we think of this natural affinity as a tool to employ—one human being (the writer) identifying with another human being (his or her character)—then we can begin to understand the responsibility a writer has to create characters with complex personalities and contradictory make-ups. This complexity is especially important in creating protagonists, the heroes of the story, the character we want our readers to root for. While it's true that the most richly rewarding stories are populated with protagonists, or heroes, whose efforts and intentions are admirable, no credible fictional character is entirely admirable, purely heroic. This becomes obvious when, remembering Forster, we think of our fictional creations as human. The most virtuous of human beings is flawed. That's what it means to *be* human. So, too, with our protagonist heroes.

The Exercise

Here's one way to consider creating heroic characters, employing that affinity Forster described, which helps to guard against making them impossibly good. Think of this exercise as a credit-and-debit sheet.

First, write a brief synopsis of your hero's personality, highlighting his or her best qualities. Then make a list of those highlighted qualities: for example, fairness, integrity, charitable impulses, modesty, etc.

Next, imagine a not so admirable, offsetting personality trait that your hero has to struggle to control, and match it with the admirable trait. He may or may not be conscious of that struggle. If you listed "fairness," for instance, you might place next to it something like, "pride." If you listed "integrity," you might list, on the debit side, "intolerance." And so on.

Finally, mix the good and the bad, so that, in the first case, you have a hero who is, indeed, fair in the end, but who occasionally self-servingly makes clear to one and all that he is one who has to suppress the impulse to do so.

Perhaps he boasts, if only to himself, about some objectively scrupulous action he's taken. He's fair, but he's sometimes a bit pleased with himself.

Or, if your hero resists the temptation to cheat and thereby profit in the process, perhaps she harbors a suspicion that her business partner isn't behaving quite so honorably, interpreting her actions as suspect, even if there's no clear evidence. She's honest as the day is long, but is apt to define that quality too strictly.

The Objective

The key is to make the admirable aspect the dominant of the two, but also to remember, as you set your protagonist heroes free to determine the outcome of the story, that they have that negative component lurking in their personalities as well. Maybe the hero is aware of his flaws and consciously fights back their emergence. Maybe someone else in the story perceives the hero's flaws. In any case, by mixing the two ingredients, one from the credit and one from the debit side of the ledger, you'll be helped to resist creating the unconvincing and—equally damning—uninteresting saintly hero.

Hate the sin but love the sinner.
—St. Augustine

30

Creating a Character's Background, Place, Setting, and Milieu

from Robie Macauley

You are what you buy, own, eat, wear, collect, read, and create; and you are what you do for a living and how you live. If somebody broke into your home or apartment while you were away, chances are he could construct a good profile of who you are. You should be able to do exactly that for your characters even when they are "offstage."

The Exercise

Create a setting for one or more of the following and furnish a place with his character—you create the character through observation of the setting. The place can be any kind of locale—house, a specific room in a house, outdoor grounds, an office, a cell, even a bed. The description must incorporate enough characteristic things so that the reader can visualize the absent dweller accurately. Try to avoid stereotypes.

> An unsuccessful painter
> A member of a lunatic fringe political group
> A former movie star who still thinks she's famous
> A foster child
> A high school senior about to flunk out
> A fugitive from the law
> A social climber
> A cocktail waitress down on her luck
> A blind person
> A paraplegic
> A paranoid person
> A supermarket checkout woman who just won the state lottery

The Objective

To be able to select details that will create a character and furnish the world of that character. Note which details indicate the circumstances of the subject—such things as success or lack of success, social status and habits. Which details indicate emotions, personality, intelligence, character, and outlook on life?

Student Example

Jeremy told me that after the accident his mother set up his room like the face of a clock. As I stand in the doorway, at what must be six o'clock, I see what he means.

Straight ahead, against the far wall is Jeremy's bed—twelve o'clock. His mom made the bed with tight hospital corners and his pajamas, black and white striped like a prisoner's uniform, are laid out for him.

His desk is at three o'clock. Braille copies of *A Tale of Two Cities* and *Wuthering Heights* sit next to small cassette recordings of our Psych textbook. Tapes for American History, Econ., and Chemistry are stacked alongside.

I move to five o'clock and touch his empty bookcase. On the third shelf up, his initials, J.M.—Jeremy Malone—are etched deep in the wood. I close my eyes and run my fingers over them. Jeremy made this bookcase a year ago—about two months before his motorcycle accident on Route 9. Jeremy told his parents to take his books away.

The closet door, at nine o'clock, has been scrubbed with Murphy's Oil Soap. His stereo sits at ten o'clock, power off, but the volume turned nearly to its maximum. His posters of *Easy Rider* and the Budweiser girl are gone.

—Christy Veladota

It's astonishing how accurate intuition and imagination can be when given their heads.
—Sydney Lea

31

Funny—You Don't Look Seventy-Five

Readers need to know certain basic facts about your characters. They should have some idea of their appearance and approximately how old they are. A writer can, of course, say something direct, like "Marvin Highsmith, sixty-eight years old, owned a Chevy pickup." But it's more interesting and dramatic to *suggest* a character's age, rather than to present the reader with a naked number. In the following passage from *Memento Mori* by Muriel Spark, an aged woman makes herself a pot of tea; the entire enterprise is made to seem Herculean—as indeed it is for a very old person. Spark never steps in to "tell" the reader that Charmian is in her eighties; it's all done through Charmian's perceptions.

> Charmian made her way to the library and cautiously built up the fire which had burnt low. The effort of stooping tired her and she sat for a moment in the big chair. After a while it was tea-time. She thought, for a space, about tea. Then she made her way to the kitchen where the tray had been set by Mrs. Anthony in readiness for Mrs. Pettigrew to make the tea. But Mrs. Pettigrew had gone out. Charmian felt overwhelmed suddenly with trepidation and pleasure. Could she make tea herself? Yes, she would try. The kettle was heavy as she held it under the tap. It was heavier still when it was half-filled with water. It rocked in her hand and her skinny, large-freckled wrist ached and wobbled with the strain. At last she had lifted the kettle safely on to the gas ring. She had seen Mrs. Anthony use the automatic lighter. She tried it but could not make it work. Matches. . . . At last the gas was lit under the kettle. Charmian put the teapot on the stove to warm. She then sat down in Mrs. Anthony's chair to wait for the kettle to boil. She felt strong and fearless.
>
> When the kettle had boiled she spooned tea into the pot and knew that the difficult part had come. She lifted the kettle a little and tilted its spout over the teapot. She stood as far back as she could. In went the hot water, and though it splashed quite a bit on the stove, she did not get any over her dress or her feet. She bore the teapot to the tray. It wafted to and fro, but she managed to place it down gently after all.
>
> She looked at the hot-water jug. Should she bother with hot water? She had done so well up to now, it would be a pity to make any mistake and have an accident. But she felt strong and fearless. A pot of tea without the hot-water jug beside it was nonsense. She filled the jug, this time splashing her foot a little, but not enough to burn.

When all was set on the tray she was tempted to have her tea in the kitchen there in Mrs. Anthony's chair.

But she thought of her bright fire in the library. She looked at the tray. Plainly she could never carry it. She would take in the tea-things one by one, even if it took half-an-hour.

. . . First the teapot, which she placed on the library hearth. Then the hot-water jug. These were the dangerous objects. Cup and saucer; another cup and saucer in case Godfrey or Mrs. Pettigrew should return and want tea; the buttered scones; jam; two plates, two knives, and two spoons. Another journey for the plate of Garibaldi biscuits which Charmian loved to dip in her tea. . . . Three of the Garibaldi biscuits slid off the plate and broke on the floor in the hall. She proceeded with the plate, laid it on a table, and then returned to pick up the broken biscuits, even the crumbs. . . . Last of all she went to fetch the tray itself, with its pretty cloth. She stopped to mop up the water she had spilt by the stove. When she had brought everything into the room she closed the door, placed the tray on a low table by her chair and arranged her tea-things neatly upon it. The performance had taken twenty minutes.

When you start thinking about it you'll realize how many instant calculations you make when you first meet someone, assessing hair, eyes, girth, jaw line, and wrinkles. There are literally scores of clues on the human body. There are also indirect clues, like what sort of clothes the person is wearing, her verbal style and idiom; even the way she meets your eyes.

The Exercise

Complete the following sentences to suggest the age of a character, keeping in mind that there are subtle ways to convey this (moral attitude, general psychology, physical surroundings, styles of speech, etc.) as well as the direct (condition of skin and hair, physical mobility, tone of voice, etc.).

I figured Carol was as old as my grandmother because _____

We knew that Janet was not far from retirement because _____

Although Daphne wouldn't admit being over thirty she gave it away by _____

Tom was obviously approaching the big four-oh because _____

The Harrisons were your unmistakable yuppy baby boomers. They _____

You could tell that Jamie was using a fake I.D. because his _____

The Objective

To make the best use of your powers of observation. To render important information by indirection and subtlety. To use age in conjunction with characterization; age isn't simply a number—it's also an attitude.

Student Example

1. her fingers trembled when she lifted her coffee cup and she made me read Daddy's letter to her twice, all the while accusing me of mumbling.
2. management started giving her jobs to other people in the department and she had so many pictures of her grandchildren on her desk there wasn't even room to set down an envelope.
3. ladling on the make-up like a floozy. And when she came back to work after the flu, you could tell she hadn't gone for her weekly touch-up at the beauty parlor.
4. his belly hung over his belt and he complained that the cleaner had shrunk two of his best jackets.
5. had a CD player, a cellular phone, a state-of-the-art fax, and a bread machine and when I asked them about kids, Marie Harrison said, "Thank god the old biological clock is just about to wind down."
6. cheeks were as smooth and pink as a dismissal slip and they flushed when he lowered his voice to ask for a "brew."

—STANLEY MONROE

I think this whole division about realism and magical realism is pointless. Hasn't literature always been magical realism— whether you're talking about the Bible or Kafka? In fact, when you are writing realism—isn't that a kind of "magical realism" in a way? They are words on a page—how real is that. The divisions are arbitrary. I've always been interested in the possibilities underneath the everyday. That's what makes writing fascinating to me—to think about what could be rather than what is. The natural world is the most magical thing of all. Think about death—how hard is that to get your mind around: one minute a person is there and then—where did they go?
—ALICE HOFFMAN

32

Put Your Characters to Work

Have you ever worked as a carpenter, cabdriver, bouncer, dentist, bar pianist, actor, film critic, drummer, teacher, domestic, waiter, coach, stockbroker, plumber, therapist, minister, policeman, or mailman? If not any of these, you have probably worked at one or several jobs and have a job now. Have you ever used a job as background for a story? Better yet: Have you ever put a character to work in a job you've never had?

Work seldom finds its way into the stories of beginning writers, although this is fertile ground for harvesting the details of language, setting, socioeconomics, and "machinery." In an interview in *StoryQuarterly*, Grace Paley is asked about her statement that "the slightest story ought to contain the facts of money and blood." Paley replies:

> It really means family, or the blood of ordinary life. . . . As for money, it's just that everybody makes a living. And that's one of the things that students forget entirely. . . . [I]t's just that they never go to work. The story takes place between eight in the morning and eight the next morning with nobody ever leaving the room! And those are the things that our life in this world and in this society and in every other society is really made up of. . . . Our family relationships are of the utmost importance, and when they don't exist they're equally important—and how we live, how we make a living. The money in our lives: how we either have it or we don't. . . . If people live without working, that is very important. It's called "Class." And that really is another way of saying that you really DO write about classes, whether you know it or not.

Ethan Canin's first collection of stories, *Emperor of the Air,* is a good example of work as foreground and background. His characters teach astronomy, biology, and English, coach basketball and baseball, sell movie tickets and run the projector, make prints, or play the horn. Other characters are a hospital orderly, a medical student, a grocery store owner, and a retired auto upholstery salesman. Some of these jobs are central to their stories and others are simply what his characters do for a living, but each job is given the respect of particularity.

Every writer should have on his bookshelf Studs Terkel's *Working.* It is a gold mine of people talking, explaining, and complaining about their respective jobs. Listen to their talk:

A DOORMAN: "If tenants came by, you had to stand up. If you were sitting down, you'd stand up. As a doorman then, you couldn't sit like this. When I was first hired, I sat down with my legs crossed. The manager came over and he said, 'No, sit down like this'—arms folded, legs stiff. If tenants came in, you had to stand up quick, stand there like a soldier."

A NURSERY ATTENDANT: "I now work in a greenhouse, where we grow nothing but roses. You can walk in there and the peace and quiet engulfs you. Privacy is such that you don't even see people you work with for hours on end. It is not always pretty. Roses have to have manure put around their roots. So I get my rubber gloves and there I go."

A PHARMACIST: "All we do is count pills. Count out twelve on the counter, put 'em in here, count out twelve more. . . . Today was a little out of the ordinary. I made an ointment. Most of the ointments come already made up. This doctor was an old-timer. He wanted something with sulphur and two other elements mixed together. So I have to weigh it out on the scale. Ordinarily I would just have one tube of cream for that."

JOCKEY: "You go to the barn and start as a hot walker. He's the one that walks the horse a half-hour, after he's been on the track for his training, while he drinks water. About every five minutes, you gotta do about two or three swallows. Then you keep with him until he's completely cooled down, until he's not sweating any more. You do this every day. You might walk six, seven horses, which starts building your legs up. We all started this way. There's no short cuts. . . . Willie Shoemaker's the greatest. He has the old style of the long hold. He has a gift with his hands to translate messages to the horse. He has the gift of feeling a horse's mouth. But it's a different style from ninety percent of us. We've gone to the trend of the South American riders. They ride a horse's shoulder, instead of a horse's back."

DENTIST: "Teeth can change a person's appearance completely. It gives me a sense of satisfaction that I can play a role. The thing that bugs me is that you work hard to create, let's say, a good gold bridge. It requires time, effort, and precision. Before I put them in place, I make the patient look at them. An artist can hang his work on the wall and everybody sees it. No one sees mine except me." (Read Jane Smiley's *The Age of Grief.*)

AN INTERSTATE TRUCKER: "Troopers prey on truck drivers for possible violations—mostly regarding weight and overload. It's extremely difficult to load a steel truck legally to capacity. . . . You have to get around the scales. At regular pull-offs, they'll say: Trucks Must Cross Scales. You pull in there and you find, lo and behold, you're five hundred or a thousand pounds over. You've got to pay a ticket, maybe twenty-five dollars, and you have to move it off. This is a great big piece of steel. You're supposed to unload it. You have to find some guy that's light and break the bands on the bundle and transfer the sheets or bars over on the other truck. Occasionally it's something that can't be broke down, a continuous coil that weighs ten thousand pounds. . . . You wish for the scale to close and you close your eyes and you go like hell to try to get out of the state. You have a feeling of running a blockade in the twenties with a load of booze."

Books on work make fascinating reading; one example is *Seven Days a Week: Women and Domestic Service in Industrializing America* by David Katzman. Do research for your stories; talk to people about their jobs. Judith Rossner must have spent weeks reading for her novel *Evangeline*. John Updike sent away for manuals on how to run a car dealership when he was writing *Rabbit Is Rich*. Work is at the heart of everyone's day. Faulkner said, "You can't eat for eight hours a day nor drink for eight hours a day nor make love for eight hours a day—all you can do for eight hours a day is work. Which is the reason why man makes himself and everybody else so miserable and unhappy."

The Exercise

Read twenty or thirty pages of *Working*—just enough to whet your appetite for writing fiction about the workplace. Then write a story in which a character is having a personal problem that is being played out where he or she works. You might want to choose a job that you haven't had so you can bring a fresh eye to its language, its details.

The Objective

To put your characters back to work so we meet them at work—and play.

Student Example

The whole thing started when Sparky came unglued in the trunk of my car. That's the number one thing a ventriloquist never does—leave his dummy in ninety-six degree heat in a parking lot. And that's the first thing Lester ever told me. Lester's my older brother and he's a professional ventriloquist. He works the Carmen Miranda room at the Chelsea Hotel on Monday nights. It's the kind of place that keeps its Christmas lights strung up year round. I like to go there and order something ritzy, like a Manhattan, and watch him. Lester's a wizard.

His lips are never more than a quarter inch apart. He can drink a whole glass of water and the Colonel keeps jabbering away. The Colonel's the name of his dummy. The rack of medals above the Colonel's pocket—those are Dad's medals from WW II, and Dad would be proud to have them on display in such a classy place as the Carmen Miranda room. Lester says ventriloquism is going to make a comeback, just like everything.

Lester and I live together. When he saw Sparky was falling apart, he really blew his top. He asked me to repeat the most important rule a ventriloquist must remember.

"Keep your buddy clean," I said. "Sparky is my life-time partner."
Lester's scrunched-up face went back to normal.
We worked on Sparky in silence, gluing the bottom half of his mouth again.

—MATT MARINOVICH, FROM "SPOKEN FOR,"
PUBLISHED IN *THE QUARTERLY*

Fiction is nothing less than the subtlest instrument for self-examination and self-display that mankind has invented yet.
—JOHN UPDIKE

33

He/She: Switching Gender

As a writer of fiction you're seriously handicapped if you can't write convincingly about people unlike yourself. You should be able to assume the voice (or, at least, the point of view) of a child, an old person, a member of the opposite gender, or someone of another race. An accomplished writer assumes as many shapes, sizes, colors, etc., as the fictional occasion demands. This requires you to do what actors do when taking on a role: They not only imagine what it's like to be another person, they transform themselves, they get inside their character's skin.

In a *Paris Review* interview, Nadine Gordimer says, "Look at Molly Bloom's soliloquy. To me, that's the ultimate proof of the ability of either sex to understand and convey the inner workings of the other. No woman was ever 'written' better by a woman writer. How did Joyce know? God knows how and it doesn't matter." Here is an excerpt from *Ulysses:*

> . . . I smelt it off her dress when I was biting off the thread of the button I sewed on to the bottom of her jacket she couldn't hide much from me I tell you only I oughtnt to have stitched it and it on her it brings a parting and the last plumpudding too split in 2 halves see it comes out no matter what they say her tongue is a bit too long for my taste your blouse is open too low she says to me the pan calling the kettle blackbottom and I had to tell her not to cock her legs up like that on show on the windowsill before all the people passing they all look at her like me when I was her age of course any old rag looks well on you then. . . .

Sue Miller in "Inventing the Abbotts" establishes early in the story that she is writing in the first person from the point of view of a teenage boy when she writes, ". . . at least twice a year, passing by the Abbotts' house on the way to school, we boys would see the striped fabric of a tent. . . ." And here is Doug coming upon his older brother Jacey:

> When I got home that night, I saw the light on in my brother's room. I went in and stood awkwardly in his doorway. He was reading in bed, the lower part of his body covered with a sheet, the upper part naked. I remember looking at the filled-in, grown-up shape of his upper body and momentarily hating him.

In "Gemcrack," Jayne Anne Phillips uses the first person to create a serial killer who was abused by his uncle as a boy. Here is one of his early school memories:

> The girls twirled, seeing how big their skirts became. I lay on the floor inside the circle of chairs. Above me the skirts volumined like umbrellas. I saw the girls' legs, thin and coltish. Pale. The ankle socks chopped their calves above the ankle and gave the illusion of hooves. I saw their odd white pants and their flatness. They were clean like dolls. They smelled of powder. They flashed and moved. I turned my face to the hard blond legs of the chairs.

In *Professor Romeo,* Anne Bernays uses the third person to write from the point of view of a man accused of sexual harassment:

> "Why do all you girls think you're fat? [Barker asks] Even you skinny ones?"
> "You really think I'm skinny?"
> Barker saw Kathy's teeth for the first time as she grinned at him. He had almost forgotten that bit of magic: Tell a female she's thin and she's yours for life.

The Exercise

Write a page in the first person, assuming the voice of someone of the opposite gender. This can be a description, a narrative, or a segment of autobiography. The main point is to completely lose yourself and become another.

The Objective

To learn how to draw convincing verbal portraits of characters different from yourself and to make them sympathetic, rounded, and complex even though you don't especially "like" them or admire what they represent.

Successful characters are not merely invented, but should emerge from a writer's latent, even secret anxieties, hungers, and obsessions.
—MARIA FLOOK

34

My Pet

from Alison Lurie

The following exercise works best if it is done first and discussed and analyzed afterward.

The Exercise

Write a composition on the subject "My Pet." The only requirement is that this must be a pet you have never owned. It can be anything from a kitten to a dinosaur, from a fly to a dragon. Describe what your pet looks like, how you acquired it, what it eats and where it sleeps, what tricks it can do, and how it gets on with your family, friends, neighbors, or the people at work.

Notes For Discussion

We are, we are told, a nation of pet lovers, and more than half the households in America include an animal, bird, or fish. What are the motives for keeping a pet? Possible suggestions are need for protection, need for affection (a creature you can love and/or one that will love you), aesthetic appreciation (the beautiful pet as interior decoration), parental feeling (a child substitute), sadistic impulses (something to maltreat), etc. What is the function of the pet in your exercise?

A portrait of a pet is also one way of creating a portrait of its owner. What does this exercise tell us about the pet's owner (for instance, that he is kind, timid, affectionate, loves beauty, etc.)?

It has also often been remarked that some people come to resemble their pets, or vice versa. Why does this happen? In other cases, the pet is extremely different from the owner; possibly it may express impulses that its owner does not want to or cannot express (for example, the actively aggressive dog with an apparently passive and peaceful owner). Is the pet in your composition like or unlike its owner, and how?

Animals can play an important part in fiction, and not only in so-called animal stories. Some classic examples are Balzac's "A Passion in the Desert," Kafka's "The Metamorphosis," D. H. Lawrence's *The Fox*, and

Ursula K. Le Guin's "The Wife's Story." What is the character and function of the pet in your exercise? What is its relation to its owner? How could this description be the basis for a short story?

The Objective

To expand your conception of characters and relationships.

Appealing workplaces are to be avoided. One wants a room with no view, so imagination can meet memory in the dark. When I furnished this study seven years ago, I pushed the long desk against a blank wall, so I could not see from either window. Once, fifteen years ago, I wrote in a cinder-block cell over a parking lot. It overlooked a tar-and-gravel roof. This pine shed under trees is not quite so good as the cinder-block study was, but it will do.

"The beginning of wisdom," according to a West African proverb, "is to get you a roof."

—ANNIE DILLARD

PART FOUR

Perspective, Distance, and Point of View

Some stories occur to us with the point of view already decided and their writing proceeds smoothly to the end. Other stories need a more considered decision about who is going to tell the story and at what distance from the reader; these require trial and error to get it right. We hope you have both experiences; writing feels like magic when you only have to think "story," but there is power to be drawn from making a deliberate and well thought-out choice from the wide array of possibilities presented by point of view.

Henry James called the point of view in fiction a "central intelligence." By this, he meant that point of view operates as eyes, ears, memory, and understanding through which the narrative makes its progress.

There are various forms of point of view—often referred to as POV: the first-person "I," as in Herman Melville's *Moby Dick*, Margaret Atwood's *The Handmaid's Tale*, J.D. Salinger's *The Catcher in the Rye*, F. Scott Fitzgerald's *The Great Gatsby*, and Molly Keane's *Good Behavior*; the "we," used rarely, as in Joan Chase's *During the Reign of the Queen of Persia*; the second-person singular—"you," rarer still, but used by Jay McInerny in his novel *Bright Lights, Big City*; and the third person—"he" or "she"—which gives the writer the most latitude.

The third person is also flexible. You can use the third-person subjective, which is similar to first person in that it's limited to one POV, such as in Rachel Ingalls's novel *Mrs. Caliban*; the difference is the use of "she" or "he" rather than "I." This POV cannot move outside the person through whom you're telling your story. For instance, a subjective character can't describe what he or she looks like from behind. You can use the third-person objective, as Hemingway does in his short story "Hills Like White Elephants." Finally, there is the omniscient POV, in which the author moves from distant description and scene setting to commenting on what is happening to the thoughts of various characters. Tolstoy's *War and Peace* is told via this omniscient POV, as are Alice Hoffman's *White Horses* and *Turtle Moon*.

When deciding on what POV to use in any story or novel, ask yourself two questions: Whose story should this be? Whose vision is most dramatic and effective?

A third consideration concerns psychic distance, defined by John Gardner as "the distance the reader feels between himself and the events of the story." In the exercise on page 91 psychic distance is further explored and explained.

For more discussion of point of view we suggest you read Wayne C. Booth's *The Rhetoric of Fiction*, John Gardner's *The Art of Fiction*, and Macauley and Lanning's *Technique in Fiction*.

When you are writing you are not conscious of the reader, so that you don't feel embarrassed. I'm sure Joyce had a most heady and wonderful time writing the last fifty pages of Ulysses—*glorious Molly Bloom. He must have written it in one bout, thinking: I'll show the women of the world that I am omniscient.*

—EDNA O'BRIEN

35

First Person or Third

When you begin a story, you are faced with the immediate decision of point of view and more often than not you will choose either the first or third person. For some writers, this decision is a conscious choice involving questions and answers about the most effective "central intelligence." For other writers, point of view is a given—it seems to come with the story they are about to tell.

The first-person point of view has the advantage of immediacy and a clear, singular voice—think of John Dowell in Ford Madox Ford's *The Good Soldier,* Captain Charles Ryder in Evelyn Waugh's *Bridehead Revisited,* Benjy, Quentin, and Jason in William Faulkner's *The Sound and the Fury,* Grendel in John Gardner's *Grendel,* Ruthie in Marilynne Robinson's *Housekeeping,* Antonio in Rudolfo Anaya's *Bless Me, Ultima,* Philip Carver in Peter Taylor's *Summons to Memphis,* Anne August in Mona Simpson's *Anywhere But Here,* and Jing-Mei Woo in Amy Tan's *The Joy Luck Club.* Each of these first-person narrators has a special voice that draws us in to his or her world. The limitation of this point of view is that the "I" should be present when most of the action takes place and is the only interpreter, aside from the reader, of what happened.

The third-person point of view is a familiar and reliable kind of central intelligence, one that allows the writer greater latitude in terms of distance and the authority to shift point of view. Several novels using third person are Joseph Heller's *Catch-22,* Christina Stead's *The Man Who Loved Children,* Leslie Epstein's *King of the Jews,* and Charles Baxter's *First Light,* whose chapters alternate between a brother and sister's point of view.

The decision whether to use first person or third is often a difficult one. (Anne Bernays wrote her novel *Growing Up Rich* using the third-person point of view, then realized it belonged in the first person and rewrote it, starting on page one; it took a year. Changing point of view like this involves a great deal more than simply turning all the "she's" into "I's"; the author must step completely away from the story and let I's voice speak for itself.) Too often writers begin a story in the first person because it makes them feel closer to the story, yet the voice isn't unique enough to warrant first person. In general, if you can substitute "he" or "she" for "I," then your story should be in third person.

The Exercise

Begin a story with a third-person point of view, making a conscious decision about distance. Write two or three pages. Then begin this same story again using a first-person point of view, rewriting the same two or three pages. Do the same in reverse—changing a first-person narrative into third.

The Objective

To understand the limitations and powers inherent in both the first- and third-person points of view. To make you more aware of the choices available to you as author and storyteller.

I remember standing on a street corner with the black painter Beauford Delaney down in the Village waiting for the light to change, and he pointed down and said, "Look." I looked and all I saw was water. And he said, "Look again," which I did, and I saw oil on the water and the city reflected in the puddle. It was a greater revelation to me. I can't explain it. He taught me how to see, and how to trust what I saw. Painters have often taught writers how to see. And once you've had that experience, you see differently.
                                        —JAMES BALDWIN

36

John Gardner on Psychic Distance

In the introduction to this section, we said that understanding and controlling "psychic distance" was as important to fiction as choosing a point of view. John Gardner's superb chapter "Common Errors," from *The Art of Fiction*, illustrates the range of psychic distance in five possible openings for a story:

1. It was winter of the year 1853. A large man stepped out of a doorway.

2. Henry J. Warburton had never much cared for snowstorms.

3. Henry hated snowstorms.

4. God how he hated these damn snowstorms.

5. Snow. Under your collar, down inside your shoes, freezing and plugging up your miserable soul.

Note how the first opening begins at a great distance from the reader in terms of time and space as it places the year of the story and introduces its character as "a large man." Isaac Bashevis Singer often begins his stories at this distance:

> It was during the summer of 1946, in the living room of Mrs. Kopitzky on Central Park West.
>
> —"THE SEANCE"

> In the town of Shidlovtse, which lies between Radom and Kielce, not far from the Mountains of the Holy Cross, there lived a man by the name of Reb Sheftel Vengrover.
>
> —"THE DEAD FIDDLER"

Then, like a camera zooming in on a scene, in each of the above stories Singer draws the reader closer to his characters and into their thoughts. At other times Singer begins stories closer in:

> Harry Bendiner awoke at five with the feeling that as far as he was concerned the night was finished and he wouldn't get any more sleep.
>
> —"OLD LOVE"

I never learned his name.

—"Two Markets"

I often hear people say, "This cannot happen, that cannot be, nobody has ever heard of such a thing, impossible." Nonsense!

—"Zeitl and Rickel"

As you can see, there is enormous elasticity available in distance but it must be carefully controlled—especially since you can change the distance within a story. In general, the distance at which you begin a story or novel is the outer boundary beyond which you cannot go within that story. For example, if you begin a story at distance 3, as Singer did with Henry Bendiner in "Old Love," you cannot then draw back to the more formal stance of distance 1 by saying "The large man had never slept well." But if you begin at distance 1, as Singer does with " . . . there lived a man by the name of Reb Sheftel Vengrover," you can "zoom in" like a camera within the story, even into a character's thoughts, to say "Reb Sheftel was almost speechless with terror, but he remembered God and recovered." Then you can pan back out to "Reb Sheftel was the first to die" and "More years went by, but the dead fiddler was not forgotten."

A careless shift in psychic distance would be to begin with "It was winter of the year 1853. A large man stepped out of a doorway" and move to "God how he hated these damn snowstorms." Although both employ the third-person point of view, the psychic shift from one to the other is jarring. Gardner's example of a shift in psychic distance that doesn't work is this: "Mary Borden hated woodpeckers. Lord, she thought, they'll drive me crazy! The young woman had never known any personally, but Mary knew what she liked."

The Exercise

First, go back to the list of beginning sentences on page 91, and read each sentence to determine its psychic distance from the reader—from 1, the greatest distance, to 5, where the psychic distance almost disappears.

Next, begin a new story five times using as your guide Gardner's five beginnings.

Finally, begin a new story at distance 1 or 2 and within 200 words gracefully decrease the psychic distance until you have reached distance 4.

The Objective

To understand how psychic distance works so that you can make conscious decisions about the range of psychic distance to use in each story or novel you write.

37

Shifts in Point of View

New writers are often told to use one point of view when telling a story—and for good reason. Shifts in point of view are difficult to do and depend on the writer's absolute control of language, detail, and observation. Four writers who shift point of view are Flaubert in *Madame Bovary,* Shirley Hazzard in *The Transit of Venus,* Alice Hoffman in *White Horses,* and Alice Adams in many of her short stories. Also, shifts in point of view must be warranted. The reader has to learn something from each character's viewpoint that he cannot learn from the perspective and interpretation of one character. Note in Kate Wheeler's story "Under the Roof" on page 462 how each character has information and perceptions the other characters couldn't possibly know.

Some writers indicate a shift in viewpoint by putting the narrator's name at the beginning of their sections, as Faulkner does in *As I Lay Dying,* Anne Tyler in *Celestial Navigation,* and Rosellen Brown in *The Autobiography of My Mother.*

Other writers, such as Sharon Sheehe Stark in *The Wrestling Season,* depend on indications in the narrative for us to know that we are now in a different character's point of view. Chapter 28 ends with Louise: "No wonder she hadn't heard the usual ferocious kabooms of some engine racing before takeoff. He had gone, yes, but not so far. As usual he was camping just outside the thumping, ridiculous mystery of her wifely heart." Chapter 29 begins with Michael: "And Michael woke early to dread. Sometimes that stalled-heart dream of his left him heavy like this, dejected. Yet he was quite certain the night had passed without fatality, dreamlessly indeed."

In Pamela Painter's story "Intruders of Sleepless Nights," the point of view shifts among three characters—a husband and wife pretending to be asleep in their bedroom and a burglar on his way there to steal the wife's jewelry. Each section begins with an observation that tells the reader whose point of view we are in. The burglar is first: "They own no dogs; the maid sleeps out. The catches on the windows are those old-fashioned brass ones, butterfly locks. No alarm system or fancy security." A few sentences later, the wife is next: "Her husband is asleep—finally. His back is to her, his right shoulder high, and now his breathing has slowed to a steady pace like some temporarily regulated clock." After more of the wife's observations, the husband's section is next: "His wife thinks he is sleeping. He knows this by the way she begins to move, adjusting the sheets, almost gaily like a puppet released to live." The story then returns to the original order: the burglar, the wife, and the husband throughout.

Shifts in point of view from paragraph to paragraph, or within the same paragraph, are more difficult to do and few writers attempt this. One writer who does is Alice Adams. For example, her story "The Party-Givers" opens with three people sitting around at the end of a party. In the space of the first two pages, the point of view shifts from Josiah, to his wife, Hope, to Clover, a former lover of Josiah's. Adams writes:

> Josiah liked the party; he smiles to himself at each recounted incident.
>
> Hope, Josiah's small, blond and very rich newlywed wife, during the noisy hours of the party has been wondering if she should kill herself. . . . This is Hope's question: if she killed herself, jumped off one of the bridges, maybe, would Josiah fall in love with Clover all over again? marry her? or would her death keep them guiltily apart?
>
> Clover, a former lover of Josiah's, of some years back, is a large, dark, carelessly beautiful woman, with heavy dark hair, a successfully eccentric taste in clothes. In the intervals between her major love affairs, or marriages, she has minor loves, and spends time with friends, a course that was recommended by Colette, she thinks. This is such an interval, since Josiah who was once a major love is now a friend, and maybe Hope is too; she can't tell yet.

Adams accomplishes her many point-of-view shifts by skillfully weaving attributions for thought into her narrative: "smiles to himself at each recounted incident," "has been wondering," "this is Hope's question [thought]," "she thinks," and "she can't tell yet."

Graceful transitions are worth all the time and energy you invest in them.

The Exercise

Write a scene involving two or three characters who have secrets from each other—or possess different perspectives on what they are doing or have just done. Or write a story using several points of view. Remember that the point of view shifts must be warranted by the information and perspective each brings to the story.

The Objective

To experience how a shift in point of view works and what conditions of the situation make it necessary.

38

An Early Memory,
Part One: The Child
as Narrator

"Write what you know" is by now such a cliché that people tend to ignore it. For the beginning writer it's pretty good advice. Your own life—and your memories of it—have an intensity and immediacy useful in creating fiction. It's not just what you know, however, but how you see it, shape it, and enhance it with your imagination. This is the crucial difference between fiction and fact. Fiction is always sifted through a singular set of perceptions, feelings, and wishes, while fact can be recorded by a machine designed for that purpose—a tape recorder or camera. Furthermore, the fiction writer often supplies an implicit rather than an explicit moral attitude.

Keep in mind when doing this exercise that even though you are writing from the point of view of a child or a young adult your audience is still an adult audience. Christine McDonnell, author of the young adult book *Friends First,* which has a fourteen-year-old narrator, makes this distinction:

> In adult fiction, when a story has a child's point of view, usually the child is scrutinizing the adult world, trying to make sense of adult behavior or adult society, as in J. D. Salinger's *Catcher in the Rye,* the childhood chapters in Anne Tyler's *Dinner at the Homesick Restaurant,* the children in Dickens's novels or Susan Minot's *Monkeys.* Children's points of view can add humor—O'Henry—or moral commentary—Mark Twain's Huck Finn. Sometimes, from a child's point of view, the situation seems more frightening or dangerous, as in Robb Forman Dew's *The Time of Her Life,* when the child is caught in her parents' ugly, boozy separation, and in Suzanna Moore's *My Old Sweetheart,* about a mentally unstable mother and philandering father. In all of these, the scope of the story is larger than childhood. Children are windows onto a larger picture, and that larger picture is of interest to adults.

The young narrators in Sharon Sheehe Stark's "Leo" and Charles Baxter's "Gryphon" are child narrators trying to make sense of the larger adult world at the point it intersects with their own.

The Exercise

Using the present tense, write an early memory in the first person. Choose something that happened before you were ten. Use only those words and perceptions appropriate to a young child. The memory should be encapsulated in a short period of time—no more than an hour or so—and should happen in one place. Don't interpret or analyze; simply report it as you would a dream. When you can't remember details, make them up; you may heighten the narrative so long as you remain faithful to the "meaning" of the memory—the reason you recalled it in the first place. Limit: 550 words.

The Objective

A fiction writer should be able to present a narrative without nudging the reader or in any way explaining what she has written. The narrative should speak for itself. In using a child's voice you are forced not to analyze but merely to tell the story, unembellished.

In probing my childhood (which is the next best to probing one's eternity) I see the awakening of consciousness as a series of spaced flashes, with the intervals between them gradually diminishing until bright blocks of perception are formed, affording memory a slippery hold.
—VLADIMIR NABOKOV

39

An Early Memory, Part Two: The Reminiscent Narrator

Something crucial to remember: The story doesn't exist until you tell it, and the same holds true for when and how your narrator chooses to tell her story. Eudora Welty in *One Writer's Beginnings* speaks of this ordering of time:

> The events in our lives happen in a sequence of time, but in their significance to ourselves they find their own order, a timetable not necessarily, perhaps not possibly, chronological. The time as we know it subjectively is often the chronology that stories and novels follow: it is the continuous thread of revelation.

This is especially true of the reminiscent narrator, a narrator who is looking back and reinterpreting or confronting the past because it has a special pointed meaning for her—a meaning that has often eluded the narrator until this particular telling of the story.

The reminiscent narrator of Peter Taylor's story "The Old Forest" is telling his story from a vantage point of forty-plus years. The tone and distance from past events are established immediately with the first line, "I was already formally engaged, as we used to say, to the girl I was going to marry." The narrator goes on to recount events that occurred when he was in an accident with another young woman a week before his wedding. At one point he wonders why these events and the images of Lee Ann's footprints in the snow and of his own bloody hand have stayed with him. "In a way it is strange that I remember all these impressions so vividly after forty years, because it is not as though I have lived an uneventful life during the years since." He goes on to list his World War II experiences, the deaths of his two younger brothers in Korea, the deaths of his parents in a terrible fire, and also the deaths of his two teenage children. As he continues the story, he learns perhaps for the first time to speak of his failures—the most important perhaps was the failure to follow his own heart. He has had a good, long life with the girl he was engaged to. He learned to follow his heart when he left the Memphis social and business community to become an English professor, but it was a lesson he learned through the events of this particular story—and with the help of Caroline his wife.

Alice Munro is another writer who brilliantly employs the reminiscent narrator to tell her story in such stories as "Friend of My Youth," "Wigtime," "Hold Me Fast, Don't Let Me Pass," and "Differently"—stories in which the present is informed by the past.

The Exercise

In no more than two pages, use the incident of "An Early Memory, Part One" and tell it from the vantage point of who you are today, that is, inject it with adult vocabulary, insight, subtlety, and comprehension. For example, "My father was obviously confused" replaces "funny look." Change the way the incident is told without altering its content. Use the past tense but keep it a first-person narrative. As in the first part of this exercise, try to let the material speak for itself. We draw up out of the well of our unconscious those things that have emotional significance. In contrast to the previous exercise, this one will force you to search—with an adult sensibility—for the underlying "meaning" of the event you simply reported in "An Early Memory, Part One" (page 96). What have you learned in the interim? What can be gained—or lost—by hindsight?

The Objective

As in many of these exercises, the idea is to empower the writer with the knowledge that he controls the material, and not the other way around. There are countless ways to tell the same story and each way says something and reveals something a little different, not only about what happened but also about how the teller feels about it.

Planning to write is not writing. Outlining . . . researching . . . talking to people about what you're doing, none of that is writing. Writing is writing.

—E. L. DOCTOROW

40

The Unreliable Narrator

You may find that you want to create a character who says one thing and unwittingly reveals another—for example, a teacher who claims to love all her students, even those with "funny, hard-to-pronounce names and weird haircuts." The unreliable narrator—between whose lines the author invites you to read—is a classic fixture in works of fiction. Eudora Welty's narrator in "Why I Live at the P.O." is a wonderful example of unreliability. So is the narrator of Ford Madox Ford's *The Good Soldier*. And more recently, Stevens, the butler of Kazuo Ishiguro's *The Remains of the Day*, totally deludes himself about the pre–World War II politics of his employer, Lord Darlington, and about his own feelings for another servant, Miss Kenton. And consider the voice of the narrator in Jenefer Shute's acclaimed first novel *Life Size*. Josie has been hospitalized for starving herself and is told that she cannot yet begin psychotherapy because she is "a starving organism" whose brain is "not working the way it should." She thinks to herself, "On the contrary, it's never been purer and less cluttered, concentrated on essentials instead of distracted by a body clamoring for attention, demanding that its endless appetites be appeased. . . . One day I will be pure consciousness, traveling unmuffled through the world; one day I will refine myself to the bare wiring, the irreducible circuitry that keeps mind alive." Were Josie allowed to have her way, she would surely die.

The Exercise

Using the first person, write a self-deceiving portrait in which the narrator is not the person she thinks she is—either more or less admirable. You must give your readers clues that your narrator is skewing the truth.

The Objective

To create a narrator who unwittingly reveals—through subtle signals of language, details, contradictions, and biases—that his or her judgment of events and people is too subjective to be trusted. The reader must thus discount the version of the story offered by the narrator and try to re-create a more objective one for himself.

PART FIVE

Dialogue

Dialogue is what people do to each other.

—Elizabeth Bowen

Dialogue is, basically, two or more characters talking to each other. It is also an ideal, compact way to advance your story by having one character tell another what's happening—to reveal, admit, incite, accuse, lie, etc.

Furthermore, dialogue is an economical way of defining a character, the way someone speaks—accent, vocabulary, idiom, inflection, etc.—tells us as much about what he is like as his actions do.

Dialogue is never a faithful rendering of the way human beings really speak. At its most poetic it is the iambic pentameter of Shakespeare's plays; at the other end of the spectrum it is Mark Twain's Huckleberry Finn using the Mississippi Valley vernacular of the 1840s. Both authors omit the hesitations, repetitions, false starts, meanderings, and aborted phrases that make actual human talk so much less compelling. Read a transcript of testimony or of a taped telephone conversation or listen attentively to the next person with whom you have a conversation and you will realize that fictional dialogue is only an approximation of true speech, having been shaped, pointed, and concentrated.

Paradoxically, dialogue is often useful for getting across *what is not said*, what we call the subtext. For instance, if you want to show that someone in a story or novel wants to avoid an unpleasant encounter, you can indicate this by having them talk around the topic uppermost in their mind but never quite touching it. In using dialogue this way, you're asking the reader to read between the lines. This is a tricky maneuver but if you think about how you talk to someone yourself when you're angry at them but don't want to tell them exactly why—by being sarcastic, arch, nitpicky, overly solicitous, etc.—you'll get it right.

It's important, too, to learn when to use direct discourse—*he said, she said*—and when to summarize by indirect discourse. This is partly a matter of what "feels" right and partly of how important the actual words used are to your narrative. For example, forcing character A to answer the phone "Hello," and then having character B say "Hello" back isn't essential. It is flat, and boring—everyone knows how you answer the phone. Far better to cut to the chase: What did character A learn from B's phone call that moves the story along or tells us something crucial about either or both A and B?

> The phone rang. It was George wanting to borrow the jeep. I told him, "Don't bring it back without a full tank of gas."

Dialogue generally goes for the heart of the story, the exchange that matters, the confrontation.

One must *avoid ambition* in order *to write. Otherwise something else is the goal: some kind of power beyond the power of language. And the power of language, it seems to me, is the only kind of power a writer is entitled to.*
    —Cynthia Ozick

41

Speech Flavor, or Sounding Real

from Thalia Selz

Here comes your character. She's Irish—Hispanic—Vietnamese, a Maine congresswoman, a shrimp boatman from Louisiana, or a black professor of English in an Ivy League college who retains traces of her Chicago slum childhood in her speech. Your character is eager to have the conversation that the structure of the story demands. Or maybe she wants to tell the story, as in a first-person narrative. Either way, you want that speech to have its own flavor, to suggest the character and background of the person uttering it, without using much phonetic spelling because it can be hard to read. Characters in fiction, like real people, have to come out of a context to be convincing and intriguing—even when that context is imaginary, like post–atomic holocaust England in Russell Hoban's *Riddley Walker.*

The Exercise

Observe how the following speech fragments convey a sense of accent or national, regional, race, class, or cultural distinctions mainly through word choice and arrangement. Easily understood foreign words or names can help, too. What do these fragments suggest about the individual speakers by conveying the flavor of their speech?

My mama dead. She die screaming and cussing.
—ALICE WALKER, *THE COLOR PURPLE*

"'I won't keep you,' I says. 'You must get a job for yourself.' But, sure, it's worse whenever he gets a job; he drinks it all."
—JAMES JOYCE, "IVY DAY IN THE COMMITTEE ROOM"

"*Muy buenos,*" I said. "Is there an Englishwoman here? I would like to see this English lady."
"*Muy buenos.* Yes, there is a female English."
—ERNEST HEMINGWAY, *THE SUN ALSO RISES*

" . . . the working mens one Sunday afternoon taking they only time off.
They laying around drinking some moonshine, smoking the hemp, having
a cock fight."

—PETER LEACH, "THE CONVICT'S TALE"

"My own wife is seven years older than me. So what did I suffer?—Nothing. If Rothschild's daughter wants to marry you, would you say on
account her age, no?"

—BERNARD MALAMUD, "THE MAGIC BARREL"

"Why me?" she rumbled. "It's no trash around here, black or white, that
I haven't given to. And break my back to the bone every day working.
And do for the church."

—FLANNERY O'CONNOR, "REVELATION"

"Father says for you to come on and get breakfast," Caddy said. "Father
says it's over a half an hour now, and you've got to come this minute."
I ain't studying no breakfast," Nancy said. "I going to get my sleep out."

—WILLIAM FAULKNER, "THAT EVENING SUN"

"Copy our sister-in-law," Brave Orchid instructed. "Make life unbear-
able for the second wife, and she'll leave. He'll have to build her a second house."
    "I wouldn't mind if she stays," said Moon Orchid. "She can comb my
hair and keep house. She can wash dishes and serve our meals . . . ."

—MAXINE HONG KINGSTON, *THE WOMAN WARRIOR*

Now write five of your own speech fragments.

The Objective

In this case, it is threefold: to help reveal character, to convince your reader
by making your dialogue sound credible, and to add variety. Differences in
speech aren't just realistic; they're interesting and provocative, and they can
give vitality to your story. Speech without flavor is like food without savor.

---

*[Do] not suspend the rest of the world while dialogue takes
place. "Let the sounds of the world continue," I tell them,
"almost like method acting. If you don't, you'll end up with
those amputated-seeming, isolated exchanges in which the rest of
the world has withdrawn out of deference. Much of the conversation that takes place has a background of assorted noises, and
actions too. O for peace and quiet, but not in fiction."*

—PAUL WEST, *MASTER CLASS*

42

Who Said That?

Well, often we're not quite sure because the attribution is faulty or even missing. Yet, it is crucial to know who is saying what to whom because dialogue is central to a scene's drama and forward movement. We need to know whether the wife or the husband says, "I've decided to leave—and no further discussion is necessary." Whether the teenager or the parent says, "You're always taking something the wrong way." Whether the mugger or the victim says, "Don't let things get out of hand here."

There are various ways of attributing speech to make it clear to the reader who is talking. The easiest way is to use *he said* or *she said* or the person's name as in the following example:

"I've decided to leave," George said. "No further discussion necessary."
"So, no discussion," Mary said. "I'll just list all the reasons I'll be glad to see you gone."
"Tell it to the dog," he said.
"That's number one. The dog goes too," she said.

"Said" works most of the time and does not draw attention to itself. Occasionally use "asked" and "replied," but avoid words like "hissed," "trumpeted," "rejoined," "growled," etc. Trust the growl to be inherent in what is said and how the person is described.

Other ways to attribute dialogue to a character are:

- Use the name of the person being spoken to:
  "Jesus, Benjy, my job's more important than your marathon Monopoly game."
  "Aw mom, you're always taking something the wrong way."

- Use emotional clues:
  His head was fizzing and he had trouble keeping the gun pointed at the man's tie. Didn't know who was scareder. "Don't let things get out of hand here."
  The man nodded and nodded. "Take it all, you can have it all."

- Use action:
  She filled a grocery bag with dog food and topped it off with a can of draino. "You getting the picture."

■ Use physical description:
Benjy's t-shirt said "Death by Doughnuts" and his hair rode his shoulders, Christ-like. "Monopoly is teaching me real estate, banking, investment."

"Just don't get too attached to those dice." Her t-shirts never said anything and her hair had been shorter than his for the past five years.

■ Use thinking by the point of view character:
He should have stuck up some woman first. "Just turn around and start walking."

Attribution doesn't only tell you who is speaking. It also provides a way for pacing a scene, for juxtaposing speech with thought, for slowing the action so the reader can absorb what is going on, for including physical details of the scene, for providing emotional clues, and for adding to the rhythm of the sentences.

Finally, most dialogue important to the drama and forward movement of a story is set off by itself, with its method of attribution. When the speaker changes, you begin a new paragraph as in the above examples. However, sometimes exchanges of dialogue are woven into a paragraph, as in the following passage from Anne Tyler's *Celestial Navigation:*

He held out his hand and said, "Well, goodbye for now, Mrs.—Mary," and she said, "Goodbye, Jeremy." Her hand was harder than his, and surprisingly broad across the knuckles. While he was still holding it he said, "Um, may I come back sometime?"—the final hurdle of the visit. "Well, of course," she said, and smiled again as she closed the door.

When dialogue or what is said is not central to a scene's forward movement, but you still want to include the characters' voices, place the dialogue inside a paragraph. Be sure that we know who is saying what. This alternative way of presenting dialogue is an important tool for controlling the pace and shaping the drama of a scene.

The Exercise

Highlight all the dialogue in one of your own stories. Next, find out how many methods of attribution you have used. Remember that attribution contributes a lot more to a scene than just telling us who said what. Then, examine how you have presented your dialogue. Would some lines of dialogue serve your story better inside a paragraph? Are the important lines presented in a dramatic way? Now, rewrite the scene using the tools you have acquired in this exercise.

The Objective

To learn to shape a scene with the tools of dialogue placement and attribution.

43

Telling Talk: When to Use Dialogue or Summarized Dialogue

One of the most important decisions a writer must make is whether to use dialogue or to summarize what is said. Too often dialogue is incorrectly used to provide information that could have been artfully done in summarized dialogue. Or else the reader is given pages of an entire scene—for example, the full escalation of an argument—when in fact only the closing lines are important to hear verbatim.

Summarized dialogue allows the writer to condense speech, set the pace of the scene, reveal attitudes, use understatement, make judgments, describe the talk, avoid sentimentality, and emphasize crucial lines of actual dialogue.

Study the following passages to learn what summarized dialogue accomplishes. If writing summarized dialogue eludes you, type out some of the following examples to *feel* how it works. Then transform the summarized dialogue into dialogue to understand why the author chose to condense it.

> So this ordinary patrolman drove me home. He kept his eye on the road, but his thoughts were all on me. He said that I would have to think about Mrs. Metzger, lying cold in the ground, for the rest of my life, and that, if he were me, he would probably commit suicide. He said that he expected some relative of Mrs. Metzger would get me sooner or later, when I least expected it—maybe the very next day, or maybe when I was a man, full of hopes and good prospects, and with a family of my own. Whoever did it, he said, would probably want me to suffer some.
>   I would have been too addled, too close to death, to get his name, if he hadn't insisted that I learn it. It was Anthony Squires, and he said it was important that I commit it to memory, since I would undoubtedly want to make a complaint about him, since policemen were expected to speak politely at all times, and that, before he got me home, he was going to call me a little Nazi cocksucker and a dab of catshit and he hadn't decided what all yet.
>   —KURT VONNEGUT, JR., *DEADEYE DICK*

> She sits in the visitor's chair beside the raised bed, while Auntie Muriel, wearing an ice-blue bed-jacket, cranked up and propped up, complains. They put extra chlorine in the water here, she can taste it. She can remember when water was water but she doesn't suppose Elizabeth can tell the difference. At first she could not get a private room. Can Elizabeth imagine?

She had to share a room, share one, with a terrible old woman who wheezed at night. Auntie Muriel is convinced the woman was dying. She could hardly get any sleep. And now that she's finally here in her private room, no one pays any attention to her. She has to ring and ring, three times even, before the nurse will come. They all read detective novels, she's seen them . . . . She will speak to Doctor MacFadden, tomorrow. If she has to stay here for a little rest and some tests, which is what he says, the least he can do is make sure she's comfortable. She's never been sick a day in her life, there's nothing really wrong with her now, she isn't used to hospitals.

Elizabeth thinks this may be true.

—Margaret Atwood, *Life Before Man*

That afternoon, Dr. Fish sent a psychiatrist to my bed. He spoke to me kindly in a low voice, and he had a white beard that I found reassuring. He didn't ask about Mrs. O. until the very end. Instead, he inquired about my studies, my parents, my friends. He wanted to know when my headache started and what my other symptoms were. He touched on the subject of my love life with great delicacy and registered my response that it was nonexistent with half a nod. I tried to speak in good sentences and to enunciate clearly. My head hurt, but my breathing was much improved, and I think I convinced him that I was sane. When he finally asked me why I had been screaming at Mrs. O., I told him very honestly that I didn't know, but that at the time it had seemed important to do so, and that I hadn't been screaming but calling. He didn't seem at all shocked by this answer, and before he left he patted my hand. I think I would have enjoyed my talk with him had I not worried about what the conversation was going to cost. He looked expensive to me, and I kept wondering if his sympathy was covered by my insurance.

—Siri Hustvedt, "Houdini"

Papa-Daddy woke up with this horrible yell and right there without moving an inch he tried to turn Uncle Rondo against me. I heard every word he said. Oh, he told Uncle Rondo I didn't learn to read till I was eight years old and he didn't see how in the world I ever got the mail put up at the P.O., much less read it all, and he said if Uncle Rondo could only fathom the lengths he had gone to to get me that job! And he said on the other hand he thought Stella-Rondo had a brilliant mind and deserved credit for getting out of town. All the time he was just lying there swinging as pretty as you please and looping out his beard, and poor Uncle Rondo was pleading with him to slow down the hammock, it was making him as dizzy as a witch to watch it.

—Eudora Welty, "Why I Live at the P.O."

They poured me more wine and I told the story about the English private soldier who was placed under the shower bath. Then the major told the story of the eleven Czechoslovaks and the Hungarian corporal. After some more wine I told the story of the jockey who found the penny. The major said there was an Italian story something like that about the duchess who could not sleep at night. At this point the priest left and I told the story about the travelling salesman who arrived at five o'clock in the morning at Marseilles when the mistral was blowing. The major said he had heard a report that I could drink. I denied this. He said it was true and by the corpse of Bacchus we would test whether it was true or not. Not Bacchus. Yes, Bacchus, he said.

—ERNEST HEMINGWAY, *A FAREWELL TO ARMS*

One evening, Cole and I lay side-by-side on our big brass bed after dinner. Our bellies were full, and the swelter of the day still stuck to us. We lay with our heads toward the foot of the bed, our legs in the air, as we rubbed our feet against the cool white surface of the wall, leaving black smears from the dirt on our soles. We could hear our parents fighting through the heating vent. Muted obscenities. You pompous prick. You fat white mammy. We were trying to block them out with talk of Elemeno. Cole was explaining to me that it wasn't just a language, but a place and a people as well. I had heard this before, but it never failed to entertain me, her description of the land I hope to visit some day. We whispered questions and answers to each other like calls to prayer. *Shimbala matamba caressi. Nicolta fo mo capsala.* The Elemenos, she said, could turn not just from black to white, but from brown to yellow to purple to green and back again. She said they were a shifting people, constantly changing their form, color, pattern, in quest for invisibility. According to her, their changing routine was a serious matter—less a game of make-believe than a fight for survival of their species. The Elemenos could turn deep green in the bushes, beige in the sand, or blank white in the snow, and their power lay precisely in their ability to disappear into any surrounding. As she spoke, a new question—a doubt—flashed through my mind. Something didn't make sense. What was the point of surviving if you had to disappear? I said it aloud—*peta marika vadersa?* But just then the door to our room flew open.

—DANZY SENNA, *CAUCASIA*

Note how telling stories lends itself to summarized dialogue in the Hemingway and Senna passages.

When I went to the school in S for the first time the following morning, the snow lay so thick that I felt a kind of exhilaration at the sight of it. The class I joined was the third grade, which was taught by Paul Bereyter. There I stood, in my dark green pullover with the leaping stag on it, in front of fifty-one fellow pupils, all staring at me with the greatest possible curiosity, and, as if from a great distance, I heard Paul say that I had arrived at precisely the right moment, since he had been telling the story of the stag's leap only the day before, and now the image of the leaping stag worked into the fabric of my pullover, could be copied onto the blackboard. He asked me to take off the pullover and take a seat in the back row beside Fritz Binswanger for the time being, while he, using my picture of a leaping stag, would show us how an image could be broken down into numerous tiny pieces—small crosses, squares or dots—or else assembled from these.

—W.G. SEBALD, *THE EMIGRANTS*

There is *only* summarized dialogue in Sebald's extraordinary book, yet its varied voices are as distinct as any we might hear in literature.

Not all summarized dialogue occurs in blocks. In the following passage, from "Saul and Patsy Are Getting Comfortable," Charles Baxter summarizes a number of phone calls from Saul's mother before he comes to a particular conversation that he puts into actual dialogue:

> Saul's mother, Delia, a boisterous widow who swam a mile a day, played bridge on Tuesdays, tennis on Fridays, called her son every other weekend. When Patsy answered, Saul's mother talked about recipes or the weather; when Saul answered, she discussed life and the nature of fate. In February, after Saul and Patsy had been in Five Oaks for nine months, she said that she had heard from a friend that wonderful teaching jobs were opening up outside Boston, and even closer, right here, outside Baltimore. I heard this, she said, from Mrs. Rauscher. Saul listened to his mother go on for five minutes, and then he stopped her.
> "Ma," he said. "We're staying."
> "Staying? Staying for what? For how long?"
> "For as long as it takes."
> "As long as what takes? Honey, you'll never have a normal life as long as you stay there."
> "What's normal?"

Alice Munro often intersperses dialogue with summarized dialogue. In the following passage from Munro's "Hold Me Fast, Don't Let Me Pass," two people who have just met are dining in a hotel at separate tables. Antoinette owns the hotel.

> Dudley said that he would not eat fish. Hazel, too, had refused it.
> "You see, even the Americans," Dudley said. "Even the Americans won't eat that frozen stuff. And you'd think they'd be used to it; they have everything frozen."
> "I'm Canadian," Hazel said. She thought he'd apologise, remembering he'd been told this once already. But neither he nor Antoinette paid any attention to her. They had embarked on an argument whose tone of practiced acrimony made them sound almost married.
> "Well, I wouldn't eat anything else," Antoinette said.

Another example of dialogue combined with indirect discourse occurs in Munro's story "Differently," when two friends meet at a "hippie restaurant" where they wear "cheap, pretty Indian cotton dresses and pretended to be refugees from a commune. . . ." Munro writes:

> When they weren't playing these games, they talked in a headlong fashion about their lives, childhoods, problems, husbands.
> "That was a horrible place," Maya said. "That school."
> Georgia agreed.
> "They were poor boys at a rich kids' school," Maya said. "So they had to try hard. They had to be a credit to their families."

Georgia would not have thought Ben's family poor, but she knew that there were different ways of looking at such things.

Maya said that whenever they had people in for dinner or the evening, Raymond would pick out beforehand all the records he thought suitable and put them in a suitable order. "I think sometime he'll hand out conversational topics at the door," Maya said.

Georgia revealed that Ben wrote a letter every week to the great-aunt who had sent him to school.

"Is it a nice letter?" said Maya.

"Yes. Oh, yes. It's very nice."

They looked at each other bleakly, and laughed. Then they announced—they admitted—what weighed on them. It was the innocence of these husbands—the hearty, decent, firm, contented innocence. That is a wearying and finally discouraging thing. It makes intimacy a chore.

"But do you feel badly," Georgia said, "talking like this?"

Note in the first passage how summarized dialogue dispenses in one sentence with the business of Antoinette offering each character fish. And how summarized dialogue allows Hazel to ignore the facts of the argument Antoinette and Dudley are having and instead to describe its tenor as having the "practiced acrimony" of marriage. In the second passage, summarized dialogue summarizes what the women usually talk about before it gives way to specifics in dialogue. It also describes the pace of their talk as "headlong." Notice how words like "agreed," "revealed," "insisted," "wailed," "announced," "squealed," "accused," and "admitted" go well with summarized dialogue but are almost never used with actual dialogue.

The Exercise

Highlight the dialogue in a story by a writer you admire. Then determine how much dialogue is summarized rather than presented in quotation marks.

Next, set up a situation in which one character is going on and on about something—complaining about grades, arguing with a spouse about the children, or recounting an accident to a friend. Summarize the dialogue, occasionally interspersing it with comments and stage directions.

The Objective

To understand what summarized dialogue accomplishes and how it affects tone, pace, and the shaping of a scene.

Student Example

No one could be certain whether Kadi had died by accident or by her own design, yet it was much debated over smoky fires far into the humid West

African night, in the manner peculiar to the Fula people. Adulai Embalo, speaker for the village elders, cited the evidence indicating an accident: that Kadi had often slipped at the muddy, sloping edge of the well as she drew water; that she had been up that morning before first light and could not have seen clearly where the bucket-ropes of other women had worn a new incline at the lip of the well; and that her sandals were found nearby, but not her enormous tin washbasin, suggesting that she had been mounting the heavy load on her head when her wet bare feet lost their hold on the slick clay.

The others listened respectfully to this, and paused in silence to consider it in the glow of the dying coals. Mamadu then proposed the facts that suggested Kadi had taken her own life: that she had quarreled with her husband Demba the night before; that she had been ashamed not to have conceived since her third miscarriage the previous rainy season; and that her rice plot had been damaged by wandering cattle so that her harvest would be less than half of what she and Demba needed toward the purchase of medicine to fertilize her womb, or toward the purchase of a second wife for Demba. But little could be done about Kadi now, except to discuss and turn over each point cited by the speakers, which is what the other village elders did as the fire slowly died, savoring the joy of conversation in the arcane Fulani of older men.

—CAMERON MACAULEY, "THE WOMAN AT THE WELL,"
PUBLISHED IN *PRISM INTERNATIONAL*

Recently, I was engaged in a profoundly meaningful conversation in one corner of a large common room. In the corner opposite somebody was trying to conduct some silly group discussion. Presently, a young man strode briskly across the floor and tapped me on the shoulder. "Can you try and keep it down?" he said. "You can't imagine how your voice carries." . . . It carries. Yes, that's the idea, isn't it? You say what you have to say the way you have to say it and hope to hell you're bothering somebody.
—SHARON SHEEHE STARK, *OTHER VOICES*

44

The Invisible Scene: Interspersing Dialogue with Action

Flannery O'Connor, in her essay "Writing Short Stories," says that in beginning stories,

> dialogue frequently proceeds without the assistance of any characters that you can actually see, and uncontained thought leaks out of every corner of the story. The reason is usually that the student is wholly interested in his thoughts and his emotions and not in his dramatic action, and that is he is too lazy or highfalutin to descend to the concrete where fiction operates.

When you are writing a scene in a story, it might help to think of your characters as being onstage. Your reader will want to know what they look like and what the stage setting looks like. Next, your reader will want to have a sense of how your characters move around and interact with the furniture of their stage world—in other words the stage business, body language, or choreography. Characters live in a concrete world and it is your job as a fiction writer to keep them there.

The Exercise

Write a scene in which a character's body, as well as his mind, is engaged in doing something—stage business. Here are some possibilities:

Repairing something
Playing solitaire or a game involving other players
Doing exercises
Painting a canvas or a wall
Cutting down a tree
Giving someone a haircut

Come up with your own suggestions.

Explore how various activities and settings can change what happens within a scene. For example, what happens when characters are planning their honeymoon while they are painting an apartment or while one of them ıs cutting the other's hair? Or what happens when characters are having a confrontation in public—say in a fancy restaurant—rather than in the privacy of their home?

It is also instructive to analyze how a writer you admire handles the interweaving of dialogue and body language. Go through one of your favorite stories and highlight all the body language and choreography. We guarantee this will teach you something.

The Objective

To give concrete life to the scenes our characters inhabit. To understand how action and choreography relate to the objects in the scene and how all of these relate to and help shape dialogue and the engagement of the characters.

Student Example

The church was condemned last week, so my sister Marion decided to have the wedding in Mom and Ivan's backyard, in front of the herb garden. I drove by the church yesterday to see the steeple that was sitting on a trailer in the parking lot. Luckily they found that it was rotting and took it down before it fell on people. Marion should take the hint.

An hour ago Mom put me in charge of weeding the old patch of dirt. "It's the least you can do for your sister's special day," Mom said. It had rained last night, so the garden was thick mud. The knees of my new red sweat pants would be stained and I'd need a hairbrush to get it out from under my fingernails.

"Colleen! Where are the car keys?" Marion called, her face pressed against the window screen.

"I put them on the counter," I said.

"They aren't there. Come in here and find them."

I threw another weed on the weed pile and slammed the screen door into the kitchen. Marion's face was pink and her hands shook. "Don't do this to me, Colleen. Mom and I need to leave now." The wedding was two days away and Marion had the whole house preparing. Ivan was at Woolworth's getting new lawn furniture and Mom was at the sink drowning a pot of peeled potatoes.

I wiped my hands on my jeans and pulled the keys from the Union Trust mug next to the sugar bowl. I threw them at her left hand. "Where's Gabe?" Her fiancé lived in the apartment buildings across town. He was nearly thirty, but he still mowed lawns and delivered papers for a living. Instead of a bike, he drove a red Mustang. I figured he should be here weeding the parsley too.

"Shut up, Colleen," Marion said. She bent down to look at her reflection in the microwave door.

"Girls," Mom said, turning off the water hard. She gave me a look and left to get her coat.

—KIM LEAHY

45

A Verbal Dance:
Not Quite a Fight

Good dialogue is not at all the way human beings speak to each other—it's an approximation. Dialogue takes human speech and renders it condensed, highlighted, and pointed. Dialogue is extremely useful when you want to show what a character is thinking and want to avoid the leaden "she thought" formulation. Simply bring on another character and have the two of them hold a conversation. Dialogue reveals character—as anyone who has ever seen a decent play knows. It is also good for breaking up long paragraphs and provides an opportunity to use common idioms. The way a character talks—vocabulary, tone, style, and sense of humor—can tell your readers exactly what you want them to know in a "showing" way that narrative can only "tell."

The Exercise

Write a dialogue between two people who know each other, each taking the opposite side of an issue or problem. This should be a verbal dance, not a shouting match. The issue you choose should be something immediate and particular (like whether to spend money on a vacation or put it in the savings account) rather than abstract (terrorism will be with us for a long time). The speakers should be equally convincing. That is, you, the author, can't load the argument on one side or the other. Make each person distinctive in her oral style, for example, in vocabulary and tone. Keep in mind that the subtext—what the conversation reveals about the speakers' relationship to each other—is as important as the manifest text. For example, in the what-shall-we-do-with-the-money conversation the subtext is about which of the two speakers has more power—and is willing to exploit it. Limit: 550 words.

The Objective

To learn to use dialogue to reveal character and human dynamics and to understand that speaking style says as much about a person as her behavior does. Incidentally, you should also recognize that dialogue should not be used for the following: for lengthy exposition, to furnish your stage, as a substitute for action, and as a vehicle for showing off your own vocabulary and education. A false line of dialogue can ruin an entire scene.

46

Text and Subtext:
Psychic Clothing

Most of us cover the nakedness of our true intentions with layers of psychic clothing. Our smile disguises a grimace; our laugh chokes a sob. The so-called text is right out there; the subtext is what is really going on. The two things don't necessarily have to contradict each other—they may vary only slightly. But it's important for the writer to be aware that subtexts exist, operating on a deeper, hidden level, along with overt action and dialogue.

In John Updike's story "Still of Some Use," Foster and his former wife are cleaning out the attic of a house they once lived in together and which she is now selling.

> "How can you bear it?" [Foster] asked of the emptiness.
> "Oh, it's fun," she said, "once you get into it. Off with the old, on with the new. The new people seem nice. They have *little* children."

Nothing but pain lies beneath the wife's flippancy.

In Anne Tyler's novel *The Accidental Tourist,* a couple, Sarah and Macon, whose son has recently been killed by a deranged gunman, are riding together in a car.

> Macon sped ahead, with his hands relaxed on the wheel.
> "Did you notice that boy with the motorcycle?" Sarah asked. She had to raise her voice; a steady, insistent roaring sound engulfed them.
> "What boy?"
> "He was parked beneath the underpass."
> "It's crazy to ride a motorcycle on a day like today," Macon said. "Crazy to ride one any day. You're so exposed to the elements."

Exposed, just as their son was exposed, as we all are—to whatever "elements" lurk in the world, waiting to finish us off.

The Exercise

Write two very short examples of text, in which the true meaning of the action or dialogue is hidden in a subtext. Under each text explicate the subtext.

The Objective

To learn to use indirection to illustrate the power of hidden meaning. This is something like a double exposure, a photograph that shows two images simultaneously.

The wastepaper basket is the writer's best friend.
—ISAAC BASHEVIS SINGER

PART SIX

The Interior Landscape of Your Characters

Hate is a failure of Imagination.

—GRAHAM GREENE

Characters reveal themselves through what they say, through their actions and body language, and also through the shape of their mental landscape. In story after story, novel after novel, a character's interior landscape is one of the most powerful resources in the art of fiction. Anything is possible when you allow your characters, through the use of their imaginations, to explore their worlds, their relationships, occasionally to transcend the confines of their point of view, and experience the full range of how they lead their inner lives. We all lead inner lives that run parallel to what we are actually doing or saying. For example, while you are driving west to start a new job, you might recall the disaster of the last job, regret past mistakes, make plans for your first day at work, entertain fears and hopes—all this while also listening to Miles Davis, mentally revising the last story you wrote, obsessing about the welfare of the cat in his cage in the backseat, and traveling at seventy miles per hour. You might also be carrying on a lively conversation with an amiable hitchhiker, while divulging none of your misgivings about this move. In dialogue much goes unsaid, but it needn't go unthought. The same is true for your characters. Every point-of-view character has an interior landscape, and you as author must respect this landscape (as distinct from your own) and allow her full access to its terror, mystery, and beauty.

Your characters can explore or chart their interior landscapes in many ways—they might examine their own motives for doing something, or wonder what might happen in the future, or remember the past, or follow an obsession to the point of folly, or project what is happening in the life of someone important to them *at that very moment,* or even imagine the life of another character. Below are other ways in which your characters might engage with their interior landscapes and lead their inner lives. They will:

imagine	fear	wonder	yearn
dread	suspect	project	grieve
plan	judge	plot	envy
lie	repress	pray	relive
regret	dream	fantasize	compose
associate	brood	doubt	feel guilt
speculate	worry	wish	analyze
glorify	romanticize	scheme	hate
interpret	obsess	compare	extrapolate
hallucinate	recreate	guess	hope
feel anything	realize	fret	interpret
misinterpret	decide	envision	posit

Literature thrives on characters who imagine, brood, fantasize, remember, and regret. The following examples of characters exploring their interior landscapes, using their imagination to enlarge their understanding of the world, or even falling victim to their imaginings should serve as the beginning of your own exploration of this powerful and useful tool in the art of fiction.

In *Beloved,* Toni Morrison's Sethe is haunted by the past and laments that her mind just won't stop:

> She shook her head from side to side, resigned to her rebellious brain. Why was there nothing it refused? No misery, no regret, no hateful picture too rotten to accept. Like a greedy child it snatched up everything. Just once, could it say, No thank you. . . . I don't want to know or have to remember that. I have other things to do: worry, for example, about tomorrow, about Denver, about Beloved, about age and sickness not to speak of love.
>
> But her brain was not interested in the future. Loaded with the past and hungry for more, it left her no room to imagine, let alone plan for the next day. . . . Other people went crazy, why couldn't she?

And in this wondrous way, Morrison leaves it to the reader to decide just how far Sethe travels into her interior landscape.

Margaret Atwood's novel *Bodily Harm* ends entirely in the mind of her character Rennie, who says, "This is what will happen." She goes on to imagine being saved in passages that alternate with the terrible reality of her situation. Rennie knows there is no real hope—but still she keeps imagining salvation in spite of herself.

Charles Baxter's story "Gryphon," which appears on page 317, is told by a young boy fascinated with a substitute teacher's lessons, lessons both true and false—such as her claim that Beethoven only pretended to be deaf to make himself famous. Her lessons grow more and more fantastic, and finally she makes a dire prophecy about one of the protagonist's classmates. To behold this teacher's interior landscape as she calmly predicts his death is to witness a dramatic and terrible event.

A story can end with a character imagining the future. Ray Carver's story "Where I'm Calling From" ends in the story's future. The first-person narrator imagines calling first his wife and then his girlfriend. He pulls change from his pocket. He imagines his conversation with his wife. It is enough to make him think that he might call his girlfriend first: "'Hello, sugar,' I'll say when she answers. 'It's me.'"

The young narrator in Don Lee's story "Casual Water" imagines what he'll do with an old seaplane that belongs to his profligate father, who has abandoned his teenage sons just as his wife did. "He would take it out to sea, far off the coast. He would remove the drain plugs from the pontoons, pour gasoline over the cabin, and throw in a book of lit matches. Then he would run the boat some distance away and drift with the swell, watch the fire accumulate, the gas cans erupt. He would wait until the seaplane began to crumple into the water, and then he would move the boat a little closer and watch it sink." And with it, all of his father's things—because he knows that father is never coming home.

Marilynne Robinson's novel *Housekeeping* also ends in the imagination of Ruthie, its first-person narrator. Ruthie, together with her Aunt Sylvie, is a drifter now, moving from one town to the next, working occasionally as a waitress until her fellow workers become suspicious of her silence in the face of their own stories, until it is as if Ruthie puts "a chill on the coffee by serving it." Ruthie's sister Lucille has opted for respectability and stayed behind. Ruthie imagines the house they tried to burn down. "Someone plants sunflowers and giant dahlias at the foot of the garden. I imagine it is Lucille, fiercely neat, stalemating the forces of ruin." Then she says she knows that Lucille is not at their home and wishes she could see the people who do live there. "Seeing them would expel poor Lucille, who has, in my mind, waited there in a fury of righteousness, cleansing and polishing all these years. She thinks she hears someone on the walk, and hurries to open the door, too eager to wait for the bell . . . sometimes she dreams that we come walking up the road in our billowing raincoats, hunched against the cold, talking together in words she cannot quite understand." A few sentences later Ruthie ends the book still thinking of Lucille and imagines her in a restaurant in Boston, waiting for a friend. "No one watching this woman smear her initials in the steam on her water glass with her first finger, or slip cellophane packets of oyster crackers into her handbag for the sea gulls, could know how her thoughts are thronged by our absence, or know how she does not watch, does not listen, does not wait, does not hope, and always for me and Sylvie." Ruthie and Sylvie are separated from Lucille forever, yet Ruthie's mind renders them together in the only way she knows how: in her imagination.

The character's capacity to imagine anything is again at work in William Gass's novella "The Pedersen Kid" when the narrator, a teenager, goes down to the crib to see where they found a half-frozen, but still living boy. "Who knows, I thought, the way it's been snowing, we mightn't have found him till spring. . . . I could see myself coming out of the house some morning with the sun high up and strong and the eaves dripping, the snow speckled with drops and the ice on the creek slushing up . . . and I could see myself . . . breaking through the big drift that was always sleeping up against the crib and running a foot right through into him, right into the Pedersen kid curled up, getting soft. . . ." Notice how even though the narrator speculates in his imagination, he uses concrete, sensory language.

On your own, look for examples of a character's interior landscape in stories and novels you admire. Look for characters having dreams or nightmares, looking forward to an event with anticipation or apprehension, imagining what another character is doing, or telling the reader how they feel about what is happening at a crucial point in the story—often the moment of realization, of epiphany. For example, in Theodore Weesner's story "Playing for Money," we see how narrating a character's feelings at a moment of epiphany can employ wondering and speculation about another character's feelings. Glenn has finally won money at pool, but his feelings surprise us and him. "He has never won big before, and the feeling within him now, to his surprise is closer to disappointment than satisfaction. He feels unclean picking up the nickel. Why is it he wonders, that his pride seems shaky and Jim Carr's pride seemed okay?" We would not have known this from only seeing Glenn's actions; we needed access to his interior landscape. The story ends as ". . . Glen sits hearing the music, looking away, and can see that he is on the wrong side of something, maybe of everything. This is what he can see. Looking for a dream to get started, he thinks. That's what he's doing. Looking for a dream to get started, to have somewhere nice to go." For further discussion of how the art of "telling" is connected to a character's interior landscape in a story, turn to "Show and Tell," on page 177.

Characters can also be tragically wrong in what they think—they can misinterpret the actions of others, misjudge the world in which they live, as Othello tragically does in *Othello,* and Stevens, the perfect butler and unreliable narrator, does in Ishiguro's *The Remains of the Day.*

Sometimes entire novels are the figment of a character's imagination or dreams—such is the case in Elizabeth Jolley's *Foxy Baby,* whose narrator imagines the entire action of the novel after there is an accident and she has a bump on her head. The same is true for Tim O'Brien's *Going After Cacciato,* in which the narrator wakes at the novel's end and realizes the entire story has been a dream.

And sometimes, one character feels compelled to try to understand another character by imagining the life and point of view of that other character. Russell Banks' novel *Affliction* is narrated by Rolfe Whitehouse, whose older brother has gone on a killing spree. In the first chapter, Rolfe begins the novel by saying, "This is the story of my older brother's strange criminal behavior and his disappearance. No one urged me to reveal these things; no one asked me not to." He says he feels separated from their family, from all who loved Wade. "They want through the telling to regain him; I want only to be rid of him. His story is my ghost life, and I want to exorcise it." Soon the narrator asks the reader to "Imagine with me that on this Halloween Eve up along the ridge east of the settlement it was still and silent and very dark." He describes the movements of a group of boys who are stealing jack-o-lanterns, then he begins Chapter Two with the same instructions to the reader. "Let us imagine that around eight o'clock on this Halloween Eve, speeding west past Toby's and headed toward town on Route 29 from the interstate turnoff . . ." is Wade Whitehouse, his brother, with his daughter Jill in the car. The novel continues with Wade's story up to the last sentences before the Epilogue, when Wade kills for the second time. The shifts in point of view are Rolfe's way of reminding us from time to time ("Picture, if you will . . .") that he is telling the story and imagining Wade's interior landscape in order to understand both of their stories, and to rid himself of Wade's ghost.

Imagination can almost kill, too. The narrator of Tim O'Brien's story "The Man I Killed" is paralyzed by imagining the life of the young man lying dead before him. "His jaw was in his throat, his upper lip and teeth were gone, his one eye was shut, his other eye was a star-shaped hole. . . ." The narrator says, "He had been born, maybe, in 1946," and goes on to imagine his early years in the village, listening to heroic stories of war. He imagines the young man wanted to be a teacher of mathematics, he imagines the seventeen-year-old girl he fell in love with. "One evening, perhaps, they exchanged gold rings." He goes on to imagine that the young man hoped the Americans would go away, that he hoped he would never be tested because he was not a fighter. Finally, the narrator imagines that this soldier— a soldier for a single day—had returned from university to his village "where he enlisted as a common rifleman with the 48th Vietcong Battalion. He knew he would die quickly. He knew he would see a flash of light. He knew he would fall dead and wake up in the stories of his village and people." "Talk," Kiowa says, desperately, to the narrator. And he did, and now we have his story, this collection, *The Things They Carried*.

Another of the most astonishing examples of a character's use of his imagination is the imagined dialogue that the narrator carries on with God at the end of Andre Dubus's story, "A Father's Story." Early on in the story the protagonist tells the reader he talks to God every morning, and then he goes out to the stable with an apple or a carrot for his horses. When his daughter causes a car accident, he proceeds to cover up for her and is himself possibly responsible for the young man's death. He soon sends his daughter to Florida and now lives with the terrible secret of what he has done—a secret he must keep from his best friend, Father Paul. Again, he tells us that he talks to God in the mornings. "Of course He has never spoken to me, but that is not something I require. Nor does He need to. I know Him, and I know the part of myself that knows Him, that felt Him watching from the wind and the night as I knelt over the dying boy. Lately, I have taken to arguing with him." Indeed, such an exchange ends this marvelous story as the father tells God, "I would do it again," not for his sons, but for his daughter. Then he tells God:

> But you never had a daughter and, if You had, You could not have borne her passion.
> So, He says, you love her more than you love Me.
> I love her more than truth.
> Then you love in weakness, He says.
> As You love me, I say, and I go out with an apple or carrot out to the barn.

In this imagined exchange—fully a rendering of the narrator's interior landscape—is the narrator's understanding that he and God love in the same flawed, abiding way.

A work of art has no importance whatever to society. It is only important to the individual.
—VLADIMIR NABOKOV

47

The Interior Landscape
of Vision and Obsession

Have you ever been captivated by a story or an idea and subsequently had this story take over your life—to the extent that your imagination is running your life? Alice Hoffman's novel *White Horses* is about such a character, Dina, who, as a child, was fascinated by her father's tales of Arias. Arias were outlaws, "men who appeared out of nowhere, who rode white horses across the mesas with no particular destination other than red deserts, the cool waterholes. . . ." Men who weren't lost but "never turned back, never went home, they were always traveling west, always moving toward the sun." Dina runs away with King Connors, a man she thinks is an Aria—even though her father belatedly tells her, "I don't even know if there is such a thing. I may have invented Arias." No matter that Arias were an invention of her father's imagination, Dina believes in Arias even when her husband turns out not to be one. "When Dina discovered that she was wrong about King, that he was as far from an Aria as a man can be, it was too late, she could never have admitted her error to her father. But these days, Dina felt it had not all been in vain; these days, she was certain her father had been describing someone not yet born." This someone is her son, Silver, whom she describes as "the perfect stranger she had known forever."

Literature is rich with such characters who get carried away by their imaginations. Such characters are useful to writers because their journeys are so compelling.

Remember the grandmother in Flannery O'Connor's story "A Good Man is Hard to Find," who brings her family to doom through her obsession with finding a plantation she incorrectly remembers from her past. "It's not much further," the grandmother said and just as she said it, a horrible thought came to her. An accident ensues that precipitates the climax of the story. Then we are once more in the grandmother's mind as she thinks, "The horrible thought she had had before the accident was that the house she had remembered so vividly was not in Georgia but in Tennessee." Think of Nabokov's novel *Pale Fire*. Charles Kinbote, the narrator, is obsessed with his neighbor, John Shade, and this obsession has led him to murder Shade. Subsequently, Kinbote tries both to confess to the murder and also cover it up in his commentary of Shade's poem, "Pale Fire."

The Exercise

Write a story about a character whose imagination is taken over with an obsession—an obsession with an idea, a tale, a vision—that determines the way in which your character lives his or her life, and acts out the forward movement of your story.

The Objective

To understand how longing and obsession can drive a story. To explore, through our characters, the mind's capacity to believe in the unbelievable, to long for something glimpsed but not seen, to imagine anything.

If the work weren't difficult I'd die of boredom. After The Recognitions, *where there is a great deal of authorial intrusion and little essays along the way, on alchemy or what have you, I found it was too easy and I didn't want to do it again. I wanted to write something different. I wanted to do something which was challenging, to create other problems, to force this discipline on myself.*

—WILLIAM GADDIS

48

What Mayhem or Scene
Is Happening Elsewhere?

Point of view can be as narrow or as all-encompassing as you want it to be because your characters can imagine anything. They can imagine scenes that are *simultaneously* happening elsewhere. This works best when a character knows or suspects how other characters would react in a given situation.

Early in John Irving's novel *Hotel New Hampshire*, John, the young narrator, goes off to bed while his parents leave for a walk. The novel is in the first person, so John, who is in bed, is not there when his parents talk to Howard Tuck, a policeman, and walk past the old Thompson Female Seminary, which they decide to buy and turn into a hotel. But John can imagine this crucial scene and proceeds to do so—he delivers this passage to the reader in the conditional tense:

> "Wutcha *doin'* here?" old Howard Tuck must have asked them.
>
> And my father, without a doubt, must have said, "Well, Howard, between you and me, we're going to buy this place."
>
> "You *are?*"
>
> "You betcha," Father would have said. "We're going to turn this place into a hotel."

A little further along in the scene, Irving reminds us that his young narrator is imagining this conversation, with clues such as "anyway" and "remember." The narrator says:

> Anyway, it was the night duty town patrolman, Howard Tuck, who asked my father, "Wutcha gonna call it?"
>
> Remember: it was night, and the night inspired my father . . . . There in Elliot Park, with the patrol car's spotlight on him, my father looked at the four-story brick school that indeed resembled a county jail—the rust-iron fire escapes crawled all over it, like scaffolding on a building trying to become something else. No doubt he took my mother's hand. In the darkness, where the imagination [his own young imagination] is never impeded, my father felt the name of his future hotel, and our future coming to him. "Wutcha gonna call it?" asked the old cop.
>
> "The Hotel New Hampshire," my father said.
>
> "Holy Cow," said Howard Tuck.
>
> "Holy Cow" might have been a better name for it, but the matter was decided: the Hotel New Hampshire it would be.

After this, there is a space break and we are back with the young boy who says, "I was still awake when Mother and Father came home. . . ." Note that his imagination takes us into this scene so convincingly that toward the end he drops the conditional. Also note that the young narrator says, "In the dark where the imagination is never impeded . . . ," which should serve as instruction to all writers: Allow your characters to imagine scenes that inform their own lives, just as they inform the reader's knowledge of their story.

The Exercise

From the point of view of your main character, have him or her imagine a scene that is happening elsewhere—a scene that IS happening without your narrator being there, except in his or her imagination. For example, a father might be driving home after a hard day's work and imagining that his son is stealing money from his top drawer, something he has suspected for a long time. Then he gets home and the money is gone—and the reader realizes that the imagined scene was most probably true. Or a roommate might be watching TV and feeling abandoned by the other two roommates who urged him or her to go to a party. He or she might then imagine the party where they do outrageous things before the police are called in. And sure enough when he is called to post bail he says "their account of the party is just what he imagined." Keep in mind that the crucial word is "simultaneously"—the scene IS HAPPENING, but elsewhere, and your character is imagining it happening.

The Objective

To transcend the traditional confines of point of view. To allow your characters' imaginations to take them and you into scenes that are simultaneously happening elsewhere, into scenes that matter to our enjoyment of and understanding of the story.

Student Examples

Italics indicate what the character is imagining.

In this passage, a young man is thinking about his girlfriend (the "you") and what she is doing:

> I've been on this train for seven hours and the only interesting thing I've seen is seven drowned, bloated cows. Some guy in the back thought he was having a heart attack near Tuscaloosa, but it was a false alarm and now he's sending his wife back to the club car for more beer. It's seven o'clock in Boston. Antennas blink on the horizon. *Voices are trying to get to you. Through your television. Through your radio. Even your answering machine is turned off. The cat prowls between your legs. You are reading love poems, point-*

ing to words you love though no one is reading over your shoulder. The crazy lady who lives next door to you is singing in the hallway again, but her own opera is beyond her tonight. The air conditioner clicks on and your lamp dims for a split second.

You turn another page.

A bag of groceries sits on your kitchen counter. The frozen yogurt is melting and the snow peas are defrosting, but it will be hours before you notice. I want to speak to you. Tell you about the baby in front who is finally asleep, about my damp socks, about the slight delay in Birmingham, and all the other minor details I wish you lived for.

—MATT MARINOVICH

In this example, a man has returned home for his father's funeral and imagines what it will be like. After imagining the scene (for himself and for the reader) he decides not to go, but because he has imagined the scene so vividly we feel like we have been there—and indeed it is important for the reader to know what Leonard is missing by not going.

Yet Leonard did not feel pressed for time. He had been deliberately vague with his sisters regarding his return home and knew he was not expected at any specific hour. He imagined the scene awaiting him: *his older sister Carla standing at the door in a business suit would direct the mourners along the receiving line. She would submerge her contempt for her father in a display of sober piety while adjusting her skirt every minute or so. Sandy would resent her sister's command of the situation and sit by their mother, sighing more in frustration than in loss, yet gratified by Carla's increasing weight—stock ammo at family gatherings. Their mother, handkerchief in hand, would sob and shake her head at the flower-encircled casket. Her hair would be up in a bun held in place with a silver pin. Between sobs she would say that her husband had been allergic to flowers and would never allow them in the house, meaning: he never brought any home for her. On her left, Dennis, the youngest, would clasp and unclasp his mother's hands, attempting to console her, though she'd shrug off his hands and ask for Leonard, the very image of his father. Then the siblings would have their moment of solidarity, eyes meeting like lifted glasses, for Leonard would certainly receive the lion's share of the inheritance, and would surely be there soon to take it.*

—JONATHAN KRANZ FROM "WAKE" PUBLISHED IN *ASCENT*

I never desire to converse with a man who has written more than he has read.

—SAMUEL JOHNSON

49

"I Know Just What She'll Say"

And you probably know just what he'll say, too. Often, we imagine a conversation with someone we know really well—well enough to be able to imagine just what they will say about a given subject or situation. Your point of view characters do too, and they are capable of imagining what another character would say, and of delivering this imagined conversation to the reader, without the need to bring this character on stage or to shift the point of view.

In Philip Roth's novel *Zuckerman Unbound*, Nathan Zuckerman is reaping the rewards of the success of his novel *Carnovsky* at the same time that he is regretting his hasty departure from his marriage on the eve of *Carnovsky's* publication. Early in the novel, Zuckerman says, "How could you not love generous, devoted, thoughtful, kindhearted Laura? How could he not? Yet during their last months together in the Bank Street floor-through, virtually all they had left in common was the rented Xerox machine at the foot of their tub in the big tiled bathroom." Their estrangement was made even more final because Zuckerman used so much from their marriage in his novel. Toward the end of the book, he wants her back and imagines an entire conversation with Laura on the way to see her. He jumps in a cab and heads for the village with "Time enough, however, for Zuckerman to gauge what he'd be up against with Laura. *I don't want to be beaten over the head with how boring I was for three years.* You weren't boring for three years. *I don't please you anymore, Nathan. It's as simple as that.* Are we talking about sex? Let's then. *There's nothing to say about it. I can do it and you can do it. I'm sure there are people both of us could call in to verify that. The rest I refuse to hear. Your present state has made you forget just how much I bored you. My affectless manner, as it is called, bored you . . . The way I make love bored you. Not making love bored you.* The way you make love did not bore me. Far from it. *But then it did. Something did, Nathan. You have a way of making things like that very clear."* This imagined conversation goes on for several pages until finally Nathan says, "He could only hope that she wouldn't be able to make the case against him as well as he himself could. But knowing her, there wasn't much chance of that." And Zuckerman has presented her part of the case so well, that Roth doesn't even bring her on stage. Nathan's wife is not home and she never appears in the book, although we feel as if we know her from Nathan's projection of what she might have said to him.

The Exercise

Add an imagined conversation to one of your own stories from the point of view of your main character. This imagined conversation should be one that will never happen, but it should tell us something important about a character whose point of view we are not privy to, and about a situation that is enlarged by our "hearing" what is "said." It can also cause the character imagining the conversation to act or not act, depending on what they know the other person will say. Note how the names "Nathan" and "Laura" are used to remind us who is being addressed. Note also, how an imagined conversation doesn't need setting or body language, just italics to keep it all straight.

The Objective

To use the imagination of your characters to deliver scenes and conversations that are important for the reader to see and hear, but which may never happen.

The answer is never the answer. What's really interesting is the mystery. If you seek the mystery instead of the answer, you'll always be seeking. I've never really seen anybody find the answer—they think they have, so they stop thinking. But the job is to seek mystery, evoke mystery, plant a garden in which strange plants grow and mysteries bloom.
—KEN KESEY

50

Mixed Motives
and Maybes

Have you ever been asked: Why did you do that? And you couldn't honestly answer the question. You don't know why you acted in such a way or why you did such a dastardly thing. You just did it. You might be able to come up with several possible reasons for your behavior—yet still not know precisely which one is the truth. Allow your own characters the same latitude you allow yourself. W.H. Auden said, "Art is writing clearly about mixed emotions."

The narrator in Pam Houston's story "Selway" uses the word "maybe" to explore her motives for making a dangerous highwater trip down the Selway River. She says, "And I knew it was crazy to take a boat through that rapid and I knew I'd do it anyway but I didn't any longer know why. Jack said I had to do it for myself to make it worth anything, and at first I thought I was there because I loved danger, but sitting on the rock I knew I was there because I loved Jack. And maybe I went because his old girlfriends wouldn't, and maybe I went because I wanted him for mine, and maybe it didn't matter at all why I went because doing it for me and doing it for him amounted, finally, to exactly the same thing. And even though I knew in my head there's nothing a man can do that a woman can't, I also knew in my heart we can't help doing it for different reasons." Later in the same story, the narrator wonders if the trip's danger would make Jack propose to her. She says, "Maybe he was the kind of man who needed to see death first, maybe we would build a fire to dry ourselves and then he would ask me and I would say yes because by the time you get to be thirty, freedom has circled back on itself to mean something totally different from what it did at twenty-one." Examining one's motives leads to insight and self-knowledge, and often determines how a character acts or reacts to a situation.

In Richard Ford's story "Privacy," the narrator questions his motives when he begins to watch, through opera glasses, a woman disrobe night after night in a window across from his bedroom. "I don't know all that I thought. Undoubtedly I was aroused. Undoubtedly I was thrilled by the secrecy of watching out of the dark. Undoubtedly I loved the very illicitness of it, of my wife sleeping nearby and knowing nothing of what I was doing. It is also possible I even liked the cold as it surrounded me, as complete as the night itself, may even have felt that the sight of the woman—whom

I took to be young and lacking caution or discretion—held me somehow, insulated me and made the world stop and be perfectly expressible as two poles connected by my line of vision. I am sure now that all of this had to do with my impending failures." What a place for this soul-searching to bring him: it had to do with his "impending failures."

A character in Rosellen Brown's novel *Before and After* imagines what her father is thinking about her mother as the family sits together in front of the TV replaying their recent, unbelievably painful ordeal—her brother's trial for murder, with his parents on opposite sides of the question. "Somewhere along the way I saw that my father, there on the couch beside her, had turned to my mother and was staring at her, not at her flat image out there in front of him. He would do that awhile, and she'd keep her eyes closed, just listening to her own voice going over this terrible ground, and then he'd switch back to the set, and his lips would move a little but I couldn't hear any words. Then he'd look back at her again, the real, solid woman in her purple bathrobe with the television light flickering high and low over her face. She looked totally different and yet wasn't—and was—and I thought how we had all dragged through so much together and I still couldn't dare guess what he was thinking about her. If deep down he respected her or hated her for what she was saying, or if he could even understand it. Was he, like, trying to lay one image on the other and see if they really matched? Or guess what she felt when he looked at her that way, he seemed so astonished and hurt and familiar and far away, right there at her side?"

Note that both Ford's and Brown's characters profess to not know what they thought or to be incapable of guessing, but they in fact go right on to do just that.

The Exercise

Return to one of your stories in which your character's behavior has puzzled you or your classmates. Then come up with four or five reasons your character might have acted in such an abominable or deceptive or ingratiating or _____ (you choose the adjective) way—from your character's POV. Next, in another story, have your point-of-view character wonder why another character did what she did. Often, the reasons are varied and sometimes wrong, but it is also easy to tuck in to this list what might be an unpleasant truth on its own.

The Objective

To understand that people rarely have only one motive for an action—hence the term "mixed motives." And to allow our characters to explore their own motives as well as those of other characters important to their story world.

51

The Need to Know:
The Solace of
Imagination

Our characters are often haunted by dramatic events that have happened to someone else, and the only way they can come to terms with them is to imagine how those events unfolded for that other character. In the Introduction to this section, we referred to Russell Banks's novel *Affliction,* in which one brother is compelled to imagine the life of his violent and doomed brother. In *The Great Gatsby,* Nick Carroway imagines Gatsby and Daisy's first kiss:

> Now it was a cool night with that mysterious excitement in it which comes at the two changes of the year. The quiet lights in the houses were humming out into the darkness and there was a stir and bustle among the stars. . . . His heart beat faster and faster as Daisy's white face came up to his own. He knew that when he kissed this girl, and forever wed his unutterable visions to her perishable breath, his mind would never romp again like the mind of God. So he waited, listening for a moment longer to the tuning-fork that had been struck upon a star. Then he kissed her. At his lips' touch she blossomed for him like a flower and the incarnation was complete.

Nick pretends to have summarized what Gatsby told him, but this scene is clearly Nick's own imagined version of it.

In Margaret Atwood's novel, *Cat's Eye,* her point-of-view character is haunted by a tragic event and so she must imagine it. This novel is told from the first-person point of view of Elaine, an artist, whose beloved brother was killed in an airplane hijacking. His death haunts Elaine, as it haunts the novel, and finally toward the novel's end, she imagines the precise details of his death. This chapter begins: "My brother Stephen died five years ago. I shouldn't say died: was killed. . . . He was sitting on a plane. He had a window seat. This much is known. In the nylon webbing in front of him was an inflight magazine with an article in it about camels, which he'd read, and another about upgrading your business wardrobe, which he hadn't." It is with that sentence that she begins to imagine his ordeal. He's traveling to a conference to deliver a paper on the "probable composition of the universe" and is "having doubts" about his theories. At this point Elaine is now imagining what her brother is thinking, has slipped into his point of view. The plane has been hijacked by men wearing pillowcases over their heads. Elaine imagines her brother thinking: "They're like those characters in old comic books, the ones with two identities. These men have been caught halfway through their transformation: ordinary bodies but with powerful, supernatural heads, deformed in the direction of heroism, or villainy." Then she reminds us that she is the one imagining this by immediately saying: "I don't know whether or not this is what my brother thought. But it's what I think for him, now." She continues to imagine the scene, the other passengers, her brother's curiosity about what country they are in, and finally the appearance from the cockpit of a new hijacker. The next paragraphs read:

> The new man starts to walk down the aisle of the plane, his oblong, three-holed head turning from side to side. A second man walks behind him. Eerily, the taped music comes on over the intercom, saccharine, soporific. The man pauses; his oversized head moves ponderously left, like the head of some shortsighted, dull-witted monster. He extends an arm, gestures, with the hand: *Up.* It's my brother he points to.
>
> Here I stop inventing. I've spoken with the witnesses, the survivors, so I know that my brother stands up, eases himself past the man in the aisle seat saying "Excuse me." . . . Perhaps they have mistaken him for someone else. Or they may want him to help negotiate, because they're walking toward the front of the plane, where another pillowhead stands waiting.
>
> It's this one who swings open the door for him, like a polite hotel doorman, letting in the full glare of day. After the semidarkness it's ferociously bright, and my brother stands blinking as the image clears to sand and sea, a happy vacation postcard. Then he is falling, faster than the speed of light.
>
> This is how my brother enters the past.

And this is how Elaine renders her brother's death for herself and for the reader. Atwood is a genius in her use of her characters' interior landscapes and her books should be read for immense pleasure and for their brilliant instruction in the art of fiction.

The Exercise

Return to a draft of a story or begin a new story in which your point-of-view character needs to understand events that have happened to someone they care deeply about. Then have that character imagine those events from the point of view of the character who experienced them.

The Objective

To explore how a character can be drawn to imagine the life of someone important to his or her life—someone who will or can no longer speak for herself.

52

The Power of "Seemed" and "Probably"

Beginning writers often think they have to go into the heads of all their characters in order for the reader to know what they are thinking. They forget that people can reveal themselves in a myriad of ways: dialogue, body language, and so forth. They also forget that in reality no one has access to another person's thoughts and that, in addition to listening to what those close to us say and observing how they act, we are constantly assuming, suspecting, projecting, and imagining what they think.

Learn to give your characters (especially the point-of-view character) the same imagination that you have. An example of this occurs in a Bartholomew Gill mystery novel, *McGarr and the Politician's Wife*. The entire plot turns on the word *seemed*. A man, Ovens, has a head injury and is lying in a coma. The detective goes to see him and needs to know if he might have just fallen or if there was foul play. He asks the doctor if Ovens can speak and the doctor says not for another forty-eight hours.

The author writes, "Ovens' eyes, however, seemed to contradict the assessment of the insouciant young doctor. Dark brown, almost black, they told McGarr that Ovens knew the score: that his was not merely a medical problem that a favorable prognosis could eliminate, that whoever had done this to him had a very good reason, and those eyes, suddenly seeming very old, realized his troubles weren't over." So McGarr doesn't have to wait forty-eight hours. He starts his investigation immediately.

Ann Beattie's use of the word *probably* in her story "Afloat" indicates that the story is not third person from the point of view of the 16-year-old child who is introduced at the beginning of the story. Beattie writes, "When she was a little girl she would stand on the metal table pushed to the front of the deck and read the letters aloud to her father. If he sat, she sat. Later, she read them over his shoulder. Now she is sixteen, and she gives him the letter and stares at the trees or the water or the boat bobbing at the end of the dock. It has probably never occurred to her that she does not have to be there when he reads them." The "probably" is a clue that someone else is making this conjecture. Sentences later, after the letter is presented, the first-person narrator comes in with "he hands the letter to me, and then pours club soda and Chablis into a tall glass for Annie and fills his own glass with wine alone."

The Exercise

Write a scene that involves two characters. Now allow the point of view character to suspect or imagine what the other character might be thinking. Or have your point-of-view character imagine something that is probably true.

The Objective

To show how your characters can use their imaginations to interpret the behavior and dialogue of other characters.

Student Examples

She *probably* expects me to keep on mowing her lawn and trimming her hedge all summer even though I told her there was no way that dog and me were going to be friends. She *probably* thinks it's something we can work out, me and the dog, like I got time for throw and fetch.

—Jack Neissen

Benny *seemed* uneasy about leaving her right after their fight, packing his duffle slowly, two things in and one thing back out, and Darl appreciated this, but she had a whole weekend of plans made—repainting their bedroom and packing up and dragging his collection of beer cans down to their storage bin in the basement.

—Patty Sinclair

My early life was very strange. I was a solitary; radio fashioned my imaginaton. Radio narrative always has to embody a full account of both action and scene. I began to do that myself. When I was seven or eight, I'd walk through Central Park like Sam Spade, describing aloud what I was doing, becoming both the actor and the writer setting him into the scene. That was where I developed an inner ear.

—Robert Stone

PART SEVEN

Plot

Except for the first few exercises in this section, most have as much to do with characterization as with plot. When we had completed the manuscript for *What If?* and were in the process of creating a table of contents, someone asked, "Where is plot?" Plot was missing. We did have exercises that fit this category, but we had placed them elsewhere. This led us to realize, however, that for both of us plot is subordinate to characterization. In a *Paris Review* interview, William Kennedy speaks to this issue. He says:

> Hemingway's line was that everything changes as it moves; and that that is what makes the movement that makes the story. Once you let a character speak or act you now know that he acts this way and no other. You dwell on why this is so and you move forward to the next page. This is my method. I'm not interested in formulating a plot to which characters are added like ribbons on a prize cow. The character is the key and when he does something which is new, something you didn't know about or expect, then the story percolates. If I knew, at the beginning, how the book was going to end, I would probably never finish.

Thus the forward movement of a story or novel derives from how a character observes—acts or reacts—and the more surprising the better.

In their book *Technique in Fiction*, Robie Macauley and George Lanning suggest that Heracleitus's observation that "character is destiny" should be "written on the wall of every novelist's study." They go on to say that character is only half the dynamics of plot, that a given situation is the other half. How a particular character observes and deals with the circumstances of that situation and chooses to act or not act moves the story forward into plot.

Macauley and Lanning discuss plot in these terms: In the beginning you present a particular character in a situation. The situation should have opposing forces and alternatives, and your central character should have choices—ways of acting or not acting. The situation should grow more complicated,

more grave, and finally reach a point of crisis. Thereafter follows the resolution of the crisis—or at the least "something happens." Almost always
things will have changed.

Writer/teacher Ron Carlson asks his students to answer this question:
"Into what life has this trouble come?" and goes on to say that the "trouble is the engine that drives the story. But before the trouble begins, your
character has a life apart from the trouble. No one is a blank tablet waiting for trouble. Everyone has an agenda, even children and dogs." Doug
Glover, another writer/teacher, uses the term "unstable situation" when discussing plot. Consider how writers have placed certain characters in an
unstable situation and set them in motion, from which point they move forward, driven by the force of their own personalities: Isabella Archer in
Henry James's *Portrait of a Lady,* Humbert Humbert in Vladimir Nabokov's
Lolita, Hester Prynne in Hawthorne's *The Scarlet Letter,* and Yossarian in
Joseph Heller's *Catch-22.*

Janet Burroway, in *Writing Fiction,* makes the distinction between story
and plot. She says, "A story is a series of events recorded in their chrono-
logical order. A plot is a series of events deliberately arranged so as to reveal
their dramatic, thematic, and emotional significance." She notes that E.M.
Forster makes the same distinction in *Aspects of the Novel,* in elaborating on
the difference between "and then" and "why." Burroway says:

> The human desire to know why is as powerful as the desire to know what
> happened next, and it is a desire of the highest order. . . . When "noth-
> ing happens" in a story, it is because we fail to sense the causal relation
> between what happens first and what happens next. When something does
> "happen," it is because the resolution of a short story or a novel describes
> a change in the character's life, an effect of the events that have gone
> before. This is why Aristotle insisted with such apparent simplicity on "a
> beginning, a middle, and an end." A story is capable of many meanings,
> and it is first of all in the choice of structure—which portion of the story
> forms the plot—that you offer us the gratifying sense that we "understand."

It is in this discussion that Burroway also speaks to the difference
between the short story and the novel. She says:

> Many editors and writers insist on an essential disjunction between the form
> of the short story and that of the novel. It is my belief, however that, like
> the distinction between story and plot, the distinction between the two forms
> is very simple, and the many and profound possibilities of difference pro-
> ceed from that simple source: A short story is short, and a novel is long."

In our minds, Burroway has the final word on the matter.

Most discussions of plot recognize the importance of conflict and here
we defer to Rust Hills' discussion of "mystery," "conflict," and "tension,"
in his book titled *Writing in General and the Short Story in Particular.* (This
is another book that should be on every writer's shelf.) He argues that
tension is the most effective technique for creating suspense and derives

from the Latin verb *tendere*, meaning stretch. He says, "Tension in fiction has that effect: of something that is being stretched taut until it must snap. It has the quality of force under pressure, as for instance when it is achieved through characterization in a 'coiled motive'—tightly wound motivation in a character that we know must spring loose on the action. The most obvious way to create it is by simply saying something is going to happen, and then putting it off." Tension, he says, "both foreshadows and creates suspense." The beginning of Andrea Barrett's story "Servants of the Map" is a brilliant example of tension at its most effective and artful.

Once you have placed a character in an unstable situation, our exercise "What If?" is designed to provide you with several organic ways to move your story forward toward complication and resolution. Always, always, with character in motion. In her wonderful book *Mystery and Manners*, Flannery O'Connor recalls lending some stories to a neighbor who, when she gave them back, said, "Well them stories just gone and shown you how some folks would do." And O'Connor comments, "I thought to myself that that was right; when you write stories, you have to be content to start exactly there—showing how some specific folks will do, will do in spite of everything." And that doing becomes your plot.

53

The Skeleton

The simplest stories are fairy tales and myths in which a central character—who is on some sort of quest or journey—is continually on stage and secondary characters only appear to assist or thwart her. This is what we call a "skeleton" story—you can see its bones. There are no subtleties, motivation is a given, emotions are unanalyzed, and the narrative proceeds in a linear way. In the skeleton the world and its people are viewed in morally black-and-white terms. The temptation to stray will be almost irresistible, but if you do, you will drag your reader into thickets of subplots and gangs of minor characters. (The following exercise is based on a suggestion by folklorist Lawrence Millman.)

The Exercise

Write a linear story, in which a strong main character is on a quest for something important and specific (e.g., a shelter for the baby, medicine for a sick mother, or the key to the storehouse where a tyrant has locked away all the grain from a starving populace). The object is a given—don't explain its importance. The main character starts acting immediately. She then meets a (specific) obstacle; finally she triumphs over the obstacle by means of a magic or supernatural element that comes from the outside (like Dorothy's red shoes in *The Wizard of Oz*). You may introduce minor characters but the narrative should never abandon your main character. This story should be told through action and dialogue. Limit: 550 words.

The Objective

Like a medical student who must learn the names and location of human bones before going on to more complex systems, a beginning writer must be able to handle and control basic plot before moving on to more subtle elements like motivation, subtext, and ambiguity. Many of the greatest novels incorporate a quest (*Moby Dick*), a journey (*David Copperfield*), and triumph over an obstacle (*The Old Man and the Sea*). These works also concentrate on one protagonist and end, if not happily, at least on an emotionally satisfying note of resolution.

Student Story

The Nanny—A Fairy Tale

There once was a young woman who wanted a baby. The urge to produce another life in her own body hit suddenly, like a squall or a virus.

"A baby," said her husband. "You don't know a diaper from a linen handkerchief. Babies are loud, they're smelly, and they cramp your sex life. We're fine as we are."

She worked on him. Walking through the park, she'd point out babies sleeping like sacks in strollers, crowing and waving from backpacks, or toddling on creased legs. "Let's eat Chinese tonight," he said. If only she could find the secret crack in his heart, the place where the gates would swing open when the magic words were said, letting the idea of their own baby enter like the children of Hamlin.

She took to sitting on playground benches, thinking. She could leave him and find a man who shared her longing. But she loved the fullness of his laugh, the way he sang as he cooked, the curls behind his ears when his haircut was overdue.

One day as the young woman sat on a bench near a wading pool, a gray-haired nanny sat down beside her, starched uniform gleaming in the sun. "Have any children?" she asked, starting to knit.

The young woman smiled and shook her head.

"Too bad. You'd like a child, wouldn't you? Not married? Men are hard to find these days, they say."

Though partly put off by the nanny's presumptuousness, the young woman shared her problem. "My husband doesn't want children. At least not yet."

"Stalled adolescence," the nanny said. "See it more and more. Want a solution?" Without waiting for an answer, she pulled a pomegranate out of her knitting bag. "Serve him this for dessert tonight and for the next two nights and have some for yourself, too. Be sure he sucks the sweet red part, and doesn't eat the seeds. If he balks, tell him it's better than kiwi."

The young woman did as she was told, carefully watching her husband savor the sweet sharp taste and spit the seeds on his plate. At first she noticed no change in her husband. But on the third day, while sipping cappuccino in an intimate Italian restaurant, he said "What the Hell. You want a baby? What are we waiting for?" And he took her home to bed.

Months later, her stomach full as a spinnaker, the young woman sat again on the bench near the wading pool, resting her legs. The nanny sat down next to her as she had before, uniform crisp, oxfords firmly tied. Eyeing the young woman's belly with a smile, she pulled out her knitting and said, "Looking for a nanny?"

—Christine McDonnell

Fiction has traditionally and characteristically borrowed its form from letters, journals, diaries, autobiographies, histories, travelogues, news stories, backyard gossip, etc. It has simply pretended to be one or the other of them.

—William Gass

54

From Situation to Plot

If you haven't read our introduction to the section on plot, please go back and read it now before doing this exercise. It is important that you understand our preference for character-driven—not plot-driven—stories.

This exercise is designed to illustrate how easy it is to come up with characters in particular situations from only a few given details.

The Exercise

Begin a story using one of the following as your main character:

- A young boy whose father is in jail
- A waitress who likes her menus to rhyme
- A policeman with ten cats
- A sixteen-year-old in the hospital
- The driver of a hit-and-run accident

(Do you see how a policeman with ten cats is a situation in itself just waiting for a little opposition?)

Now, complicate your character's life with opposing forces, with tension and conflict, and offer your character alternatives within that situation. Ask: What does my character want? What would my character do? How will he act or react? How will those actions propel the story forward?

Then experiment with creating your own sets of details involving character and situation. Do ten or fifteen as fast as you can.

The Objective

To understand how the most effective plots are those driven by character. To see how a character within a given of any situation creates his own destiny.

Student Story

Intelligence
I'm eight years old. But I have the mind of a nineteen-year-old. Mom says it's making up for all the wrong Dad did. Today there's going to be

a whole camera crew here. They're going to film different angles of me beating myself at chess. Then they want me to walk around the neighborhood in my Eagle Scout uniform. Dad doesn't want to talk to them. So I guess they'll do an exterior of the penitentiary.

Dad called a few hours ago. Mom handed me the phone. She never wants to talk to him. I end up answering all the questions he wants to ask her. He asked me when was the last time Mom talked about him. I told him she said something at the bowling alley because we were having trouble keeping score. Mom doesn't care how much I lie to him because she says he's going to rot in jail. I miss him. But I can't tell him that. Mom would hit the roof and call me a traitor and start that whole thing about who's bringing me up and who's the slob behind bars. With Mom, eventually everything comes down to physical appearances. "It was a choice between your Dad and Henry Lee," she says when she reminisces about marrying Dad. "And Henry Lee had hair on his back."

On the phone, I asked Dad what he made in woodshop, and he asked me if I was eating lots of peas and carrots because the brain is just another muscle and you can't feed it junk. Dad thinks he's grooming me for the Nobel Prize. I made a few reading suggestions. I send him books and tell him to highlight the difficult parts. He's not very easy to explain things to. If he doesn't get it the first time, he gets angry—and when he gets angry, he automatically thinks of Mom and says, "Don't sign anything. Not even your homework. I own the rights to you. Every single cent you make, you freak of fucking nature."

I never hang up on him, no matter what he says.

I wait until he calms down, and then give him an update on how many sparrows have moved into the birdhouse we built.

But it's really sitting in the basement.

The camera crew is here. Taping down cable and knocking over chairs. Mom's on the phone right now because the producer wants a shot of me playing with my friends. I told him I could punch up some people on my computer. But he wants the real thing. So Mom's on the phone, asking Mrs. Milgram if she can borrow her son for the afternoon. That's the same kid who smashed up my invention for the Science Fair last year. The key grip is showing me how to throw a frisbee. The producer is suggesting a shot of me bicycling down Quarry Lane with my dog running after me. But Einstein has arthritis and bleeding gums. He can barely stand up.

The whole neighborhood's watching us. Kids on mountain bikes and skateboards are casing our house, making circles in the road. When Dad was taken away, Mom ran out and aimed the sprinkler at them. Now she's too busy. She's even got a pencil behind her ear.

I tell the producer I know what people want to see. They want to see me in my tiny apron making a white sauce. Or me playing the piano. A little Vivaldi and maybe the camera panning to my sneakers dangling a foot from the floor while my mother turns the pages and presses the pedal. I love it when she steps on the pedal, when the notes run together and take too long to end.

I lower my head and pretend that this is sadness.

—MATT MARINOVICH, PUBLISHED IN *THE QUARTERLY*

55

Peter Rabbit and Adam and Eve: The Elements of Plot

from Thomas Fox Averill

For the fiction writer, telling a whole story—and not just writing dialogue, or setting scene, or creating character—is crucial. Yet, plotting is often difficult for beginning writers. One way to practice plotting is to work with story elements, putting them in patterns, and writing a story to their specifications. By "story elements" I mean basic plot moves—those things that have nothing to do with specific character, setting, or even conflict.

For example, Peter Rabbit and the Genesis garden story share plot elements. In both, an authority figure tells the character what not to do (eat fruit from the tree of knowledge of good and evil, or go into Farmer McGregor's garden). In each story, the prohibited "does" the "don't." Anything else and the story would be over, of course. "Doing the don't" has two levels of consequence in each story—the personal consequences and the consequences with the authority/prohibitor.

In Peter's case, he enjoys the garden, but, once spotted, he is chased, he gets wet, he loses his clothes and he finally escapes, sick and tired and naked; his mother puts him to bed with a cup of tea. His sisters eat bread, milk, and blackberries.

Adam and Eve, on the other hand, are immediately ashamed of their nakedness, and try to hide from God; they are punished with work, pain, and death and made to leave the garden.

The Exercise

Write a story that uses these four elements as a basic plot line:

- A prohibition
- Doing the prohibited
- Personal/immediate consequences
- Long-term/authority consequences

Note that the first and the final elements have to do with the pro-hibitor/authority, the middle two with the character who is doing the don't.

Note that simple variations are possible, by beginning the story with advice, warning, or prediction.

The Objective

To help you understand basic elements that underlie plots. For further read-ing, you should become familiar with the stories collected by the Grimm Brothers, with *The Canterbury Tales*, with the *1001 Arabian Nights*, with the *Decameron*, and with books of myths, legends, and religious stories. The purpose is not to get you to write to formula, but to be aware of elements of structure and patterns that commonly appear together. Think, for exam-ple, of how many stories begin with either "lack" or "desire." Think of how often kindness is rewarded unexpectedly. Think of the role of luck and coincidence in stories. Think of how many stories turn on a lie. Think of how many stories reveal hypocrisy. Of how many require an arduous jour-ney. All of these, used over and over by fiction writers, show us how few plot elements we have to work with, and yet they allow us infinite possibilities to tell our stories. The more we know them, the more we're in control of what and how we write.

Student Example

My father does not talk about Vietnam.

As a child, I would sometimes wonder what he had done there, or why he was there. He was married before my mother, but he doesn't talk about that, either. Sometimes, I made up stories about my father. I'd flop down in my dad's favorite chair, watch John Wayne annihilate masses of North-ern Vietnamese, and dream about my father. He wasn't a big man, but he was stern. My family boasts many generations of warriors, and I wanted to be one.

One day, I picked open my dad's special suitcase. He had hidden it from us boys. We all thought he was hiding his nudie magazines, whatever we thought those were. Letters tumbled out, along with medals and pictures. After reading the letters, I realized that my father very much loved my mother. I also realized that my father had been a cold-blooded killer.

A picture caught my eye. My father and a black man had their arms around a sickly-looking Vietnamese man. It was an odd picture; I had never seen my father smile before. For an instant I was proud of my father, until I noticed the Vietnamese man's left ear. It was missing. The man was dead.

I looked up from the picture to see my father staring blankly at me from the doorway. My father does not talk about Vietnam.

—JASON PUFF

56

What If? How to Develop
and Finish Stories

Writers sometimes have story blocks—they begin a story easily enough, but then they run into trouble when they try to finish it. Well, one possible reason is that some stories don't have enough forward motion to become a successful story—and these should be abandoned. On the other hand, many story beginnings just need to be examined and explored for their inherent possibilities. As François Camoin says, "A story needs to take a narrative fork."

The Exercise

Look in your files for a story that seems stuck, a story that has a story block. Next, write at the top of a separate sheet of paper the two words *What If*. Now write five ways of continuing the story, not ending the story, but continuing the story to the next event, scene, etc. Let your imagination go wild. Loosen up your thinking about the events in the story. Your what if's can be as diverse as your imagination can make them. More than likely, and this has proved true through years of teaching and writing, one of the what if's will feel right, organic, to your story and that is the direction in which you should go. Sometimes you will have to do several groups of what if's per story, but that's okay as long as they keep you moving forward.

The Objective

To illustrate that most story beginnings and situations have within them the seeds of the middle and end—seeds that spark not only your creativity but also your curiosity. You just have to allow your imagination enough range to discover what works.

Student Example

One writer began a story about a young boy, Paul, who shoplifts with a cousin. The story opens when they take something more expensive than they have ever taken before. This raises the stakes immediately. After writing a superb opening scene of two and a half pages, the writer didn't know where to go with the story. Below are her five what if's for this beginning.

1. Paul decides to admit to shoplifting, but hopes not to implicate his cousin.
2. Paul is excited by shoplifting something more expensive, and talks his cousin into going back again soon.
3. The store security guard notices their theft and decides to set a trap. (Involves some point-of-view issues.)
4. Paul feels brave now and steals something from his stepfather—something Paul has wanted for a long time.
5. There is a time shift to five years later when Paul commits a major burglary.

The writer continued the story with the fourth idea because she felt it was a more complex development of Paul's situation. If she hadn't explored several alternatives, she might not have arrived at this story line.

Writer's block is only a failure of the ego.
—NORMAN MAILER

57

There's a Party and You're Invited

from Margot Livesey

We all know the standard workshop questions—Whose story is this? What do they want? What prevents them from getting what they want?—questions designed to help bring the story into focus, for both reader and writer, and to heighten both the forward movement and the conflict. These questions are genuinely helpful and they work particularly well for certain kinds of stories, especially plot-driven ones. Sometimes, though, I find it more useful to think in terms of the occasion of the story. Why are these characters showing up here, now, for these events? Why are we, as readers, being invited today rather than yesterday or tomorrow?

In the best fiction the occasion nearly always turns out to be more complicated than we first expect. Katherine Mansfield's "The Garden Party" declares its occasion in the title; there's a party and we're invited. But other people, the poor people who live down the lane, are not and this painful juxtaposition between luxury and poverty becomes the true occasion of the story.

Sometimes a story turns out to have two distinct occasions—the one that we discover in the opening pages and the other that gradually surfaces. In Charles D'Ambrosio's "The Point" the first occasion of the story is yet another party given by the teenage narrator's mother after which he ends up escorting yet another drunken adult home. But as we continue to read, we realize that behind the difficulties of maneuvering the very drunk Mrs. Gurney back to her home, lies another much darker occasion: the morning when the narrator discovered his father dead in his car by his own hand.

The Exercise

Re-read the opening scene or section of your story and answer the question: What is the occasion of this story? Now read the remainder of the story and answer the question again.

The Objective

Readers are our guests and we need to make them feel as soon as possible in a story that this is an occasion, somber or joyful, worth attending. And we need to reward that attendance by the end of the story.

I guarantee you that no modern story scheme, even plotlessness, will give a reader genuine satisfaction, unless one of those old-fashioned plots is smuggled in somewhere. I don't praise plots as accurate representations of life, but as ways to keep readers reading.
—KURT VONNEGUT, JR.

58

So, What Happened?

In his introduction to a stellar group of stories, *American Stories: Fiction from the Atlantic Monthly,* C. Michael Curtis says, "Each achieves the sort of transforming moment one looks for in the short story form, a shift in understanding, a glimpse of unexpected wisdom, the discovery of unimagined strength. . . . You will find no minimalism here, no sketches or portraits, no glimpses, merely, of 'things as they are'; these are honest-to-God stories, in which Something Happens." We also feel that *something has to happen* in a story once the original situation has been presented—something in terms of the consequences of situation and action.

In Janet Burroway's discussion of conflict and resolution, she says, "Still another way of seeing the shape of the story is in terms of situation-action-situation. The story begins by presenting us with a situation. It then recounts an action, and when that action is over, we are left with a situation that is the opposite of the opening situation. This formula seems oversimplified, but it is very difficult to find a story it does not describe."

Keep in mind that "opposite" can mean that the narrator at the beginning of the story does not understand her situation, but after a scene or several scenes (action), and by the end of the story, she does. Or she might understand something about another person, an event, or a relationship. Note that Curtis talks about the "transforming moment" in terms of "a shift in understanding," a "glimpse of wisdom," and the "discovery of unimagined strength"—all internal changes, cerebral transformations. James Joyce calls such a moment the "epiphany."

Burroway goes on to say that the "moment of recognition" must be manifested or externalized in an action, in the concrete world of the story: the prince recognizes Cinderella, and the shoe fits. (See page 177, "Show and Tell.")

And what of those stories in which "nothing happens"? Rust Hills, in *Writing in General and the Short Story in Particular,* discusses the "kind of story that seems at first to be a character sketch." The character seems unaltered at the end of the story—more firmly entrenched in his situation than ever. Yet, what has happened is that his "capacity for change" has been removed. There is no longer any hope for him: that is the change. Janet Burroway uses the metaphor of war to explain this type of story—a story that began with two sides hopeful about victory ends with two survivors, one from each side, grasping the border fence with bloodied fists. "The 'resolution' of this battle is that neither side will ever give up and that no one will ever win; there will never be a resolution." In both instances, possibility and hope are gone. What happens, happens for the reader who has witnessed this failure.

The Exercise

One by one, review five or six of your stories and look for "what happened" in each story. Mark the moment of transformation, the moment of recognition, the epiphany in each—and then look for the corresponding action that makes these moments manifest.

The Objective

To write stories in which something happens.

Student Example

(In "Matrimony," the first-person narrator finally realizes that she and her ex-husband should stay parted. This is made manifest by the last lines of the story.)

> That night Phillip went back to his own apartment, and I played the videotape of our wedding. I watched the whole thing through, and then again as it rewound. I watched as our lips disengaged from our first kiss as husband and wife, as we made frenzied, backward steps down the aisle, and finally walked out of the church at different times, alone.
>
> —DINA JOHNSON

59

Plot Potential

The main thing to keep in mind as you're doing plot is that *you're the boss* and not the other way around. It's your story, and you have an infinite number of choices. As a creator of fiction, you should feel supremely at ease in the role of storyteller.

The Exercise

Write five mini-stories (limit: 200 words each) to account for a single event or set of circumstances, such as a man and woman standing on a city sidewalk, hailing a cab. Each story should be different—in characters, plot, and theme—from the others.

The Objective

To loosen the bonds that shackle you to a single, immutable version; to underscore the fact that plot is not preordained but something you can control and manipulate at will, like the strings of a marionette; and to demonstrate once more that there are many ways to skin a cat.

Student Example

1. At 2:00 in the afternoon, John, a forty-four-year-old man in a business suit, and Dawn, a twenty-two-year-old woman in a tight skirt and high heels, came out of the Hancock Building. While John stood in the street trying to hail a cab, Dawn stayed on the sidewalk, sobbing. John is Dawn's boss and she is his secretary. At 1:45 she'd gotten a call from the hospital; her mother had a heart attack and was in intensive care. When Dawn told John why she had to leave so suddenly, he looked as though it was his mother who was in the hospital. Dawn could not understand why he was so concerned, and why he was going with her to the hospital. John held Dawn's hand in the cab and said, "Oh God, oh God." And he wondered how he was going to tell Dawn that he was her mother's lover, that they'd fallen in love the night Dawn brought her mother to the company Christmas party.

2. As usual, Pauline had been totally humiliated by her father, and now he was making a fool of himself trying to hail a cab. He'd insisted on coming to her interview with her. He insisted on sitting in the waiting room while she was in with the personnel director, and he pestered the receptionist with stories about how cute Pauline had been as a child and how smart she was as an adult. Pauline knew he did it with good intentions—he wanted her to be safe in the city, but it was driving her crazy.

3. Maggie hated the city, the people in it, the noise, the dirt, and especially that man who had stepped out in front of her and was trying to flag down the cab she had been waiting for. When a cab finally pulled up and he put his hand on the door, she banged him so hard with her hip that he fell to the street. "Get your own cab, buster."

   "Maggie?" he said, still on the ground. "Maggie Pillbox? Is that you?"

   "Wow," she said. "It's you, Doctor Pantry. Gosh, if I'd known it was you, I never would have hit you so hard."

   "Still hostile, eh?" he said. Doctor Pantry had been Maggie's psychiatrist. She helped him up, and for the next fifty minutes, they stood on the sidewalk, Doctor Pantry listening carefully and taking notes as Maggie told him all her life's woes.

4. The man and woman trying to hail down a cab, the ones dressed like insurance sales people, had just pulled off their greatest crime to date. It wasn't the big time, but eleven wallets, a watch, and a solar calculator weren't bad for five minutes' work. Once in the cab, they started going through the loot, unaware that the cabdriver was watching in his rearview mirror. The woman talked about how they could finally afford Cindy's braces. The man said he could now pay the rent, and the cabdriver took them on a circuitous route to the police station.

5. Joe had been driving a cab for only two weeks and still found the job intoxicating. He liked trying to figure out what each person was like before they got into his cab, though he was usually wrong about people. His last fare had turned out to be a transvestite so convincing that he'd almost asked him/her out on a date. Now this couple, the man in the three-piece suit waving him down and the much younger woman on the sidewalk, worked together and were lovers dying to get away for an afternoon of hot passion. Why else the unlikely pair? "Forest Lawn Mortuary," the man said as he got into the car. "And step on it. We don't want to be late."

—TERRY FRENCH

A story isn't about a moment in time, a story is about the moment in time.
—W. D. WETHERELL

60

The End Foretold

Few readers are tempted to turn to the end of a novel to find out "what happens," because the journey to the end is one of the pleasures of being inside that particular story. However, some writers tell future events at the beginning of their story or novel, trusting their story-telling abilities to keep the reader reading. Early on in his story "White Angel," Michael Cunningham writes about two brothers, the younger of whom adores his older brother, Carlton. "I was, thanks to Carlton, the most criminally advanced nine-year-old in my fourth-grade class. I was going places. I made no move without his counsel." The next sentence begins, "Here is Carlton several months before his death, in an hour so alive with snow that earth and sky are identically white." And we continue reading on for that "hour so alive"—alive even more so in the face of Carlton's impending death.

Rudolfo Anaya also foretells events in his novel *Bless Me, Ultima.* In the first pages his narrator tells us, "The attic of our home was partitioned into two small rooms. My sisters, Deborah and Theresa, slept in one and I slept in the small cubicle by the door. The wooden steps creaked down into a small hallway that led into the kitchen. From the top of the stairs I had the vantage point into the heart of our home, my mother's kitchen. From there I was to see the terrified face of Chavez when he brought the terrible news of the murder of the sheriff; I was to see the rebellion of my brothers against my father; and many times late at night I was to see Ultima returning from the Llano where she gathered the herbs that can be harvested only in the light of the full moon by the careful hands of a curandera." Note how murder and his brothers' rebellion are woven into a sentence that brings us through to his adored Ultima.

In the beginning of *Stones for Ibarra,* Harriet Doerr writes, "Here they are, a man and a woman just over and just under forty, come to spend their lives in Mexico City and are already lost as they travel cross-country over the central plateau. The driver of the station wagon is Richard Everton, a blue-eyed, black-haired stubborn man who will die thirty years sooner than he now imagines. On the seat beside him is his wife, Sara, who imagines neither his death nor her own, imminent or remote as they may be."

In the first paragraph of Howard Norman's novel *The Bird Artist,* Fabian Vas makes a startling revelation. It begins: "My name is Fabian Vas. I live in Witless Bay, New Foundland. You would not have heard of me. Obscurity is not necessarily failure, though; I am a bird artist, and have more or less made a living at it. Yet I murdered the lighthouse keeper, Botho August, and that is an equal part of how I think of myself." The murder doesn't occur till almost the end of the novel.

Other works of fiction that foretell their endings are Elizabeth Jane Howard's "The Long View" and Gabriel García Márquez's *Chronicle of a Death Foretold*.

The Exercise

Select one of your own stories that has an ending that is final—a story in which someone leaves a place or person forever, someone dies, or something irrevocable and irreparable takes place. Now move this "news" to the beginning of your story. Be brief. Then read your story again to see if the journey through the story is rewarding in itself.

The Objective

To put pressure on the story—sentence by sentence—by "giving away" the ending. To understand that chronology is fluid and sometimes irrelevant to the experience of the story.

> *I write in longhand. My Baltimore neighbor Anne Tyler and I are maybe the only two writers left who actually write with a fountain pen. She made the remark that there's something about the muscular movement of putting down script on that paper that gets her imagination back in the track where it was. I feel that too, very much so. My sentences in print, as in conversation, tend to go on a while before they stop: I trace that to the cursiveness of the pen. The idea of typing out first drafts, where each letter is physically separated by a little space from the next letter, I find a paralyzing notion. Good old script, which connects this letter to that, and this line to that—well, that's how good plots work, right? When this loops around and connects to that . . .*
>
> —JOHN BARTH

61

The Double Ending:
Two Points in Time

Have you ever finished a short story only to feel that perhaps there is more to the story—but at a future time, past your story's current ending? This dilemma—the need for more—calls for the solution of the double ending. It isn't that the first ending is wrong, but rather it is a necessary stepping-stone on the way to the final ending. And once you have written this second ending to the story—at a future time that is past the current ending—you might find that the first ending no longer satisfies the story's arc. The following stories by three superb storytellers illustrate the elegant art and architecture of the double ending.

Sharon Sheehe Stark's story "The Appaloosa House," on page 454, begins with this first sentence: "My father's girlfriend's name was Delores and my mother went by Dusie because she was one." The daughter narrates the story with biting good humor as she tells how the father is kicked out of the house because of his philandering, but eventually is allowed to return. As a surprise, her "dusie" of a mother paints the house like an Appaloosa horse and is riding the peak when the father arrives home. He joins her on the roof in a joyful reunion, which the daughter has been longing for, but ultimately doesn't trust. There is a space break and the story continues with the daughter jumping ahead to her father's death in the company of a woman not his wife (page 461). And then it returns to the moment of joy—a joy that ends the current time of the story, but alas will not last.

Alice Munro's story "Post and Beam" is the story of Lorna, a young mother of two children, married to an older academic who is "very proud" of their post-and-beam house. Lorna has become infatuated with one of her husband's students, Lionel, who hangs around the house and writes her poems. As the story proceeds, Lionel disappears for a while and Polly, Lorna's disgruntled dissatisfied cousin, comes to visit. Near the end of the story, when the family is on a vacation, Lorna imagines that Polly, who was left behind, is going to commit suicide. In order to head this off, Lorna thinks:

> Make a bargain. Believe that it was still possible, up to the last minute it was possible to make a bargain.
>
> It had to be serious, a most final and wrenching promise or offer. Take this. I promise this. . . . Not the children. She snatched that thought away as if she were grabbing them out of the fire. Not Brendan, for an opposite

reason. She did not love him enough. . . . Herself? Her looks. . . . It occurred
to her that she might be on the wrong track. In a case like this, it might
not be up to you to choose. Not up to you to set the terms. You would
know them when you met them. You must promise to honor them without knowing what they were going to be. Promise.

When the family arrives home, in fact, Polly is doing quite well for
herself and seems to have caught the fancy of Lionel. Lorna hears their
companionable voices in the back yard and thinks, "Lionel. She had forgotten all about him." She had forgotten to exempt him when bargaining.
The story nears its end with Lorna, isolated and bereft, looking down from
an upstairs window on her assembled family and the new duo of Polly
and Lionel, who is now lost to her. There is a space break. And then this:

> It was a long time ago that this happened. In North Vancouver, when
> they lived in the post-and-beam house. When she was twenty-four years
> old and new to bargaining.

Clearly, Lorna has learned to bargain better—and this no doubt has
had something to do with why they no longer live in the post-and-beam
house. This is a crucial detail; surely only death or divorce could have moved
her husband out of it.

In Jean Thompson's story "Mercy" a divorced and lonely policeman
sleeps with a woman after he tells her that her son has been killed in a car
accident. He continues to call her, but she avoids him until finally, at the
end of the story, he waits outside the place where she works. When he
accosts her, she tells him, "Christ. I felt sorry for you. You and your sad-
sack face and your stupid badge. It was a mercy fuck. OK." He is devas-
tated. Then a few sentences later the story continues:

> Much later, after he had met and married his second wife, and left the
> force, and had become accustomed to his new happiness, he was able to
> see that moment more clearly. She might have been cruel, but she had
> not been unwise to cast him off. He had only wanted to fill himself up with
> her grief, because it would take up more space in him than his own imper-
> fect grief . . . But he didn't know that yet, or that things would get bet-
> ter, or that he would not always feel his shame like a sickness. He started
> the car, and she gave him a little fluttering wave, and the rain dropped
> like a curtain over the windshield glass and blurred the red of her skirt.
> She made a pantomime of dodging the rain, turned, and disappeared
> into the shop. He had been set free from something, although that was
> another thing he did not yet know.

And there the story ends—although we know that a better future is in
store for him.

Note that the double ending allows the writer to use an *extreme* ending
for the first ending because it will be mitigated by the one to follow. In
"Mercy" the policeman hits bottom in the first ending, when the woman

tells him that their earlier encounter was a "mercy fuck." In "Post and Beam" the young wife is also in despair at losing Lionel, at "acquiring Polly," and at returning to her previous situation of a young mother married to a pompous academic. In "The Appaloosa House" the daughter sees her parents at their best: her mother's craziness beguiling the father into coming home once again. Their immense joy on that roof. But it is too extreme to last—and the father's character (character is destiny) asserts itself and he once again cheats on his wife and he and his young fling die in an accident.

The extreme is acceptable in the first ending for some of the following reasons:

- Sometimes, what happens to a character needs time to sink in—to make a character act (as in "Post and Beam").

- A character needs time to heal, but can't immediately (as in "Mercy").

- A character needs enough to time make a decision (again as in "Post and Beam") or for the inevitable to happen (the break up of the "Post and Beam" marriage).

- It allows a character to have a satisfying BUT TEMPORARY change of character (as in "The Appaloosa House"), but that temporary change cannot last.

The Exercise

Look at your stories that are in draft form and consider whether one of them would benefit from just such a double ending. How might the future of the characters be quite different and produce a truer ending to their story than the current ending? Be sure to set the "second" ending at least two to five years in the future.

The Objective

To give the way you think about your characters' lives—the arc of their stories—more latitude. To understand how the future can be foretold within the confines of the first ending.

PART EIGHT

The Elements of Style

Style is the feather in the arrow, not the feather in the cap.

—GEORGE SAMPSON

John Updike once grumbled to an interviewer that his prose always sounded like John Updike no matter how hard he tried to sound like someone else. Most of us try our entire writing lives to achieve a unique and recognizable style—and he complains! We have borrowed the title of this section from E.B. White and William Strunk's writing bible of the same name. White said during an interview, "I don't think style can be taught. Style results more from what a person is than from what he knows." He went on to say that there are a "few hints that can be thrown out to advantage. They would be the twenty-one hints I threw out in Chapter V of *The Elements of Style*. There was nothing new or original about them, but there they are, for all to read." Everybody should have a copy of this book on his shelf, but as a reminder we have listed the section headings of Chapter V below:

1. Place yourself in the background; 2. Write in a way that comes naturally; 3. Work from a suitable design; 4. Write with nouns and verbs; 5. Revise and rewrite; 6. Do not overwrite; 7. Do not overstate; 8. Avoid the use of qualifiers; 9. Do not affect a breezy manner; 10. Use orthodox spelling; 11. Do not explain too much; 12. Do not construct awkward adverbs; 13. Make sure the reader knows who is speaking; 14. Avoid fancy words; 15. Do not use dialect unless your ear is good; 16. Be clear; 17. Do not inject opinion; 18. Use figures of speech sparingly; 19. Do not take shortcuts at the cost of clarity; 20. Avoid foreign languages; 21. Prefer the standard to the offbeat.

Strunk and White is a good place to begin, but it isn't the whole story of style in fiction. What would John Barth be without his instructional presence; Didion without Didion; Vladimir Nabokov without his complicated, high style; Alice Adams without her qualifiers; Laurie Colwin without her breezy manner; Russell Hoban without his unorthodox spelling; Nicholson Baker without his explanations; Flannery O'Connor without her inventions in dialect; Joseph Conrad without his opinions; John Updike without his figures of speech; Thomas Mann and Sandra Cisneros without their foreign languages; and Donald Barthelme without the upbeat?

Begin with Strunk and White, but as you grow more experienced in writing and life, you will grow into a more individual style. Style is a kind of personal signature, made up of the writer's particular vocabulary, sentence structure, subject matter, inflection, attitude, tone, and vision.

Cyril Connolly, the English critic, said, "Style is manifest in language. The vocabulary of a writer is his currency, but it is a paper currency and its value depends on the reserves of mind and heart which back it. The perfect use of language is that in which every word carries the meaning that it is intended to, no less and no more."

Jazz great Miles Davis said, "You have to play a long time to play like yourself." The same is true of writing fiction. The exercises in this section are designed to make you more aware of the elements of style, style in language—sentence structure, word choice, diction, tone, etc.—in your own work and the work of writers you admire. And what we say in Exercise 13 "Put Your Heart on the Page" is worth repeating here: Know yourself. Write from the heart. Ellen Glasgow said of style that it "should be [like] a transparent envelope which changes color in response to the animation within." Profound advice from a master of fiction.

In conversation you can use timing, a look, inflection, pauses. But on the page all you have is commas, dashes, the amount of syllables in a word. When I write I read everything out loud to get the right rhythm.
—FRAN LEBOWITZ

62

A Style Of Your Own

from Rod Kessler

Students are often surprised to discover patterns within their own writing styles. Sometimes the patterns reveal strengths of style, but sometimes the patterns uncover easy-to-fix problems, such as "having the as's"—using too many "as he was walking" constructions.

The Exercise

Make a photocopy of a page from a story you've already put into final form. This can be the opening of the story or a page from the middle, it doesn't matter—but be sure the page is typed neatly. Also bring in a copy of a page from a fiction writer you admire. Analyze your page for:

1. Sentence length. From the top of your page count down ten sentences. Make a list indicating the word length of each sentence. How varied in length are your sentences? Do you have a mix of short and long, or are your sentences around the same length?

   Next, add up all the words in your ten sentences and divide by ten—which gives you your average sentence length.

   Now perform the same counts on the page from the writer whose work you admire—writer X. How varied are these sentences compared with your own? What is the writer's average length?

2. Modifier density. On your own writing sample, mark all of the adjectives and adverbs you've used in the first 100 words and add them up. This gives an approximate percentage of modifiers. (If you counted 5, that's 5 out of 100 or 5 percent).

   Perform the same count on the page from writer X. How do your styles compare?

3. Sentence structure. Does each of your paragraphs contain a mixture of simple, complex, and compound sentences? Or are they all of the same structure? How many times do you begin, say, with participial phrases (Running to the station, Jack. . . . Looking up at the sky, Joan. . . .)? How many times do you use "subject-verb" constructions? How many times do you use "as" as a conjunction? (Jerry

turned to go as the bell chimed.) (Read John Gardner's discussion of "The Sentence" in *The Art of Fiction,* in which he teaches the lesson of the sentence by example.)

4. Diction. How many of the first 100 words exceed two syllables? Three syllables? More than three? (Again, read Gardner's section "Vocabulary," same book.)

5. Verbs. What percentage of your verbs are forms of the boring verb "to be"? How often do you use the passive voice?

The Objective

To enable you to regard your own prose style objectively and decide if you need to make changes—perhaps vary your sentences or cut out an obvious mannerism. Some students might want to go beyond ten sentences and one hundred words to do a closer study of their "natural" prose.

A true work of fiction does all of the following things, and does them elegantly, efficiently: it creates a vivid and continuous dream in the reader's mind; it is implicitly philosophical; it fulfills or at least deals with all of the expectations it sets up; and it strikes us, in the end, not simply as a thing done but as a shining performance.

—JOHN GARDNER, "WHAT WRITERS DO"

63

Taboos: Weak Adverbs and Adjectives

Voltaire said the adjective is the enemy of the noun and the adverb is the enemy of the verb. Thus war ensues on both—with the object of banishing adjectives and adverbs forever. Banishing them precipitously and unfairly. John Gardner said, "Adverbs are either the dullest tools or the sharpest tools in the novelist's toolbox." Adverbs are not meant to augment a verb—as in walked *slowly*—but to create friction with the verb or alter its meaning. For example, pair the following adverbs with different verbs to see how they change those verbs: relentlessly, conscientiously, chastely, uncharacteristically, reluctantly, gratuitously, erroneously, furtively, and inadequately. This is what Mark Twain wrote to a young admirer: "I notice that you use plain simple language, short words [brief sentences. That is the way to write English. . . . Stick to it] don't let fluff and flowers creep in. When you catch an adjective, kill it. No, I don't mean that, utterly, but kill most of them—then the rest will be valuable. They weaken when they are close together, they give strength when they are wide apart."

Adjectives may seem to bolster nouns when in fact they often weaken them. Yet some adjectives have everything to do with style and meaning. Whenever you use an adjective try to make it unexpected; it should pull away from the noun, giving the two words a sort of delicious tension. The same goes for the adverb.

The following are examples of adverbs and adjectives that are used well:

She had been to Germany, Italy, everywhere that one visits *acquisitively.*
—ELIZABETH BOWEN, *THE LAST SEPTEMBER*

Within the parson's house death was *zealously* kept in view and lectured on.
—ISAK DINESEN, "PETER AND ROSA"

She jammed the pedal to the floor, and like something huge and prehistoric and pea-brained, the Jeep leapt *stupidly* out of its stall.
—SHARON SHEEHE STARK, *A WRESTLING SEASON*

I have always enjoyed gestures—never failing to bow, for example, when I finished dancing with a woman—but one attribute I have acquired with age is the ability to predict when I am about to act *foolishly.*

—ETHAN CANIN, *EMPEROR OF THE AIR*

She reached again for the door and kept her eyes on him, like a captive who edges *watchfully* towards escape.

—SHIRLEY HAZZARD, *THE TRANSIT OF VENUS*

So closely had we become tied to the river that we could sense where it lay and make for it *instinctively* like cattle.

—W. D. WETHERELL, *CHEKHOV'S SISTER*

When Sula first visited the Wright house, Helene's *curdled* scorn turned to butter.

—TONI MORRISON, *SULA*

With a *bladdery* whack it [the boat] slapped apart and sprang away.

—SHARON SHEEHE STARK, *A WRESTLING SEASON*

Charmian sat with her eyes closed, attempting to put her thoughts into *alphabetical* order.

—MURIEL SPARK, *MEMENTO MORI*

Hank was not accepted at Harvard Law School; but *goodhearted* Yale took him.

—JOHN UPDIKE, "THE OTHER"

On the far side of the room, under the *moiling* dogs the twins are playing.

—FRANÇOIS CAMOIN, "BABY, BABY, BABY"

"Perhaps the Beauforts don't know her," Janey suggested, with her *artless* malice.

—EDITH WHARTON, *AGE OF INNOCENCE*

And he contemplated her absorbed young face with a thrill of possessorship in which pride of his own masculinity was mingled with a tender reverence for her *abysmal* purity.

—EDITH WHARTON, *AGE OF INNOCENCE*

The Exercise

Part One

Circle all the adverbs and adjectives in a published story and decide which ones work. Then, exchange all weak adverbs and adjectives for strong ones of your own. Consider omitting them altogether. Now do the same exercise with one of your own stories.

The Objective

To be alert to the power—and the weakness—of these verbal spices. To avoid them except when they can add something you really need.

To underscore the fact that verbs and nouns are stronger alone than when coupled with modifiers that add nothing to nuance or meaning and are about as useful as a pair of broken crutches.

Student Examples

Hunched over, scissors clasped in her hands, the old woman passed like a shadow behind a screen of young birch and stepped *possessively* into her neighbor's garden.

—COLLEEN GILLARD

I clatter Sparkey's mouth and make him laugh *demonically,* or have him insult the guy who is sitting too near the stage.

—MATT MARINOVICH

Magdalen was the woman who'd managed to turn her passion *sacred.* She was the saint who turned the flesh *Divine.*

—MARIETTE LIPPO

Part Two

Write a two-page scene or description using only one adjective and one adverb, with the exception of colors. You should try to make this piece so fluid that anyone reading it without knowing the exercise should not be aware of its nature.

Read, read, read. And write every day. Never compare yourself to anyone but yourself. The question you ask of yourself each evening is: Did I write, did I spend time? Show up for work every day, like any good citizen.
—RICHARD BAUSCH

Word Packages Are Not Gifts

A word package is a group of neutral words strung together into a hackneyed phrase. Word packages are used by lazy writers searching for an easy way out of a difficult or slippery thought. (Frequently they are found at the beginnings of sentences.)

The Exercise

Stay away from the following word packages. They signal to the smart reader that you lack freshness and are an uninteresting writer.

> Better than ever
> For some curious reason
> A number of . . .
> As everybody knows
> She didn't know where she was
> Things were getting out of hand
> It came as no surprise
> It was beyond him
> Needless to say
> Without thinking
> He lived in the moment
> Well in advance
> An emotional roller coaster
> Little did I know
> To no avail
> The only sound was

The Objective

To learn to write without word packages until your use of them is absolutely deliberate and to some purpose.

Boxcars and Mechanical Stylistics
from David Madden

The functional usefulness of conjunctions and connectives is obvious. Their mechanical and clumsy use in first drafts, even by the most skillful writers, is not so obvious. The effect is to drug the reader's responses. Phrases pass before the reader's eyes like boxcars hooked together, rather than a flowing stream.

The Exercise
In the revision phase of the creative process, make a raid on your story to arrest the overuse of conjunctives and connectives such as "but," "and," "as if," "which," "when," "or," "so," "nor," "yet," "for," "after," "because," "if," "since," "where," "while," "as," "although," "unless," "until," "also," "finally," "however," "therefore," and "moreover."

The Objective
To maximize the sense of experience happening now, to sustain a sense of immediacy. The words cited above, when overused or used too mechanically, call attention to the fact that you are constructing sentences—as if you were, in the lingo of a lawyer, only dealing out facts to reach a verdict.

I don't feel that it's plot that is moving my stories along from the start to their finish. I know it's not plot. It's language largely . . . and the characters' observations.
—AMY HEMPEL

Practice Writing Good, Clean Prose

from Christopher Keane

Too often new writers think in terms of story, rather than in terms of words—of building a story with words. As a result, their early efforts are often overwritten and flowery. The following exercise will challenge your use of language—and it might change the way you write.

The Exercise

Write a short story using words of only one syllable.

The Objective

To make you conscious of word choice.

Example

Fire

I see her in a red dress, a red bow in her hair. She would have on black shoes and white socks. The socks would be up to her knees. She would have been, say, five years old at the time the fire broke out. It would have still been dark; it would have been cold.

She would be in her room at the time.

She would have waked from a deep sleep as if pushed or shoved. She would have known what to do. She was that way, they tell me. She was that kind of child.

I see her leave her room, stand at the top of the stairs in the front hall, smell the smoke. She would be dressed; she put on her clothes when she climbed out of bed. When she smelled smoke she would scream a fire scream that would start at the base of her throat, pass through her lips in a howl. The howl would wake those in the rest of the house. It would curl through the rooms, ride the smoke that climbed the stairs, seep through doors, cloud the glass.

The man got up first and woke his wife. They heard the child's howl filled with smoke, and they raced to the cribs of the twins, they raced to their room. Flames licked the closed doors, climbed the walls.

The man and his wife crept down the back stairs. They heard the girl's scream but there was no way to reach her. There was no time. They did not want to leave the house, but they had to. While there was still time. They must save at all cost what they had in their arms. Each held one of the twins that they took from the cribs. The twins slept on. They slept a dead sleep, safe in the arms that held them.

I see her red dress. I see a red bow in her hair. She would be told she saved them all, and she would be glad. She would have scars on her face and arms. The scars would hurt. The fire would be with her through life.

She would see the red dress and the red bow in her dreams, the white socks up to her knees. In her dreams, she would stand at the top of the stairs in the front hall. She would smell smoke and start to howl. The scars would not have come yet, nor the pain.

—ANNE BRASHLER, EDITOR, *StoryQuarterly*

The difference between the right word and the nearly right word is the same as that between lightning and the lightning bug.
—MARK TWAIN

67

Reading Your Work Aloud

John Updike says that the best way to get the kinks out of your prose is to read it aloud. Reading aloud what you have written reveals its flaws in the same way a magnifying glass reveals blemishes on your skin.

Keep in mind that the eye and ear are connected and that what the reader sees will somehow be transmitted to his inner ear. Too many sentences with a similar construction will make your reader yawn. Too many unintended repetitions of words of phrases will also displease the reader's ear. Know which words you use too often, such as "and," "just," "look," "even," and so on. You should always read your work aloud before showing it to anyone. Doing this will help you avoid monotony, repetition, flatness, unintentional alliteration, and other impediments to smooth, fluid prose. Your teachers, fellow students, and future editors will know when you have not read your work out loud.

The following passage from Mavis Gallant's story "The Four Seasons" is an example of prose that sings when read both silently and aloud. "The sea was greener than anything except Mrs. Unwin's emerald, bluer than her sapphire, more transparent than blue, white, transparent glass. Wading with a twin in each hand, she saw their six feet underwater like sea creatures. The sun became white as a stone; something stung in its heat, like fine, hard, invisible rain."

The Exercise

Write a description in which the sentences are variously built. The subject should not always be the first word; some sentences should be longer than others. Read aloud the work of an author you admire and see how he or she accomplishes this. It's all right to imitate.

The Objective

Prose is both utilitarian and decorative. Unless you're deliberately reaching for a flat, monotonous tone, you should try for variation in the sound of your prose.

PART NINE

A Writer's Tools

As we said in our introduction—and we think it's worth repeating—a writer must think like a writer and also master the tools needed to write smoothly, with feeling, and control. Thinking like a writer means being open, skeptical, curious, passionate, forgiving, and truthful. Writing like a writer involves learning specific techniques of the craft and, not incidentally, shedding bad habits such as using stale or approximate language, wasting words, and working in haste.

What we call "tools" includes solving the problems presented by time and space, bringing abstract ideas to life, learning to show more and tell less, handling transitions, and naming everything from diners to dogs.

A few blessed people seem able to sit down and turn out polished and exciting prose. Most of us, however, must go through a long apprenticeship, trying one way after another until our fiction falls into the right place; there is no substitute for trial and error. And as you revise you will find yourself being a ruthless self-editor, cutting and shaping until you get it the way you want it. The following exercises were designed to provide you with company along the way. They should help take you from the uncertainty and disarray of a first draft to a finished piece of work you have every right to be proud of.

68

Handling the Problems of Time and Pace

from Robie Macauley

The traditional rule is that episodes meant to show important behavior in the characters, to make events dramatic as in theater, or to bring news that changes the situation, should be dealt with in the scenic, or eyewitness, manner. Stretches of time or occurrences that are secondary to the story's development are handled by means of what is called a narrative bridge. Dialogue is the direct report of speech; indirect discourse is the summary of what was said. Some examples:

Scenic
Now they were at the ford, the rain was still falling, and the river was in flood. John got out of the jeep and stared at the white violence of the water they must cross to reach the place where the muddy road picked up again.

Narrative Summary
The journey to Punta Gorda took two days by near-impossible road. At one point, they had to cross a raging river and follow a muddy track that only a jeep could manage.

Dialogue
"Now how are we going to get across this monster?" Lisa asked.
    "Easy," said John. "We take the rope over, get it around that big tree and use the winch to pull the jeep across."
    "But who swims the flood with the rope?"
    "Well, I can't swim," he said, "but you're supposed to be so good at it."

Indirect Discourse
When they came to the swollen river, John suggested that they put a rope across and then use the jeep's winch to pull the vehicle to the farther bank. Because Lisa had talked so often about her swimming ability, he suggested ironically that she be the one to take the rope over.

The Exercise

As a class, come up with a plot or a series of events that might make a long short story. Next, write a scenario in which you indicate

- Where you would place a full scene or incidental scene
- Where you would use summaries, either narrative summaries or summarized scenes

The Objective

To learn to identify which parts of a story should be presented in a scene and which parts of a story should be summarized. To develop an understanding of pace.

A writer is someone for whom writing is more difficult than it is for other people.
                                        —THOMAS MANN

69

Show and Tell:
There's a Reason
It's Called Storytelling

from Carol-Lynn Marrazzo

Beginning writers have often been told "show don't tell," and sometimes by writers who tell plenty. Flannery O'Connor observed that "fiction writing is very seldom a matter of saying things; it is a matter of showing things." But there is a difference, however, between "saying" and "telling," and the wise writer is not afraid to tell. As the following story excerpts illustrate, O'Connor and other fine writers blend telling and showing in their stories and novels—and for good reason. When a writer depends solely on showing and neglects the narrative that artfully shapes, characterizes, qualifies, or in some other way informs the character's actions, the reader is forced to extrapolate meaning based upon what is observed—for example, a character's sweating palms or nervous twitch—and the reader, rather than the writer, then creates the story.

Contrary to what you may think or have been led to believe, writers tell their stories and even O'Connor tells plenty. In "Good Country People," the main character, Joy, a cripple and self-cultivated cynic, is transformed by a moment of vulnerability with a Bible salesman. O'Connor shows the action, but tells Joy's transformation. In this and examples that follow, first read the plain text, then read the complete passage including the narrative in italics.

> She sat staring at him. *There was nothing about her face or her round freezing-blue eyes to indicate that this had moved her; but she felt as if her heart had stopped and left her mind to pump her blood. She decided that for the first time in her life she was face to face with real innocence. This boy, with an instinct that came from beyond wisdom, had touched the truth about her.* When after a minute, she said in a hoarse high voice, "All right," *it was like surrendering to him completely. It was like losing her own life and finding it again, miraculously, in his.*
> Very gently he began to roll the slack leg up.

The sentence that begins "There was nothing" explains why the "show, don't tell" rule so often fails. We are told that we cannot know through observation alone what is happening within Joy. If you are unconvinced, read just the showing alone again. Ask: Is there any indication Joy has changed? In this passage, telling not only heightens the moment, it reveals it as a moment of rapture.

"Good Country People" and other stories prove that a complementary interplay between telling and showing at the transforming moment in the story is often crucial to the reader's understanding. Following is a key passage from Eudora Welty's "Livvie is Back." This is the story of a girl married to a sickly old man named Solomon. When Livvie holds and kisses Cash, a young laborer, Welty tells the reader exactly what Livvie realizes about herself and marriage:

> She gathered the folds of his coat behind him and fastened her red lips to his mouth, and *she was dazzled at herself then, the way he had been dazzled at himself to begin with. In that instant she felt something that could not be told— that Solomon's death was at hand, that he was the same to her as if he were dead now.* She cried out, and uttering little cries, turned and ran for the house.

Here the reader is told Livvie's thoughts and feelings about Solomon "that he was the same to her as if he were dead." Welty chose not to leave the moment to showing alone.

Another quick example. In Jane Smiley's story "Lily," Smiley tells in one word what Lily experiences when she betrays her good friend:

> Lily broke into a sweat the moment she stopped speaking, *a sweat of instant regret.*

Lily's response is characterized as "regret." The whole story would be changed if Lily reacted with a sweat of "confusion" or "triumph."

There is nothing economical or reticent about James Joyce's telling in "The Dead" during Gabriel's epiphany, the moment when he internalizes that all with his wife is not as he thought—she was loved once by a boy, a love Gabriel knew nothing about. The physical manifestations of Gabriel's new awareness are, in contrast, quite modest.

> "He is dead," she said at length. "He died when he was only seventeen. Isn't it a terrible thing to die so young as that?"
> "What was he?" asked Gabriel, *still ironically.*
> "He was in the gasworks," she said.
> *Gabriel felt humiliated by the failure of his irony and by the evocation of this figure from the dead, a boy in the gasworks. While he had been full of memories of their secret life together, full of tenderness and joy and desire, she had been comparing him in her mind with another. A shameful consciousness of his own person assailed him. He saw himself as a ludicrous figure, acting as a penny-boy for his aunts, a nervous well-meaning sentimentalist, orating to vulgarians and idealizing his own clownish lusts, the pitiable fatuous fellow he had caught a glimpse of in the mirror. Instinctively* he turned his back more to the light *lest she might see the shame that burned upon his forehead.*
> *He tried to keep his tone of cold interrogation but* his voice when he spoke was humble and indifferent.

Telling is also used to good effect in Amy Hempel's story, "In The Cemetery Where Al Jolson Is Buried," in which the first-person narrator is visiting a dying friend in the hospital. Hempel writes:

"I have to go home," I said when she woke up.

She thought I meant home to her house in the Canyon, and I had to say No, *home* home. *I twisted my hands in the time-honored fashion of people in pain. I was supposed to offer something. The Best Friend. I could not even offer to come back.*

I felt weak and small and failed.

Also exhilarated.

Hempel's narrator tells exactly how she feels—conflicted.

A wonderful example of balanced and complementary interplay between showing and telling is the transforming movement in Peter Taylor's "The Gift of the Prodigal." In order to appreciate how remarkable the telling is, first read only those portions of the passage that are NOT italicized.

I say to myself, "He really is like something not quite human. For all the jams and scrapes he's been in, he's never suffered any second thoughts or known the meaning of remorse. I ought to have let him hang," I say to myself, "by his own beautiful locks."

But almost simultaneously what I hear myself saying aloud is "Please don't go, Rick. Don't go yet, son." *Yes, I am pleading with him, and I mean what I say with my whole heart.* He still has his right hand on the door-knob and has given it a full turn. Our eyes meet across the room, *directly, as they never have before in the whole of Ricky's life or mine. I think neither of us could tell anyone what it is he sees in the other's eyes, unless it is a need beyond any description either of us is capable of.*

Presently Rick says, "You don't need to hear my crap."

And I hear my *bewildered* voice saying, "I do . . . I do." And "Don't go, Rick, my boy." My eyes have *even* misted over. But I still meet his eyes across the *now too silent* room. He looks at me *in the most compassionate way imaginable. I don't think any child of mine has ever looked at me so before. Or perhaps it isn't really with compassion as he is viewing me but with the sudden, gratifying knowledge that it is not, after all, such a one-sided business, the business between us.* He keeps his right hand on the doorknob a few seconds longer. Then I hear the latch click and *know he has let go.* Meanwhile, I observe his left hand making that *familiar gesture,* his fingers splayed, his hand tilting back and forth. I am out of my chair now. I go to the desk and bring out two Danlys cigars from another desk drawer, which I keep locked. He is there *ready to receive my offering when I turn around.* He accepts the cigar without smiling, and I give it without smiling, too.

Now ask: If only the "showing" portion of this passage were available, would a reader have any idea what subtle understanding has transpired between father and son? Study the passage carefully and observe Taylor's strategy as he grounds the passage through the father's keen senses (showing) and at the same time gives the reader access to the father's most intimate thoughts and feelings (telling)—all while the action keeps moving forward.

The Exercise

Choose a story in which you think the transforming moment is effectively rendered. Underline the telling portions of that moment and read the passage without the underlined portions. Do this for a number of stories.

Then, turn to a story draft of your own in which you think the transforming moment is not yet effectively rendered. Underline the telling portions of that moment. If you have no "telling," add some, but try to balance the showing and telling to their best combined effect. Do not be afraid to use the world "felt." Note how many times it appeared in the previous examples.

If it seems impossible to tell anything, then you might not know your characters well or you might not know what your story is about.

The Objective

To be able to both show and tell. To experiment with different combinations of showing and telling to enhance your narrative technique and to illuminate the final meaning of your story.

A story is a way to say something that can't be said any other way, and it takes every word in the story to say what the meaning is.

—FLANNERY O'CONNOR

70

Separating Author, Narrator, and Character

from Frederick Reiken

Many students have experienced the problem of a short story or novel that feels flat because the protagonist is really nothing more than a passive observer of the action, and hence winds up being not so much a character as either a once-removed narrator (in the case of first-person POV) or the so-called "brain in a room" (in the case of third-person POV) in which the character sees and ruminates but never becomes the focus of the action. Often this is because the student is unconsciously "merged" with the protagonist in his or her imagination, whether the story is autobiographical or not.

When you are writing a conventionally character-driven story or novel, it is crucial to understand that the function of a narrator is to present and somehow to translate the action of the story, such that the reader can understand objectively what's happening, even if the protagonist does not. For example, in *Emma* by Jane Austen, Emma Woodhouse is quite sure that Mr. Knightly is wooing her friend Harriet, and over a sequence of scenes urges Harriet, who has not interpreted Mr. Knightly's actions toward her as such, to believe that Knightly is indeed building up to a marriage proposal. If read carefully, however, all the scenes involving Emma, Harriet, and Mr. Knightly demonstrate objectively—and to comic and ironic effect—that Knightly is actually interested in Emma and that Emma has drastically misread the situation. Without overtly stating anything, the third-person omniscient narrator presents the drama in such a way that we, as readers, can see exactly what's happening, even as the protagonist Emma remains blind.

The same separation holds true for successful first-person narratives, even in the case of the most voice-driven and unreliable of narrator/protagonists. Holden Caulfield, for instance, narrates J.D. Salinger's *The Catcher in the Rye* from a vantage point beyond the timeline of the story, alternately dramatizing himself as a character and then effortlessly moving back to the mode of narrator, in which he makes expository commentary about himself and the little odyssey he is unfurling. But even if Holden is absolutely sure of every last thing he asserts, author Salinger, who exists outside of Holden and the novel, has envisioned the narrative so that we see

Holden objectively as a boy who is quite lost. The rift between Holden's perceptions and our objective perception—which has been built into the narrative through Salinger's ability to separate himself from Holden in his imagination—creates pathos as well as narrative tension.

The Exercise

Part One

Write the words "Once upon a time there was a(n)" on a sheet of paper and then continue, letting yourself write whatever story automatically ensues. Take five to ten minutes and then restart using the same "Once upon a time" prompt.

Part Two

Choose one of your two favorite fairy tales. Remove the "Once upon a time" from the beginning of the story and rewrite at least the first paragraph in a realistic manner, adding character details, realistic setting, modern syntax, etc.

The Objective

The phrase "Once upon a time" is a storytelling convention that we've all internalized. The words "Once upon a time" also prompt us to envision whatever character we choose to invent with an implicit separation between the time of story and the future vantage from which it is told. As a result, three things tend to happen automatically:

1. We do not mix ourselves up with the narrator

2. We do not mix the scene up with our present-day lives

3. We are oriented outward and hence cued to invent some character and/or place that is distinctly envisioned in our imagination.

Whether the story starts out with "Once upon a time there was a very sad turtle who lived in a dying lake," or with something more realistic such as "Once upon a time there was a woman who was dying of leukemia," or even something self-reflexive such as "Once upon a time I was walking down the street in Brooklyn," the separation will, in almost all cases, be apparent.

Of course, the separation is not always going to be this obvious in a realistic literary narrative, and while many authors will at times intentionally merge narrator and character for various rhetorical effects (one example of this is the free indirect discourse employed by writers such as Virginia Woolf and Alice Munro), a successful separation of author, narrator, and character is still the key to a work's texture, depth, and dimensionality. By translating your "Once upon a time" fairy tale to a more realistic narrative, which generally entails providing the characters with more specific and singular details as well as going deeper into a character's point of view, you should be able to see how the separation is structured into any good piece of fiction. Keep in mind that the separation begins in your head, and that no amount of tinkering with sentences is going to fix the problem unless you are able to envision your character, autobiographical or not, on the screen of your imagination. As John Berger writes in his essay "Lost Off Cape Wrath," the moment a writer "simply repeats facts instead of imagining the experience of them, his writing will be reduced to a document."

Life knows us not and we do not know life—we don't even know our own thoughts. Half the words we use have no meaning whatever and of the other half each man understands each word after the fashion of his own folly and conceit. Faith is a myth and beliefs shift like mist on the shore; thoughts vanish; words, once pronounced, die; and the memory of yesterday is as shadowy as the hope of to-morrow—only the string of my platitudes seems to have no end.
—JOSEPH CONRAD

71

The Pet Store Story: Exposition

from Ron Carlson

A fair beginning of the discussion of any story would be to determine the percentage of exposition; this sounds clinical, but it is a useful way to offer an exact description of the story's components, and identify where further evidence is required. We're defining exposition as anything that happens before the first moment of the current story; it also could be anything that happens after the current story—sometimes offered in conditional or future tenses (look for would). Some stories have almost no stated exposition (it is implied—as in Hemingway's "Hills Like White Elephants") and some stories are dominated by exposition. Many stories have multiple layers of exposition, that is many time periods that are being brought to bear on the current story. (See the Alice Munro story "Save the Reaper.") While the plot (the current story) remains the motor of any story, the characters are the freight.

This assignment will result in a short short story, 600 to 1000 words in length. If it is under 600 words, you will need your instructor's permission. If it is over 1000 words, you will need your instructor's permission. If it goes onto the fifth page—oh, just make it short.

The story will feature two people (opposite sex, any relationship) who go to a pet store on a mission.

The Exercise

It is a three-part story; it starts in the middle, goes back to the beginning, and jumps to the ending. In the story (1) two people approach the pet store; (2) we find out their recent and not-so-recent history; (3) they go into the pet store.

1. Write one page in which two people approach a pet store, any pet store except Mammals and More, because that's been used. It can be free-standing or in a mall. The duty of this page is to convince us that two actual people are in an actual place. There can be dialogue, but this section should be at least 90 percent outer story: the day, the sounds, the imagery through which two people approach the pet store.

2. Write one page in which we discover from where they've come most recently (today) and what their larger history is.

3. Write one to two pages in which they enter the store and pursue their objective. This section will include current story and flashback as necessary. There probably will be another character introduced. The two people either will or will not fulfill their mission.

The Objective

The value of the current story is established/determined/colored by the exposition. The dynamic between current action and the past is a key operating feature of every story.

Student Example

Fish

The hood tightens around my neck as I pull at the strings of my Sedro Valley Sparklers sweatshirt. As the hood tightens, the string gets longer. I put the ends together and wrap them around my fingers.

"Dad?" I say. He is facing straight ahead, hands on the steering wheel, even though we have parked and he has taken the keys out of the ignition.

"Right," he says, smiling, looking over at me. He pulls at the handle of his door. It screeches as it opens. The sound makes me think of a cat yowling in pain, like when you accidentally step on its fur.

"Don't we have any WD-40?" I ask, but he is already out and can't hear me.

Letting go of my sweatshirt strings, I pull at my handle and push my shoulder against the door, but before I can get it open my father comes around and opens it for me. Sometimes it gets a little sticky, so you have to kind of put some muscle into it.

I make my strides as long as possible as we walk toward the front door of the Sedro Valley Pet Store. It feels strange, coming here without my mother. This fish thing was her idea, her way of showing support, I think. Her nickname was Goldie, but only my father called her that. It was something between them. She loved goldfish, loved filling bowls and water pitchers and glass vases with them, spreading them throughout the house so thickly that everywhere you looked there was movement— orange and glint-y like the flames flickering from her and my father's fancy cigarette lighters. When she came to my games, she would wave bags of goldfish up in the air. "Go, Baby!" she would shout. If I scored, there'd be more.

One time, when I was waiting for the Hot Peppers to throw the ball in, I looked over and saw her holding a fish bag straight out in front of her in one hand. With the other, she was sprinkling chalk from the field lines all over the bag, as if to bless the fish inside. Mr. Hergus, our coach, hated if we messed up the field lines. I remember thinking this as the team threw the ball in and Heather Hardwick passed it to me, and I kicked it in past the goalie. I remember looking back at my parents, like most kids do if they score, but my father was involved in watching my mother bless the fish, involved in the something between them. Heather Hardwick tried to slap my hand, but I wasn't paying attention. Even Mr. Hergus was smiling at my mother. She had started waving her hand higher, spreading clouds of the chalk in the air. A foot of line was missing from the end of the field. She had a sweater tied around her waist and it was falling off and you should've seen the smile on my father's face as he reached down, caught it, wrapped it around her neck, and hugged her. If I had passed the ball back to Heather, she could have kicked it in. She would have probably gotten ice cream from DairyFreeze. That was the normal thing to do. I've never told anyone this, but sometimes I worry that I look a bit like a fish. My face, anyway. I've gone through all the photo albums and looked real close at all the pictures of me, and you can see it, a little, that fish resemblance, especially in the eyes and mouth, even when I don't suck in my cheeks and mush my lips out.

Beverly sees us coming through the window and waves. She is talking into her telephone, but as we get closer, she pushes a button on it and sets it down near the credit card machine.

"Hi, Sweetie," she says to me after my father opens the door and I slide inside in front of him. "How'd you do?"

"Three goals," my father says.

"Three goals!" Beverly says. "You're going to need a new bowl!"

"Oh, yes," my father says. "Maybe a tank!"

"We'll see," I say.

Two tabby cats sitting on a carpeted cat tree raise their heads at blink at me. One lifts a paw and begins to lick it.

I walk to the back of the store, back to where the fish are. The goldfish flit around in their tanks with the bubbles. I read on a popsicle stick once that fish have memories that last only two seconds. My mother told me if you make eye contact with them for more than that, they explode. Sticking my face up close to the glass, I try to look at their flat black eyes, but they just burble past. I wonder if sideways eye contact counts. The fish look paranoid and high-strung, like the cokeheads we pass on Virginia Avenue on our way to soccer practice.

I look back and see my father talking with Beverly. He pulls on his earlobe and looks down at his shiny tassled shoes. Beverly puts a hand on his arm. I try to imagine what she's saying: yes, I know, I know, it's okay, of course, sure, mm-hmmm. Looking back at the tank, I try to pick three fish. One seems to be struggling. It keeps floating up to the top of the tank, then struggling back down, like a balloon being tugged. It wears me out, watching it. Gas, I think, and wonder if I should tell Beverly. Goldfish have so many problems.

Fish. I hate that word. I hate fish.

I pull my hood over my head and step closer to the tank. The air from my nose hits the glass and it begins to fog up. I pull the strings of my sweatshirt down and the hood tightens against my eyes. The harder I pull, the blurrier the fish get.

Look at me, I think. I let go of my strings and tap the glass with my fingers. Over here. Look.

—Josie Milliken

72

Bringing Abstract Ideas to Life

One of the principal problems in writing stories is to make abstract ideas come to life. It is not enough to talk of poverty or ambition or evil, you must render these ideas in a concrete way with descriptive sensory details, similes, and metaphors. Examine how growing old is handled in Muriel Spark's *Memento Mori,* poverty in Charles Dickens's *Bleak House* and Carolyn Chute's *The Beans of Egypt, Maine,* racism in Ralph Ellison's *Invisible Man,* growing up in Frank Conroy's *Stop-Time,* ambition in Theodore Dreiser's *An American Tragedy,* and evil in William Golding's *Lord of the Flies.*

The Exercise

Make several of the following abstractions come to life by rendering them in concrete specific details or images.

racism	poverty
injustice	growing up
ambition	sexual deceit
growing old	wealth
salvation	evil

The Objective

To learn to think, always, in concrete terms. To realize that the concrete is more persuasive than any high-flown rhetoric full of fancy words and abstractions.

Student Examples

Racism
referring to others as "you people"

—FRED PELKA

Poverty
checking for change in the telephone booth

—SANFORD GOLDEN

Sexual Deceit
splashing on Brut to cover the smell of a woman's perfume

—SANFORD GOLDEN

Evil
purposely running down animals on the road

—SANDY YANNONE

Prejudice
Victoria slipped the camphor between her skin and her undershirt before opening the library door. Her mother made her wear it from Rosh Hashanah to Passover, a guard against winter colds. "In Poland it was colder," she always said, "yet we never got sick in the winter." It was useless for Victoria to point out that one aunt and uncle had died in Polish winters despite their health charms.

She placed her bag of books on the library's high stone counter where "Returns" was written in a beautiful penmanship. "I hope you didn't tear any of these," Mrs. Holmes said, pausing in her friendly chat with a woman who looked like Betty Crocker. One by one she checked in the ragged copies of kids' classics saying that sometimes it looked as if Victoria had eaten her dinner on these books. She smiled to the woman. "Everything turns into rags in their hands, you know."

Victoria went to sit in the children's section of the library. Three new books were displayed on the table. She might get through them by closing time. She knew Mrs. Holmes wouldn't let her take out these books till yellow tape obscured some of the words. She wondered if it might make a difference if Mrs. Holmes knew that she was the best reader in the whole fifth grade.

—BARBARA SOFER

Writing about what you know does not usually mean writing about your own life. Writing about what you know means writing about the girl whose fierce-looking father picked her up from school on his Harley-Davidson motorcycle, about the Rhode Island red hens on your aunt Beulah's farm, or the way a carburetor works on a 1950 Plymouth. Writers are meant to peer outward at others with an inward passion and sympathy.
—RON HANSEN

73

Transportation: Getting There Isn't Half the Fun—It's Boring

This isn't strictly an exercise: It's more of a reminder. When moving characters from one place to another, write about how they got there only if it's crucial. Think of the movies—rarely do we see a character on a bus or in a train *unless the trip itself tells us something we absolutely need to know about the story or the character.* The lovers are in bed; next thing we see they're in a little bistro, smooching over a glass of Pernod. Who cares how they got from bed to bistro? Avoid stairs, sidewalks, subways, planes, trains, and automobiles if you can tell your story as richly without them.

The whole secret of a living style and the difference between it and a dead style, lies in not having too much style—being, in fact, a little careless, or rather seeming to be, here and there. It brings wonderful life into the writing . . .
— THOMAS HARDY

74

Naming the Diner, Naming the Diet, Naming the Dog

In an earlier exercise, "Naming Your Characters" (page 67) you learned how to choose a character's name with care and respect for the essence of that character.

Likewise, during the course of writing stories set in counties and towns with restaurants and mortuaries, stories in which characters play in rock bands, buy race horses, play on football teams, or found new religions, you are going to have to name them all. Think of William Faulkner's Yoknapatawpha County, Thomas Hardy's Wessex, Willa Cather's Red Cloud, Marilynne Robinson's Fingerbone Lake, Anne Tyler's Homesick Restaurant and travel-guide series, *The Accidental Tourist,* and Oscar Hijuelos's Mambo Kings. Names matter.

The Exercise

In your notebook, keep a list of unusual names for potential characters. In fact, every writer should have a collection of old yearbooks, benefit programs, phone books, and so forth to browse through when he needs to name a character. And don't stop there. Keep lists for things you might need to name in a story sometime.

Name the following things. Imagine stories they might go in. Remember that tone is important, so choose both an earnest name and a farcical one.

a desert town	a football team
a race horse	a diner
a literary magazine	a new religion
a new disease	a new planet
a rock band	a polluted river
a summer cottage	a poetry collection
triplets	a chihuahua
a liqueur	a burglar

a beauty salon   a bar
a new diet   a lipstick color
a soap opera   a yacht

The Objective

To loosen up your imagination by naming things you wouldn't ordinarily have to name—never mind "own."

Student Examples

Clearly, the students had more fun with the farcical names.

Desert Town
Drymouth   Noren Caceres

Racehorse
Windpasser   Sam Halpert
Race Elements   Jay Greenberg

Summer Cottage
Bric-a-Brac   Karla Horner

Triplets
Farrar, Straus
and Giroux   Robert Werner

Beauty Salon
Tressed for Success   E. J. Graff

Diner
Crisco   David Zimmerman

New Religion
People of the Tree   Karla Horner

Planet
Pica   Dawn Baker

Polluted river
Floop River   Daniel Bigman

Chihuahua
Bruno's Lunch   Karen Brock

Burglar
Nick Spieze   Greg Duyck

Diet
Body Carpenter   David Zimmerman

Soap Opera
The Rammed
and the Damned
(on cable TV)   Sanford Golden

Yacht
Waves Goodbye   Molly Lanzarotta

---

*The best training is to read and write, no matter what. Don't
live with a lover or roommate who doesn't respect your work.
Don't lie, buy time, borrow to buy time. Write what will stop
your breath if you don't write.*
                                        —GRACE PALEY

CHAPTER 75

Transitions: Or White Space Does Not a Transition Make

Often in the course of a story or novel you need a transition to indicate a flashback, a movement in time, a movement in space, or a movement from scene to narrative summary. Many writers have trouble with transitions. They either treat them too elaborately so that they jar the reader out of what Gardner calls "the vivid and continuous fictional dream," or they ignore them altogether and use white space to indicate that some shift has occurred. In either case, writers neglect the very medium they are using—language—to do it for them, and do it gracefully.

Here's Ray Carver, in "Where I'm Calling From," moving from the present to the past:

> ". . . If, if you ask for it and if you listen. End of Sermon. But don't forget. If," he says again. Then he hitches his pants and tugs his sweater down. "I'm going inside," he says. "See you at lunch." "I feel like a bug when he's around," J. P. says. "He makes me feel like a bug. Something you could step on." J. P. shakes his head. Then he says, "Jack London. What a name. I wish I had me a name like that. Instead of the name I got."
> WHITE SPACE
> Frank Martin talked about that "if" the first time I was here.

Notice how Carver not only uses "first time I was here" to indicate that there has been a shift, but he also reuses the "if" to make it graceful. Here's another example from the same story where Carver moves from past to the present *without* white space:

> Then I noticed a bunch of us were leaning over Tiny, just looking at him, not able to take our eyes off him. "Give him air!" Frank Martin said. Then he ran into the office and called the ambulance.
> Tiny is on board again today. Talk about bouncing back.

Notice how he brings us back to the present with the word "today" tucked into the sentence that focuses on Tiny's return.

In Alice Munro's "Differently," there is a time shift after a woman lies to her babysitter:

> "My car wouldn't start," she told the babysitter, a grandmother from down the street. "I walked all the way home. It was lovely, walking. Lovely. I enjoyed it so much."
>
> Her hair was wild, her lips were swollen, her clothes were full of sand.
>
> WHITE SPACE
>
> Her life filled up with such lies.

Sometimes it is more efficient to use phrases to indicate a shift in time or place. Here are several phrases that Carver uses in his story "Fever": "all summer, since early June," "In the beginning," "in the livingroom," "That evening, after he'd put the children to bed," "After he'd hung up," "After Eileen had left," "This was the period when," "Just before the incident with Debbie," "Over the summer," "But a few hours later," "Once, earlier in the summer," "The next morning," "In a little while," "For the first time in months," "During first-period art-history," "In his next class," "As he moved down the lunch line in the faculty dining room," "That afternoon," "That evening," "It was the middle of the fall term," and "The next time he awoke." All of these phrases are used to move the story along in space and time. Note how the school day is gracefully moved along from "first-period art history" to "next class" to "the lunch line."

The Exercise

Turn to a third or fourth draft of a story and examine your transitions. Is what is happening clear? Do your transitions employ language or are you depending on white space and your reader's imagination? Do your transitions gracefully connect the sections being bridged? Now rewrite your transitions, using language as a bridge to lead the reader from here to there to there.

The Objective

To be able to lead the reader gracefully over and around unnecessary parts of the story and to bridge skillfully the shifts in time, memory, and space.

76

Noises Off: The Beauty
of Extraneous Sound

from Laurence Davies

In our lives, background noise may be annoying, sometimes maddening, but in our fiction it can work for us. A single interruption from a creaking stair, a song, a blast of radio, a whining fan-belt, sharpens the most intense encounter. When cunningly paced, a whole sequence of extraneous sounds can make a stretch of dialogue resonate. Rather than distracting from it, patterns of noises, words, or music from outside the immediate scene create a sense of depth, giving the speakers in the foreground context and urgency. Noises off, as actors call them, may contradict your reader's first impressions or may reinforce them. Perhaps they will seem more menacing, or more vulnerable, even perhaps more ridiculous, but in any case your characters will spring to life.

In Part Two, Chapter Eight, of Gustave Flaubert's *Madame Bovary*, Rodolphe is in the town hall wooing Emma Bovary with romantic cadences, while bombastic speeches in the square mark the opening of an agricultural show. "Why castigate the passions?" asks Rodolphe. "Are they not the only beautiful thing there is on earth, the source of heroism, enthusiasm, poetry, music, art, of everything?" As Emma's would-be lover celebrates the passions, a local dignitary honors rustic produce: "Here the vine; there, the cider-apple trees; there, the rape-seed; further afield, cheese; and flax; gentlemen, let us not forget flax! Which has in recent years made great headway and to which I would most particularly draw your attention" (translation by Geoffrey Wall). From every field of expression, Flaubert collected clichés; here he gambles with his trophies, letting two kinds of banality create a scene that is anything but banal. At its climax, Rodolphe seizes Emma's hand just when the judges announce the winners of contests for best pig, best merino ram, and best manure heap. Does this episode of small-town claustrophobia make Emma seem foolish, pitiable, or both? Everything depends on Flaubert's exquisite sense of timing and his delight in counterpointed voices. We often talk about a writer's vision; perhaps we need a word for how an author *hears* the world.

Another outrageous juxtaposition occurs in Chapter Four of Joseph Conrad's *The Secret Agent*. Two anarchists meet in a basement restaurant, the Silenus. As they discuss police surveillance, the shortcomings of conventional morality, explosive chemistry, and a bomber's accidental death, a player-piano hammers out mazurkas. Then the Professor, who always keeps his hand around a detonator, leaves; Ossipon, an ineffectual terrorist but an energetic womanizer, lingers: "The lonely piano, without as much as a music stool to help it, struck a few chords courageously, and beginning a selection of national airs, played him out at last to the tune of 'The Bluebells of Scotland.'" Ossipon's visions of "horrible fumes . . . and mutilated corpses," ethical and pyrotechnic speculations, the plinking of a piano with a mind of its own: the whole sequence mingles irony and melodrama, horror and absurdity.

The background of the last example is seen as well as heard. The title character in James Baldwin's "Sonny's Blues" is a jazz pianist and heroin user. Sonny's fecklessness troubles the narrator, his hard-working schoolteacher brother. In this scene, Sonny has just been arrested for possession. The teacher walks through Harlem with one of Sonny's street acquaintances, a down-and-out young man. Just in front of a bar, they stop:

> The juke box was blasting away with something black and bouncy and I half watched the barmaid as she danced her way from the juke box to her place behind the bar. And I watched her face as she laughingly responded to something someone said to her, still keeping time to the music. When she smiled one saw the little girl, one sensed the doomed, still-struggling woman beneath the battered face of the semi-whore.
>
> "I never *give* Sonny nothing," the boy said finally, "but a long time ago I come to school high and Sonny asked me how it felt." He paused, I couldn't bear to watch him, I watched the barmaid, and I listened to the music which seemed to be causing the pavement to shake. "I told him it felt great." The music stopped, the barmaid paused and watched the juke box until the music began again. "It did."
>
> All this was carrying me some place I didn't want to go. I certainly didn't want to know how it felt. It filled everything, the people, the houses, the music, the dark, quicksilver barmaid, with menace; and this menace was their reality.
>
> "What's going to happen to him now?" I asked again.
>
> "They'll send him away some place and they'll try to cure him." He shook his head. "Maybe he'll even think he's kicked the habit. Then they'll let him loose"—he gestured, throwing his cigarette into the gutter. "That's all."
>
> "What do you mean, that's *all*?"
>
> But I knew what he meant. . . .
>
> . . . I felt that ice in my guts again, the dread I'd felt all afternoon; and again I watched the barmaid moving about the bar, washing glasses, and singing. "Listen. They'll let him out and then it'll just start all over again. That's what I mean."

Although his brother "didn't want to know how it felt," Sonny will later tell him that heroin feels like hearing gospel music. By the story's end, the unnamed teacher will recognize that the power of Sonny's music, as of other kinds of African-American music, grows from centuries of insult and abuse, and that music is a way of keeping going. In the background figure of the woman dancing to "black and bouncy music," Baldwin anticipates these insights, even as the brother sees her as both an equivalent to Sonny and as a representative of a whole community caught between experience and innocence.

The Exercise

Take a page or two of dialogue between two intensely engaged characters— preferably an entire scene. Work in some noises off. Experiment with different placings in your scene, and listen hard. Whatever their nature, the sounds should help control the pace, postponing the scene's resolution without losing momentum. They should also relate to something in the dialogue, strengthening or undercutting a theme, making a speaker sound more passionate, more pompous, or more poignant, adding oil to vinegar or vinegar to oil.

You might try: an auction; a television fundraiser; an ice-cream truck (playing what tune?); the passing of a very long and rumbly freight train; a trumpet lesson in the next apartment; the organ at a baseball game; a wedding reception (in the tradition of your choice); a grade-school arithmetic class; a political rally; doormen on duty at a club; a squabble over a parking space

The Objective

To hear the difference between incidental noise and cunning discord. To vary the pacing of your dialogue. To put your characters in the buzz of life around them. Although this exercise has you playing with sound, think what you could do with smell (fish fried in garlic, honeysuckle, rain-drenched earth, hot metal), touch (satin, canvas, blistered hands), or sight.

Nothing is less real than realism. Details are confusing. It is only by selection, by elimination, by emphasis that we get the real meaning of things.
—GEORGIA O'KEEFE

77

Titles and Keys

A title is the first thing a reader encounters, and the first clue to both the initial meaning and the final meaning of the story. Look back to the sentences in the exercise "First Sentences." Notice how many first lines play off the title of the story.

Titles can also be a way of finding stories. Blaise Cendrars once said in an interview, "I first find a title. I generally find pretty good titles, people envy me for them and not only envy me but quite a few writers come to see me to ask for a title."

And until your book is in galleys, you can still change the title. Below are the titles of some famous novels, along with their original titles.

War and Peace—All's Well That Ends Well, by Leo Tolstoy
Lady Chatterley's Lover—Tenderness, by D. H. Lawrence
The Sound and the Fury—Twilight, by William Faulkner
The Great Gatsby—Hurrah for the Red, White and Blue, by F. Scott
    Fitzgerald
The Sun Also Rises—Fiesta, by Ernest Hemingway

New York Magazine has published a competition for many years. One example is a game in which you were asked to change some famous (and successful) title just enough to make it a loser rather than a winner. The difference between the true ring of the real title and the false note of the parody suggests how good titles are the ultimate test of the exact word, *le mot juste.* Here are some examples.

A Walk on the Wild Side, by Nelson Algren: *A Hike Through Some Dangerous Areas*
One Hundred Years of Solitude, by Gabriel García Márquez: *A Very Long Time Alone*
Girls of Slender Means, by Muriel Spark: *Minimal-Income Young Women*
The Naked and the Dead, by Norman Mailer: *The Nude and the Deceased*
A Farewell to Arms, by Ernest Hemingway: *A Good-bye to War*

The best titles convey some immediate picture or concept to the reader and they do it with an exciting, tantalizing juxtaposition of words.

Finding the ideal title might take time—and effort. Ernest Hemingway says, "I make a list of titles after I've finished the story or the book—sometimes as many as a hundred. Then I start eliminating them, sometimes all of them."

The Exercise

Part I

Have a place in your writer's notebook where you play around with titles and start a list of possibilities for future stories.

Part II

When you need a title for a new story or novel, make a list of possible titles from inside the story and from just thinking about the story. (Try for a hundred.) Then start eliminating titles you know you won't use and see what is left. Chances are that the title you choose will not be the first one that occurred to you or the "working" title of the story.

The Objective

To learn how titles can lead you to stories and to sharpen your instincts for a good title.

Student Examples

Company Time

—ANNE SPALEK

Sunday Funnies

—ELLEN TARLIN

Silence Between Songs
—FRANK BACH, FROM "CURES," A POEM BY DAVID RIVARD

Nights Take Care of Themselves
—LAINA JAMES, FROM "THE SATISFACTION COAL COMPANY,"
A POEM BY RITA DOVE

PART TEN

Invention and Transformation

Where do your stories originate? From a pool so wide it has no boundaries. Writers get their ideas for stories or novels from memory, from stories they've been told from the time they were very young, from what is seen and heard around them—including the daily newspaper, the tragedy next door, the overheard conversation, or the arresting image. Joan Didion began *Play It As It Lays* after seeing a young actress being paged in a Las Vegas casino. Didion says, "A young woman with long hair and a short white halter dress walks through the casino at the Riviera in Las Vegas at one in the morning. She crosses the casino alone and picks up a house telephone. . . . I know nothing about her. Who is paging her? Why is she here to be paged? How exactly did she come to this? It was precisely this moment in Las Vegas that made *Play It As It Lays* begin to tell itself to me." Other writers start with a situation (e.g., a person taking a shower hearing a strange noise beyond the bathroom door). Although we don't especially endorse it, some writers begin with an abstraction—injustice, war, divorce, child abuse, etc.—and proceed to make up the story and characters that dramatize the idea.

The exercises in this section are here mainly to help the beginning writer recognize effective fictional triggers. Here is a situation—now compose a story growing directly out of it. While some of these triggers are general (e.g., "Sunday") others are quite specific and ask for different "versions" or "accounts" of particular incidents. Another exercise challenges you to inhabit the mind and heart of your enemy. This is a delicate but powerful operation, about which Rosellen Brown says, "Fiction always has an obligation to the other side, whatever it is." The exercise "It's a Laugh" asks you to write about a past event that wasn't funny when it happened and is only funny in retrospect. And then there's the exercise on writing a compelling sex scene. Is being "explicit" necessary? To answer this, read John Fowles's *The Ebony Tower.*

In other words, these exercises are imagination stretchers and should help writers who feel they don't know what to write about learn how to recognize fictional potential. Often, seemingly difficult guidelines are more liberating than being asked to write about "anything." The most important thing to remember in creating your fictional world is that you have a lifetime of experience to call on; all of it is potentially useful. Relax, have fun. It's all out there, floating free, waiting for you to pull it down and anchor it in story.

A short story is like a flare sent into the sky. Suddenly and startlingly, it illuminates one portion of the world and the lives of a few people who are caught in its glare. The light is brief, intense, and contrasts are likely to be dramatic. Then it fades quickly and is gone. But, if it is worth its moment of brilliance, it will leave an afterimage in the mind's eye of the beholder.
—ROBIE MACAULEY

78

The Enemy's Life

from Lore Segal

Your first job as writer of a story is to make up the people to whom your story will happen. Not one character, but several, many, all of whom live inside their own bodies, look out of their own eyes at a different world.

The Exercise

Week One

Write a scene that brings to fictional life someone you hate. Make the reader hate her. It might be someone who annoys you—someone whose manner you can't stand, whose voice grates on you. Or it might be someone who has offended you or done you some harm, or someone to whom you have done some harm—there are many reasons to hate people. If you have the courage, take on someone who is evil on the grand scale. It can be someone you know, someone you know about, or, best of all, invent a real nasty.

Week Two

Write the same scene, from the point of view of the nasty, and write it in the first person.

The Objective

Story and only story is the peaceable kingdom where you and I and the next fellow can lie down on the same page with one another, not by wiping our differences out, but by creating our differences on the page. Only on the page of a story can I look out of your and my and the other fellow's eyes all at the same time.

Student Example

Week One

"Doctor" Andrews, as he styled himself, was one of those white men who can be taken seriously no place in the world except an obscure bush country in Africa. He was a Canadian health program administrator, trained as a nurse, with a minimal knowledge of medicine, yet blessed with a kind of bureaucratic power in the Republic of Songhai by virtue of his control over the medical aid program provided by a generous Canadian government. He was a plump, rosy, voluble man with tiny white teeth in an insincere smile.

I met him when he arrived one day to inspect my clinic. He bustled around, looked over the shoulder of one of my Mandinka aides who was sewing up a gash in a boy's leg and said superciliously, "Not very sterile, you know. But I suppose they've never heard of the concept." I mentioned that we did use antiseptics, kept the surgery room as clean as possible, and did scrub before even minor procedures, but he paid no attention.

He inspected my three shelves of medicines and sniffed. "What do you call this?" he asked.

I took the opportunity to put in my oft-frustrated request. "We have lots of infections here," I said, "and one of the things we could use is a supply of penicillin. I know the Canadian program has a steady supply and I wonder if you could spare me some from time to time?"

He turned and looked at me as if I had demanded his wallet. "Really!" he said. "You do have grandiose ideas about practicing in the bush. I think you should realize that we need every gram of medication we have for the government hospital in the city. For the kind of patient who counts."

Week Two

The first day I met him in a remote Mandinka village, he was asking for penicillin. The American hadn't even been here a month yet, and already he thought he could set our whole health care system on its head and shake miracles out of its pockets. I knew he would blunder ahead and upset the Africans with his persistent demands; Peace Corps is full of self-important American youngsters who little realize the damage they're capable of inflicting on fragile, carefully constructed development projects like ours—initiated a decade before anyone even thought of inviting the USA in.

The Canadians make a point of sending qualified people here, and of briefing us meticulously. But the American knew little about the health care system over which he raged; he couldn't see the impossibility and the dangers of shipping penicillin out to a bush clinic where the natives had never even seen a Band-Aid; he thought that just because he had arrived, we would scramble to meet his every need—he had no notion of how hopelessly overworked we are, and will be for many years to come, in the involved process of establishing this system. If Peace Corps had courteously offered his services to us in advance, instead of flinging him pointlessly out into the bush, he could have become a useful member of our team. Now he's no more than a gadfly—another obstacle to be worked out. It wouldn't take much to get him transferred—or better yet, deported.

I still wonder why we didn't go ahead and get rid of him.

—CAMERON MACAULEY

It's All in Your Head

Avoiding the obvious when writing about extreme states of mind is a real challenge for any writer. Resorting to such clichés as "his heart was in his mouth," "she was on cloud nine," and "he flew off the handle" is far easier than figuring out what is really happening to someone scared, happy, or angry. You must translate the emotion or feeling into fresh, interesting language, rendering precisely or metaphorically what is taking place within the character. Here is Mrs. Dalloway, in Virginia Woolf's novel, experiencing pleasure. "The cook whistled in the kitchen. She heard the click of the typewriter. It was her life, and, bending her head over the hall table, she bowed beneath the influence, felt blessed and purified, saying to herself, as she took the pad with the telephone message on it, how moments like this are buds on the tree of life."

The Exercise

Write three short paragraphs, the first "fear," the second "anger," and the last "pleasure," without using those words. Try to render these emotions by describing physical sensations or images. If you want, write mini-stories, dramatizing these emotions. Try to make your language precise and fresh.

The Objective

To learn to render emotional states without falling back on tired and imprecise language.

Student Example

Pleasure
Jillie thought the ice cream sundae was beautiful, and she let it sit in front of her for a minute before starting to eat. The ice cream made her think of being rolled in soft blankets, and the cherry looked like her cat's nose. She took her first spoonful, and as the hot fudge and ice cream made her mouth both hot and cold, she shut her eyes. A trickle ran from the corner of her mouth because she was smiling so much. It hung off the side of her chin like an ice cream tear.

—BRIAN FOSTER

Illustrations

from Margot Livesey

I was talking to a poet friend about the difficulty of judging my work. "I have the same problem," he said. "If you ask me flat out which is my best poem, I'll shilly-shally and complain that it's like asking me to choose between my children. But if you ask me which poems I'm sending to the *New Yorker* and which to the *Ontario Nugget*, I can answer you in a flash."

We do know about our own work, its flaws and virtues, but it can be hard to gain access to this knowledge. One strategy that I use with myself and my students is to illustrate a story. Instead of beginning a workshop with a critique or a description of the work, we each draw a picture. When I suggest this, people always complain that they can't draw. But everyone does draw something and the pictures are wonderfully revealing. Some people sketch the climactic scene: Sonny playing the piano in the bar at the end of "Sonny's Blues." Some people draw something more metaphorical: a hearse and a cat for "A Good Man is Hard to Find." Some people put together several scenes or draw crucial images—a hypodermic, say, for Dennis Johnson's "Emergency"; a beaten up Cadillac for Louise Erdrich's *Love Medicine*.

The Exercise

Drawing pictures can be useful at various stages. You might start by drawing pictures to illustrate your own work over the last couple of years. (If you're part of a writers' group you might also do this for the work of your colleagues, and vice versa.) Then turn to your work in progress and draw an illustration for each scene or section of narration.

The Objective

Whatever the results in aesthetic terms (and usually they're much better than the artist expects), the pictures provide a highly useful map of the energy of a story and what has stayed with you as both author and reader. More importantly, I think, they provide information that might not come up if you'd simply plunged into verbal discussion.

Faraway Places

Many writers have written about places they have never been—Franz Kafka about America in *Amerika,* Saul Bellow about Africa in *Henderson the Rain King,* Thomas Pynchon about postwar Germany in *Gravity's Rainbow,* W. D. Wetherall about the Crimea in *Chekhov's Sister,* Oscar Hijuelos about Cuba in *Mambo Kings Play Songs of Love,* and Hilding Johnson about India in her BASS story "Victoria"—yet their descriptions of these places persuasively transport the reader there. Below are passages from a novel and a short story.

> Finally one morning we found ourselves in the bed of a good-sized river, the Arnewi, and we walked downstream in it, for it was dry. The mud had turned to clay, and the boulders sat like lumps of gold in the dusty glitter. Then we sighted the Arnewi village and saw the circular roofs which rose to a point. I knew they were just thatch and must be brittle, porous, and light; they seemed like feathers, and yet heavy—like heavy feathers. From these coverings smoke went up into the silent radiance.
> —SAUL BELLOW, *HENDERSON THE RAIN KING*

> Flowers stayed tight in the bud, drying in crisp pods and rattling to the ground one by one in the still night.
> The bearers brought half as much water, then still less. The children on the wards slid from whining into torpor.
> A sacred cow wandered into the hospital courtyard and could go no further. It was chalky, white, fleshless, its loose dry hide scarred in random constellations, a dessicated wreath of twisted flowers digging into its neck. It stood, eyes closed and head nearly to the ground, for a day and night. Early the next morning I came upon Richard holding a bucket of water beneath the animal's nose.
> I said, "We don't have much of that."
> "It's what I was allotted for shaving."
> I shrugged. "Suit yourself."
> In the afternoon the cow knelt, shuddered and died. The sweepers came with great hooks and dragged it out of the courtyard, leaving thin trails of scarlet in the pale dust.
> At supper, Richard said, "If they think so much of the beasts, how can they let them suffer?"
> "To them they're gods. In general, people don't care much about the suffering of a god. You should know that by now."
> —HILDING JOHNSON, "VICTORIA"

The Exercise

Choose a country where you have always longed to go but haven't yet been and set a story there. Read old and new Fodor's guides as well as other recent travel guides and *National Geographic*; buy a map; study the country's politics, religion, government, and social issues; read cookbooks—always, always looking for the persuasive detail, something you would almost have to be there to know.

The Objective

To write with authority and conviction about a place to which you have never been.

Student Example

One of the reasons Tess had come to Japan was to visit the fish auction by the Sumidagawa River, where her father probably went during his business trips when he wanted to feel at home. He'd run an auction in the back parking lot of St. Leonard's Church till Tess was ten. Near the marketplace, she knelt on the slick pavement and pulled heavy trash bags around each of her yellow sneakers. The auctioneers had already begun and the wholesalers were placing their bids. She spotted another tourist with plastic bags up to his knees. A brochure had advised wearing the bags because hoses would continually be pumping water over the pavement, washing away stray bits of raw sea food. Tess wove in and around the people and crates of tuna and crab. She took in small breaths through her mouth. Jake should have come with her to see this.

Jake was the first stranger Tess spoke with on her vacation. Her friend, Marlene, had worked late last night, so Tess had made her way to a sushi bar with a large fish tank at its center. She was wondering if the tank was in place of a printed menu. That was when Jake came up and asked if she'd like to join him. He was in Tokyo for three days on business.

The fish they ordered that night was sliced ribbon-thin, and shaped like roses. Jake used one chopstick to push some raw tuna into the green smudge of wasabi. He choked and rubbed his tongue on his sleeve. "That's a nasty little paste," he said. He coughed and took a long drink of beer. She looked at the paper lanterns over the bar. Her father used to attach one yellow balloon to a wooden sign that read "The Everything Auction." "It's horseradish," Tess said.

—KIM LEAHY

I don't invent characters because the Almighty has already invented millions. . . . Just like experts at fingerprints do not create fingerprints but learn how to read them.
—ISAAC BASHEVIS SINGER

82

It's a Laugh

---

*Humor is emotional chaos remembered
in tranquility.*

—JAMES THURBER

Styles of humor seem to change shape and kind more quickly than any other form of writing. From Ring Larder through James Thurber, S. J. Perelman, Ogden Nash, Nathanael West, Joseph Heller, John Kennedy O'Toole, and Woody Allen, we have American humor that ranges from gentle reminiscence to the grimmest shade of black. It may be true partly because one man's meat is another man's poison (or, as Ogden Nash said, "One man's Mede is another man's Persian"), and it's hard to get any large number of people to agree on what's a laugh. So, the writer of humor has to depend largely on her own sense of what is funny about life. As E. B. White said, "Humor can be dissected as a frog can, but the thing dies in the process and the innards are discouraging to any but the pure scientific mind."

Just as humor defies analysis, it seems to defy any rules—rules of tolerance or good taste. One of the classics of English satire is Jonathan Swift's cruel "A Modest Proposal"; W. C. Fields made fun of marriage, sobriety, and family values; Lenny Bruce relied heavily on racial slurs and intolerance to amuse his audiences. Some writers and comedians even risk scatology—traditionally the most despised form of humor.

All of which is to say that if you take a sardonic view of the world ("the world is a comedy to those who think, a tragedy to those who feel") and can express it with humor and wit, you should do your own thing. Read Lawrence Sterne, Kingsley Amis, Dave Barry, P. G. Wodehouse, Nicolai Gogol, Kurt Vonnegut, Lorrie Moore, Ilf and Petrov, Mark Twain, Michael Frayn, Evelyn Waugh, Somerville and Ross, Molly Keane, Oscar Wilde, George Saunders.

The main thing a writer should remember is that written humor is quite a different thing from comedy on the stage or that delivered by a stand-up comedian. Oral humor largely depends on timing, tone of voice, body language, and the infection of laughter in an audience. Written humor depends on language alone—words create the joke. Thus the writer of fiction should not imitate—in fiction—what came off so uproariously or wittily on the stage, in a movie, or on TV. His nuances, allusions, surprises, parodies all come from verbal skill and shrewdness. Good narrative, fresh language, succinct expression, the juxtaposition of incongruities—these are the heart of written humor. Or, as Shakespeare said it better, "Brevity is the soul of wit."

The Exercise

Write about something that happened to you that didn't seem funny at the time, for example, the day you were stuck in a traffic jam and a bee flew in through the car window or the time your tenant set your stove on fire and the firemen wrenched it from the wall and tossed it into the backyard. Bring the incident under the humor spotlight and transform it so as to emphasize things that will make your reader smile or laugh. Pacing is important, as are crucial surprising details, and your own confidence that the story does not need analysis or authorial nudging. Limit: 550 words.

The Objective

Because humor resides largely in the attitude you assume toward your material, you must be able to discover and exploit those elements that highlight the comic, the exaggerated, and the unlikely. Keep in mind that you could just as easily take the bee story and make it tragic (bee bites driver, driver crashes into another car, killing infant in back seat).

Writing is a hard way to make a living but a good way to make a life.

—Doris Betts

83

Sunday: Discovering Emotional Triggers

Most of the time it doesn't matter on what day of the week you set your action—unless it's a Sunday (remember the movie *Sunday Bloody Sunday?*). Most people feel at loose ends on this day, even those who spend the morning in church. Instead of using the freedom wisely, a lot of us tend to overdo it—overeat, oversleep, overreact. Sundays bring out the worst in people. Children grow anxious as the weekend draws to a close and they realize they haven't done their homework. During football season, another possible area of tension opens up. Then there is the obligatory trip to grandma and grandpa's house for a large heavy meal and some equally heavy recriminations. Things happen on Sundays that wouldn't happen on weekdays. So if you want to examine domestic dynamics close up, set some action on a Sunday and let her rip.

The Exercise

Title it "Sunday." Write 550 words.

The Objective

Certain words and ideas, such as *retirement, in-laws, boss, vacation, pneumonia,* and *fraud,* serve as triggers for stories or scenes in fiction. *Sunday* is one of these. Try to think of others.

84

Five Different Versions:
And Not One Is a Lie

We tell stories every day of our lives. But *how* we tell the story is often determined by who we are telling the story to. Think of the range of people in one's life—parents, spouse, children, friends, lovers, priests, rabbis, in-laws, social workers, parole officers (come on—use your imagination), doctors, claims adjusters, lawyers, judges, juries, therapists, talk-show hosts, astrologers—the list goes on and on. And as we tell these people our story, we add or subtract, exaggerate or play down, tolerate or condemn, depending on the identity of the person to whom we are telling our tale.

The Exercise

Here is the situation: You have just come out of the movie theater at around seven in the evening and you are mugged—a person asks for your money, then knocks you to the ground before running away. Or make up your own situation.

Next, pretend you are telling the account of this event to five different people:

Your mother
Your best friend
Your girlfriend or boyfriend (or wife or husband)
A therapist
A police officer

The Objective

To become conscious of how we shape and shade the stories that we tell to each other according to the listener. Your characters also tell stories to each other and make selections about content according to whom they are telling the story, the effect they want the story to have, and the response they want to elicit from the listener. A lot of dialogue in fiction, in real life, is story telling—and there is always the story listener who is as important to the tale as the tale itself.

Student Example

Telling My Mother

No, I wasn't wearing my black mini. Anyway, I'd asked this guy—some kid from school—what time it was and he told me 7:10. Don't worry. He wasn't the mugger. It was Johnny Something from my morning Lit. 121. So I'm just walking down the sidewalk, heading for the car and it happened. Johnny Whozit must have heard it. He's a big kid, probably a football player or something, and that's all I could think about there, sitting sprawled all over the ground. That kid could've helped me out.

Telling My Boyfriend

Listen, I have never, not once, taken anything so hard. They found me sitting on the sidewalk in front of the Tivoli, my dress up around my bottom, crying, just out of my head. The policeman told me I was going to have to calm down, tell him some facts. But I couldn't even remember what film I'd been to. (I'd gone to *Hairspray* for the third time. I've got this thing about John Waters.)

Telling a Police Officer

I was just minding my business, leaving a little early. School tomorrow. I teach, you know, and he must have come out from one of those cars over there because I didn't see him in the building. He was real big, lots of muscles. I didn't get a good look at his face, but he was dressed like a street person and smelled like one. Strong, you know, in more ways than one.

—KARLA HORNER

While short stories often tell us things we don't know anything about—and this is good of course—they should also, and maybe more importantly, tell us what everybody knows but what nobody is talking about. At least not publicly.

—RAYMOND CARVER, INTRODUCTION TO *BASS 1986*

85

Psycho: Creating Terror

You like scary? Here's an exercise students have so taken to heart that they report terror-filled, sleepless nights. Many writers shy away from extremes when in fact it's those very tense situations and moments that give fiction its excitement and singularity. You should be able to handle violence, passion, and terror as easily as you do two people having a friendly conversation over a couple of burgers.

The Exercise

You're taking a shower in your house or apartment. You are not expecting anyone and the front door is locked (the bathroom door is not). You hear a strange noise in a room beyond the bathroom. Now, take it from there for no more than two pages. This can be in either the third or the first person. Don't spend any time getting into the shower; you're there when the action begins.

The Objective

To tell a convincing story centered on speculation and terror.

Student Example

Ajax, my cat, must have crawled on top of the refrigerator again and knocked over the basket of onions. And now he's playing with the onions—that's the scraping noise—and when I get out of the shower they're going to be all over the floor. Sometimes when Ajax sees another cat he starts to moan and howl, like he's doing now—but he sounds strange. Maybe he's hurt himself.

I pull back the shower curtain and stick my head out to listen. The noise has stopped but I think I just saw something move in the hall. I can't see much from here, but I'm sure a shadow darted past the door. I let the water run over my head again and shut my eyes as the soap runs by, and all of a sudden I feel a draft of cold air. I open my eyes through the soap and hold my breath; the soap stings my eyes. Everything is quiet. All I can hear is the sound of the water, but again I think I see a shadow change.

I turn off the water and now I'm breathing fast. I'm standing on the bath mat and Ajax comes in and rubs against my wet legs and then the moaning starts again but it's not the cat, who jumps in fright. I clutch a towel to my chest. I don't know whether to look out into the hall or shut the door. I freeze. Things are crashing in the kitchen, glass breaks; a chair is moved. I slam the bathroom door and manage to lock it even though my fingers are trembling. I'm whimpering. Ajax is hunched in the corner, behind the toilet. The moans grow louder; they're coming closer.

What can I use as a weapon? A disposable razor? A tube of shampoo, a toilet brush, a bottle of Fantastik? I hold this bottle like a gun, my finger on its trigger. I've dropped the towel and I get into the other corner, making small sobbing noises. The moans stop abruptly; then the pounding on the door begins.

—HESTER KAPLAN

When I used to teach creative writing, I would tell students to make their characters want something right away even if it's only a glass of water. Characters paralyzed by the meaninglessness of modern life still have to drink water from time to time. One of my students wrote a story about a nun who got a piece of dental floss stuck between her lower left molars, and who couldn't get it out all day long. I thought that was wonderful. The story dealt with issues a lot more important than dental floss, but what kept readers going was anxiety about when the dental floss would finally be removed. Nobody could read that story without fishing around in his mouth with a finger.
—KURT VONNEGUT, *PARIS REVIEW* INTERVIEW

86

One in the Hand

How and why are proverbs born? Most of us say them without giving them a second's thought. But if we look at them carefully we see that they contain a human drama, condensed. "A rolling stone gathers no moss." "A stitch in time saves nine." "A bird in the hand is worth two in the bush." Each of these suggests choices, conflict, and resolution. Narrative is everywhere; training yourself to see and catch it is one way of refining your craft.

The Exercise

Take one of the proverbs above (or another one you like) and outline a short story that uses it as both plot and theme.

The Objective

There are two here. The first is to make yourself super-sensitive to ordinary things that contain the essence of drama. The second is to transform what at first seems just another piece of old-fashioned wisdom into a shapely narrative.

Student Example

A Rolling Stone Gathers No Moss
While my two sisters and two brothers and I were growing up, we were nearly smothered by activities that never seemed to stop, not even on Sundays. There was baseball for Dave and Michael, soccer for me and Susan, violin for Rebecca, Hebrew lessons for all of us and—I can hardly believe it myself—etiquette for all of us; mom insisted. By the end of a typical day I was so tired I would fall asleep on top of the covers with my clothes on.

As a trouble-shooter for the gas and electric company, Dad was on call twenty-four seven. Mom was one of those women who thought that if you didn't start every meal from scratch it wasn't worth eating. Maybe I'm exaggerating a little but not that much. We tried to talk her into short-cuts in the kitchen. "What's wrong with using canned broth instead of boiling an entire fowl?" Dad would ask. "It's just not the same," she told him.

One day, after soccer practice, I walked into the kitchen for a snack and there was Mom, frozen in a pose that summed up our overprogrammed lives. Mom had her hand on the door of the toaster oven, about to pop in a homemade leftover Belgian waffle. She had been zapped by some loose current and could not move. She looked at me, opened her mouth and, tried to say something. Her eyes pleaded for help; I called 911.

After the EMT guys loosened her grip on the toaster oven, they loaded her in an ambulance to be treated for second-degree burns and a mild state of shock.

Dad kissed her ashen face and then told us to get ready for Hebrew school. He herded us into the SUV and as we drove away he said, "I hope your mother won't have to stay there very long. We need her." Then he said that after class we probably still had time to rake some leaves and feed the compost heap before it got dark. "What do you guys say to a trip to Burger King after we're finished?" Just then his beeper went off.

—POLLY TIGGES

A good title should be like a good metaphor: It should intrigue without being too baffling or too obvious.
—WALKER PERCY

87

Notes and Letters

The first novels in the English language were in the form of letters—so-called epistolary novels, like Samuel Richardson's *Pamela* and *Clarissa*. Recent epistolary novels are Hal Dresner's *The Man Who Wrote Dirty Books*, Lee Smith's *Fair and Tender Ladies,* and Alice Walker's *The Color Purple*. And then there are the novels that employ letters. Herzog in Saul Bellow's novel by that name writes letters to Spinoza; to Willie Sutton, the famous bank robber; and to presidents. In Ann Beattie's novel *Love Always,* Lucy Spenser receives and replies to letters as Cindi Coeur, the Miss Lonelyhearts of a magazine called *Country Daze.* Sam Hughes, a feisty seventeen-year-old girl in Bobbie Ann Mason's *In Country,* meets the father, who died before she was born, in the diary he kept in Vietnam and his letters home. Tucked into the narrative of a work of fiction, a letter allows the author an especially intimate tone—somewhat like talking into the reader's ear. It's also useful at crucial moments in a plot—in it things get told economically and with a sense of urgency. A letter is often a quick way of delivering exposition, characterization, and voice.

The Exercise

Here are several situations and the letters they might engender. You're a senior in college writing home to tell your parent(s) that you're dropping out of school. You want them to understand, if not exactly approve of, your reason(s) for leaving. Make these reasons specific and persuasive. Then write the answer, either from one or both of the parents. Or, you're writing a letter to your landlord to tell him you are withholding the rent until he addresses problems in your apartment. Or you are leaving behind a note for your spouse explaining why you are leaving him or her. Or you are writing literary graffiti on the walls of a toilet stall in the Library of Congress. Limit: 500 words.

The Objective

To get inside the head of another person, someone you have invented, and assume her voice to vary your narrative conveyance.

Student Example

Cher Mom and Dad,

I hope you two know how to speak a little French, because I have some news for you that's going to knock your berets right off. Remember I told you that I was taking French this semester? Well, I didn't tell you that my teacher's name was Mademoiselle Pipette and I didn't tell you that I had a crush on her. It turns out that she had a crush on me too, and now we are madly in love. We want to get married so little Pierre or little Gigi will have a dad when he or she arrives at the end of May. I'm going to be a *père*! (That's "father" in French.)

Jeannette can't support us on her teaching salary, so I'm dropping out of college. You've always taught me to be responsible for my actions and this seems like the correct thing to do. I'm going to get a job to support my family and make a home for us. Someday I'll go back to school. The dean assured me I can reapply later and finish my degree.

You two are going to be grandparents! I'm sure you're as excited by all this as I am. College seems unimportant at the moment in the face of these great changes. I know you'll love Jeannette and she sends a *bonjour* to you.

Avec amour (that's "with love"),
Teddy

Dear Teddy,

Forget it. No son of mine is going to drop out of college and get married just because a schoolboy crush on his French teacher went a little too far. I think I know better than you when I say that a twenty-one-year-old boy has no conception of what it means to be a responsible father and husband. And what kind of job do you imagine yourself getting? Who's going to hire a boy whose only work experience was mowing his parents' lawn?

I, too, talked to the dean. At the end of the semester, your Mademoiselle Pipette will say good-bye to teaching and to you. I have arranged for her go back to France and have the baby there. I have also gotten her assurance that she and you will have no more contact.

I've spared your mother the news of this mess. It would only make her sicker. Though you don't think so now, you will thank me in years to come for getting you out of this situation. In the meantime I suggest you get back to your studies and work hard toward that all-important degree.

Fondly,
Dad

—BRIAN FOSTER

Memo from Atlantic *editors*

Subject: Articles and stories we do not want to read or edit

Short stories which ask the reader to blame society for misfortunes inflicted on the characters by the author.

PART ELEVEN

Revision: Rewriting Is Writing

Revision is just that: a chance to reenvision your work, to revise your story or chapter until it feels finished. By revision, we mean building on that first draft, revising it with various strategies until it becomes a second draft, and continuing to revise your story or chapter or novel until it is finished. It is important to note that when you finish a draft and move on to the next one, you put the previous draft(s) aside. You do not want six different versions of the same story; you want one draft—although it may be your sixth draft. Although there might be writers who start over again and again, we don't advise this. There is almost always something wonderful in what Frost calls "that first melting" that must be saved, and revised around. Often the difference between a good story and a publishable story is revision. Ted Solotaroff, in his essay "Writing in the Cold," says:

> Writing a first draft is like groping one's way into a pitch-dark room, or overhearing a faint conversation, or telling a joke whose punchline you've forgotten. As someone said, one writes mainly to rewrite, for rewriting and revising are how one's mind comes to inhabit the material fully. In its benign form, rewriting is a second, third, and nth chance to make something come right, to "fall graciously into place," in Lewis Hyde's phrase. But it is also a test: one has to learn to respect the misgiving that says, This still doesn't ring true, still hasn't touched bottom. And this means to go back down into the mine again and poke around for the missing ore and find a place for it and let it work its will.

We didn't understand the reluctance of beginning writers to rewrite—and in fact ascribed it to a lack of commitment—until one student wrote in her class evaluation: "The most important thing I learned this semester was that rewriting is writing. Although I understood in theory the importance of revising work, somehow I felt guilty unless I produced something new—and preferably something good—the first time. Rewriting felt like cheating." When we brought this up in subsequent classes, most students admitted that they mistrusted the degree to which established writers say they revise. "Surely Saul Bellow doesn't have to rewrite!" Yet Bellow rewrote *Herzog* twenty times. "The first chapters of Gish Jen's novel flow so smoothly that they must have come right the first time." Yet Jen rewrote her opening chapters forty times. From that class on, we have made it a point to show students that *rewriting is writing* and that revising a story or novel—two, ten, or forty times—is part of the pleasure of writing. We also encourage our students to see rewriting as a continuum. One must write the next draft in order to get to the point in the process to go on to the next draft—and the next draft. It is analogous to the hiker who looks up to the top of the mountain, then sets off to arrive there, only to find that she has reached a false summit. The real summit, which had been hidden behind the false one, looms ahead—or perhaps once there it is discovered to be another false summit. But don't be discouraged; you are making progress—and each successive draft, though it may prove to be a false summit, is moving the story closer and closer to completion.

When William Faulkner was asked what advice he would give to young writers, he said:

> At one time I thought the most important thing was talent. I think now that the young man or the young woman must possess or teach himself, training himself, in infinite patience, which is to try and to try until it comes right. He must train himself in ruthless intolerance—that is to throw away anything that is false no matter how much he might love that page or that paragraph.

We have found that students often lose interest in revision because they merely go back over a story from start to finish—making a few changes as they go. They fail to see that an early draft is in a fluid state and can be totally redrafted and/or rearranged: the final scene might be moved to the beginning; the first person might be changed to third; present tense might be changed to past; characters might be dropped or invented; language, scene length, imagery, body language, description, etc., all are evaluated—often separately.

We chose not to include sample pages from a work in progress or examples of successive drafts because how something finds its way on to the page or is changed or deleted is a mysterious, complicated, and always personal process. The most successful "reproductions" of the revision process appear in Janet Burroway's *Writing Fiction* and David Madden's *Revising Fiction*, and in *A Piece of Work*, edited by Jay Woodruff, in which Tobias Wolfe and Joyce Carol Oates speak to interviewers about revising their stories. The exercises in this section are designed to take you through various aspects of the revision process, and to help you discover how revision works best for you. Bernard Malamud said, "Revision is one of the true pleasures of writing."

88

Exploring the Creative Writing Process

from Tony Ardizzone

When I talk to students about the writing process and how they might become more productive and even happier writers, I tell them it's best to write in stages. It's like washing a linoleum floor. Then I describe the process step by step.

I say start in one corner and clear off a small section, not too much, maybe the top four tiles and the next four down. Sweep these sixteen tiles thoroughly. Then prepare a bucket full of warm, soapy water and wash the sixteen tiles until they're clean. Wait for the sixteen tiles to dry. After they're dry, check to see if dirt from the other tiles has gotten on them, and if so, sweep the dirt off. Then pour on the polish. Wait for the polish to dry. Then buff the polish until it shines. Then move onto the next section of sixteen tiles.

By this time students are shaking their heads. They tell me that's no way to wash a floor. You'd go crazy washing floors like that, they say. You're repeating every little step. The way to wash a floor, they say, is to do it in big stages: to clear the floor entirely of furniture, to sweep the tiles all at once, then wash the entire floor, wait for it dry, then polish the entire floor, wait for the polish to dry, then buff and shine it.

Do it in big stages, they say, not in a series of repetitions that attempts to perfect each and every little thing as you go along.

I agree with them. Then I add that I was really talking about writing by describing how *not* to write.

The Exercise

Read one of the many volumes of *Writers at Work: The Paris Review Interviews,* and take notes on the sections in which writers talk about the process they follow as they write. Then look at your notes for similarities, as well as differences, in the writing processes they describe. Consider which writer works most like the way you write. Which writer works most differently from you? Discover ways that you might change how you go about writing fiction in order to work more happily and successfully.

The Objective

To learn that while there is no single correct way to write fiction, there is a series of stages that most writers inevitably follow. These stages begin with a spark or germ and then include *discovering* the preliminary or first draft, *exploring* further possibilities of character and action in one or more middle drafts, then *editing and polishing* the work in a satisfying manner. Most successful writers do what is more or less appropriate to the stage they are working on. Writers who attempt to do too much too soon often end up feeling frustrated. There is a time to discover and take risks and explore unforseen possibilities, and another (usually later) time to polish the work's syntax and diction.

INTERVIEWER: *How much rewriting do you do?*
HEMINGWAY: *It depends. I rewrote the ending to* Farewell to Arms, *the last page of it, thirty-nine times before I was satisfied.*
INTERVIEWER: *Was there some technical problem there? What was it that had stumped you?*
HEMINGWAY: *Getting the words right.*
            —WRITERS AT WORK

89

Opening Up Your Story

When stories are in an early draft they sometimes feel thin, in need of more texture—in need of something. This is the precise time when your story is most flexible and capable of being opened up; successive drafts weave the sentences ever more tightly together. At first glance this exercise on opening up your story might seem the most artificial, the most intrusive foray into your work. Keep in mind, however, that even when suggestions come from "outside" the story, your own imagination is still in control of selecting the material, the details, the language, to make many of these suggested additions absolutely organic to your story.

The Exercise

Choose a story to work with that is still in an early draft form. Read it through so you are thoroughly familiar with it and with the characters. Then find a place in the story to complete and insert the following sentences (change the pronoun as necessary).

The last few nights she had a recurring dream (or nightmare) about _____.

Her mother always warned her that _____.

The one thing I couldn't say was _____. (Put this insert in a dramatic scene with two or more characters.)

The telephone rang. It was a wrong number but the caller refused to hang up. Instead, he _____. (Have at least five or six exchanges.)

She made a list: _____ To do, or _____.

Something seemed different _____.

The last time he had worn this _____ was when _____.

If someone said make a wish, she would wish for _____.

As for God, _____.

So this is what it's all about: _____

People were probably saying _____. (You can use this as a reality check—that what is being said is true. Or the character can report what people think and then refute it.)

This time last year she was _____.

Secretly, I collected _____. (What is collected, where is it kept, and from whom is it hidden?)

Outside, it was _____. (Make the weather do something—play off the inside atmosphere. Choose a season.)

Suddenly, she remembered she had forgotten to _____.

On TV (or the radio or a CD player) _____ was _____.

She suspected that _____.

The smell of _____ brought back _____.

It became a family story _____.

As a child, he had learned _____.

Five years from now I'll probably be _____. (If you insert this sentence at the beginning of the story, the entire story can "work" to prove it wrong—with your character rejecting that as his fate. If you insert this near the end, then it is probably prophetic about that character's future, beyond the end of the story.)

Now come up with some of your own inserts.

The Objective

To experience how your semiconscious imagination is capable of conjuring up material that is absolutely organic to your story for each "fill-in" from the above list. Writers who do this exercise are always amazed at how something so seemingly artificial can provide them with effective additions to their stories.

Student Examples

Last night Bobby had *the dream* again that Albert was down in the basement, he had all the bodies in the basement, everyone strapped to a chair in a big circle, and the washer was going, rumbling and ticking like there were rocks in it, and Albert was in the middle of the circle with a beer in his hand and he was singing, spinning around and singing to each body, bending, bowing to each one and Bobby yelled to him Albert what the fuck, what the fuck Albert and Albert sang to him too, sang get your own beer, get your own beer brother Bobby, and that's when he realized what the bumping noise was, it was their shoes, all of their shoes, Albert was washing their shoes in the washer, all their feet were bare, purple, and Albert was still singing to him, singing now I'm cleaning their shoes.

—JIM MEZZANOTTE, "BROTHERS"

The one thing I can't say is that I have a feeling we might not make it. A negative attitude in the mountains is a taboo. There were two guys who got lost in a snowstorm on this same mountain just a week before and froze to death. But Donnie knows what he's doing.

—TOM BRADY

He was calling for a Mrs. Patterson to tell her that she might win a million dollars in a vacuum-cleaner catalog sweepstakes. I said, "There is no Mrs. Patterson here."

"Can I talk to your mom?" he asked.

"No," I said. "Her name's not Mrs. Patterson."

He said, "Your mother must be Mrs. Luckman. She promised she'd call me back." My mother was Mrs. Luckman but what the man didn't know was that my mother was always promising everyone everything. She had no time for all her promises. I tried not to hurt his feelings. "Mister," I said, "Promises are easy to forget when there's more important things to be remembered." Later I often wondered if he understood me.

—DORY ELZAURDIA

That summer we saw twelve movies. We went on two-mile walks. We ate out at least one meal a day, sometimes two. *Secretly I collected* paper menus from the restaurants, stacking them neatly underneath the coloring books in my suitcase. I circled the food I ate, adding up the calories. If it was breakfast I usually ordered two poached eggs (160 calories), dry whole-wheat toast (140), and a glass of orange juice (100 to 120). Then I highlighted the foods I wanted to eat, but couldn't.

—ABBY ELLIN

Secretly I'd taken all the engraved matchbooks from the tables—Lorraine and Gregory, April 29, 1952—and smuggled them out of the reception in the pockets of my coat, in my purse. They were stacked, one up one down, in a box of Totes on the top of my closet.

—JANET TASHJIAN

The smell of fresh coffee *always brings back memories* of teacher's lounges where we'd try to relax between classes, exchanging stories about students and complaints about the principal. We pretended we were friends, but I truly wonder if we ever were.

—CHRISTOPHER HORAN

Middles have the double and contradictory function of delaying the climax while at the same time preparing the reader for it and fetching him to it.
—JOHN BARTH, *LOST IN THE FUNHOUSE*

90

Gifts to Yourself

In addition to bringing your characters and story alive, details are first and foremost gifts to yourself as a writer, something to be used and reused, and quite possibly something that will determine the course of the story. Flannery O'Connor speaks to the mystery and power of the telling detail. "I doubt myself if many writers know what they are going to do when they start out. When I started writing that story ["Good Country People"], I didn't know there was going to be a Ph.D. with a wooden leg in it. I merely found myself one morning writing a description of two women that I knew something about, and before I realized it, I had equipped one of them with a daughter with a wooden leg." And that wooden leg became central to the story.

It is true that a story's powerful details often take on symbolic significance, but we never encourage students to insert symbols into their stories. A symbol is something that stands for something else—it is usually smaller and more mundane than the larger truth it represents. Symbols can arise from a number of things—real details, personal attitudes, habits, acting, and so on. The important thing to remember is that significant detail adds to the texture of the story. It makes the story a more interesting (or surprising) account of what-if reality. A symbol should be a subtle hint about the author's ultimate meaning for the fiction. Do not confuse the two uses. Details, when used and reused well, have a way of becoming symbols without the writer's self-conscious effort to make them so.

The Exercise

Make a list of the important details in an early draft of a story. Then consider if there are any details—gifts to yourself—that have unexplored potential for opening up your story, for taking plot in a different direction. Can you delete superfluous details? How can you reuse an important detail? In fiction, $1 + 1 + 1 = 23$, not 3.

The Objective

To learn what Flannery O'Connor means when she says, "To say that fiction proceeds by the use of details does not mean the simple, mechanical piling-up of detail. Detail has to be controlled by some overall purpose, and every detail has to be put to work for you. Art is selective."

Student Examples

Christopher Horan says, "I don't know what possessed me to have the narrator scrubbing the toilet bowl and wearing rubber gloves when his landlord shows up at the door, but when I had to decide what the narrator had invented, I didn't have to look very far."

> That afternoon the landlord appeared at my door and said he'd waited long enough. I took off my rubber gloves (for the first time in months I'd been scrubbing the toilet bowl) and shook his hand. I thanked him for his patience, told him that of course I sympathized with him and understood that he, too, had bills to pay. Fortunately, I assured him, he wouldn't have to wait much longer. By the end of the week I expected to receive the first payment for my invention, which would make me solvent enough to give him a year's rent if he liked. He let out a deep sigh. Then, as if he knew he would later regret it, he repeated the word "invention." So I told him, trying desperately to sound as if I weren't making it up on the spot, about my patent—my patent for the self-cleaning toilet bowl.

Another student says, "In my story, 'Objects in Mirror Are Closer Than They Appear,' I made my main character a toll collector on the Mass Pike. Because of the repetitive motion of the job, her doctor prescribes special gloves for her carpal tunnel syndrome. As the story progresses, these constricting gloves begin to represent everything that has been repressing her (her mother, religion, etc.). And I use them to end the story."

> The gloves slowed me down a bit but Dr. Larson insisted I wear them all day, every day, to help my throbbing wrists. They reminded me of the way my mother used to tie a long piece of yarn to each of my mittens, thread it through the sleeves of my winter jacket, behind my neck then down the other sleeve.
> —JANET TASHJIAN, PUBLISHED IN *MASSACHUSETTS REVIEW*

The story's last sentence is: "I hung the gloves on the handle of my door and fastened the straps. They immediately filled with the wind and exhaust of the highway, like the automatic reflex of hands, waving goodbye or hello."

A love story has to implicitly include a definition of love.
—BRIAN HINSHAW

91

A Little Gardening,
A Little Surgery

When a story or novel isn't working, it often helps to look at it in a new way—not just on your computer screen or even in hard copy manuscript—but with scissors and tape and a conference table or wall.

In her book *The Writing Life,* Annie Dillard says she has often "written" with the "mechanical aid of a twenty-foot conference table. You lay your pages along the table's edge and pace out your work. You walk along the rows; you weed bits, move bits, and dig out bits, bent over the rows with full hands like a gardener."

Novelist E. L. Doctorow, formerly an editor, when asked about the relationship between editing and the craft of writing, said, "Editing taught me how to break books down and put them back together. . . . You learn how to become very free and easy about moving things around, which a reader would never do. A reader sees a printed book and that's it. But when you see a manuscript as an editor, you say, 'Well this is chapter twenty, but it should be chapter three.' You're at ease in the book the way a surgeon is at ease in a human chest, with all the blood and the guts and everything. You're familiar with the material and you can toss it around and say dirty things to the nurse." Thus, one method for revising, or "reenvisioning," a story is to become very self-conscious about its shape and its components when it is laid out in front of you in pieces.

The Exericse

Choose a story that doesn't seem to be working and cut it apart into the separate components of scenes and narrative passages and flashbacks. Number each piece in the order in which it appears in your story. Then hang the pieces across a wall with tape and absorb what is in front of you. Ask:

- How many scenes are there? Are there too few or too many?

- Are too many of the components the same length?

- Does each scene accomplish something? Can some be combined? Deleted?

- Are there any missing scenes? Unexplored territory?

- Is the material from the "past" in the right places?

- What would happen if you rearranged the sequence of events?

- What would happen if you begin with the ending scene and use it to frame the story? Or to foretell the end?

As you ask yourself these questions, pace back and forth and move your story pieces around. Play with them. Experiment. If you have missing scenes, add a piece of paper that says "add scene about _____." Then, when you are satisfied with the order of your story, number the sections again—ignoring the original numbers. Then compare the old order—and numbers—to the new order. Chances are 9 might now be 3 and 2 and 4 might be combined. Finally, instead of doing "cut and paste" on your computer, retype the story again from scratch—using your new arrangement. Feel the difference, the power of the revised word.

The Objective

To see an early draft of a story as something that isn't etched in stone. Not only are the words and lines capable of being revised, but the story structure itself is often still fluid enough to rearrange and analyze for the questions listed above.

Student Examples

I asked one class to write about this "scissors and tape" process and below are several responses:

> The class suggested that I drop a character, but I wanted to keep her. Then I saw that I could remove each of her components without affecting—at all—the heart of the story. It's hard to see a scene objectively until you separate it from the rest of the story and dare it to stand on its own. Cutting up a story liberates you; it gives you a kind of "fuck it" attitude when you see how easy it is to shape and move things around.
>
> —LEE HARRINGTON

> Mainly I learned that any story is fluid. I will do this for every story now. I've also cut up other stories—in particular, a couple of Alice Munro's, since many of her stories dip into the past. I'm amazed at how long some of her sections of the past really are (like mine!), but in hers every word counts.
>
> —MARYANNE O'HARA

Dynamic Scening

from Thalia Selz

The playwright Harold Pinter writes about creating drama from the "battle for positions." He pointed out that threat—and thus the necessary tension—arises from having people in a confined space battling over dominance and over "what tools they would use to achieve dominance and how they would try to undermine the other person's dominance." Pinter's scene dynamics work not only for plays but equally well for short fiction and novels.

The Exercise

Examine a scene you are having trouble with, one that (1) demands action, although not necessarily physical action, and (2) provides a turning point in your story. If you don't yet have such a scene in your story, try writing one. Make it at least three pages long, although five pages will give you a greater chance to develop the personal dynamics and show how the balance of power can keep changing. Tish, discovering that Mort has cheated her in a business deal, confronts him with evidence that would stand up in court, forcing him to return funds he has stolen. Alycia, a charming jewel thief, is caught in the act by her intended victim—an attractive diamond merchant—and seduces him, ensuring both his silence and the gift of a handsomely insured necklace.

The Objective

To show that by the time the scene is over the position of dominance has changed while the characters remain consistent and credible throughout.

The only way, I think, to learn to write short stories is to write them, and then try to discover what you have done. The time to think of technique is when you've actually got the story in front of you.

—FLANNERY O'CONNOR

Magnifying Conflict
from David Ray

Great fiction is tense with conflict—between characters, within characters, between characters and forces opposing them. We need only think of Ernest Pontifex's struggles with his father in the Victorian classic *The Way of All Flesh* or Raskolnikov's struggle between his fixation on murder and his impulse to love and remain loyal to his family and its values in *Crime and Punishment*—or more accurately, his struggle between sanity and insanity. We might recall the heroine of *Pamela,* struggling against the wiles of her employer-seducer. Or we might think of Huck Finn, in his perplexity about the racism he's been taught and his more trustworthy intuition and loyalty to his friend Jim, a runaway slave. In *Moby Dick* there is conflict on many levels, but primarily between hunter and hunted, malefic force and the innocent violence of nature. Any solid work of fiction will provide ready examples. The Japanese poet Kobayashi Issa found a storm of raging conflict even within a dewdrop, the most peaceful thing he could find in nature when he sought a retreat from his grief. The writer who loses touch with his responsibility to energize his fiction with conflict will probably have a very limited or temporary audience.

The Exercise

Go through a completed story and intensify the conflict, magnifying the tension and shrillness at every turn, even to the point of absurdity or hyperbole. Add stress wherever possible, both between characters and within them as individuals. Exaggerate the obstacles they face. Be extreme.

The Objective

To create an awareness of the need for a high level of tension while encouraging a healthy regard for how easily it can become excessive. This exercise is not meant to "improve" the story, although it often provokes new and more dynamic descriptions and dialogue. It raises the writer's consciousness about the need for conflict in fiction.

What's at Stake?

from Ken Rivard

What's at stake in your story? What is in jeopardy in your story? What is at risk? What do your characters stand to win or lose—custody of the kids, a place on a starting line-up, the approval of a tyrannical boss?

Once you can answer that question, then ask if your stakes are high enough to keep readers reading. When they are too low, the story fails to move us. The survival of a tenuous relationship, a minor personal insight, getting through one more day at a tedious job—it's difficult to make such familiar scenarios come alive. You have to overcome the reader's skepticism that the lousy husband, crappy job, or minor realization is worth the fuss and bother in the first place. Why not create a dilemma that immediately snags and holds our attention? Consider the following situations:

- A six-year-old boy disappears for a few hours. Eventually, he's discovered, unharmed, a few blocks from his home, with no memory of what has happened to him. Years later, as a university student on vacation, he drives by the street where he disappeared, notices a young boy, and acts on an irresistible compulsion to lure him into his car. (Ruth Rendell's "The Fallen Curtain")

- An eccentric substitute teacher subverts the $2 + 2 = 4$ universe of her fourth-grade students by introducing them to "substitute facts" (such as $6 \times 11 = 68$), Egyptian cosmology, and the curse of the Hope diamond. One afternoon she explains the use of Tarot cards, and predicts the early death of a particular student. (Charles Baxter's "Gryphon" on page 317.)

- For years, a reticent working-class white woman has allowed a devil-may-care friend to talk her into "adventures" without their husbands' knowledge, including slipping away once a week to go tea dancing. At the ballroom, they make the acquaintance of a young black man who becomes their regular dance partner. When the more daring woman dies, her friend screws up her courage for one last afternoon of escape. This time, their dance partner begins communicating gentle, but unmistakable signals of sexual interest. (William Trevor's "Afternoon Dancing")

Inexperienced writers often forget that readers are essentially voyeurs, peering through the window of a story into its characters' lives. Though quite different in structure and style, each of the three stories described above involves us in circumstances full of promise for events to come. How strange will the substitute teacher get before the school administration finds her out? Will the adult kidnapper remember what happened to him as a boy, and is he doomed to replay some dreadful scene? What will the woman do, confronted with possibilities for new adventure, now that her spunky friend isn't there to encourage her?

Beginning writers often agree in principle that high stakes are good, but balk when it comes to actually upping the ante in their own stories. This natural inclination to avoid tension and/or conflict and to avoid putting anything at risk or in jeopardy is a survival skill in the real world, but a death knell to fiction. In order to create a story with high stakes you must make a leap of imaginative faith—that some things, at least for your characters, are unambiguously worth fighting for.

The Exercise

Examine some of your favorite stories and novels and ask: What's at stake? Then examine your own fiction and ask: What's at stake? If you can't answer then you don't know enough about your characters or their lives.

The Objective

To understand that compelling stories are about characters motivated to take risks, to put something in jeopardy, to gamble for high stakes, in order to get what they want. And to incorporate a sense of urgency into your own fiction.

When you're in a workshop, your manuscript is given the time of day.
—EDWIN HILL

95

Writing Outside the Story
from Elizabeth Libbey

Sometimes a story feels as if it hasn't reached its full potential. You know it isn't finished yet, but you are not sure how to proceed in revising it. Another draft doesn't seem to be the answer, nor do you want to put it aside for a while. This is the time when "writing outside" the story might be the way to return to working inside it.

There are different ways to write outside a story. You might explore the interior life of your main character through diary entries, letters, dreams, or lists. Or you might write a scene that occurred before the beginning of the story. Or perhaps your story ended too soon. Even if you don't use this material in the story, it will, as Hemingway said, make itself felt.

The Exercise

Pull out a story that doesn't feel finished. Have your main character do the following exercises—as if she had her own notebook. Maybe you write with a number 2 pencil, but your character prefers a Rapidograph pen. Go with the pen. Remember, your character is doing this exercise— not you, the author!

So, as your main character:

- Make a diary entry for the time of the story

- Make a diary entry for the time preceding the story

- Write a letter to someone not in the story about what is happening in the story

- Write a letter to someone in the story

Or you might explore places in the story that you haven't either dramatized or summarized. Examples:

- Have your characters avoided a confrontation? (We are all nonconfrontational and, therefore, we often allow our characters to avoid the very scenes and confrontations that we would avoid.)

- What events happened before the beginning of the story? Before page one? Write scenes of those events. How would they affect the story?

- Write past the ending. Maybe your story isn't really finished. Try the double ending from Exercise 61.

The Objective

To explore aspects of a story that may seem to be on the periphery, but at closer look can deepen or open it up. Nothing is ever lost by more fully knowing the individual world of each story, and allowing your characters to speak for themselves.

I try to leave out the parts that people skip.
—ELMORE LEONARD

With Revision Comes
Final Meaning

Meaning isn't something you start from; it's something you work toward through successive drafts of your story or novel. Chances are if you tell a story to present some general principle, some truth about life, then your story is never going to come alive with specific characters living their specific lives. In *Mystery and Manners,* Flannery O'Connor says, "A story is a complete dramatic action—and in good stories, the characters are shown through the action and the action is controlled through the characters, and the result of this is meaning that derives from the whole presented experience."

So it's okay to write the first draft of a story without knowing what the story is about. Again, O'Connor says it best: "In fact, it may be better if you don't know what before you begin. You ought to be able to discover something from your stories. If you don't, probably nobody else will."

Stanley Elkin has an effective method for finding out what a story means. He suggests that, after five or six drafts, you should write what the story means in one sentence. Then use that sentence to cut, revise, add, adjust, or change the next drafts. Use that sentence as a filter, or a window, to the whole piece.

The Exercise

Write one sentence for a story that is in its fourth or fifth draft. Then revise the story to heighten and illuminate this final meaning.

The Objective

To make you aware of how you come to final meaning slowly, slowly, as you revise a story. To bring you through this process to what you intend the story to mean and what you want to convey to the reader. And finally, to make everything in the story accrue to this final meaning.

It Ain't Over
Till It's Over

When men and women began telling tales around evening campfires, surely the most frequent words from their audience were "And then what happens?" Perhaps the only assurance these storytellers had that their story was truly over was someone in the audience saying "Tell us another one." It is this last response—"Tell us another one"—that you want from your readers at the end of your story or novel. If your reader is still saying "And then what happened?" clearly your story isn't over and hasn't achieved the emotional resolution necessary in most stories.

A complete short story should be like a suspended drop of oil, entire unto itself. Or, viewed another way, it should be psychically "resolved." That is, when the reader gets to the last sentence she will understand that the story ends here—she doesn't have to know what happened to the characters beyond this final moment.

The Exercise

Examine each of your stories carefully to make sure it has this psychic resolution. Read them to a friend or fellow student and ask if they think it's finished. One of the hardest things to learn is how to judge your own work; it's eminently reasonable to try it out on a sympathetic—but objective—listener.

The Objective

To master the art of tying up narrative and thematic threads.

> "[One must] learn to read as a writer, to search out that hidden machinery, which it is the business of art to conceal and the business of the apprentice to comprehend."
> —MARGOT LIVESEY

In-Class Revision

In spite of good intentions, writers often don't put enough time into revising a story, so they never learn to trust the process, and their stories' potential remains unexplored. This exercise suggests ways to revise and shows you how to relax into the revision process. Ideally, the exercise should be done in two consecutive workshops or classes, totaling six to eight hours. Although all questions and suggestions for revision will not apply to all stories, enough will speak to each writer's individual story to make the session rewarding and even fun. Writer Laurence Davies calls this exercise "strategic derangement."

The Exercise

Bring to class a first or second draft of a story—a story you care about enough to spend six to eight hours revising. (Caring about the story is crucial to this exercise's success.) Also bring several highlighters, scissors, and tape. The teacher or workshop leader will ask questions, give instructions, and direct you to various exercises. You will probably find questions and problems that can't be answered or resolved during this session; jot down notes as reminders for the next time you revise this particular story.

- Whose story is it? How does the story reflect this? Is the point of view right for the story? (The point-of-view character owns the story.)

- What does your main character want? Where do you indicate this in the story? How does this drive the story? See Exercise 28, "What Do Your Characters Want?"

- Can you answer the question, "Into what life has this trouble come?" for your point-of-view character?

- What does the reader learn about your main characters in the first third of the story? Is any crucial information withheld from the reader? Do Exercise 25, "What Do You Know About Your Characters?"

- Do your characters have an inner life? See Part 6, "The Interior Landscape of Your Characters." Have you allowed them to use their imaginations?

- Does your story both show and tell, especially toward the end of the story? See Exercise 69, "Show and Tell: There's a Reason It's Called Storytelling."

- How many scenes does your story have? See Exercise 91, "A Little Gardening, A Little Surgery." Now for the scissors: Cut your story apart into its components and spread it out somewhere to peruse.

- What is the unstable situation of your story? See the introduction to Part 7, "Plot," on page 139.

- Does your story start in the right place—in the middle? What is the story's "history?" See Exercise 2, "The Story's History."

- Is your beginning sentence the best way to start your story? See Exercise 3, "Ways to Begin a Story."

- What is at stake in your story? What is at risk? What can be won or lost? See Exercise 94, "What's at Stake?"

- Does your story have tension, conflict? See Exercise 93, "Magnifying Conflict."

- Does something happen in your story? Something that is significant, that carries everything? Is there a change? See Exercise 58, "So, What Happened?" You might not be able to determine this until you cut your story apart.

- How well have you choreographed your scenes? Highlight the body language in your most important scenes. See Exercise 44, "The Invisible Scene."

- Does your dialogue serve the story well and move the plot along? Do you use indirect discourse where needed? See Exercise 43, "Telling Talk."

- Have you developed your story's gifts to yourself? Make a list of the significant details and check to see if you have reused them. See Exercise 90, "Gifts to Yourself."

- Does your story have enough texture? Open up your story with Exercise 89, "Opening Up Your Story." This exercise should take a while to do. Spend about four minutes each on six to eight "inserts." Have students create other "inserts."

- Underline the first interesting sentence in your story—interesting for language, characterization, setting, atmosphere—for something. (It should be the first or close to the first sentence.)

- Is the language of your story interesting? See the introduction to Part 8, "The Elements of Style," page 161.

- Do your adjectives and adverbs enhance your nouns and verbs? Circle all the adjectives and adverbs in the first two pages. See Exercise 63, "Taboos: Weak Adjectives and Adverbs."

- Do your sentences vary in length and complexity? See Exercise 62, "A Style of Your Own."

- Do you know how your story ends? Are there unanswered questions? See Exercise 97, "It Ain't Over Till It's Over."

- What final meaning are you working toward in your story? See Exercise 96, "With Revision Comes Final Meaning."

- Was your title thrown at the top of the page or chosen with care? Make a list of fifty or one hundred possible titles—take some from within the story. See Exercise 77, "Titles and Keys."

You've accomplished a lot in the past few hours. Now, think about what you have discovered about this story, and sometime in the next day or two return to this story for further revision. Then bring a new draft in to the next class. Include a page or two in which you discuss the revision process and how it worked for you. How will you proceed in the future?

The Objective

To relax into the revision process and give your story your undivided attention. To see the process as a fluid one—made up of components that are variable, manageable, and yours alone.

If you tell yourself you are going to be at your desk tomorrow, you are by that declaration asking your unconscious to prepare the material.

—Norman Mailer

PART TWELVE

Games

We have included three games using words partly for your amusement and partly as a demonstration that the combination and recombination of the twenty-six letters of the alphabet don't always have to end in so-called deathless prose. Words are magical playthings as well as instruments of persuasion, entertainment, enlightenment, social change, and uplift. These games are more fun than going to the movies, watching television, or playing poker.

CHAPTER 99

Learning To Lie

Beginning writers often resist their imaginations as something childish, exotic, or out of reach when in fact everyone has at some time told a lie. So for this exercise think of writing fiction as telling a lie. (This exercise, actually a late-night parlor game, is particularly good for the first session of a class or workshop.)

The Exercise

In two or three sentences, write down three unusual, startling, or amusing things you did or that happened to you. One must be true, the other two must be lies. Use details. Here are three from one writer.

> Elvis Presley wrote me a two-sentence letter after I sent him a poem I'd written about him and a picture of my younger sister in a bikini.
> The first time I heard him play, Buddy Rich threw me a drumstick during a drum roll and never missed a beat.
> I asked Mick Jagger to sign a program for me, but he said he'd prefer to sign my left white shoe. And he did.

Now everybody do one.

Then one by one read them to the group. The group is allowed to ask questions pertaining specifically to the details. For example, someone might ask the above person, "Why did you send your sister's photograph instead of your own?" Or "What was Buddy Rich playing?" Or "Do you still have your shoe and, if so, where is it?" The "author" has to be able to think on her feet, to make up more convincing details, to "lie." Then ask for a vote as to which story is true and which stories are fictions. It is surprising how many people are already good storytellers, capable of finding the concrete persuasive detail. (By the way, in the above example, the second "lie" is true.)

The Objective

To understand how we can exaggerate events in our lives, appropriate the lives of others—friends, enemies, strangers—or just plain out-and-out lie. All these are ways of using what we see and experience to produce fiction.

The Dictionary Game

In one sense, all fiction writing is artifice: dialogue isn't like real speech: stories are, for the most part, invented; singing prose is as carefully crafted as a glass bowl. The following calls on you to exercise pure inventiveness and pure craft.

The Exercise

A game for four to six players. Using a standard English dictionary, each player takes turns being *it*. The *it* finds a word that none of the other players knows the meaning of (everyone is on his honor to tell the truth about this). The *it* then writes down the real definition, while the other players invent and write down a definition they hope will be construed as the real one. They then pass their papers in to the *it,* who gives each definition a number, making sure they are all legible. The *it* reads each one in turn. The players make up their minds about which definition is real and then they vote by holding up the number of fingers corresponding to the number of the definition they choose. You may not vote for your own definition. Scoring: You get one point for each player who thinks yours is the correct definition. If you guess the real definition you get one point. If no one guesses the real definition, the *it* gets one point.

The Objective

Words are what it's all about. You can play around with them in much the same way you play around with plot and with ideas.

NEWSLETTER INTERVIEWER, EMERSON COLLEGE: Do you have any rituals, such as a particular time or place you write, or specific tools?

MARGOT LIVESEY: I did when I was first starting, but rituals became a handicap rather than a support. Now I write whenever and wherever I can.

Fictionary: A Variation of Dictionary

It can be fun to try to invent sentences that another writer might have written. This game is played using the books of writers who are fairly well known to all the players—say books by Paul Auster, James Baldwin, T.C. Boyle, Sandra Cisneros, Alice Hoffman, Henry James, Bobbie Ann Mason, Flannery O'Connor, Isaac Bashevis Singer, Mark Twain, Virginia Woolf. Choose writers with a very distinct style.

The Exercise

Choose one sentence, preferably one with four to ten words, from a story or a novel. Next, call out the first letter for each word in the sentence. For example, if you were to use this sentence from John Gardner's *Grendel*, "Pick an apocalypse, any apocalypse," you would call out P A A A A. Then ask the players to make up a sentence containing words beginning with those letters. After that, the same rules apply as those for Dictionary (see page 246).

The Objective

To have fun with language and try to imitate or outwrite the published author.

I can't write without a reader. It's precisely like a kiss—you can't do it alone.
                                        —JOHN CHEEVER

PART THIRTEEN

Learning from the Greats

Everywhere I've been a poet has been there first.

—FREUD

*The great guides were the books I discovered in the Johns
Hopkins library, where my student job was to file books away.
One was more or less encouraged to take a cart of books and
go back into the stacks and not come out for seven or eight
hours. So I read what I was filing. My great teachers (the best
thing that can happen to a writer) were Scheherazade,
Homer, Virgil, and Boccaccio; also the great Sanskrit
taletellers. I was impressed forever with the width as well as
the depth of literature—*

—JOHN BARTH

We hope this book will take you in two directions: first, into your own well
of inspiration, your own store of forgotten or overlooked material, and
into your own writing and, second, back to the greats who are your true
teachers.

One of these teachers, F. Scott Fitzgerald, names his own teachers in
the following passage:

By style, I mean color. . . . I want to be able to do anything with words:
handle slashing, flaming descriptions like Wells, and use the paradox with
the clarity of Samuel Butler, the breadth of Bernard Shaw and the wit of
Oscar Wilde, I want to do the wide sultry heavens of Conrad, the rolled
gold sundowns and crazy-quilt skies of Hichens and Kipling as well as

the pastelle [*sic*] dawns and twilights of Chesterton. All that is by way of example. As a matter of fact I am a professional literary thief, hot after the best methods of every writer in my generation.

In a letter Fitzgerald again pays homage to a "teacher." He says, "The motif of the 'dying fall' [in *Tender is the Night*] was absolutely deliberate and did not come from the diminution of vitality but from a definite plan. That particular trick is one that Ernest Hemingway and I worked out—probably from Conrad's preface to *The Nigger* [*of the Narcissus*]." Madison Smartt Bell echoes this sense of learning tricks from a master in his dedication for *The Washington Square Ensemble*. He says, "This book is dedicated to the long patience of my parents with a tip of the trick hat to George Garrett."

The exercises in this next section are meant to show you how to read for inspiration and instruction. Study the letters and journals of writers to discover how they grappled with problems you will encounter in your own fiction. For example, Flaubert worried about the "lack of action" in *Madame Bovary*. In a letter to Louise Colet he says, "The psychological development of my characters is giving me a lot of trouble; and everything, in this novel, depends on it." And he immediately comes up with the solution, "for in my opinion, ideas can be as entertaining as actions, but in order to be so they must flow one from the other like a series of cascades, carrying the reader along midst the throbbing of sentences and the seething of metaphors."

And read what writers say about writing, for example John Barth's *Lost in the Funhouse*, Elizabeth Bowen's *Collected Impressions*, Raymond Carver's *Fires*, Annie Dillard's *Living by Fiction* and *The Writing Life*, John Gardner's *The Art of Fiction* and *Becoming a Novelist*, E. M. Forster's *Aspects of the Novel*, William Gass's *On Being Blue*, Henry James's prefaces to his novels, Flannery O'Connor's *Mystery and Manners*, Eudora Welty's *The Eye of the Story*, and Virginia Woolf's *A Room of One's Own*, among others. And now on to our exercises for learning from the greats.

We're supposed to be able to get into other skins. We're supposed to be able to render experiences not our own and warrant times and places we haven't seen. That's one justification for art, isn't it—to distribute the suffering? Writing teachers invariably tell students Write about what you know. That's, of course, what you have to do, but on the other hand, how do you know what you know until you've written it? Writing is knowing. What did Kafka know? The insurance business? So that kind of advice is foolish because it presumes that you have to go out to a war to be able to do war. Well, some do and some don't. I've had very little experience in my life. In fact, I try to avoid experience if I can. Most experience is bad.

—E.L. DOCTOROW, *THE WRITER'S CHAPBOOK*

102

Finding Inspiration in Other Sources — Poetry, Nonfiction, Etc.

A writer is someone who reads. We recommend that you read the letters and notebooks of writers, biographies and autobiographies, plays and poetry, history and religion. Reading for writers has always engendered a cross-pollination of ideas and forms. For the writer, everything is a possible source for an epigraph, a title, a story, a novel.

Following are some well-chosen epigraphs.

Joseph Conrad, *Nostromo*
So foul a day clears not without a storm.

—SHAKESPEARE, *KING JOHN*

Joseph Conrad, *Lord Jim*
It is certain my Conviction gains infinitely, the moment another soul will believe in it.

—NOVALIS

Charles Baxter, *First Light*
Life can only be understood backwards; but it must be lived forwards.

—SØREN KIERKEGAARD

Arundhati Roy, *The God of Small Things*
Never again will a single story be told as though it's the only one.

—JOHN BERGER

John Hawkes, *The Blood Oranges*
Is there then any terrestrial paradise where, amidst the whispering of the olive-leaves, people can be with whom they like and have what they like and take their ease in shadows and in coolness?

—FORD MADOX FORD, *THE GOOD SOLDIER*

Margot Livesey, *Homework*
. . . it is children really, perhaps because so much is forbidden to them, who understand from within the nature of crime.

—RENATA ADLER, *PITCH DARK*

James Alan McPherson, *Elbow Room*
> I don't know which way I'm travelin'—
>> Far or near,
> All I knows fo' certain is
>> I *cain't* stay *here.*
>
> —STERLING A. BROWN, "LONG GONE"

Nadine Gordimer, *Burger's Daughter*
> I am the place in which something has occurred.
>
> —CLAUDE LÉVI-STRAUSS

Joyce Carol Oates, *Them*
> . . . because we are poor
> Shall we be vicious?
>
> —JOHN WEBSTER, THE WHITE DEVIL

Tim O'Brien, *Going after Cacciato*
> Soldiers are dreamers.
>
> —SIEGFRIED SASSOON

Amy Hempel, *Reasons to Live*
> Because grief unites us,
> like the locked antlers of moose
> who die on their knees in pairs.
>
> —WILLIAM MATTHEWS

T. Coraghessan Boyle, *If the River Was Whiskey*
> You know that the best you can expect is to avoid the worst.
>
> — ITALO CALVINO, IF ON A WINTER'S NIGHT A TRAVELER

One final example: the "Etymology" and "extracts" preceding the first chapter of Herman Melville's novel *Moby Dick*. In them, Melville quotes from Hakluyt, *Genesis*, Holland's *Plutarch's Morals*, Rabelais, *King Henry*, *Hamlet*, *Paradise Lost*, *Thomas Jefferson's Whale Memorial to the French minister in 1778*, *Falconer's Shipwreck*, Hawthorne's *Twice Told Tales*, and *Whale Song*, among others.

The Exercise

Read widely for inspiration and then use an original text as an epigraph for your own story or novel. For example, think of Stanley Kunitz's wonderful line: "The thing that eats the heart is mostly heart." This would make a superb epigraph to a story collection or novel titled *Mostly Heart*. Begin a story with this line in mind. Or write a story that illustrates this line from John le Carré's *Tinker, Tailor, Soldier, Spy:* "There are moments that are made up of too much stuff for them to be lived at the time they occur."

Choose several of your favorite poems and reread them with an eye toward finding a title or using a line as an epigraph to a story. Or choose a sentence from an essay or popular song.

Read, read, read. Then write, write, write. Sometimes in reverse order.

The Objective

To absorb what we read in a way that allows it to spark our own creativity, to use it as inspiration for our own writing. To build on what has gone before.

The important thing for a writer is to get to your desk before you do.

—HERB GARDNER

103

The Sky's the Limit: Homage to Kafka and García Márquez

from Christopher Noël

In a *Paris Review* interview, Gabriel García Márquez says,

> At the university in Bogotá, I started making new friends and acquaintances, who introduced me to contemporary writers. One night a friend lent me a book of short stories by Franz Kafka. I went back to the pension where I was staying and began to read *The Metamorphosis*. The first line almost knocked me off the bed. I was so surprised. The first line reads, "As Gregor Samsa awoke that morning from uneasy dreams he found himself transformed in his bed into a gigantic insect. . . ." When I read the line I thought to myself that I didn't know anyone was allowed to write things like that. If I had known, I would have started writing a long time ago. So I immediately started writing.

The Exercise

For inspiration read Kafka's story, or perhaps García Márquez's "A Very Old Man with Enormous Wings." Then if you are part of a group, each member should write a fantastical first line and then pass it to the left (or right). Each person, after receiving a first line from her neighbor, should then try to make good on its implicit riches, to open up a world from this seed, one that is different from the everyday world but nonetheless full of concrete detail and clear and consistent qualities, rules of being.

Next, write a story of your own.

The Objective

To loosen up your thinking, to countenance a greater range of possibilities, and to see that sometimes even the most apparently frivolous or ludicrous notions, completely implausible even for the slanted implausibility that writers use, can turn out to be just the ticket. What's strange can be made to seem necessary in a story; you can work to solidify the strangeness if, while you're writing, you keep a sort of grim faith at those pivotal moments—whether the first line or the third chapter or the final paragraph—when it seems you are betraying or trivializing your authentic vision of the world.

Student Examples

I scream each time I see that the house is surrounded, and I know this makes Carmen's patience wavery, like the heat mirages. Carmen has always lived in this desert and tells me that it is the normal way for Joshua trees to behave. But how am I to get used to them, all standing there with their arms raised each time I pass the window and forget not to look out. The Joshua trees are moving closer every day, and to me this is ominous, Carmen or no Carmen.

This house, this desert, are supposed to be for my health. Carmen, too, is supposed to be for my health. The doctor in Boston told my son so. Warm climate, a companion, and the old lady will be all set. Well, that doctor didn't know about the ways of the desert. I watch as the Joshua trees group and regroup like some stunted army, never quite making up their minds that they are going to advance. Bradford gets upset on the phone if I talk about the Joshua trees, how they are preparing for some sort of final march. Carmen can see it in the moon, although I don't tell Bradford this lest he think Carmen a bad influence.

—MOLLY LANZAROTTA, "RUNNING WITH THE JOSHUA TREE"

When Rene returned from the army, I felt at first that we should not contradict him, although the letter that had come weeks before clearly stated he was dead.

And sure enough, my cousin Rene did not at all wish to discuss the manner of his dying, which had been described in great detail in the letter from his friend in the army, how he had been dismembered by the rebels in the mountains, how he'd been skinned and scalped, his eyes gouged out and any number of things, to the point that there was nothing left to send home of him, nothing for us to mourn but the letter. I was practiced at this, this sudden grief with no ceremony, and wondered whether soon I would be the last one of this family, too, just one young girl left from so many.

And then Rene wandered in on a night that was gray with the glow of distant explosions, gray himself, covered with the dirt of the mountains and the dust of the desert our town has become. Little Yolanda shrieked when he pulled back the burlap we'd hung over the door of our collapsing home, and, of course, none of us could finish our meal. Rene sat down and ate everything on each of our plates, while his brother Evelio shouted, paced the room and questioned him, and his mother, Luisa, wept and kissed him and pulled on her rosary until it snapped, showering us all with tiny black beads. It seemed that they had cut the voice out of Rene as well, when they killed him, because he did not want to talk at all.

—MOLLY LANZAROTTA, "THE DEATH OF RENE PAZ,"
FROM *CAROLINA QUARTERLY*

If it hadn't been for my long serpentine tail, I wouldn't have lost my job as a cabdriver. It wasn't that management objected so much, God knows good help is hard to find these days, but eventually passengers complained, especially when I became agitated, say, in heavy traffic and whipped my tail into the backseat. I even struck a passenger once, but not on purpose or forcefully, and no permanent damage was done. I apologized afterward. I didn't get many tips.

I tried to make a virtue of my tail by decorating it on holidays, tying bright ribbons around its circumference until it looked like a barber pole, or the lance of a medieval knight. Things seemed to be working, at least until that incident with the motorcycle cop.

"Believe me, Melvin, it's not you," the dispatcher said. "Well, actually, it is you, in a way. But it's not personal," he pleaded, larding his voice with concern to avoid a class action suit. "Insurance is eating me up, man. That pedestrian you hit the other day . . ."

"I can explain that. I was giving a left turn signal . . ."

"Melvin, go to a doctor. Get it taken off. You're a good driver. You got a future."

"But it's part of me. It kind of gives me something to lean against."

He shrugged his shoulders toward the picture of the near-naked woman embracing a tire on the Parts Pups calendar on the wall. "He likes it," he said, as if to her. Then he looked at me. "Okay, Mel, you like it. You live with it. But not here."

And so I was out of a job.

—Gene Langston, "Fired"

I read Shakespeare directly I have finished writing. When my mind is agape and redhot. Then it is astonishing. I never yet knew how amazing his stretch and speed and word coining power is, until I felt it utterly outpace and outrace my own, seeming to start equal and then I see him draw ahead and to things I could not in my wildest tumult and utmost press of mind imagine.
—Virginia Woolf, *A Writer's Diary*

104

Learning from the Greats

Most writers can look back and name the books that seemed to fling open doors for them, books that made them want to go to the typewriter and begin to write one word after another. When asked if one writer had influenced her more than others, Joan Didion replied:

> I always say Hemingway, because he taught me how sentences worked. When I was fifteen or sixteen I would type out his stories to learn how sentences worked. . . . A few years ago when I was teaching a course at Berkeley I reread *A Farewell to Arms* and fell right back into those sentences. I mean they're perfect sentences. Very direct sentences, smooth rivers, clear water over granite, no sinkholes.

While teaching at several writing conferences, we noticed that fiction writers tend to remember what other writers have said about writing—and said eloquently—while poets have memorized the poem itself. "Not memorized," the poet Christopher Merrill says, "Committed to heart"—something he requires of all his students. The style and cadences of the Bible verses Abraham Lincoln learned as a boy emerged in his "Gettysburg Address."

The Exercise

Choose a writer you admire, one who has withstood the test of time. Type out that writer's stories or several chapters from a novel. Try to analyze how the sentences work, how their vocabulary differs from your own, how the structure of the story emerges from the language. Feel in your fingers what is different about that prose.

Then commit your favorite passages to heart.

Next, in a story or novel by the writer you admire, find a place between two sentences that seems like a "crack" that could be "opened up." Next, write your own paragraph or scene and insert it into this place. Now read the entire story including your addition.

The Objective

To understand just how much you need to know to really understand another person's story and how it works—and then add to it. The answer: everything—characterization, plot, tone, style, etc.

Student Examples

Two consecutive sentences from "A Very Old Man with Enormous Wings," by Gabriel García Márquez:

> The Angel was no less stand-offish with him than with other mortals, but he tolerated the most ingenious infamies with the patience of a dog who had no illusions. They both came down with chicken pox at the same time.

A student inserted the following addition between the above two sentences.

> The child hung dried crabs and lizards off the fallen Angel's wings, climbed onto his back to grasp the crow feathers in his tiny hands. The child tried to pull the enormous wing wide, imagining they were flying as the chickens ticked his muddy toes. He thought of the Angel as a great, broken doll and spent hours tying colored rags around his dried fig of a head, hanging rosaries around his neck and painting the crevices of his face with soot and red earth, the Angel all the while mumbling in his befuddled sailor's dialect.
>
> When the wise neighbor woman heard words of the Angel's language coming out of the child's mouth, she shook her head and threw more mothballs into the chicken coop. She told Elisenda, "Your child will grow wings or be carried off. He will disappear into the heavens." For a while, Elisenda tried to keep the child in the garden and Pelayo repaired the broken wires of the chicken coop. But the child continued to play on the other side of the wire and the Angel remained so inert that Elisenda ceased to believe it was the Angel's tongue her child spoke at all, but his own made up child's language. Soon the child was once again playing inside the coop, flying on the back of the old man.
>
> —MOLLY LANZAROTTA

Two consecutive sentences from *Lost in the Funhouse,* by John Barth:

> Ambrose's former archenemy.
>   Shortly after the mirror room he'd groped along a musty corridor, his heart already misgiving him at the absence of phosphorescent arrows and other signs.

One student inserted this between the above two sentences.

> Ambrose wanders aimlessly, loses sight of Peter as Magda chases him beyond the mirrors, into the darkness of the next room. Their laughter echoes and he cannot tell the direction from which it comes. He will not

call out to them. He is not lost yet. He will find his way out on his own. The smudges of hand prints on the mirrors reassure Ambrose that he is not the only one to follow this path through the funhouse. In one of the reflections, his arm is around the waist of an exquisite young woman with a figure unusually well developed for her age. He is taller, wearing a sailor's uniform. The image moves away, but Ambrose remains. Glass. *Not a mirror.* Sentence fragments can be used to emphasize discoveries or thoughts that suddenly occur to a character. The point is communicated to the reader without saying "he thought . . ." The fragmented thought may be used in combination with italics to create a feeling of urgency. Ambrose tries creating a path parallel to the one taken by the others but is constantly forced to change direction as the mirrors obscure his goal. At an unordained moment he reaches out to touch what he thinks is another mirror, but turns out in fact to be a passageway.

—ZAREH ARTINIAN

Whenever I sit down to write and can't think of anything to say, I write my name—W. Somerset Maugham—over and over again until something happens.

—W. SOMERSET MAUGHAM

Borrowing Characters

Authors have been borrowing characters from other authors' works for years. Some well-known examples are Jean Rhys's wonderful novel *Wide Sargasso Sea*, which provides an account of the early life of Mrs. Rochester, the wife of Mr. Rochester in Charlotte Brontë's *Jane Eyre*. George Macdonald Fraser uses Tom Brown and Flashman from Thomas Hughes's novel, *Tom Brown's School Days*. And there have been any number of continuations of the adventures of Sherlock Holmes; Nicholas Meyer's *The Seven Percent Solution,* Rick Boyer's *The Giant Rat of Sumatra*, and Sena Jeter Nasland's *Sherlock in Love* are three of the best. John Gardner wrote a novel titled *Grendel* about the beast in *Beowulf.* Joseph Heller brought King David once again to life in *God Knows.* Mark Twain also turned to the Bible for *The Diary of Adam and Eve.* Playwright Tom Stoppard borrowed characters from Shakespeare's *Hamlet* for *Rosencrantz and Guildenstern are Dead. Ahab's Wife*, by Sena Jeter Nasland, begins with this tantalizing sentence: "Captain Ahab was neither my first husband nor my last." David Foster Wallace takes on Lyndon Baines Johnson in "LBJ." In Kafka's short short story "The Truth about Sancho Panza," we learn that Don Quixote was really Panza's demon, whom he called Don Quixote, and then followed "on his crusades, perhaps out of a sense of responsibility, and had of them a great and edifying entertainment to the end of his days."

The Exercise

Take an antagonist or a minor character from a story or novel by someone else—a character who has always intrigued you. Make that person the protagonist in a scene or story of your own. For example, what would Allie Fox's wife say if she were to tell her version of Paul Theroux's *Mosquito Coast*, or write a story about their courtship? And what would Rabbit's illegitimate daughter, from Updike's *Rabbit* novels, say if she could tell her story?

The Objective

To enter into the imaginative world of another writer, to understand that particular world, and to build from it.

What Keeps
You Reading?

In *The Eye of the Story,* Eudora Welty writes, "Learning to write may be part of learning to read. For all I know, writing comes out of a superior devotion to reading."

Part of the apprenticeship of being a successful writer is learning to read like a writer, discovering how a particular story catches your attention and keeps you involved right straight through to the end.

The Exercise

Halfway through a story ask yourself several questions: What do I care about? What has been set in motion that I want to see completed? Where is the writer taking me? Then finish reading the story and see how well the writer met the expectations that she raised for you.

The Objective

To illustrate how the best stories and novels set up situations that are resolved by the time you finish the story or close the book. To learn how to arouse the reader's curiosity or create expectations in the first half of your story or novel, and then to decide to what degree you should feel obliged to meet those expectations.

Mary McCarthy once lost the only manuscript copy of a novel. Interviewer Bob Cromie said to her, "But it's your novel, you can write it again." McCarthy replied, "Oh, I couldn't do that—I know how it ends."

The Literary Scene Circa 1893, 1929, 1948, or?

from George Garrett

The year 1929 saw the publication of major books (in the present view of things) by Faulkner, Fitzgerald, Thomas Wolfe, and others. The Pulitzer Prize, and the lion's share of review space, went to Oliver LaFarge for *Laughing Boy*. Another example: Throughout the 1920s one of the most productive and interesting American novelists, widely reviewed and praised, was Joseph Hergesheimer. One of the very few reviews of a work of fiction by the young William Faulkner was devoted to Hergesheimer and indicates not only that Faulkner took his work very seriously, but also that Hergesheimer influenced Faulkner's own art.

The Exercise

You are given (or draw out of a hat) a year, say 1929. You are responsible for knowing the literary history of this year as it saw itself. That is, on your honor you do not use books or histories to learn about the literary scene in 1929. You use only the newspapers and magazines of that year. In due time you report on that year to the rest of us. (To make it a bit more interesting, the student who chose 1929 might do a book report on LaFarge's *Laughing Boy*, discovering thereby that it is an excellent novel.)

The Objective

Year after year, to your surprise and to ours, you will report on all kinds of once-famous writers none of us has ever heard of. You will discover that many now-acclaimed masters were ignored or given short shrift in their own time. Thus learn a basic truth—that they did not know or accurately judge their own era and neither can we. It follows that the writer's business is to write. Reputation, or the lack of it, is out of your hands. Persevere. Endure. Maybe prevail.

PART FOURTEEN

Sudden, Flash, and Microfiction: Writing the Short Short Story

The short short story is an elusive form—perhaps more mysterious than the short story or novel. In *Sudden Fiction*, Stuart Dybek addresses the editors' question of what is a short short as opposed to a short story. He says, ". . . the short prose piece so frequently inhabits a no-man's land between prose and poetry, narrative and lyric, story and fable, joke and meditation, fragment and whole, that one of its identifying characteristics has been its protean shape. Part of the fun of writing them is the sense of slipping between the seams. Within the constraint of their small boundaries the writer discovers great freedom. In fact, their very limitations of scale often *demand* unconventional strategies. . . . Each writer makes up the form. Each piece is a departure. A departure—but from what?"

The elusiveness of the short short story especially makes itself felt in the workshop. When discussing longer stories or novel excerpts in class we use the language of the art of fiction, asking if the characters are fully fleshed out, does the plot have forward movement, does the metafictional aspect of the story enlarge our understanding of fiction, has the story found its own balance between narrative summary and scene, and so on. When teaching a *short short* story workshop, however, we find ourselves asking only one question of each short short story: *does it work?* Irving Howe in his introduction to *Short Shorts* states, "Writers who do short shorts need to be especially bold. They stake everything on a stroke of inventiveness. Sometimes they have to be prepared to speak out directly, not so much in order to state a theme as to provide a jarring or complicating commentary. . . . And then, almost before it begins, the fiction is brought to a stark conclusion—abrupt, bleeding, exhausting. This conclusion need not complete the action; it has to break it off decisively."

As always, the best teachers are the stories themselves. Noted practitioners include Kafka, Borges, Hemingway, Kawabata, Mishima, and more recently Grace Paley, Thomas Berger, Luisa Valenzuela, and Diane Williams. Even writers known for longer work have written in this form: Joyce Carol Oates, David Foster Wallace, Tim O'Brien, among others. There are also many superb anthologies of the short short story. One of the first to appear was Irving and Ilana Wiener Howe's *Short Shorts,* mentioned above, with its informative introduction. Then came the enormously influential *Sudden Fiction,* followed by *Flash Fiction, Sudden Fiction International,* and the shortest of all, *Microfiction,* edited by Jerome Stern, which includes many of the winners and finalists of a contest started by Stern, known as the World's Best Short Short Story Contest. One winner of this contest was Brian Hinshaw, then an MFA student at Emerson College. Hinshaw's story, "The Custodian" (page 288), is discussed at length in Ron Wallace's essay "Writers Try Short Shorts" in the *AWP Chronicle* (Vol. 33, No. 6, 2001). (It can be read online by going to Google and keying in "Ronald Wallace" to find his Web site.) Other anthologies of short short stories include *Four Minute Fictions,* edited by Robley Wilson, who first published them in *North American Review,* and *Sudden Stories: The Mammoth Book of Miniscule Stories,* edited by Dinty Moore. Finally, two new magazines by former Emerson students feature the short short story: *Quick Fiction,* edited by Jennifer Cande and Adam Pieroni, publishes stories under 500 words (www.quickfiction.org), and *Night Train,* edited by Rod Siino and Rusty Barnes, runs an intriguing competition twice a year for "Firebox" fiction (www.Nighttrainmagazine.com)—a competition that shares the reading fees with the contest winners. *Esquire* often features a short short story on its last page under the title "Snapfiction." Lots of stories to read. Lessons to learn. Places to publish.

There is no absolute rule for how short or long a short short might be, but we think of it as falling somewhere between 250 words and four or five manuscript pages. It is not a condensed longer story, but rather a story that requires this length and its particular form. The most compelling short short stories often have a narrative thread.

Perhaps because the stories are so short, we encourage you to play around with the exercises—on your own or in a workshop. When assigning Ron Carlson's ABC story (see page 268) we ask students to come up with A words as fast as they can, going around and around the room until someone repeats a word. (They are amazed at how many A words there are—that they know.) Then B words. Then we move to X and Y and Z words. When students bring their ABC stories in, we ask each student to read off their AB and YZ sentences—just to hear the variety. When students are assigned the "Rules of the Game" exercise (page 275), we go around the room compiling a list of games. Sometimes we ask the students to create their own exercises based on a story they've read. One student came up with a superb "Chain" story exercise based on Francine Prose's "Pumpkins" from *Flash Fiction*. At the end of the semester each student is astonished that she has written and revised between ten and fifteen new short short stories. At this time, students put together individual collections in addition to creating a class anthology of short shorts, complete with title page and cover art. Now, it's your turn.

*The business of the poet and novelist is to show the sorriness
underlying the grandest things, and the grandeur underlying the
sorriest things.*
—THOMAS HARDY

Sudden Fiction

From James Thomas

In our introduction to *Sudden Fiction,* Robert Shapard and I recount how we solicited responses to our working first title, "Blasters," and were amazed at the "uproar." Writers not only had opinions about the word for the short short story, but also about their traditions, their present developments, the motives for writing and reading them, how they compare to sonnets, ghazals, folk tales, parables, koans, and other forms. Almost no one agreed entirely on anything, least of all what a short short was. Highly compressed, highly charged, insidious, protean, sudden, alarming, tantalizing, short shorts do confer form on small corners of chaos, and, at their best, can do in a page what a novel does in two hundred.

Question: What is shorter than "sudden fiction?"
Answer: "Flash fiction."

These even shorter stories (all under 750 words) are collected in *Flash Fiction,* edited by Tom Hazuka, Denise Thomas, and myself. Then there is the World's Best Short Short Story Contest, run by Jerome Stern at Florida State University at Tallahassee, whose winners and finalists appear in *Sundog: The Southeast Review.* Will anyone forget the "big wind" or "moiling dogs" from the 1991 winning story, "Baby, Baby, Baby," by François Camoin?

The Exercise

Read, read, read these shortest of stories with joy and amazement at their range and multiplicity of form.

Then write one—under 750 words.

The Objective

To create a world, give it shape—all of a sudden, in a flash.

Write a Story Using
a Small Unit of Time

Some short stories employ a small, contained unit of time or center on a single event that provides the story with a given natural shape. For example, in Nicholson Baker's short story "Pants on Fire," the narrator puts on a shirt and takes the subway to work—nothing else happens. Raymond Carver's story "Cathedral" takes place in one evening when an old friend comes to visit the narrator's wife (page 338). Luisa Valenzuela's "Vision Out of the Corner of One Eye" captures a fleeting encounter on a bus (page 300). Elizabeth Tallent's story "No One's a Mystery" lasts the length of time it takes for the narrator to receive a gift from her married lover Jack, who also gives her the unwanted truth of their situation, achieving a unity of time and place (page 298). Such unity is a natural for the short short story form.

The Exercise

Make a list yourself of things that are done in small units of time: naming a child or a pet, washing a car, stealing something, waiting or standing in line, packing for a trip, changing the message on an answering machine, teaching a class, getting a haircut, throwing a birthday party, etc. Now write a two-to-four-page story staying within the confines of a particular time unit. For example, a birthday party story would probably last only a few hours, or an afternoon or evening.

The Objective

To recognize the large number of shaped time units in our lives. These units can provide a natural substructure for a story and make the writing of a story seem less daunting.

Solving for X
from Ron Carlson

The following exercise works best if it is done first and discussed afterward.

The Exercise

Write a short story with the following conditions: It is exactly 26 sentences in length. Each sentence begins with a word that starts with one of the letters of the alphabet—in order. For example:

> All the excuses had been used. By the time the school doctor saw me, he'd heard everything. Coughing, I began to tell him about the lie which I hoped would save us all. AND SO FORTH.

Also, you must use one sentence fragment. Oh, and one sentence should be exactly 100 words long and grammatically sound.

The Objective

The objective here is initially obscured by how confused everyone is to have such a strange mission. Tell them to get over it. What the assignment illuminates is form's role in process. Since the imposed form has nothing at all to do with the writer's real agenda, the exercise becomes a fundamental exploration of our sense of story, narrative rise and fall, and process—process most prominently. What a challenge and a comfort knowing how that next sentence begins! The discussions we've had over these ABC stories are some of the strongest and most central, and the issues that arise follow us all semester.

To make a more dramatic point about structure and its relationship to process, divide any group of writers in two and assign only half the above exercise to the first group. Assign the second group the same exercise but make it clear that the twenty-six sentences do not have to be in alphabetical order. Any bets on who has the more difficult task?

Student Story

Tasteful

Anton, my wife's French lover, has been leaving me clues in the kitchen sink. Before I realized what was at work I thought them to be merely lazy with their adulterous business. "Careless, careless," I thought, on finding the clamshells piled on the countertop, some rimmed with lipstick, a red kind I'd never seen before. Determined to leave them to their affair, I said nothing and cleaned up, scrubbing the sauce pots and plates (Anton would sometimes have the courtesy to rinse the blackest of the bunch and these gestures were to me like little reliefs).

Eventually, however, a line was crossed, or rather, a line was drawn. For the record, I'd like to put that my initial reaction was not violent in nature; I tore no hair, or cursed or banged my chest in heartfelt agony—in truth, I flinched. Getting home late one evening I found the house in a state of measured disarray: chairs carefully overturned, shelves upset of their volumes (mostly mine), pictures skewed on their hooks, etc., etc. . . . but the dining room was ruined for me alone. Honestly, it appeared as though they had gone to some trouble to give me a show, as the walls were speckled with soup (a pork and potato potage, I determined, after much finger-licking), the plates and their contents scattered across the floor (swordfish, in a light virgin oil with mixed greens) while the table itself was strewn with the wreckage of a planned passion; a snow angel of wine stains and silverware to document their deliberate bad fun. In the heart of this scene was a heavy line of salt, running lengthwise down the table, dividing the house into territories of mine and theirs, but like a challenge as well—a dare, if you will. Justifiably, I remained a gentleman and made no effort to erase the line or its litter, but switched off the lights instead, the salt strip illuminating the room like a tail of phosphorus. Knowing hunger myself, I righted a chair and fell to, picking through the leftovers.

Later, weeks later, the taste of this food would remain in my mouth, blooming at the back of my throat into a kind of perpetual gag reflex, an unshakable sweetness, there, just behind my tongue, trimmed out with the unmistakable sting of stomach bile. Momentarily, I believed the nausea to be the announcement of a great nest of ulcers, all growing fat from my ample stress and rotten habits—a consequence of adulthood with which I have learned to live. Nevertheless, the symptoms here refused to match up—they were more violent, unpredictable and stretched to include bouts of strenuous retching, night fever, insomnia and a general bad temper. Of course, no conventional remedy could slake the tides of digestive fluid; chalk tablets, milk of magnesia—even a strong belt of castor oil did nothing but discolor my teeth and extinguish my appetite. Polite as you please, I spent each night splayed across the cool tiles of our shared bathroom, stifling my moans and thumbing eagerly through a French dictionary, my ear pressed to the wall, conjugating his irregular and exclamatory verbs with all the severity of a death sentence.

Quite by accident, I discovered my own antidote.

Regarding the innocence of my intentions, I must say that reckless knife-play has never been customary in my kitchen—however, fortunate slips of the hand are. So, one afternoon, while straying admittedly too far from my task at the chopping block (dicing fresh rhubarb for rhubarb pie), I found myself wandering the house, knife in hand, apparently seeking out some hidden rhubarb, or some such thing. This long and seemingly aimless search ended at last (surprisingly) in my wife's private bed chambers. Under oath (were I ever to find myself in such a civil bind), I would feel obligated to include in my testimony a brief description of my wife's habit of discarding useless and quite obtrusive items onto the floor of her bedroom (including clothes, suitcases, boxes and books—all manner of item and accessory laid out like an obstacle course), as it sheds, I believe, some light on how I managed to plunge, or rather, trip, knife-first into the bed.

Very much by coincidence, the bed was unoccupied and none were duly slain—but oh, those sheets—those stained and soiled and sinned-upon sheets, they did get a running through, by god! Without love, I gathered the tattered remnants of my wife's beloved bed sheets and, seeing no further use for them, and being myself a bit short on rhubarb, I saw no better course than to include them in my pie. XXL Egyptian cotton bed sheets, it turns out, need only a good dousing of sherry before being sealed under a cinnamon crust and put to bake for more than two hours at a medium heat. Yes, and it came out marvelous, tasting in the end something like almond or arsenic, like a poison you build yourself up against, becoming stronger by every bite until the last of the acid is snuffed out and you are at once full—full up forever. Zero states, in the stomach and the heart and all the rest, full up and empty forever, never again to feel hunger or pain, free to eat now for reasons of your own.

—DERRICK ABLEMAN, *NIGHT TRAIN*

111

The Journey of the Long Sentence

The following exercise came from a conversation with the poet Richard Jackson, who values exercises and always does each exercise with his students. He tells his class to write a poem that is one sentence long. He says the sentence should keep pushing and gain momentum. Even in the midst of suspension and qualification, the sentence has to move forward—not just repeating—but adding new information and achieving new emotional levels to finish on a different emotional note at the end. He says that what goes along with this assignment is the assumption that the sentence should radiate out to embrace more of the world, of the complications surrounding details and events and observations and feelings. Then the details become a part of an intricate set of relationships, giving and taking from that set.

Below is the beginning of the poem, printed with permission, without its line breaks from *Alive All Day,* that Jackson wrote with his class for this exercise:

THE OTHER DAY

I just want to say a few words about the other day, an ordinary day I happen to recall because my daughter has just given me a yellow flower, a buttercup, for no reason, though it was important that other day, that ordinary one when the stones stayed stones and were not symbols for anything else, when the stars made no effort to fill the spaces we see between them, though maybe you remember it differently, a morning when I woke to find my hand had flowered on the breast of my wife, a day so ordinary I happened to notice the old woman across the street, hips so large it's useless to try to describe them, struggle off her sofa to pull down the shade that has separated us ever since, her room as lonely as Keats' room on the Piazza di Spagna where there was hardly any space for words, where I snapped a forbidden photo that later showed nothing of his shadow making its way to a window above Bernini's fountain . . .

For other examples of long sentences intrinsic to a writer's style, turn to the work of William Faulkner, Julio Cortazar, Marcel Proust, David Foster

Wallace, all of whom explore and express continuing action with qualification and complication. Jamaica Kincaid's story "Girl," on page 289, is one sentence long.

The Exercise

Write a short short story that is only one sentence.

The Objective

To develop a sense of how syntax can qualify, develop, and provide an expansive context for our observations in much the same way the brain does, finding a linear order for what are often simultaneous aspects of an observation.

Student Story

One Day Walk Through the Front Door

It got so the only place I could cry was the freeway since traffic jams and the absence of curves made driving and crying less dangerous, unlike surface streets which scattered the pile of flyers on the passenger seat, jumbling the printed images of my sister's face and frightening me beyond tears with the sight of a life slipping out of reach as I pulled into gas stations, cafés, rest stops, a mad woman slapping flyers on walls, in people's faces, blurting *Have you seen her?* . . . until soon I only made calls from phone booths, avoiding the empty apartment I shared with her, talking to police, friends, reporters, even giving phone interviews so sometimes it was my own voice on the news as I drove, *I just hope she's safe, I want her home,* other times my voice shouted back at the radio, *say her name, don't drop the story, oh Jesus, please,* then I'd cry more and believe how alone I felt, surrounded by hundreds of people encased in tinted-glass worlds that could neatly hide any individual horror, until I could only whisper, *please even just her body,* because I had to know or I'd be stranded in this moment forever and I'd never sleep again, but wait, always wait to see her one day just walk through the front door . . . then, finally, my last hope was to hear it from our priest, but it was the car, detached reporting from that radio on the fifth day: they'd found a body, floating in the bay.

—MOLLY LANZAROTTA, HONORABLE MENTION, WORLD'S BEST SHORT SHORT STORY CONTEST

112

How to Use Juxaposition to Write a Short Short Story

from Peter Jay Shippy

Beautiful is the chance encounter, on an operating table,
of a sewing machine and an umbrella.

—COMTE DE LAUTREAMONT

Many surrealist writers and artists effectively used the technique of juxtaposition to infuse their work with mystery, rough beauty and humor. Juxtaposition, in this case, means using disparate objects, ideas, or incongruous characters on the same canvas or in the same short story. Think about Salvador Dali's paintings. In Dali's work you may find melting clocks hanging off trees or giraffes, their necks ablaze, galloping across department store mezzanines. Writers like Jorge Luis Borges, Eugene Ionesco, Julio Cortazar, and Donald Barthelme have used juxtaposition to create masterpieces of contemporary literature.

The Exercise

Look in newspapers or magazines for a few items that wallop your fancy. Choose ones with an absurd story or an arresting subject. These need not be long exposes or essays; just a few paragraphs will suffice.

Next, choose one of your finds to develop into a fiction, with one important change. Transfer your father or mother into that item's protagonist. Also, if possible, change the location to that parent's home. So if the newspaper piece were about teens in Madagascar spray painting their names on wild animals, you will write a story about your adult mother tagging her initials on squirrels in her backyard. At first, stick to the news item and be true to your parents, physically and emotionally, the way they are now. Later, feel free to amend the assignment if your story calls for it. If your first attempt doesn't pan out, try another item or another parent.

Teachers: this exercise may work better if you divide the assignment. That is, ask the students to find the news items before you explain what they will do with them. This way, they don't tailor the item to a subject.

The Objective

To give free reign to the unexpected as a source for inspiration within the reigns of character and plot.

Student Example

One writer found an item about the *Otaku*, a Japanese word meaning hobbyist. It's used specifically to describe the extreme fans of *anime* and video games. The article explained that some *Otaku* live only virtually. They skip school and meals; they've lost their friends and stay in their rooms for days on end at their computers. The writer found this topic fascinating. In particular, he was intrigued by the case of a young boy whose obsession with Pokemon had so polluted his life that the wall between reality and fantasy had turned to a thin veil. The lifestyles of the young Japanese were far different than that of his own family in the American suburbs, especially his parents. So the writer melded the plight of Pokemon *Otaku* to the character of his own businessman father.

The writer only had to use his father's personality and the plot of his day to write his story. As the father eats breakfast with his family he dreams about becoming Ash Ketchem, Pokemon Master. He speeds to work in his SUV, believing that the monsters, Zubat and Drowzee, pursue him. We can see where this will end. No? Good.

Juxtaposing the *Otaku* obsession with fantasy to the drone of American work made for a riotous but dark story.

113

Rules of the Game

As we mentioned in the introduction, except for length the short short story doesn't have any rules. But the "rules of a game" and the accoutrements that accompany many games—boards, chessmen, checkers, a dictionary—are good material for the short short story form In this exercise, we want you to write a story that somehow uses a familiar game and its rules.

The Exercise

Go around the class and have each person name a game. Continue doing this, round and round, till you have run out of games. You will be surprised how many games there are that most of us know. Shut this book right now and begin. When you return to this exercise, see how many of the following games the class named: Scrabble, Life, Risk, Poker, Candyland, Parchesi, Monopoly, Trouble, Clue, Trivial Pursuit, bridge, Dictionary, crossword puzzles, Mousetrap, Othello, Chutes and Ladders, checkers, chess, Sorry, backgammon, hearts, canasta, Go, Boggle, Stratego, mah jong, telephone, and so on.

Next, write a story that uses a game in some way. Are the players playing the game? Is the game writing new rules for itself? Is someone calling Parker Brothers to adjudicate a Monopoly move?

The Objective

To show how rules lend themselves to the freedom of the short short story form.

Student Story

Alfalfa

The fight started with a simple cryptogram in the Sunday edition of the *New York Times*: Find a word with the letter combination XYZXYZX, but things escalated, as they inevitably did, and soon it was no longer a friendly contest to see who could solve the puzzle first but a battle fought tooth and nail across a glass coffee table, the outcome of which would be the surest sign yet of who was smarter, thus settling a furtive rivalry that loomed over their new marriage like a cartoon anvil and had recently intensified thanks to comments such as, Oh come on, my twelve-year-old niece knows Bismarck is the capital of North Dakota, Thirty-five across is harebrained, not "hairbrained," and Well sure, I used to think existentialism was interesting too, but that was back in high school, and even though they were both educated and believed themselves to be above the things about which most newlyweds bickered, they still found themselves arguing over equally trivial matters—the significance of SAT scores, who had actually read Baudelaire in French, or the proper pronunciation of Nabokov—at the same time they both knew these subjects had little to do with the questions they really wanted to ask, the answers they wanted to hear, so now here they were in the middle of a row over a word game, saying nasty things about each other's parents and threatening to give up on the whole damn marriage, emphasizing each point by pounding the tabletop when suddenly the glass surface shattered into a thousand tiny pieces and they were left wondering what just happened, until one of them figured it out.

—TERRY THEUMLING, *StoryQuarterly*

I'm just trying to look at something without blinking.
—TONI MORRISON

114

Ten to One

from Hester Kaplan

Part of writing well is the ability to reduce a story to its linguistic essence, while still allowing for rich and complex ideas and images. Imagination and control meet to create effective fiction. Sometimes less really is more. This exercise is always a hit; thanks to Tracy Boothman Duyck for passing it on to me.

The Exercise

Write a complete story in fifty-five words. Your first sentence should have ten words, your second nine, your third eight, and so on until your final sentence consists of a single word.

The Objective

To illustrate that writing's power can often be found in its economy; that precision can lead to surprisingly original results.

115

Make a List

Do you keep a list? A grocery list? A "to do" list? a list of errands to run, people to call, letters to write, items to pack, books you've read, places you've lived? Almost everyone at some time or other resorts to a list. It might be a list to organize one's day or chores, or a list that is meant to provide you with information about yourself: women you have loved; men you have left; friends who are no longer friends; or excuses you have used, as in Antonia Clark's short short story, "Excuses I Have Already Used." on page 286. One can almost imagine the "protagonist" making up the list in Gregory Burnham's superb story, "Subtotals," from *Flash Fiction.* Interesting correspondences: "Number of dogs: 1. Number of cats: 7." All subtotals, because of course the progagonist is still counting. Then there are the books that are themselves lists: Alexander Theroux's *The Primary Colors* and John Mitchell's *Euphonics: A Poet's Dictionary of Sounds.*

The Exercise

Write a story about a list or write a story that is a list. The list must tell us something about the person making the list, and have an organic structure of its own.

The Objective

To be able to use an ordinary list as a microcosm of your character's life.

Student Examples

List Within a Story
". . . or I'll be some kind of super hero, straight out of the comic books, and my superpower, be it death, breath, magma vomit, hypnosehair, or telekinetic control over mops, pasta, curtains, dishwashers, applesauce, doorknobs, earlobes, comic books, burlap, fog, and monkeys, will allow the elderly and timid to walk through even the toughest neighborhoods with a strut of confidence . . ."

—BRIAN RUUSKA

Story

"Love and Other Catastrophes: A Mix Tape"

"All By Myself" (Eric Carmen). "Looking for Love" (Lou Reed). "I Wanna Dance With Somebody" (Whitney Houston). "Let's Dance" (David Bowie). "Let's Kiss" (Beat Happening). "Let's Talk About Sex" (Salt N' Pepa). "Like A Virgin" (Madonna). "We've Only Just Begun" (The Carpenters). "I Wanna Be Your Boyfriend" (The Ramones). "I'll Tumble 4 Ya" (Culture Club). "Head Over Heels" (The Go-Go's). "Nothing Compares To You" (Sinéad O'Connor). "My Girl" (The Temptations). "Could This Be Love?" (Bob Marley). "Love and Marriage" (Frank Sinatra). "White Wedding" (Billy Idol). "Stuck in the Middle with You" (Steelers Wheel). "Tempted" (The Squeeze). "There Goes My Baby" (The Drifters). "What's Going On?" (Marvin Gaye). "Where Did You Sleep Last Night?" (Leadbelly). "Whose Bed Have Your Boots Been Under?" (Shania Twain). "Jealous Guy" (John Lennon). "Your Cheatin' Heart" (Tammy Wynette). "Shot Through the Heart" (Bon Jovi). "Don't Go Breaking My Heart" (Elton John and Kiki Dee). "My Achy Breaky Heart" (Billy Ray Cyrus). "Heartbreak Hotel" (Elvis Presley), "Stop, In the Name of Love" (The Supremes). "Try a Little Tenderness" (Otis Redding). "Try (Just a Little Bit Harder)" (Janis Joplin). "All Apologies" (Nirvana). "Hanging on the Telephone" (Blondie). "I Just Called to Say I Love You" (Stevie Wonder). "Love Will Keep Us Together" (Captain and Tennille). "Let's Stay Together" (Al Green). "It Ain't Over 'Till It's Over" (Lenny Kravitz). "What's Love Got To Do With It?" (Tina Turner). "You Don't Bring Me Flowers Anymore" (Barbara Streisand and Neil Diamond). "I Wish You Wouldn't Say That" (Talking Heads). "You're So Vain" (Carly Simon). "Love is a Battlefield" (Pat Benatar). "Heaven Knows I'm Miserable Now" (The Smiths). "Can't Get No Satisfaction" (Rolling Stones). "Must Have Been Love (But It's Over Now)" (Roxette). "Breaking Up is Hard to Do" (Neil Sedaka). "I Will Survive" (Gloria Gaynor). "Hit the Road, Jack" (Mary McCaslin and Jim Ringer). "These Boots Were Made for Walking" (Nancy Sinatra). " All Out of Love" (Air Supply). "All By Myself" (Eric Carmen).

—AMANDA HOLZER, *STORYQUARTERLY*,
BEST AMERICAN NON-REQUIRED READING 2004

116

How To . . . ...

How to do what? you might ask. Well, anything. Think of all the articles written about how to grow herbs indoors, how to lose weight, how to train a dog, how to write a will, how to improve your golf game, tennis serve, swimming stroke, sales techniques, how to _____—you fill in the blank. But better yet, write a story that uses the language of "how to" as part of the story. The inspiration for this exercise came from the writer Nancy Zafris, and was passed along via Kit Irwin to Toni Clark, who wrote a hilarious story from the point of view of a food photographer titled "How to Shoot a Tomato."

The Exercise

Write a story that is about a character learning how to do something. Or telling someone else how to do it. Make the directions particular to the character and the task at hand—sometimes an inadvertent lesson, such as in Lee Harrington's "How to Become a Country-Western Singer," below.

The Objective

To use the stuff of everyday instruction as the basis for a story. It can be in the story—or the story itself.

How to Become a Country-Western Singer
First your girlfriend has to move out, taking everything from the Lovett albums to the leftover beans-and-franks. Then you rush to your secret letter drawer; sure enough, the latest from Dolly-Sue are missing. Minutes later, snow begins to fall. Ice collects on the gutters and eaves. At midnight, black water seeps through the ceiling and onto your white shag rug. Your girlfriend calls while you're on your knees, positioning pots and pans beneath the drips. "You cheat too much," she says. "You're lazy and self-ish and you never make me laugh."

You stand and cough and tell her marriage could change all that.
"Well, what about those goddamn extension cords?" she says.
"Extension cords?"

On the radio, DJ Charles Francis says something about the coldest winter in forty years.

"Can't you string them behind furniture like normal people?" she says. "Not straight across the floor?" She screams something about land-mines and subconscious sabotage and slams down the phone.

You step over a few of these cords: bass-amp, floor lamp, mike. Apparently they represent some major character flaw. You try to read them like life-lines on a palm. *Like life-lines on a palm!*

There's a song in this, you tell yourself, and open a bottle of rum. You sit on the rug and listen; if you listen, the music will come.

The popcorn bowl clacks and the mini-wok thwacks. The ice in your glass makes a tinkly-wind-chime sound. But the rhythm needs work. You'll try less ice, more rum. Then you'll add some pathetic lyrics. Later, when the bottle's empty, you can lie among the extension cords and compare the sound of water hitting skin. Maybe it will thud like a broken heart.

—LEE HARRINGTON, FINALIST, BEST SHORT SHORT STORY CONTEST

Stare. It is the way to educate your eye, and more. Stare. Pry. Listen. Eavesdrop. Die knowing something. You are not here long.
—WALKER EVANS

117

The Inside/Outside Story

This exercise owes its origin to Ron Carlson, who has his students ask of all their stories: "Into what life has this trouble come?" and goes on to say that "trouble" is the engine that drives the story. It might even be helpful to think of the trouble as often not having anything to do with the character's life—until it appears in the story. But before that trouble begins, your character has a past, a present life filled with texture and relationships—a life apart from the trouble. Keep in mind what Carlson was quoted as saying in our introduction to Part 7, "Plot": "No one is a blank tablet waiting for trouble; everyone has an agenda, even children and dogs."

The Exercise

First, think of something that might be the trouble in a story—a holdup in a store where your character is shopping, a salesperson who comes to your character's door and refuses to leave, an unexpected and unwelcome guest arrives to spend the night, or the week, and so on. Second create a character to whom this might happen. Give that character a life before they went shopping, before the unwelcome guest appeared, and also give your character an agenda. What is going on in your character's life that will be affected by the story's trouble—soon to appear on the horizon? What are your character's concerns and issues—her agenda—and how will it affect how she acts or reacts when the trouble appears? Then bring on the trouble. It can be as "small" as the splinter in Sheehan McGuirk's story "Pricks" below—or as large and "troublesome" as the blind visitor in Ray Carver's story "Cathedral" on page 338.

The Objective

To be able to imbue your characters with life and your stories with trouble. And to understand the interaction between the two—how the outside story is the engine that drives the story while the inside story is the heart of what really happens.

Pricks

After I slammed my pointer finger in the car door last week, I waited for the swelling to go down. At the tip, it is a small but perfect plum. I ask Mickey if he will take me to the emergency room.

"When? Now?" He hangs his jump rope around his neck and checks his heart rate with the gadget I bought for him last Christmas, when we moved in together.

"Today or tomorrow," I say and lean back against the garage door.

"You know," he says, "they're going to charge you for sticking a stupid pin in it."

He looks at my finger from across the room, I put my hands behind my back.

"It's giving me headaches," I say. He puts down the jump rope and lies back on the mat with his Abflex.

"Did you take the B-12 I left out for you?" he asks.

"I forgot."

He rolls his eyes in mid-ab-contraction, when his chin is tucked into his upper chest.

"Can you?" I ask.

"What, now?"

That night I try sleeping with my arm extended above my head. I prop it up with couch cushions and other pillows from around the house. I am fine for a while and then my arm begins to ache. I lie there staring at the ceiling and rubbing my finger against my lips. With my left arm, I reach over to Mickey and slip my hand beneath his pajamas, then his boxers.

"Now?" He looks over his shoulder at the pile of cushions. I tell him I can't sleep, it hurts too much.

"It's late," he says. It's a little after midnight.

"I know, I'm sorry." I move my hand down. He rolls over and tells me to get some sleep.

I am up at 5:30. After six Aspirin and a shot of Tequila I hide behind the microwave, my finger is no better. At 7:30, I call in sick to work and get Debra.

"You still haven't gone to the hospital?" she says.

"I was waiting, I thought it would go down."

"Do you need a ride?" She sounds annoyed.

"No, of course not." I have to hang up because I'm in too much pain. I lie back on the couch and raise my arm over my head. I try to read magazines, but there are only *Men's Health* and *Health and Fitness*. When I wake up Mickey is squatting beside me, inspecting my finger.

"Did you take your B-12?" he asks.

"What?" I'm still coming out of sleep. "No, I forgot I guess." He is talking funny. I lower my arm slowly so it won't throb too much. Something shines from between his lips. I sit up fast.

"I think," he says standing up, "I should go in through the nail." A sewing needle sparkles on his tongue.

"Mickey," I say, "I want to go to the emergency room." He tips my head down and looks me in the eyes.

"You don't smell like liquor," he says, "do you?"

"What?" I say. He makes a show of looking me up and down, stopping at my feet in his new socks then at the mess of magazines on the floor.

"Are you drunk?"

"Jesus, I am not drunk." I push myself up out of the couch and slip on a magazine. "I'm going to the hospital," I say, walking past him to the bedroom. He grabs my shoulder and turns me around.

"You are not driving drunk." I realize my T-shirt is wet and clinging to my back. My forehead is damp. I could faint.

"Fine," I say. "I don't care, whatever, do it."

"Go sit, I'll get something for the blood." I follow him back into the kitchen and sit down at the table. He's beside me with a rag and a lighter. Under the lamplight, he holds the needle above the flame while the tip turns black. I am watching him for signs of pleasure as I remember it is my only needle.

"Is it going to feel better though?" I ask. He doesn't answer and he doesn't look up from the flame.

—SHEEHAN MCGUIRK

Try again. Fail again. Fail better.
—SAMUEL BECKETT

PART FIFTEEN

A Collection of Short Short Stories

20/20

Linda Brewer

By the time they reached Indiana, Bill realized that Ruthie, his driving companion, was incapable of theoretical debate. She drove okay, she went halves on gas, etc., but she refused to argue. She didn't seem to know how. Bill was used to East Coast women who disputed everything he said, every step of the way. Ruthie stuck to simple observation, like "Look—cows." He chalked it up to the fact that she was from rural Ohio and thrilled to death to be anywhere else.

She didn't mind driving into the setting sun. The third evening out Bill rested his eyes while she cruised along making the occasional announcement.

"Indian paintbrush. A golden eagle."

Miles later he frowned. There was no Indian paintbrush, that he knew of, near Chicago.

The next evening, driving, Ruthie said, "I never thought I'd see a Bigfoot in real life." Bill turned and looked at the side of the road streaming innocently out behind them. Two red spots winked back—reflectors nailed to a tree stump.

"Ruthie, I'll drive," he said. She stopped the car and they changed places in the light of the evening star.

"I'm so glad I got to come with you," Ruthie said. Her eyes were big, blue, and capable of seeing wonderful sights. A white buffalo near Fargo. A UFO above Twin Falls. A handsome genius in the person of Bill himself. This last vision came to her in Spokane and Bill decided to let it ride.

Excuses I Have Already Used

Antonia Clark

He hit me first. She called me four-eyes. The dog ate it. It's not my turn. Everybody else is doing it. My alarm didn't go off. I didn't know it was due. My grandmother died. It went through the wash. My roommate threw it in the trash. He got me drunk. He said he loved me. He said he'd pull out in time. She pulled right out in front of me. I didn't know how you felt. I was only trying to help. He backed me into a corner. It just slipped out of my hand. I was in a hurry. It was on sale. I needed a little pick-me-up. It calms my nerves. They looked too good to resist. It sounded like such a good deal. Hospitals give me the creeps. He's probably tired of visitors. He didn't even recognize me last time. There were extra expenses this month. My vote wouldn't have counted anyway. The kids were driving me nuts. I didn't have time. My watch must have stopped. I couldn't find the instructions. The dishwasher's broken. Somebody else used it last. I forgot my checkbook. I gave at the office. I've got a headache. I've got my period. It's too hot. I'm too tired. I had to work late. I got stuck in traffic. I couldn't get away. I couldn't let them down. I didn't know how to say no. We were thrown together by circumstance. He made me feel like a woman again. I didn't know what I was doing. It seemed like a good idea at the time. I've been up to my eyeballs. The flight was delayed. The car broke down. My hard drive crashed. I've got a call waiting. I'm flat out. Life is too short. It's too late to go back.

Mackerel Night

Laurence Davies

In another night or so the mackerel will come, hungry for the myriad tiny creatures that live by their own light. During the highest tides of summer, when sun warms sand and sand warms sea, the warmth draws migrant plankton whose iridescent, savory foaming lures the starving fish. Last year so many mackerel shoaled and jostled in the shallows that we'd catch them with our hands. Then, in nothing but our dripping shirts, we'd race to the dark hotel, steal into the moonlit kitchen, and quietly bring out the knives. One swift slash to underbelly, two twists for gut and gills and, scales still radiant, the cleft fish slipped into the lightly buttered pan as if it were another sea.

Tonight, I shed my clothes above high-water mark and run to meet the tide. As the sea tugs at my feet, I stoop and straighten. A froth of stars sparkles in my cupped hands and drifts along the soft sides of my arms. I imagine smoothing the drift over shoulders, breasts, hips, and into my mound so stars would shine among black curls just where you loved to hunt them down.

You ply your knife in Boston now, prying open oysters, loosening the black threads of shrimp and lobster. Only a band of phosphorescent ocean lies between us. And if I swam to you, West Sou'West three thousand miles, what starry foam, what knife, what melted butter would be waiting, waiting to undo me?

The Custodian

Brian Hinshaw

The job would get boring if you didn't mix it up a little. Like this woman in 14-A, the nurses called her the mockingbird, start any song and this old lady would sing it through. Couldn't speak, couldn't eat a lick of solid food, but she sang like a house on fire. So for a kick, I would get in there with my mop and such, prop the door open with the bucket, and set her going. She was best at the songs you'd sing with a group—"Oh Susanna," campfire stuff. Any kind of Christmas song worked good, too, and it always cracked the nurses if I could get her into "Let it Snow" during a heat spell. We'd try to make her take up a song from the radio or some of the old songs with cursing in them, but she would never go for those. Although I once had her do "How dry I am" while Nurse Winchell fussed with the catheter.

Yesterday, her daughter or maybe granddaughter comes in while 14-A and I were partways into "Auld Lang Syne" and the daughter says "oh oh oh" like she had interrupted scintillating conversation and then she takes a long look at 14-A lying there in the gurney with her eyes shut and her curled-up hands, taking a cup of kindness yet. And the daughter looks at me the way a girl does at the end of an old movie and she says "my god," says "you're an angel," and now I can't do it anymore, can hardly step in her room.

Girl

Jamaica Kincaid

Wash the white clothes on Monday and put them on the stone heap; wash the color clothes on Tuesday and put them on the clothesline to dry; don't walk barehead in the hot sun; cook pumpkin fritters in very hot sweet oil; soak your little cloths right after you take them off; when buying cotton to make yourself a nice blouse, be sure that it doesn't have gum on it, because that way it won't hold up well after a wash; soak salt fish overnight before you cook it; is it true that you sing benna in Sunday school?; always eat your food in such a way that it won't turn someone else's stomach; on Sundays try to walk like a lady and not like the slut you are so bent on becoming; don't sing benna in Sunday school; you mustn't speak to wharf-rat boys, not even to give directions; don't eat fruits on the street—flies will follow you; *but I don't sing benna on Sundays at all and never in Sunday school;* this is how to sew on a button; this is how to make a buttonhole for the button you have just sewed on; this is how to hem a dress when you see the hem coming down and so to prevent yourself from looking like the slut I know you are so bent on becoming; this is how you iron your father's khaki shirt so that it doesn't have a crease; this is how you iron your father's khaki pants so that they don't have a crease; this is how you grow okra—far from the house, because okra tree harbors red ants; when you are growing dasheen, make sure it gets plenty of water or else it makes your throat itch when you are eating it; this is how you sweep a corner; this is how you sweep a whole house; this is how you sweep a yard; this is how you smile to someone you don't like too much; this is how you smile to someone you don't like at all; this is how you smile to someone you like completely; this is how you set a table for tea; this is how you set a table for dinner; this is how you set a table for dinner with an important guest; this is how you set a table for lunch; this is how you set a table for breakfast; this is how to behave in the presence of men who don't know you very well, and this way they won't recognize immediately the slut I have warned you against becoming; be sure to wash every day, even if it is with your own spit; don't squat down to play marbles—you are not a boy, you know; don't pick people's flowers—you might catch something; don't throw stones at blackbirds, because it might not be a blackbird at all; this is how to make a bread pudding; this is how to make doukona; this is how to make pepper pot; this is how to make a good medicine for a cold; this is how to make a good medicine to throw away a child before it even becomes a child; this is how to catch a fish; this is how to throw back a fish you don't like, and that way something bad won't fall on you; this is how to bully a man; this is how a man bullies you; this is how to love a man, and if this doesn't work there are other ways, and if they don't work don't feel too bad about giving up; this is how to spit up in the air if you feel like it, and this is how to move quick so that it doesn't fall on you; this is how to make ends meet; always squeeze bread to make sure it's fresh; *but what if the baker won't let me feel the bread?;* you mean to say that after all you are really going to be the kind of woman who the baker won't let near the bread?

Confirmation Names

Mariette Lippo

W e studied the saints, slipped the boys in through a break in the hockey field's fence, and led them to the woods the nuns had deemed "off-limits."

Vicky let a boy read her palm there. He told her her lifeline was short, that she'd better learn reverence for the moment. She cried for weeks before choosing the name Barbara, patron saint of those in danger of sudden death.

Susan said she would only go "so far," but no one knew what that meant. Boys went nuts trying to find out. They loved to untie her waist-long hair, to see it fan underneath her. She loved their love letters, the way they'd straighten up whenever she walked by. She chose Thecla, who'd caused the lions to "forget themselves;" instead of tearing her to shreds, they licked her feet.

Jackie couldn't wait for anything. The nuns told her impatience was her cross. Even the lunches her mother packed would be gone before ten, and she'd be left sorry, wanting more. She'd chosen Anthony, "the Finder," in a last-ditch effort to recover what she'd lost. But the nuns gave her Euphrasia, the virgin, who'd hauled huge rocks from place to place to rid her soul of temptation.

Before mass, we'd check her back for leaves.

None of us, of course, chose Magdalen, the whore. She was the secret patron whose spirit, we believed, watched over us from the trees. She was the woman who'd managed to turn her passion sacred. She was the saint who turned the flesh Divine.

It Would've Been Hot

Melissa McCracken

The first and only night he and I had sex his apartment building burned down and though the "official" cause was 2B's hotplate, I wanted to blame him as I huddled in his winter coat and boxer shorts beside the fire truck—blame him because he'd been reckless and impatient, hadn't used a condom or even the couch, instead mauling me in his hallway, all long before I said, "Do you smell that?" and he threw open the front door, drowning us in choking smoke before he slammed it shut, coughing, and I tried to yell "back stairs" but I couldn't breathe, yet I saw him reach up with the flat of his palm and place it against the now closed door (like in those old school-safety films) just to see, had he bothered, if it would've been hot—the same way he reached out, as the fireman pulled away, and placed his hand against the small of my back in a gesture I guess was meant to be tender but instead was after the fact.

My Mother's Gifts

Judith Claire Mitchell

While I sleep, my dead mother revises my poetry. I wake to find my pet adjectives—indigo, lone, cozy—deleted and my childhood traumas—a swan biting my finger, the bearded man who followed me home—inserted. I tend to write about domestic life. Raising tomatoes. Folding towels. My mother adds ice cubes cracking in scotch, wildcats roaming backyards, poets sleeping with poets.

Before she died, my mother bequeathed me her editor, an older man with eyes as blue as Johnny jump-ups and a very deep tan. He takes me to lunch when I'm in the city. He reads my work over sushi. Nice, he says. My mother sits in the chair next to mine, oblivious to my purse on the cushion. She beams when the editor tells me I resemble her. Have you ever twisted your hair in a knot? he asks. Did she leave you any of those wild earrings? My mother leans back, young, beautiful, and lights a cigarette. She never speaks but she expresses herself.

Tell me your happiest memory, the editor says. Then, waving his hand, he erases the question. No, he says. The most bitter.

I pick one at random. An evening before one of her readings. I'm eleven and stretched on her bed while she wriggles into a fuchsia sheath. Let me go with you, I say. When she shakes her head her earrings ring like a New Year's toast. You're too young, she says. Your poems still rhyme. She presses a tissue to her lips, tosses it so it floats toward me. Her goodbye kiss. A hot pink smear.

Write about it, the editor says. What is poetry, after all? Personal stuff. Gossip. My mother pulls out her notebook, starts scribbling.

Before we part, the editor takes my wineglass, rubs away my own lipstick smear with the pad of his thumb. Be safe, he says. He kisses my cheek. He is worried I'll die the same way she did, as if swallowing pills while swimming naked in a neighbor's pool runs in families like poor circulation.

On the drive back to Connecticut my mother writes a new poem for me to claim as my own. It tells how I will actually die—a very old woman with bad knees toppling down steep basement stairs while carrying an overflowing laundry basket. She writes about how embarrassed I'll be when the *Times'* obituary compares our deaths. The poem is wry and clever and hurts my feelings. When we get home I type it up and fax it to the editor. He replies at once. Now we're talking, he says.

Sometimes I question the morality of what we are doing. Other times I wonder if this is how every poet breaks in. Once I gave us both credit—by

Catherine and Erica Blessing, I wrote—but next morning there was a slash through her name, a pink lipstick kiss on mine.

My mother never questions anything, never did. Not her borrowed images, not her summers with jaded laureates, not her leaving me home with stepfathers.

Still, why hold a grudge? She's with me now, maybe to stay until I fall down the stairs. And certainly she's generous with her gifts—her talent, her time. Both are boundless.

And yet, there are times I'm ungrateful.

Tonight I lock my bedroom door so I can write a poem about sautéing onions. The words come fast. When I finish I fold the page in half, hide it beneath my pillow. I fall asleep and dream the editor has come to visit. He praises my herb garden and the shape of my calves and my subtle interior rhymes.

It isn't quite dawn when I wake up, first surprised to be alone, then reluctant to admit I'm not. I glance around my bedroom several times to confirm that the windows are locked, the key in the latch. It doesn't matter. I know what woke me: the sound of feet shuffling several inches above the carpet.

I reach under the pillow. I don't have to read the poem to know that it's better. Even the pillowcase smells of raw onion. She has turned paper torn from a notebook into the vegetable's frail husk.

I hold the onion's skin toward the window. Muffled light shines through it. A corner crumbles, scraps of peel fall to my comforter. I rub the opposite corner between my fingers. It disintegrates, too. I rub away the other corners; I rub away the poem's heart. There is still some power in flesh and unburied bones.

Pencil to lined paper, I go at that poem again. I slice away the beginning, chop off the ending, add childhood memories my mother doesn't know I have. I include all she left out, things so simple they would never occur to her. The way a paring knife's handle fits in a palm. A Vidalia's green meat, more tempting and dangerous than any apple. The cook herself—she holds her hair away from the blue burner as she bends over a pan. White slivers turn translucent. She likes how they squirm in the hot, spitting oil.

The raw juice on my fingers, the fumes and smoke in my bedroom, sting my eyes. I keep it anyway. Longer and longer. Better and better. How will I know when to stop?

Cigarette smoke haloes my head. That's easy, my mother says. When the tears come, of course.

The New Year

Pamela Painter

It's late Christmas Eve at Spinelli's when Dominic presents us, the waitstaff, with his dumb idea of a bonus—Italian hams in casings so tight they shimmer like Gilda's gold lamé stockings.

At home, Gilda's waiting up for me with a surprise of her own: my stuff from the last three months is sitting on the stoop. Arms crossed, scarlet nails tapping the satin sleeves of her robe, she says she's heard about Fiona. I balance the ham on my hip and pack my things—CD's, weights, a vintage Polaroid—into garbage bags she's provided free of charge. Then I let it all drop and offer up the ham in both hands, cradling it as if it might have been our child. She doesn't want any explanations—or the ham.

Fiona belongs to Dominic, and we are a short sad story of one night's restaurant despair. But the story's out and for sure I don't want Dominic coming after my ham.

Under Gilda's unforgiving eye, I sling my garbage bags into the trunk of the car and head west. The ham glistens beside me in the passenger's seat. Somewhere in Indiana I strap it into a seat belt.

I stop to call, but Gilda hangs up every time. So I send her pictures of my trip instead: The Ham under the silver arch of St. Louis; The Ham at the Grand Canyon; The Ham in Las Vegas. I'm taking a picture of The Ham in the Pacific when a big wave washes it out to sea. I send the picture anyway: The Ham in the Pacific Undertow. In this picture, you can't tell which of us is missing.

Wants

Grace Paley

I saw my ex-husband in the street. I was sitting on the steps of the new library.

Hello, my life, I said. We had once been married for twenty-seven years, so I felt justified.

He said, What? What life? No life of mine.

I said, O.K. I don't argue when there's real disagreement. I got up and went into the library to see how much I owed them.

The librarian said $32 even and you've owed it for eighteen years. I didn't deny anything. Because I don't understand how time passes. I have had those books. I have often thought of them. The library is only two blocks away.

My ex-husband followed me to the Books Returned desk. He interrupted the librarian, who had more to tell. In many ways, he said, as I look back, I attribute the dissolution of our marriage to the fact that you never invited the Bertrams to dinner.

That's possible, I said. But really, if you remember: first, my father was sick that Friday, then the children were born, then I had those Tuesday-night meetings, then the war began. Then we didn't seem to know them any more. But you're right. I should have had them to dinner.

I gave the librarian a check for $32. Immediately she trusted me, put my past behind her, wiped the record clean, which is just what most other municipal and/or state bureaucracies will *not* do.

I checked out the two Edith Wharton books I had just returned because I'd read them so long ago and they are more apropos now than ever. They were *The House of Mirth* and *The Children*, which is about how life in the United States in New York changed in twenty-seven years fifty years ago. A nice thing I do remember is breakfast, my ex-husband said. I was surprised. All we ever had was coffee. Then I remembered there was a hole in the back of the kitchen closet which opened into the apartment next door. There, they always ate sugar-cured smoked bacon. It gave us a very grand feeling about breakfast, but we never got stuffed and sluggish.

That was when we were poor, I said.

When were we ever rich? he asked.

Oh, as time went on, as our responsibilities increased, we didn't go in need. You took adequate financial care, I reminded him. The children went to camp four weeks a year and in decent ponchos with sleeping bags and boots, just like everyone else. They looked very nice. Our place was warm in winter, and we had nice red pillows and things.

I wanted a sailboat, he said. But you didn't want anything.

Don't be bitter, I said. It's never too late.

No, he said with a great deal of bitterness. I may get a sailboat. As a matter of fact I have money down on an eighteen-foot two-rigger. I'm doing well this year and can look forward to better. But as for you, it's too late. You'll always want nothing.

He had had a habit throughout the twenty-seven years of making a narrow remark which, like a plumber's snake, could work its way through the ear down the throat, halfway to my heart. He would then disappear, leaving me choking with equipment. What I mean is, I sat down on the library steps and he went away.

I looked through *The House of Mirth*, but lost interest. I felt extremely accused. Now, it's true, I'm short of requests and absolute requirements. But I do want *something*.

I want, for instance, to be a different person. I want to be the woman who brings these two books back in two weeks. I want to be the effective citizen who changes the school system and addresses the Board of Estimate on the troubles of this dear urban center.

I *had* promised my children to end the war before they grew up.

I wanted to have been married forever to one person, my ex-husband or my present one. Either has enough character for a whole life, which as it turns out is really not such a long time. You couldn't exhaust either man's qualities or get under the rock of his reasons in one short life.

Just this morning I looked out the window to watch the street for a while and saw that the little sycamores the city had dreamily planted a couple of years before the kids were born had come that day to the prime of their lives.

Well! I decided to bring those two books back to the library. Which proves that when a person or an event comes along to jolt or appraise me I *can* take some appropriate action, although I am better known for my hospitable remarks.

No One's a Mystery

Elizabeth Tallent

For my eighteenth birthday Jack gave me a five-year diary with a latch and a little key, light as a dime. I was sitting beside him scratching at the lock, which didn't seem to want to work, when he thought he saw his wife's Cadillac in the distance, coming toward us. He pushed me down onto the dirty floor of the pickup and kept one hand on my head while I inhaled the musk of his cigarettes in the dashboard ashtray and sang along with Rosanne Cash on the tape deck. We'd been drinking tequila and the bottle was between his legs, resting up against his crotch, where the seam of his Levi's was bleached linen-white, though the Levi's were nearly new. I don't know why his Levi's always bleached like that, along the seams and at the knees. In a curve of cloth his zipper glinted, gold.

"It's her," he said. "She keeps the lights on in the daytime. I can't think of a single habit in a woman that irritates me more than that." When he saw that I was going to stay still he took his hand from my head and ran it through his own dark hair.

"Why does she?" I said.

"She thinks it's safer. Why does she need to be safer? She's driving exactly fifty-five miles an hour. She believes in those signs: 'Speed Monitored by Aircraft.' It doesn't matter that you can look up and see that the sky is empty."

"She'll see your lips move, Jack. She'll know you're talking to someone."

"She'll think I'm singing along with the radio."

He didn't lift his hand, just raised the fingers in salute while the pressure of his palm steadied the wheel, and I heard the Cadillac honk twice, musically; he was driving easily eighty miles an hour. I studied his boots. The elk heads stitched into the leather were bearded with frayed thread, the toes were scuffed, and there was a compact wedge of muddy manure between the heel and the sole—the same boots he'd been wearing for the two years I'd known him. On the tape deck Rosanne Cash sang, "Nobody's into me, no one's a mystery."

"Do you think she's getting famous because of who her daddy is or for herself?" Jack said.

"There are about a hundred pop tops on the floor, did you know that? Some little kid could cut a bare foot on one of these, Jack."

"No little kids get into this truck except for you."

"How come you let it get so dirty?"

"'How come,'" he mocked. "You even sound like a kid. You can get back into the seat now, if you want. She's not going to look over her shoulder and see you."

"How do you know?"

"I just know," he said. "Like I know I'm going to get meat loaf for supper. It's in the air. Like I know what you'll be writing in that diary."

"What will I be writing?" I knelt on my side of the seat and craned around to look at the butterfly of dust printed on my jeans. Outside the window Wyoming was dazzling in the heat. The wheat was fawn and yellow and parted smoothly by the thin dirt road. I could smell the water in the irrigation ditches hidden in the wheat.

"Tonight you'll write, 'love Jack. This is my birthday present from him. I can't imagine anybody loving anybody more than I love Jack.'"

"I can't."

"In a year you'll write 'I wonder what I ever really saw in Jack. I wonder why I spent so many days just riding around in his pickup. It's true he taught me something about sex. It's true there wasn't ever much else to do in Cheyenne.'"

"I won't write that."

"In two years you'll write, 'I wonder what that old guy's name was, the one with the curly hair and the filthy dirty pickup truck and time on his hands.'"

"I won't write that."

"No?"

"Tonight I'll write, 'I love Jack. This is my birthday present from him. I can't imagine anybody loving anybody more than I love Jack.'"

"No, you can't." he said. "You can't imagine it."

"In a year I'll write, 'Jack should be home any minute now. The table's set—my grandmother's linen and her old silver and the yellow candles left over from the wedding—but I don't know if I can wait until after the trout à la Navarra to make love to him.'"

"It must have been a fast divorce."

"In two years I'll write, 'Jack should be home by now. Little Jack is hungry for his supper. He said his first word today besides "Mama" and "Papa." He said "kaka."'"

Jack laughed. "He was probably trying to finger-paint with kaka on the bathroom wall when you heard him say it."

"In three years I'll write, 'My nipples are a little sore from nursing Eliza Rosamund.'"

"Rosamund. Every little girl should have a middle name she hates."

"'Her breath smells like vanilla and her eyes are just Jack's color of blue.'"

"That's nice," Jack said.

"So, which one do you like?"

"I like yours," he said. "But I believe mine."

"It doesn't matter. I believe mine."

"Not in your heart of hearts, you don't."

"You're wrong."

"I'm not wrong," he said. "And her breath would smell like your milk, and it's kind of a bittersweet smell, if you want to know the truth."

Vision Out of the Corner of One Eye

Luisa Valenzuela

It's true, he put his hand on my ass and I was about to scream bloody murder when the bus passed by a church and he crossed himself. He's a good sort after all, I said to myself. Maybe he didn't do it on purpose or maybe his right hand didn't know what his left hand was up to. I tried to move farther back in the bus—searching for explanations is one thing and letting yourself be pawed is another—but more passengers got on and there was no way I could do it. My wiggling to get out of his reach only let him get a better hold on me and even fondle me. I was nervous and finally moved over. He moved over, too. We passed by another church but he didn't notice it and when he raised his hand to his face it was to wipe the sweat off his forehead. I watched him out of the corner of one eye, pretending that nothing was happening, or at any rate not making him think I liked it. It was impossible to move a step farther and he began jiggling me. I decided to get even and put my hand on his behind. A few blocks later I got separated from him. Then I was swept along by the passengers getting off the bus and now I'm sorry I lost him so suddenly because there were only 7,400 pesos in his wallet and I'd have gotten more out of him if we'd been alone. He seemed affectionate. And very generous.

—Translated by Helen Lane

PART SIXTEEN

A Collection of Short Stories

Happy Endings

Margaret Atwood

John and Mary meet.
What happens next?
If you want a happy ending, try A.

A. John and Mary fall in love and get married. They both have worthwhile and remunerative jobs which they find stimulating and challenging. They buy a charming house. Real estate values go up. Eventually, when they can afford live-in help, they have two children, to whom they are devoted. The children turn out well. John and Mary have a stimulating and challenging sex life and worthwhile friends. They go on fun vacations together. They retire. They both have hobbies which they find stimulating and challenging. Eventually they die. This is the end of the story.

B. Mary falls in love with John but John doesn't fall in love with Mary. He merely uses her body for selfish pleasure and ego gratification of a tepid kind. He comes to her apartment twice a week and she cooks him dinner, you'll notice that he doesn't even consider her worth the price of a dinner out, and after he's eaten the dinner he fucks her and after that he falls asleep, while she does the dishes so he won't think she's untidy, having all those dirty dishes lying around, and puts on fresh lipstick so she'll look good when he wakes up, but when he wakes up he doesn't even notice, he puts on his socks and his shorts and his pants and his shirt and his tie and his shoes, the reverse order from the one in which he took them off. He doesn't take off Mary's clothes, she takes them off herself, she acts as if she's dying for it every time, not because she likes sex exactly, she doesn't, but she wants John to think she does because if they do it often enough surely he'll get used to her, he'll come to depend on her and they will get married, but John goes out the door with hardly so much as a good-night and three days later he turns up at six o'clock and they do the whole thing over again.

Mary gets run-down. Crying is bad for your face, everyone knows that and so does Mary but she can't stop. People at work notice. Her friends tell her John is a rat, a pig, a dog, he isn't good enough for her, but she can't believe it. Inside John, she thinks, is another John, who is much nicer. This other John will emerge like a butterfly from a cocoon, a Jack from a box, a pit from a prune, if the first John is only squeezed enough.

One evening John complains about the food. He has never complained about the food before. Mary is hurt.

Her friends tell her they've seen him in a restaurant with another woman, whose name is Madge. It's not even Madge that finally gets to Mary: it's the restaurant. John has never taken Mary to a restaurant. Mary collects all the sleeping pills and aspirins she can find, and takes them and a half a bottle of sherry. You can see what kind of a woman she is by the fact that it's not even whiskey. She leaves a note for John. She hopes he'll discover her and get her to the hospital in time and repent and then they can get married, but this fails to happen and she dies.

John marries Madge and everything continues as in A.

C.   John, who is an older man, falls in love with Mary, and Mary, who is only twenty-two, feels sorry for him because he's worried about his hair falling out. She sleeps with him even though she's not in love with him. She met him at work. She's in love with someone called James, who is twenty-two also and not yet ready to settle down.

John on the contrary settled down long ago: this is what is bothering him. John has a steady, respectable job and is getting ahead in his field, but Mary isn't impressed by him, she's impressed by James, who has a motorcycle and a fabulous record collection. But James is often away on his motorcycle, being free. Freedom isn't the same for girls, so in the meantime Mary spends Thursday evenings with John. Thursdays are the only days John can get away.

John is married to a woman called Madge and they have two children, a charming house which they bought just before the real estate values went up, and hobbies which they find stimulating and challenging, when they have the time. John tells Mary how important she is to him, but of course he can't leave his wife because a commitment is a commitment. He goes on about this more than is necessary and Mary finds it boring, but older men can keep it up longer so on the whole she has a fairly good time.

One day James breezes in on his motorcycle with some top-grade California hybrid and James and Mary get higher than you'd believe possible and they climb into bed. Everything becomes very underwater, but along comes John, who has a key to Mary's apartment. He finds them stoned and entwined. He's hardly in any position to be jealous, considering Madge, but nevertheless he's overcome with despair. Finally he's middle-aged, in two years he'll be bald as an egg and he can't stand it. He purchases a handgun, saying he needs it for target practice—this is the thin part of the plot, but it can be dealt with later—and shoots the two of them and himself.

Madge, after a suitable period of mourning, marries an understanding man called Fred and everything continues as in A, but under different names.

D. Fred and Madge have no problems. They get along exceptionally well and are good at working out any little difficulties that may arise. But their charming house is by the seashore and one day a giant tidal wave approaches. Real estate values go down. The rest of the story is about what caused the tidal wave and how they escape from it. They do, though thousands drown, but Fred and Madge are virtuous and lucky. Finally on high ground they clasp each other, wet and dripping and grateful, and continue as in A.

E. Yes, but Fred has a bad heart. The rest of the story is about how kind and understanding they both are until Fred dies. Then Madge devotes herself to charity work until the end of A. If you like, it can be "Madge," "cancer," "guilty and confused," and "bird watching."

F. If you think this is all too bourgeois, make John a revolutionary and Mary a counterespionage agent and see how far that gets you. Remember, this is Canada. You'll still end up with A, though in between you may get a lustful brawling saga of passionate involvement, a chronicle of our times, sort of.

You'll have to face it, the endings are the same however you slice it. Don't be deluded by any other endings, they're all fake, either deliberately fake, with malicious intent to deceive, or just motivated by excessive optimism if not by downright sentimentality.

The only authentic ending is the one provided here:

John and Mary die. John and Mary die. John and Mary die.

So much for endings. Beginnings are always more fun. True connoisseurs, however, are known to favor the stretch in between, since it's the hardest to do anything with.

That's about all that can be said for plots, which anyway are just one thing after another, a what and a what and a what.

Now try How and Why.

Christmas Eve at Johnson's Drugs N Goods

Toni Cade Bambara

I was probably the first to spot them cause I'd been watching the entrance to the store on the lookout for my daddy, knowing that if he didn't show soon, he wouldn't be coming at all. His new family would be expecting him to spend the holidays with them. For the first half of my shift, I'd raced the cleaning cart down the aisles doing a slapdash job on the signs and glass cages, eager to stay in view of the doorway. And look like Johnson's kept getting bigger, swelling, sprawling itself all over the corner lot, just to keep me from the door, to wear me out in the marathon vigil.

In point of fact, Johnson's Drugs N Goods takes up less than one-third of the block. But it's laid out funny in crisscross aisles so you get to feeling like a rat in an endless maze. Plus the ceilings are high and the fluorescents a blazing white. And Mrs. Johnson's got these huge signs sectioning off the spaces—Tobacco Drugs Housewares, etc.—like it was some big-time department store. The thing is, till the two noisy women came in, it felt like a desert under a blazing sun. Piper in Tobacco even had on shades. The new dude in Drugs looked like he was at the end of a wrong-way telescope. I got to feeling like a nomad with the cleaning cart, trekking across the sands with no end in sight, wandering. The overhead lights creating mirages and racing up my heart till I'd realize that wasn't my daddy in the parking lot, just the poster-board Santa Claus. Or that wasn't my daddy in the entrance way, just the Burma Shave man in a frozen stance. Then I'd tried to make out pictures of Daddy getting off the bus at the terminal, or driving a rented car past the Chamber of Commerce building, or sitting jammed-leg in one of them DC point-o-nine brand X planes, coming to see me.

By the time the bus pulled into the lot and the two women in their big-city clothes hit the door, I'd decided Daddy was already at the house waiting for me, knowing that for a mirage too, since Johnson's is right across from the railroad and bus terminals and the house is a dollar-sixty cab away. And I know he wouldn't feature going to the house on the off chance of running into Mama. Or even if he escaped that fate, having to sit in the parlor with his hat in his lap while Aunt Harriet looks him up and down grunting, too busy with the latest crossword puzzle contest to offer the man some supper. And Uncle Henry talking a blue streak bout how he outfoxed the city council or somethin and nary a cold beer in sight for my daddy.

But then the two women came banging into the store and I felt better. Right away the store stopped sprawling, got fixed. And we all got pulled together from our various zones to one focal point—them. Changing up the whole atmosphere of the place fore they even got into the store proper. Before we knew it, we were all smiling, looking halfway like you supposed to on Christmas Eve, even if you do got to work for ole lady Johnson, who don't give you no slack whatever the holiday.

"What the hell does this mean, Ethel?" the one in the fur coat say, talking loud and fast, yanking on the rails that lead the way into the store. "What are we, cattle? Being herded into the blankety-blank store and in my fur coat," she grumbles, boosting herself up between the rails, swinging her body along like the kids do in the park.

Me and Piper look at each other and smile. Then Piper moves down to the edge of the counter right under the Tobacco sign so as not to miss nothing. Madeen over in Housewares waved to me to ask what's up and I just shrug. I'm fascinated by the women.

"Look here," the one called Ethel say, drawing the words out lazy slow. "Do you got a token for this sucker?" She's shoving hard against the turnstile folks supposed to exit through. Pushing past and grunting, the turnstile crank cranking like it gonna bust, her Christmas corsage of holly and bells just ajingling and hanging by a thread. Then she gets through and stumbles toward the cigar counter and leans back against it, studying the turnstile hard. It whips back around in place, making scrunching noises like it's been abused.

"You know one thing," she say, dropping her face onto her coat collar so Piper'd know he's being addressed.

"Ma'am?"

"That is one belligerent bad boy, that thing right there."

Piper laughs his prizewinning laugh and starts touching the stacks of gift-wrapped stuff, case the ladies in the market for pipe tobacco or something. Two or three of the customers who'd been falling asleep in the magazines coming to life now, inching forward. Phototropism, I'd call it, if somebody asked me for a word.

The one in the fur coat's coming around now the right way—if you don't count the stiff-elbow rail-walking she was doing—talking about "Oh, my God, I can walk, I can walk, Ethel, praise de lawd."

The two women watching Piper touch the cigars, the humidors, the gift-wrapped boxes. Mostly he's touching himself, cause George Lee Piper love him some George Lee Piper. Can't blame him. Piper be fine.

"You work on commissions, young man?" Fur Coat asking.

"No, ma'am."

The two women look at each other. They look over toward the folks inching forward. They look at me gliding by with the cleaning cart. They look back at each other and shrug.

"So what's his problem?" Ethel says in a stage whisper. "Why he so hot to sell us something?"

"Search me." Fur Coat starts flapping her coat and frisking herself. "You know?" she asking me.

"It's a mystery to me," I say, doing my best to run ole man Samson over. He sneaking around trying to jump Madeen in Housewares. And it is a mystery to me how come Piper always so eager to make a sale. You'd think he had half interest in the place. He says it's because it's his job, and after all, the Johnsons are Black folks. I guess so, I guess so. Me, I just clean the place and stay busy in case Mrs. J is in the prescription booth, peeking out over the top of the glass.

When I look around again, I see that the readers are suddenly very interested in cigars. They crowding around Ethel and Fur Coat. Piper kinda embarrassed by all the attention, though fine as he is, he oughta be used to it. His expression's cool but his hands give him away, sliding around the counter like he shuffling a deck of slippery cards. Fur Coat nudges Ethel and they bend over to watch the hands, doing these chicken-head jerkings. The readers take up positions just like a director was hollering "Places" at em. Piper, never one to disappoint an audience, starts zipping around these invisible walnut shells. Right away Fur Coat whips out a little red change purse and slaps a dollar bill on the counter. Ethel dips deep into her coat pocket, bending her knees and being real comic, then plunks down some change. Ole man Sampson tries to boost up on my cleaning cart to see the shells that ain't there.

"Scuse me, Mr. Sampson," I say, speeding the cart up sudden so that quite naturally he falls off, the dirty dog.

Piper is snapping them imaginary shells around like nobody's business, one of the readers leaning over another's shoulder, staring pop-eyed.

"All right now, everybody step back," Ethel announces. She waves the crowd back and pushes up one coat sleeve, lifts her fist into the air and jerks out one stiff finger from the bunch, and damn if the readers don't lift their heads to behold in amazement this wondrous finger.

"That, folks," Fur Coat explains, "is what is known as the indicator finger. The indicator is about to indicate the indicatee."

"Say wha?" Dirty ole man Sampson decides he'd rather sneak up on Madeen than watch the show.

"What's going on over there?" Miz Della asks me. I spray the watch case and make a big thing of wiping it and ignoring her. But then the new dude in Drugs hollers over the same thing.

"Christmas cheer gone to the head. A coupla vaudevillians," I say. He smiles, and Miz Della says "Ohhh" like I was talking to her.

"This one," Ethel says, planting a finger exactly one-quarter of an inch from the countertop.

Piper dumb-shows a lift of the shell, turning his face away as though he can't bear to look and find the elusive pea ain't there and he's gonna have to take the ladies' money. Then his eyes swivel around and sneak a peek and widen, lighting up his whole face in a prizewinning grin.

"You got it," he shouts.

The women grab each other by the coat shoulders and jump each other up and down. And I look toward the back cause I know Mrs. J got to be hearing all this carrying-on, and on payday if Mr. J ain't handing out the checks, she's going to give us some long lecture about decorum and what it means to be on board at Johnson's Drugs N Goods. I wheel over to the glass jars and punch bowls, wanting alibi distance just in case. And also to warn Madeen about Sampson gaining on her. He's ducking down behind the coffeepots, walking squat and shameless.

"Pay us our money, young man," Fur Coat is demanding, rapping her knuckles on the counter.

"Yeah, what kind of crooked shell game is you running here in this joint?" say Ethel, finding a good foil character to play.

"We should hate to have to turn the place out, young man."

"It out," echoes Ethel.

The women nod to the crowd and a coupla folks giggle. And Piper tap-taps on the cash register like he shonuff gonna give em they money. I'd rather they turned the place out myself. I want to call my daddy. Only way any of us are going to get home in time to dress for the Christmas dance at the center is for the women to turn it out. Like I say, Piper ain't too clear about the worker's interest versus management's, as the dude in Drugs would say it. So he's light-tapping and quite naturally the cash drawer does not come out. He's yanking some unseen dollar from the not-there drawer and handing it over. Damn if Fur Coat don't snatch it, deal out the bills to herself and her friend and then make a big production out of folding the money flat and jamming it in that little red change purse.

"I wanna thank you," Ethel says, strolling off, swinging her pocketbook so that the crowd got to back up and disperse. Fur Coat spreads her coat and curtsies.

"A pleasure to do business with you ladies," Piper says, tipping his hat, looking kinda disappointed that he didn't sell em something. Tipping his hat the way he tipped the shells, cause you know Mrs. J don't allow no hats indoors. I came to work in slacks one time and she sent me home to change and docked me too. I wear a gele some times just to mess her around, and you can tell she trying to figure out if she'll go for it or not. The woman is crazy. Not Uncle Henry type crazy, but Black property owner type crazy. She thinks this is a museum, which is why folks don't hardly come in here to shop. That's okay cause we all get to know each other well. It's not okay cause it's a drag to look busy. If you look like you ain't buckling under a weight of work, Mrs. J will have you count the Band-Aids in the boxes to make sure the company ain't pulling a fast one. The woman crazy.

Now Uncle Henry type crazy is my kind of crazy. The type crazy to get you a job. He march into the "saloon" as he calls it and tells Leon D that he is not an equal opportunity employer and that he, Alderman Henry Peoples, is going to put some fire to his ass. So soon's summer comes, me and Madeen got us a job at Leon D. Salon. One of them hushed, funeral type shops with skinny models parading around for customers corseted and strangling in their seats, huffin and puffin.

Madeen got fired right off on account of the pound of mascara she wears on each lash and them weird dresses she designs for herself (with less than a yard of cloth each if you ask me). I did my best to hang in there so's me and Madeen'd have hang-around money till Johnson started hiring again. But it was hard getting back and forth from the stockroom to this little kitchen to fix the espresso to the showroom. One minute up to your ass in carpet, the next skidding across white linoleum, the next making all this noise on ceramic tile and people looking around at you and all. Was there for two weeks and just about had it licked by stationing different kind of shoes at each place that I could slip into, but then Leon D stumbled over my bedroom slippers one afternoon.

But to hear Uncle Henry tell it, writing about it all to Daddy, I was working at a promising place making a name for myself. And Aunt Harriet listening to Uncle Henry read the letter, looking me up and down and grunting. She know what kind of name it must be, cause my name in the family is Miss Clumsy. Like if you got a glass-top coffee table with doodads on em, or a hurricane lamp sitting on a mantel anywhere near a door I got to come through, or an antique jar you brought all the way from Venice the time you won the crossword puzzle contest—you can rest assure I'll demolish them by and by. I ain't vicious, I'm just clumsy. It's my gawky stage, Mama says. Aunt Harriet cuts her eye at Mama and grunts.

My daddy advised me on the phone not to mention anything to the Johnsons about this gift of mine for disaster or the fact that I worked at Leon D. Salon. No sense the Johnson's calling up there to check on me and come to find I knocked over a perfume display two times in the same day. Like I say—it's a gift. So when I got to clean the glass jars and punch bowls at Johnson's, I take it slow and pay attention. Then I take up my station relaxed in Fabrics, where the worst that can happen is I upset a box of pins.

Mrs. J is in the prescription booth, and she clears her throat real loud. We all look to the back to read the smoke signals. She ain't paying Fur Coat and Ethel no attention. They over in Cosmetics messing with Miz Della's mind and her customers. Mrs. J got her eye on some young teen-agers browsing around Jewelry. The other eye on Piper. But this does not mean Piper is supposed to check the kids out. It means Madeen is. You got to know how to read Mrs. J to get along.

She always got one eye on Piper. Tries to make it seem like she don't trust him at the cash register. That may be part of the reason now, now that she's worked up this cover story so in her mind. But we all know why she watches Piper, same reason we all do. Cause Piper is so fine you just can't help yourself. Tall and built up, blue-black and smooth, got the nerve to have dimples, and wears this splayed-out push-broom mustache he's always raking in with three fingers. Got a big butt too that makes you wanna hug the customer that asks for the cartoons Piper keeps behind him, two shelfs down. Mercy. And when it's slow, or when Mrs. J comes bustling over for the count, Piper steps from behind the counter and shows his self. You get to see the whole Piper from the shiny boots to the glistening fro and every inch of him fine. Enough to make you holler.

Miz Della in Cosmetics, a sister who's been passing for years but fooling nobody but herself, she always lolligagging over to Tobacco talking bout are there any new samples of those silver-tipped cigars for women. Piper don't even squander energy to bump her off any more. She mostly just ain't even there. At first he would get mad when she used to act hinkty and had these white men picking her up at the store. Then he got sorrowful about it all, saying she was a pitiful person. Now that she's going out with the blond chemist back there, he just wiped her off the map. She tries to mess with him, but Piper ain't heard the news she's been born. Sometimes his act slips, though, cause he does take a lot of unnecessary energy to play up to Madeen whenever Miz Della's hanging around. He's not consistent in his attentions, and that spurs Madeen the dress designer to madness. And Piper really oughta put brakes on that, cause Madeen subject to walk in one day in a fishnet dress and no underwear and then what he goin do about that?

Last year on my birthday my daddy got on us about dressing like hussies to attract the boys. Madeen shrugged it off and went about her business. It hurt my feelings. The onliest reason I was wearing that tight sweater and that skimpy skirt was cause I'd been to the roller rink and that's how we dress. But my daddy didn't even listen and I was really hurt. But then later that night, I come through the living room to make some cocoa and he apologized. He lift up from the couch where he always sleeps when he comes to visit, lifted up and whispered it—"Sorry." I could just make him out by the light from the refrigerator.

"Candy," he calls to make sure I heard him. And I don't want to close the frig door cause I know I'll want to remember this scene, figuring it's going to be the last birthday visit cause he fixin to get married and move outta state.

"Sir?"

He pat the couch and I come on over and just leave the frig door open so we can see each other. I forgot to put the milk down, so I got this cold milk bottle in my lap, feeling stupid.

"I was a little rough on you earlier," he say, picking something I can't see from my bathrobe. "But you're getting to be a woman now and certain things have to be said. Certain things have to be understood so you can decide what kind of woman you're going to be, ya know?"

"Sir," I nod. I'm thinking Aunt Harriet ought to tell me, but then Aunt Harriet prefers to grunt at folks, reserving words for the damn crossword puzzles. And my mama stay on the road so much with the band, when she do come home for a hot minute all she has to tell me is "My slippers're in the back closet" or "Your poor tired Ma'd like some coffee."

He takes my hand and don't even kid me about the milk bottle, just holds my hand for a long time saying nothing, just squeezes it. And I know he feeling bad about moving away and all, but what can he do, he got a life to lead. Just like Mama got her life to lead. Just like I got my life to lead and'll probably leave here myself one day and become an actress or a director. And I know I should tell him it's all right. Sitting there with that milk bottle chilling me through my bathrobe, the light from the refrigerator throwing funny shadows on the wall, I know that years later when I'm in trouble or something, or hear that my daddy died or something like that, I'm going feel real bad that I didn't tell him—it's all right, Daddy, I understand. It ain't like he'd made any promises about making a home for me with him. So it ain't like he's gone back on his word. And if the new wife can't see taking in no half-grown new daughter, hell, I understand that. I can't get the words together, neither can he. So we just squeeze each other's hands. And that'll have to do.

"When I was a young man," he says after while, "there were girls who ran around all made up in sassy clothes. And they were okay to party with, but not the kind you cared for, ya know?" I nod and he pats my hand. But I'm thinking that ain't right, to party with a person you don't care for. How come you can't? I want to ask, but he's talking. And I was raised not to interrupt folk when they talking, especially my daddy. "You and Madeen cause quite a stir down at the barbershop." He tries to laugh it, but it comes out scary. "Got to make up your mind now what kind of woman you're going to be. You know what I'm saying?" I nod and he loosens his grip so I can go make my cocoa.

I'm messing around in the kitchenette feeling dishonest. Things I want to say, I haven't said. I look back over toward the couch and know this picture is going to haunt me later. Going to regret the things left unsaid. Like a coward, like a child maybe. I fix my cocoa and keep my silence, but I do remember to put the milk back and close the refrigerator door.

"Candy?"

"Sir?" I'm standing there in the dark, the frig door closed now and we can't even see each other.

"It's not about looks anyway," he says, and I hear him settling deep into the couch and pulling up the bedclothes. "And it ain't always about attracting some man either . . . not necessarily."

I'm waiting to hear what it is about, the cup shaking in the saucer and me wanting to ask him all over again how it was when he and Mama first met in Central Park, and how it used to be when they lived in Philly and had me and how it was when the two of them were no longer making any sense together but moved down here anyway and then split up. But I could hear that breathing he does just before the snoring starts. So I hustle on down the hall so I won't be listening for it and can't get to sleep.

All night I'm thinking about this woman I'm going to be. I'll look like Mama but don't wanna be no singer. Was named after Grandma Candestine but don't wanna be no fussy old woman with a bunch of kids. Can't see myself turning into Aunt Harriet either, doing crossword puzzles all day long. I look over at Madeen, all sprawled out in her bed, tangled up in the sheets looking like the alcoholic she trying to be these days, sneaking liquor from Uncle Henry's closet. And I know I don't wanna be stumbling down the street with my boobs out and my dress up and my heels cracking off and all. I write for a whole hour in my diary trying to connect with the future me and trying not to hear my daddy snoring.

Fur Coat and Ethel in Housewares talking with Madeen. I know they must be cracking on Miz Della, cause I hear Madeen saying something about equal opportunity. We used to say that Mrs. J was an equal opportunity employer for hiring Miz Della. But then she went and hired real white folks—a blond, crew-cut chemist and a pimply-face kid for the stockroom. If you ask me, that's running equal opportunity in the ground. And running the business underground cause don't nobody round here deal with no white chemist. They used to wrinkly old folks grinding up the herbs and bark and telling them very particular things to do and not to do working the roots. So they keep on going to Mama Drear down past the pond or Doc Jessup in back of the barbershop. Don't do a doctor one bit of good to write out a prescription talking about fill it at Johnson's, cause unless it's an emergency folk stay strictly away from a white root worker, especially if he don't tell you what he doing.

Aunt Harriet in here one day when Mama Drear was too sick to counsel and quite naturally she asks the chemist to explain what all he doing back there with the mortar and pestle and the scooper and the scales. And he say something about rules and regulations, the gist of which was mind your business, lady. Aunt Harriet dug down deep into her crossword-puzzle words and pitched a natural bitch. Called that man a bunch of choicest names. But the line that got me was—"Medication without explanation is obscene." And what she say that for, we ran that in the ground for days. Infatuation without fraternization is obscene. Insemination without obligation is tyranny. Fornication without contraception is obtuse, and so forth and so on. Madeen's best line came out the night we were watching a TV special about welfare. Sterilization without strangulation and hell's damnation is I-owe-you-one-crackers. Look like every situation called for a line like that, and even if it didn't, we made it fit.

Then one Saturday morning we were locked out and we standing around shivering in our sweaters and this old white dude jumps out a pickup truck hysterical, his truck still in gear and backing out the lot. His wife had given their child an overdose of medicine and the kid was out cold. Look like everything he said was grist for the mill.

"She just administered the medicine without even reading the label," he told the chemist, yanking on his jacket so the man couldn't even get out his keys. "She never even considered the fact it might be dangerous, the medicine so old and all." We follow the two down the aisle to the prescription booth, the old white dude talking a mile a minute, saying they tried to keep the kid awake, tried to walk him, but he wouldn't walk. Tried to give him an enema, but he wouldn't stay propped up. Could the chemist suggest something to empty his stomach out and soothe his inflamed ass and what all? And besides he was breathing funny and should he administer mouth-to-mouth resuscitation? The minute he tore out of there and ran down the street to catch up with his truck, we started in.

Administration without consideration is illiterate. Irrigation without resuscitation is evacuation without ambulation is inflammation without information is execution without restitution is. We got downright silly about the whole thing till Mrs. J threatened to fire us all. But we kept it up for a week.

Then the new dude in Drugs who don't never say much stopped the show one afternoon when we were trying to figure out what to call the street riots in the sixties and so forth. He say Revolution without Transformation is Half-assed. Took me a while to ponder that one, a whole day in fact just to work up to it. After while I would listen real hard whenever he opened his mouth, which wasn't often. And I jotted down the titles of the books I'd see him with. And soon's I finish up the stack that's by my bed, I'm hitting the library. He started giving me some of the newspapers he keeps stashed in that blue bag of his we all at first thought was full of funky jockstraps and sneakers. Come to find it's full of carrots and oranges and books and stuff. Madeen say he got a gun in there too. But then Madeen all the time saying something. Like she saying here lately that the chemist's jerking off there behind the poisons and the goopher dust.

The chemist's name is Hubert Tarrly. Madeen tagged him Herbert Tarey-ton. But the name that stuck was Nazi Youth. Every time I look at him I hear Hitler barking out over the loudspeaker urging the youth to measure up and take over the world. And I can see these stark-eyed gray kids in short pants and suspenders doing jump-ups and scissor kicks and turning they mamas in to the Gestapo for listening to the radio. Chemist looks like he grew up like that, eating knockwurst and beating on Jews, rounding up gypsies, saying *Sieg heil* and shit. Mrs. J said something to him one morning and damn if he didn't click his heels. I like to die. She blushing all over her simple self talking bout that's Southern cavalier style. I could smell the gas. I could see the flaming cross too. Nazi Youth and then some. The dude in Drugs started calling him that too, the dude whose name I can never remember. I always wanna say Ali Baba when I talk about him with my girl friends down at the skating rink or with the older sisters at the arts center. But that ain't right. Either you call a person a name that says what they about or you call em what they call themselves, one or the other.

Now take Fur Coat, for instance. She is clearly about the fur coat. She moving up and down the aisles talking while Ethel in the cloth coat is doing all the work, picking up teapots, checking the price on the dust mops, clicking a bracelet against the punch bowl to see if it ring crystal, hollering to somebody about whether the floor wax need buffing or not. And it's all on account of the fur coat. Her work is something other than that. Like when they were in Cosmetics messing with Miz Della, some white ladies come up talking about what's the latest in face masks. And every time Miz Della pull something out the box, Ethel shake her head and say that brand is crap. Then Fur Coat trots out the sure-fire recipe for the face mask. What she tells the old white ladies is to whip us some egg white to peaks, pour in some honey, some oil of win-tergreen, some oil of eucalyptus, the juice of a lemon and a half a teaspoon of arsenic. Now any fool can figure out what lemon juice do to arsenic, or how honey going make the concoction stick, and what all else the oil of this and that'll do to your face. But Fur Coat in her fur coat make you stand still and listen to this madness. Fur Coat an authority in her fur coat. The fur coat is an act of alchemy in itself, as Aunt Harriet would put it.

Just like my mama in her fur coat, same kind too—Persian lamb, bought hot in some riot or other. Mama's coat was part of the Turn the School Out Outfit. Hardly ever came out of the quilted bag cept for that. Wasn't for window-shopping, wasn't for going to rehearsal, wasn't for church teas, was for working her show. She'd flip a flap of that coat back over her hip when she strolled into the classroom to get on the teacher's case bout saying something out of the way about Black folks. Then she'd pick out the exact plank, exact spot she'd take her stand on, then plant one of them black suede pumps from the I. Miller outlet she used to work at. Then she'd lift her chin arrogant proud to start the rap, and all us kids would lean forward and stare at the cameo brooch visible now on the wide-wale wine plush corduroy dress. Then she'd work her show in her outfit. Bam-bam that black suede pocketbook punctuating the points as Mama ticked off the teacher's offenses. And when she got to the good part, and all us kids would strain up off the benches to hear every word so we could play it out in the schoolyard, she'd take both fists and brush that fur coat way back past her hips and she'd challenge the teacher to either change up and apologize or meet her for a showdown at a school-board hearing. And of course ole teacher'd apologize to all us Black kids. Then Mama'd let the coat fall back into place and she'd whip around, the coat draping like queen robes, and march herself out. Mama was baad in her fur coat.

I don't know what-all Fur Coat do in her fur coat but I can tell it's hellafyin whatever it all is. They came into Fabrics and stood around a while trying to see what shit they could get into. All they had in their baskets was a teapot and some light bulbs and some doodads from the special gift department, perfume and whatnot. I waited on a few customers wanting braid and balls of macramé twine, nothing where I could show my stuff. Now if somebody wanted some of the silky, juicy cotton stuff I could get into something fancy, yanking off the yards, measuring it doing a shuffle-stick number, nicking it just so, then ripping the hell out the shit. But didn't nobody ask for that. Fur Coat and Ethel kinda finger some bolts and trade private jokes, then they moved onto Drugs.

"We'd like to see the latest in rubberized fashions for men, young man." Fur Coat is doing a super Lady Granville Whitmore the Third number. "If you would." She bows her head, fluttering her lashes.

Me and Madeen start messing around in the shoe-polish section so's not to miss nothing. I kind of favor Fur Coat, on account of she got my mama's coat on, I guess. On the other hand, I like the way Ethel drawl talk like she too tired and bored to go on. I guess I like em both cause they shopping the right way, having fun and all. And they got plenty of style. I wouldn't mind being like that when I am full-grown.

The dude in Drugs thinks on the request a while, sucking in his lips like he wanna talk to himself on the inside. He's looking up and down the counter, pauses at the plastic rain hats, rejects them, then squints hard at Ethel and Fur Coat. Fur Coat plants a well-heeled foot on the shelf with the tampons and pads and sighs. Something about that sigh I don't like. It's real rather than play snooty. The dude in Drugs always looks a little crumbled, a little rough dry, like he jumped straight out the hamper but not quite straight. But he got stuff to him if you listen rather than look. Seems to me ole Fur Coat is looking. She keeps looking while the dude moves down the aisle behind the counter, ducks down out of sight, reappears and comes back, dumping an armful of boxes on the counter.

"One box of Trojans and one box of Ramses," Ethel announces. "We want to do the comparison test."

"On the premises?" Lady G Fur says, planting a dignified hand on her collarbone.

"Egg-zack-lee."

"In your opinion, young man," Lady G Fur says, staying the arm of the brand tester, "which of the two is the best? Uhmm—the better of the two, that is. In your vast experience as lady-killer and cock hound, which passes the X test?" It's said kinda snotty. Me and Madeen exchange a look and dust around the cans of shoe polish.

"Well," the dude says, picking up a box in each hand, "in my opinion, Trojans have a snappier ring to em." He rattles the box against his ear, then lets Ethel listen. She nods approval. Fur Coat will not be swayed. "On the other hand, Ramses is a smoother smoke. Cooler on the throat. What do you say in your vast experience as—er—"

Ethel is banging down boxes of Kotex cracking up, screaming, "He gotcha. He gotcha that time. Old laundry bag got over on you, Helen."

Mrs. J comes out of the prescription booth and hustles her bulk to the counter. Me and Madeen clamp down hard on giggles and I damn near got to climb in with the neutral shoe polish to escape attention. Ethel and Fur Coat don't give a shit, they paying customers, so they just roar. Cept Fur Coat's roar is phony, like she really mad and gonna get even with the dude for not turning out to be a chump. Meanwhile, the dude is standing like a robot, arms out at exactly the same height, elbows crooked just so, boxes displayed between thumb and next finger, the gears in the wrist click, clicking, turning. And not even cracking a smile.

"What's the problem here?" Mrs. J trying not to sound breathless or angry and ain't doing too good a job. She got to say it twice to be heard.

"No problem, Mrs. Johnson," the dude says straight-face. "The customers are buying condoms, I am selling condoms. A sale is being conducted, as is customary in a store."

Mrs. J looks down at the jumble of boxes and covers her mouth. She don't know what to do. I duck down, cause when folks in authority caught in a trick, the first they look for is a scapegoat.

"Well, honey," Ethel says, giving a chummy shove to Mrs. J's shoulder, "what do you think? I've heard that Trojans are ultrasensitive. They use a baby lamb brain, I understand."

"Membrane, dear, membrane," Fur Coat says down her nose. "They remove the intestines of a four-week-old lamb and use the membrane. Tough, resilient, sheer."

"Gotcha," says Ethel. "On the other hand, it is said by folks who should know that Ramses has a better box score."

"Box score," echoes Mrs. J in a daze.

"Box score. You know, honey—no splits, breaks, leaks, seeps."

"Seepage, dear, seepage," says Fur Coat, all nasal.

"Gotcha."

"The solution," says the dude in an almost robot voice, "is to take one small box of each and do the comparison test as you say. A survey. A random sampling of your friends." He says this to Fur Coat, who is not enjoying it all nearly so much as Ethel, who is whooping and hollering.

Mrs. J backs off and trots to the prescription booth. Nazi Youth peeks over the glass and mumbles something soothing to Mrs. J. He waves me and Madeen away like he somebody we got to pay some mind.

"We will take one super-duper, jumbo family size of each."

"Family size?" Fur Coat is appalled. "And one more thing, young man," she orders. "Wrap up a petite size for a small-size smart-ass acquaintance of mine. Gift-wrapped, ribbons and all."

It occurs to me that Fur Coat's going to present this to the dude. Right then and there I decide I don't like her. She's not discriminating with her stuff. Up till then I was thinking how much I'd like to trade Aunt Harriet in for either of these two, hang out with them, sit up all night while they drink highballs and talk about men they've known and towns they've been in. I always did want to hang out with women like this and listen to their stories. But they beginning to reveal themselves as not nice people, just cause the dude is rough dry on Christmas Eve. My Uncle Henry all the time telling me they different kinds of folks in the community, but when you boil it right down there's just nice and not nice. Uncle Henry say they folks who'll throw they mamas to the wolves if the fish sandwich big enough. They folks who won't whatever the hot sauce. They folks that're scared, folks that are dumb; folks that have heart and some with heart to spare. That all boils down to nice and not nice if you ask me. It occurs to me that Fur Coat is not nice. Fun, dazzling, witty, but not nice.

"Do you accept Christmas gifts, young man?" Fur Coat asking in icy tones she ain't masking too well.

"No. But I do accept Kwanza presents at the feast."

"Quan . . . hmm . . ."

Fur Coat and Ethel go into a huddle with the stage whispers. "I bet he thinks we don't know beans about Quantas . . . Don't he know we are The Ebony Jet Set . . . We never travel to kangaroo land except by . . ."

Fur Coat straightens up and stares at the dude. "Will you accept a whatchamacallit gift from me even though we are not feasting, as it were?"

"If it is given with love and respect, my sister, of course." He was sounding so sincere, it kinda got to Fur Coat.

"In that case . . ." She scoops up her bundle and sweeps out the place. Ethel trotting behind hollering, "He gotcha, Helen. Give the boy credit. Maybe we should hire him and do a threesome act." She spun the turnstile round three times for she got into the spin and spun out the store.

"Characters," says Piper on tiptoe, so we all can hear him. He laughs and checks his watch. Madeen slinks over to Tobacco to be in asking distance in case he don't already have a date to the dance. Miz Della's patting some powder on. I'm staring at the door after Fur Coat and Ethel, coming to terms with the fact that my daddy ain't coming. It's gonna be just Uncle Henry and Aunt Harriet this year, with maybe Mama calling on the phone between sets to holler in my ear, asking have I been a good girl, it's been that long since she's taken a good look at me.

"You wanna go to the Kwanza celebrations with me sometime this week or next week, Candy?"

I turn and look at the dude. I can tell my face is falling and right now I don't feel up to doing anything about it. Holidays are depressing. Maybe there's something joyous about this celebration he's talking about. Cause Lord knows Christmas is a drag. The sister who taught me how to wrap a gele asked me was I coming to the celebration down at the Black Arts Center, but I didn't know nothing bout it.

"Look here," I finally say, "would you please get a pencil and paper and write your name down for me. And write that other word down too so I can look it up."

He writes his name down and spins the paper around for me to read.

"Obatale."

"Right," he says, spinning it back. "But you can call me Ali Baba if you want to." He was leaning over too far writing out Kwanza for me to see if that was a smile on his face or a smirk. I figure a smile, cause Obatale nice people.

Gryphon

Charles Baxter

On Wednesday afternoon, between the geography lesson on ancient Egypt's hand-operated irrigation system and an art project that involved drawing a model city next to a mountain, our fourth-grade teacher, Mr. Hibler, developed a cough. This cough began with a series of muffled throat-clearings and progressed to propulsive noises contained within Mr. Hibler's closed mouth. "Listen to him," Carol Peterson whispered to me. "He's gonna blow up." Mr. Hibler's laughter—dazed and infrequent—sounded a bit like his cough, but as we worked on our model cities we would look up, thinking he was enjoying a joke, and see Mr. Hibler's face turning red, his cheeks puffed out. This was not laughter. Twice he bent over, and his loose tie, like a plumb line, hung down straight from his neck as he exploded himself into a Kleenex. He would excuse himself, then go on coughing. "I'll bet you a dime," Carol Peterson whispered, "we get a substitute tomorrow."

Carol sat at the desk in front of mine and was a bad person—when she thought no one was looking she would blow her nose on notebook paper, then crumple it up and throw it into the wastebasket—but at times of crisis she spoke the truth. I knew I'd lose the dime.

"No deal," I said.

When Mr. Hibler stood us in formation at the door just prior to the final bell, he was almost incapable of speech. "I'm sorry, boys and girls," he said. "I seem to be coming down with something."

"I hope you feel better tomorrow, Mr. Hibler," Bobby Kryzanowicz, the faultless brown-noser, said, and I heard Carol Peterson's evil giggle. Then Mr. Hibler opened the door and we walked out to the buses, a clique of us starting noisily to hawk and raugh as soon as we thought we were a few feet beyond Mr. Hibler's earshot.

Since Five Oaks was a rural community, and in Michigan, the supply of substitute teachers was limited to the town's unemployed community college graduates, a pool of about four mothers. These ladies fluttered, provided easeful class days, and nervously covered material we had mastered weeks earlier. Therefore it was a surprise when a woman we had never seen came into the class the next day, carrying a purple purse, a checkerboard lunchbox, and a few books. She put the books on one side of Mr. Hibler's desk and the lunchbox on the other, next to the Voice of Music phonograph. Three of us in the back of the room were playing with Heever, the chameleon that lived in a terrarium and on one of the plastic drapes, when she walked in.

She clapped her hands at us. "Little boys," she said, "why are you bent over together like that?" She didn't wait for us to answer. "Are you tormenting an animal? Put it back. Please sit down at your desks. I want no cabals this time of the day." We just stared at her. "Boys," she repeated, "I asked you to sit down."

I put the chameleon in his terrarium and felt my way to my desk, never taking my eyes off the woman. With white and green chalk, she had started to draw a tree on the left side of the blackboard. She didn't look usual. Furthermore, her tree was outsized, disproportionate, for some reason.

"This room needs a tree," she said, with one line drawing the suggestion of a leaf. "A large, leafy, shady, deciduous . . . oak."

Her fine, light hair had been done up in what I would learn years later was called a chignon, and she wore gold-rimmed glasses whose lenses seemed to have the faintest blue tint. Harold Knardahl, who sat across from me, whispered, "Mars," and I nodded slowly, savoring the imminent weirdness of the day. The substitute drew another branch with an extravagant arm gesture, then turned around and said, "Good morning. I don't believe I said good morning to all of you yet."

Facing us, she was no special age—an adult is an adult—but her face had two prominent lines, descending vertically from the sides of her mouth to her chin. I knew where I had seen those lines before: *Pinocchio*. They were marionette lines. "You may stare at me," she said to us, as a few more kids from the last bus came into the room; their eyes fixed on her, "for a few more seconds, until the bell rings. Then I will permit no more staring. Looking I will permit. Staring, no. It is impolite to stare, and a sign of bad breeding. You cannot make a social effort while staring."

Harold Knardahl did not glance at me, or nudge, but I heard him whisper "Mars" again, trying to get more mileage out of his single joke with the kids who had just come in.

When everyone was seated, the substitute teacher finished her tree, put down her chalk fastidiously on the phonograph, brushed her hands, and faced us. "Good morning," she said. "I am Miss Ferenczi, your teacher for the day. I am fairly new to your community, and I don't believe any of you know me. I will therefore start by telling you a story about myself."

While we settled back, she launched into her tale. She said her grandfather had been a Hungarian prince; her mother had been born in some place called Flanders, had been a pianist, and had played concerts for people Miss Ferenczi referred to as "crowned heads." She gave us a knowing look. "Grieg," she said, "the Norwegian master, wrote a concerto for piano that was . . ."—she paused— "my mother's triumph at her debut concert in London." Her eyes searched the ceiling. Our eyes followed. Nothing up there but ceiling tile. "For reasons that I shall not go into, my family's fortunes took us to Detroit, then north to dreadful Saginaw, and now here I am in Five Oaks, as your substitute teacher, for today, Thursday, October the eleventh. I believe it will be a good day: all the forecasts coincide. We shall start with your reading lesson. Take out your reading book. I believe it is called *Broad Horizons,* or something along those lines."

Jeannie Vermeesch raised her hand. Miss Ferenczi nodded at her. "Mr. Hibler always starts the day with the Pledge of Allegiance." Jeannie whined.

"Oh, does he? In that case," Miss Ferenczi said, "you must know it *very* well by now, and we certainly need not spend our time on it. No, no allegiance pledging on the premises today, by my reckoning. Not with so much sunlight coming into the room. A pledge does not suit my mood." She glanced at her watch. "Time *is* flying. Take out *Broad Horizons.*"

She disappointed us by giving us an ordinary lesson, complete with vocabulary and drills, comprehension questions, and recitation. She didn't seem to care for the material, however. She sighed every few minutes and rubbed her glasses with a frilly handkerchief that she withdrew, magician-style, from her left sleeve.

After reading we moved on to arithmetic. It was my favorite time of the morning, when the lazy autumn sunlight dazzled its way through ribbons of clouds past the windows on the east side of the classroom and crept across the linoleum floor. On the playground the first group of children, the kindergartners, were running on the quack grass just beyond the monkey bars. We were doing multiplication tables. Miss Ferenczi had made John Wazny stand up at his desk in the front row. He was supposed to go through the tables of six. From where I was sitting, I could smell the Vitalis soaked into John's plastered hair. He was doing fine until he came to six times eleven and six times twelve. "Six times eleven," he said, "is sixty-eight. Six times twelve is . . ." He put his fingers to his head, quickly and secretly sniffed his fingertips, and said, ". . . seventy-two." Then he sat down.

"Fine," Miss Ferenczi said, "Well now. That was very good."

"Miss Ferenczi!" One of the Eddy twins was waving her hand desperately in the air. "Miss Ferenczi! Miss Ferenczi!"

"Yes?"

"John said that six times eleven is sixty-eight and you said he was right!"

"*Did* I?" She gazed at the class with a jolly look breaking across her marionette's face. "Did I say that? Well, what *is* six times eleven?"

"It's sixty-six!"

She nodded. "Yes. So it is. But, and I know some people will not entirely agree with me, at some times it is sixty-eight."

"When? When is it sixty-eight?"

We were all waiting.

"In higher mathematics, which you children do not yet understand, six times eleven can be considered to be sixty-eight." She laughed through her nose. "In higher mathematics numbers are . . . more fluid. The only thing a number does is contain a certain amount of something. Think of water. A cup is not the only way to measure a certain amount of water, is it?" We were staring, shaking our heads. "You could use saucepans or thimbles. In either case, the water *would be the same.* Perhaps," she started again, "it would be better for you to think that six times eleven is sixty-eight only when I am in the room."

"Why is it sixty-eight," Mark Poole asked, "when you're in the room?"

"Because it's more interesting that way," she said, smiling very rapidly behind her blue-tinted glasses. "Besides, I'm your substitute teacher, am I not?" We all nodded. "Well, then, think of six times eleven equals sixty-eight as a substitute fact."

"A substitute fact?"

"Yes." Then she looked at us carefully. "Do you think," she asked, "that anyone is going to be hurt by a substitute fact?"

We looked back at her.

"Will the plants on the windowsill be hurt?" We glanced at them. There were sensitive plants thriving in a green plastic tray, and several wilted ferns in small clay pots. "Your dogs and cats, or your moms and dads?" She waited. "So," she concluded, "what's the problem?"

"But it's wrong," Janice Weber said, "isn't it?"

"What's your name, young lady?"

"Janice Weber."

"And you think it's wrong, Janice?"

"I was just asking."

"Well, all right. You were just asking. I think we've spent enough time on this matter by now, don't you, class? You are free to think what you like. When your teacher, Mr. Hibler, returns, six times eleven will be sixty-six again, you can rest assured. And it will be that for the rest of your lives in Five Oaks. Too bad, eh?" She raised her eyebrows and glinted herself at us. "But for now, it wasn't. So much for that. Let us go on to your assigned problems for today, as painstakingly outlined, I see, in Mr. Hibler's lesson plan. Take out a sheet of paper and write your names on the upper left-hand corner."

For the next half hour we did the rest of our arithmetic problems. We handed them in and then went on to spelling, my worst subject. Spelling always came before lunch. We were taking spelling dictation and looking at the clock. "Thorough," Miss Ferenczi said. "Boundary." She walked in the aisles between the desks, holding the spelling book open and looking down at our papers. "Balcony." I clutched my pencil. Somehow, the way she said those words, they seemed foreign, mis-voweled and mis-consonanted. I stared down at what I had spelled. *Balconie.* I turned the pencil upside down and erased my mistake. *Balconey.* That looked better, but still incorrect. I cursed the world of spelling and tried erasing it again and saw the paper beginning to wear away. *Balkony.* Suddenly I felt a hand on my shoulder.

"I don't like that word either," Miss Ferenczi whispered, bent over, her mouth near my ear. "It's ugly. My feeling is, if you don't like a word, you don't have to use it." She straightened up, leaving behind a slight odor of Clorets.

At lunchtime we went out to get our trays of sloppy joes, peaches in heavy syrup, coconut cookies, and milk, and brought them back to the classroom, where Miss Ferenczi was sitting at the desk, eating a brown sticky thing she had unwrapped from tightly rubber-banded waxed paper. "Miss Ferenczi," I said, raising my hand. "You don't have to eat with us. You can eat with the other teachers. There's a teacher's lounge," I ended up, "next to the principal's office."

"No, thank you," she said. "I prefer it here."

"We've got a room monitor," I said. "Mrs. Eddy." I pointed to where Mrs. Eddy, Joyce and Judy's mother, sat silently at the back of the room, doing her knitting.

"That's fine," Miss Ferenczi said. "But I shall continue to eat here, with you children. I prefer it," she repeated.

"How come?" Wayne Razmer asked without raising his hand.

"I talked to the other teachers before class this morning," Miss Ferenczi said, biting into her brown food. "There was a great rattling of the words for the fewness of the ideas. I didn't care for their brand of hilarity. I don't like ditto-machine jokes."

"Oh," Wayne said.

"What's that you're eating?" Maxine Sylvester asked, twitching her nose. "Is it food?"

"It most certainly *is* food. It's a stuffed fig. I had to drive almost down to Detroit to get it. I also brought some smoked sturgeon. And this," she said, lifting some green leaves out of her lunchbox, "is raw spinach, cleaned this morning."

"Why're you eating raw spinach?" Maxine asked.

"It's good for you," Miss Ferenczi said. "More stimulating than soda pop or smelling salts." I bit into my sloppy joe and stared blankly out the window. An almost invisible moon was faintly silvered in the daytime autumn sky. "As far as food is concerned," Miss Ferenczi was saying, "you have to shuffle the pack. Mix it up. Too many people eat . . . well, never mind."

"Miss Ferenczi," Carol Peterson said, "what are we going to do this afternoon?"

"Well," she said, looking down at Mr. Hibler's lesson plan, "I see that your teacher, Mr. Hibler, has you scheduled for a unit on the Egyptians." Carol groaned. "Yesssss," Miss Ferenczi continued, "that is what we will do: the Egyptians. A remarkable people. Almost as remarkable as the Americans. But not quite." She lowered her head, did her quick smile, and went back to eating her spinach.

After noon recess we came back into the classroom and saw that Miss Ferenczi had drawn a pyramid on the blackboard close to her oak tree. Some of us who had been playing baseball were messing around in the back of the room, dropping the bats and gloves into the playground box, and Ray Schontzeler had just slugged me when I heard Miss Ferenczi's high-pitched voice, quavering with emotions. "Boys," she said, "come to order right this minute and take your seats. I do not wish to waste a minute of class time. Take out your geography books." We trudged to our desks and, still sweating, pulled out *Distant Lands and Their People.* "Turn to page forty-two." She waited for thirty seconds, then looked over at Kelly Munger. "Young man," she said, "why are you still fossicking in your desk?"

Kelly looked as if his foot had been stepped on. "Why am I what?"

"Why are you . . . burrowing in your desk like that?"

"I'm lookin' for the book, Miss Ferenczi."

Bobby Kryzanowicz, the faultless brown-noser who sat in the first row by choice, softly said, "His name is Kelly Munger. He can't ever find his stuff. "He always does that."

"I don't care what his name is, especially after lunch," Miss Ferenczi said. *"Where is your book?"*

"I just found it." Kelly was peering into his desk and with both hands pulled at the book, shoveling along in front of it several pencils and crayons, which fell into his lap and then to the floor.

"I hate a mess," Miss Ferenczi said. "I hate a mess in a desk or a mind. It's . . . unsanitary. You wouldn't want your house at home to look like your desk at school, now, would you?" She didn't wait for an answer. "I should think not. A house at home should be as neat as human hands can make it. What were we talking about? Egypt. Page forty-two. I note from Mr. Hibler's lesson plan that you have been discussing the modes of Egyptian irrigation. Interesting, in my view, but not so interesting as what we are about to cover. The pyramids, and Egyptian slave labor. A plus on one side, a minus on the other." We had our books open to page forty-two, where there was a picture of a pyramid, but Miss Ferenczi wasn't looking at the book. Instead, she was staring at some object just outside the window.

"Pyramids," Miss Ferenczi said, still looking past the window. "I want you to think about pyramids. And what was inside. The bodies of the pharaohs, of course, and their attendant treasures. Scrolls. Perhaps," Miss Ferenczi said, her face gleeful but unsmiling, "these scrolls were novels for the pharaohs, helping them to pass the time in their long voyage through the centuries. But then, I am joking." I was looking at the lines on Miss Ferenczi's skin. "Pyramids," Miss Ferenczi went on, "were the repositories of special cosmic powers. The nature of a pyramid is to guide cosmic energy forces into a concentrated point. The Egyptians knew that; we have generally forgotten it. Did you know," she asked, walking to the side of the room so that she was standing by the coat closet, "that George Washington had Egyptian blood, from his grandmother? Certain features of the Constitution of the United States are notable for their Egyptian ideas."

Without glancing down at the book, she began to talk about the movement of souls in Egyptian religion. She said that when people die, their souls return to Earth in the form of carpenter ants or walnut trees, depending on how they behaved—"well or ill"—in life. She said that the Egyptians believed that people act the way they do because of magnetism produced by tidal forces in the solar system, forces produced by the sun and by its "planetary ally," Jupiter. Jupiter, she said, was a planet, as we had been told, but had "certain properties of stars." She was speaking very fast. She said that the Egyptians were great explorers and conquerors. She said that the greatest of all the conquerors, Genghis Khan, had had forty horses and forty young women killed on the site of his grave. We listened. No one tried to stop her. "I myself have been in Egypt," she said, "and have witnessed much dust and many brutalities." She said that an old man in Egypt who worked for a circus had personally shown her an animal in a cage, a monster, half bird and half lion. She said that this monster was called a gryphon and that she had heard about them but never seen them until she traveled to the outskirts of Cairo. She wrote the word out on the blackboard in large capital letters: GRYPHON. She said that Egyptian astronomers had discovered the planet Saturn but had not seen its rings. She said that the Egyptians were the first to discover that dogs, when they are ill, will not drink from rivers, but wait for rain, and hold their jaws open to catch it.

"She lies."

We were on the school bus home. I was sitting next to Carl Whiteside, who had bad breath and a huge collection of marbles. We were arguing. Carl thought she was lying. I said she wasn't, probably.

"I didn't believe that stuff about the bird," Carl said, "and what she told us about the pyramids? I didn't believe that, either. She didn't know what she was talking about."

"Oh yeah?" I had liked her. She was strange. I thought I could nail him. "If she was lying," I said, "what'd she say that was a lie?"

"Six times eleven isn't sixty-eight. It isn't ever. It's sixty-six, I know for a fact."

"She said so. She admitted it. What else did she lie about?"

"I don't know," he said. "Stuff."

"What stuff?"

"Well." He swung his legs back and forth. "You ever see an animal that was half lion and half bird?" He crossed his arms. "It sounded real fakey to me."

"It could happen," I said. I had to improvise, to outrage him. "I read in this newspaper my mom bought in the IGA about this scientist, this mad scientist in the Swiss Alps, and he's been putting genes and chromosomes and stuff together in test tubes, and he combined a human being and a hamster." I waited, for effect. "It's called a humster."

"You never." Carl was staring at me, his mouth open, his terrible bad breath making its way toward me. "What newspaper was it?"

"*The National Enquirer*," I said, "that they sell next to the cash registers." When I saw his look of recognition, I knew I had him. "And this mad scientist," I said, "his name was, um, Dr. Frankenbush." I realized belatedly that this name was a mistake and waited for Carl to notice its resemblance to the name of the other famous mad master of permutations, but he only sat there.

"A man and a hamster?" He was staring at me, squinting, his mouth opening in distaste. "Jeez. What'd it look like?"

When the bus reached my stop, I took off down our dirt road and ran up through the backyard, kicking the tire swing for good luck. I dropped my books on the back steps so I could hug and kiss our dog, Mr. Selby. Then I hurried inside. I could smell brussels sprouts cooking, my unfavorite vegetable. My mother was washing other vegetables in the kitchen sink, and my baby brother was hollering in his yellow playpen on the kitchen floor.

"Hi, Mom," I said, hopping around the playpen to kiss her. "Guess what?"

"I have no idea."

"We had this substitute today, Miss Ferenczi, and I'd never seen her before, and she had all these stories and ideas and stuff."

"Well. That's good." My mother looked out the window in front of the sink, her eyes on the pine woods west of our house. That time of the afternoon her skin always looked so white to me. Strangers always said my mother looked like Betty Crocker, framed by the giant spoon on the side of the Bisquick box. "Listen, Tommy," she said. "Would you please go upstairs and pick your clothes off the floor in the bathroom, and then go outside to the shed and put the shovel and ax away that your father left outside this morning?"

"She said that six times eleven was sometimes sixty-eight!" I said. "And she said she once saw a monster that was half lion and half bird." I waited. "In Egypt."

"Did you hear me?" my mother asked, raising her arm to wipe her forehead with the back of her hand. "You have chores to do."

"I know," I said. "I was just telling you about the substitute."

"It's very interesting," my mother said, quickly glancing down at me, "and we can talk about it later when your father gets home. But right now you have some work to do."

"Okay, Mom." I took a cookie out of the jar on the counter and was about to go outside when I had a thought. I ran into the living room, pulled out a dictionary next to the TV stand, and opened it to the Gs. After five minutes I found it. *Gryphon:* variant of griffin. *Griffin:* "a fabulous beast with the head and wings of an eagle and the body of a lion." Fabulous was right. I shouted with triumph and ran outside to put my father's tools in their proper places.

Miss Ferenczi was back the next day, slightly altered. She had pulled her hair down and twisted it into pigtails, with red rubber bands holding them tight one inch from the ends. She was wearing a green blouse and pink scarf, making her difficult to look at for a full class day. This time there was no pretense of doing a reading lesson or moving on to arithmetic. As soon as the bell rang, she simply began to talk.

She talked for forty minutes straight. There seemed to be less connection between her ideas, but the ideas themselves were, as the dictionary would say, fabulous. She said she had heard of a huge jewel, in what she called the antipodes, that was so brilliant that when light shone into it at a certain angle it would blind whoever was looking at its center. She said the biggest diamond in the world was cursed and had killed everyone who owned it, and that by a trick of fate it was called the Hope Diamond. Diamonds are magic, she said, and this is why women wear them on their fingers, as a sign of the magic of womanhood. Men have strength, Miss Ferenczi said, but no true magic. That is why men fall in love with women but women do not fall in love with men: they just love being loved. George Washington had died because of a mistake he made about a diamond. Washington was not the first *true* President, but she didn't say who was. In some places in the world, she said, men and women still live in the trees and eat monkeys for breakfast. Their doctors are magicians. At the bottom of the sea are creatures thin as pancakes who have never been studied by scientists because when you take them up to air, the fish explode.

There was not a sound in the classroom, except for Miss Ferenczi's voice, and Donna DeShano's coughing. No one even went to the bathroom.

Beethoven, she said, had not been deaf; it was a trick to make himself famous, and it worked. As she talked, Miss Ferenczi's pigtails swung back and forth. There are trees in the world, she said, that eat meat: their leaves are sticky and close up on bugs like hands. She lifted her hands and brought them together, palm to palm. Venus, which most people think is the next closest planet to the sun, is not always closer, and, besides, it is the planet of greatest mystery because of its thick cloud cover. "I know what lies underneath those clouds," Miss Ferenczi said, and waited. After the silence, she said, "Angels. Angels live under those clouds." She said that angels were not invisible to everyone and were in fact smarter than most people. They did not dress in robes as was often claimed but instead wore formal evening clothes, as if they were about to attend a concert. Often angels *do* attend concerts and sit in the aisles, where, she said, most people pay no attention to them. She said the most terrible angel had the shape of the Sphinx. "There is no running away from that one," she said. She said that unquenchable fires burn just under the surface of the earth in Ohio, and that the baby Mozart fainted dead away in his cradle when he first heard the sound of a trumpet. She said that someone named Narzim al Harrardim was the greatest writer who ever lived. She said that planets control behavior, and anyone conceived during a solar eclipse would be born with webbed feet.

"I know you children like to hear these things," she said, "these secrets, and that is why I am telling you all this." We nodded. It was better than doing comprehension questions for the readings in *Broad Horizons.*

"I will tell you one more story," she said, "and then we will have to do arithmetic." She leaned over, and her voice grew soft. "There is no death," she said. "You must never be afraid. Never. That which is, cannot die. It will change into different earthly and unearthly elements, but I know this as sure as I stand here in front of you, and I swear it: you must not be afraid. I have seen this truth with these eyes. I know it because in a dream God kissed me. Here." And she pointed with her right index finger to the side of her head, below the mouth where the vertical lines were carved into her skin.

Absentmindedly we all did our arithmetic problems. At recess the class was out on the playground, but no one was playing. We were all standing in small groups, talking about Miss Ferenczi. We didn't know if she was crazy, or what. I looked out beyond the playground, at the rusted cars piled in a small heap behind a clump of sumac, and I wanted to see shapes there, approaching me.

On the way home, Carl sat next to me again. He didn't say much, and I didn't either. At last he turned to me. "You know what she said about the leaves that close up on bugs?"

"Huh?"

"The leaves," Carl insisted, "The meat-eating plants. I know it's true. I saw it on television. The leaves have this icky glue that the plants have got smeared all over them and the insects can't get off 'cause they're stuck. I saw it." He seemed demoralized. "She's tellin' the truth."

"Yeah."

"You think she's seen all those angels?"

I shrugged.

"I don't think she has," Carl informed me. "I think she made that part up."

"There's a tree," I suddenly said. I was looking out the window at the farms along County Road H. I knew every barn, every broken windmill, every fence, every anhydrous ammonia tank, by heart. "There's a tree that's . . . that I've seen . . ."

"Don't you try to do it," Carl said. "You'll just sound like a jerk."

I kissed my mother. She was standing in front of the stove. "How was your day?" she asked.

"Fine."

"Did you have Miss Ferenczi again?"

"Yeah."

"Well?"

"She was fine. Mom," I asked, "can I go to my room?"

"No," she said, "not until you've gone out to the vegetable garden and picked me a few tomatoes." She glanced at the sky. "I think it's going to rain. Skedaddle and do it now. Then you come back inside and watch your brother for a few minutes while I go upstairs. I need to clean up before dinner." She looked down at me. "You're looking a little pale, Tommy." She touched the back of her hand to my forehead and I felt her diamond ring against my skin. "Do you feel all right?"

"I'm fine," I said, and went out to pick the tomatoes.

Coughing mutedly, Mr. Hibler was back the next day, slipping lozenges into his mouth when his back was turned at forty-five minute intervals and asking us how much of his prepared lesson plan Miss Ferenczi had followed. Edith Atwater took the responsibility for the class of explaining to Mr. Hibler that the substitute hadn't always done exactly what he, Mr. Hibler, would have done, but we had worked hard even though she talked a lot. About what? he asked. All kinds of things, Edith said. I sort of forgot. To our relief, Mr. Hibler seemed not at all interested in what Miss Ferenczi had said to fill the day. He probably thought it was woman's talk: unserious and not suited for school. It was enough that he had a pile of arithmetic problems from us to correct.

For the next month, the sumac turned a distracting red in the field, and the sun traveled toward the southern sky, so that its rays reached Mr. Hibler's Halloween display on the bulletin board in the back of the room, fading the pumpkin head scarecrow from orange to tan. Every three days I measured how much farther the sun had moved toward the southern horizon by making small marks with my black Crayola on the north wall, ant-sized marks only I knew were there.

And then in early December, four days after the first permanent snowfall, she appeared again in our classroom. The minute she came in the door, I felt my heart begin to pound. Once again, she was different: this time, her hair hung straight down and seemed hardly to have been combed. She hadn't brought her lunchbox with her, but she was carrying what seemed to be a small box. She greeted all of us and talked about the weather. Donna DeShano had to remind her to take her overcoat off.

When the bell to start the day finally rang, Miss Ferenczi looked out at all of us and said, "Children, I have enjoyed your company in the past, and today I am going to reward you." She held up the small box. "Do you know what this is?" She waited. "Of course you don't. It is a Tarot pack."

Edith Atwater raised her hand. "What's a Tarot pack, Miss Ferenczi?"

"It is used to tell fortunes," she said. "And that is what I shall do this morning. I shall tell your fortunes, as I have been taught to do."

"What's fortune?" Bobby Kryzanowicz asked.

"The future, young man. I shall tell you what your future will be. I can't do your whole future, of course. I shall have to limit myself to the five-card system, the wands, cups, swords, pentacles, and the higher arcanes. Now who wants to be first?"

There was a long silence. Then Carol Peterson raised her hand.

"All right," Miss Ferenczi said. She divided the pack into five smaller packs and walked back to Carol's desk, in front of mine. "Pick one card from each one of these packs," she said. I saw that Carol had a four of cups and a six of swords, but I couldn't see the other cards. Miss Ferenczi studied the cards on Carol's desk for a minute. "Not bad," she said. "I do not see much higher education. Probably an early marriage. Many children. There's something bleak and dreary here, but I can't tell what. Perhaps just the tasks of a housewife life. I think you'll do very well, for the most part." She smiled at Carol, a smile with a certain lack of interest. "Who wants to be next?"

Carl Whiteside raised his hand slowly.

"Yes," Miss Ferenczi said, "let's do a boy." She walked over to where Carl sat. After he picked his five cards, she gazed at them for a long time. "Travel," she said. "Much distant travel. You might go into the army. Not too much romantic interest here. A late marriage, if at all. But the Sun in your major arcana, that's a very good card." She giggled. "You'll have a happy life."

Next I raised my hand. She told me my future. She did the same with Bobby Kryzanowicz, Kelly Munger, Edith Atwater, and Kim Foor. Then she came to Wayne Razmer. He picked his five cards, and I could see that the Death card was one of them.

"What's your name?" Miss Ferenczi asked.

"Wayne."

"Well, Wayne," she said, "you will undergo a great metamorphosis, a change, before you become an adult. Your earthly element will no doubt leap higher, because you seem to be a sweet boy. This card, this nine of swords, tells me of suffering and desolation. And this ten of wands, well, that's a heavy load."

"What about this one?" Wayne pointed at the Death card.

"It means, my sweet, that you will die soon." She gathered up the cards. We were all looking at Wayne. "But do not fear," she said. "It is not really death. Just change. Out of your earthly shape." She put the cards on Mr. Hibler's desk. "And now, let's do some arithmetic."

At lunchtime Wayne went to Mr. Faegre, the principal, and informed him of what Miss Ferenczi had done. During the noon recess, we saw Miss Ferenczi drive out of the parking lot in her rusting green Rambler American. I stood under the slide, listening to the other kids coasting down and landing in the little depressive bowls at the bottom. I was kicking stones and tugging at my hair right up to the moment when I saw Wayne come out to the playground. He smiled, the dead fool, and with the fingers of his right hand he was showing everyone how he had told on Miss Ferenczi.

I made my way toward Wayne, pushing myself past two girls from another class. He was watching me with his little pinhead eyes.

"You told," I shouted at him. "She was just kidding."

"She shouldn't have," he shouted back. "We were supposed to be doing arithmetic."

"She just scared you," I said. "You're a chicken. You're a chicken, Wayne. You are. Scared of a little card," I sing-songed.

Wayne fell at me, his two fists hammering down on my nose. I gave him a good one in the stomach and then I tried for his head. Aiming my fist, I saw that he was crying. I slugged him.

"She was right," I yelled. "She was always right! She told the truth!" Other kids were whooping. "You were just scared, that's all!"

And then large hands pulled at us, and it was my turn to speak to Mr. Faegre.

In the afternoon Miss Ferenczi was gone, and my nose was stuffed with cotton clotted with blood, and my lip had swelled, and our class had been combined with Mrs. Mantei's sixth-grade class for a crowded afternoon science unit on insect life in ditches and swamps. I knew where Mrs. Mantei lived: she had a new house trailer just down the road from us, at the Clearwater Park. She was no mystery. Somehow she and Mr. Bodine, the other fourth-grade teacher, had managed to fit forty-five desks into the room. Kelly Munger asked if Miss Ferenczi had been arrested, and Mrs. Mantei said no, of course not. All that afternoon, until the buses came to pick us up, we learned about field crickets and two-striped grasshoppers, water bugs, cicadas, mosquitoes, flies, and moths. We learned about insects' hard outer shell, the exoskeleton, and the usual parts of the mouth, including the labrum, mandible, maxilla, and glossa. We learned about compound eyes, and the four-stage metamorphosis from egg to larva to pupa to adult. We learned something, but not much, about mating. Mrs. Mantei drew, very skillfully, the internal anatomy of the grasshopper on the blackboard. We learned about the dance of the honeybee, directing other bees in the hive to pollen. We found out about which insects were pests to man, and which were not. On lined white pieces of paper we made lists of insects we might actually see, then a list of insects too small to be clearly visible, such as fleas; Mrs. Mantei said that our assignment would be to memorize these lists for the next day, when Mr. Hibler would certainly return and test us on our knowledge.

Some of Our Work
with Monsters

Ron Carlson

Elaine and I had been working in the lab, dismantling the sleep research equipment, when the call came from the Secret Agency. We hadn't planned on a big project so soon. Elaine wanted to go up to Union City to see our son, Grant, and his wife, Karla, and the baby. We missed them, and we needed a break. Grant's the mayor of Union City, and they had just put his name on the water tower over the population, 2,234, and we wanted to go up there and kiss everybody and take a few photographs. Elaine and I joked about wanting some proof that we were grandparents. We'd lived a life looking for proof, and now we had a grandchild. We hadn't realized how much we wanted to be grandparents; we hadn't even thought about that word. Sometimes there's a real gap between a word and the thing, and we have learned that empirical evidence can narrow that gap. Grandfather. Grandmother. Of course, we were still young people, but we needed to see Carlisle, the baby. I had a real interest in holding the baby. A fact, our little fact.

But, when the Secret Agency calls, you listen. These people do all their contracts over the phone, and by the time we hung up the receiver, we were definitely hired. They sent a plane that night, and a driver came to our apartment while we were still packing. We didn't know if we would be gone overnight or for a couple of weeks. He stood in the bedroom doorway in his dark suit and skinny tie.

"How long will we be gone," Elaine asked him, "a day or a couple of weeks?"

"I don't know," the driver said. "I'm just the driver." Elaine is a scrupulous packer; she can pack like nobody. She's experienced at packing. She's gone everywhere and arrived with the right stuff, even Alaska. At least, we think it was Alaska. It was a ten-day job in a snow-packed place. This new job was in the Midwest. The guy on the phone, the Secret Guy, had said the Midwest. It would require warm clothing and some lighter stuff; it could get cold in the spring.

Elaine and I hadn't spoken about it, but we already knew what the job was. It had been in all the papers every day. It was the new monster. The monster was doing a lot of damage and he was responsible for a great deal of harm. Some of the things the monster had done were difficult to listen to. They were terrible. It had been going on for months, but the Secret Agency was closing in. We'd seen it like this before. It takes a while for there to be sightings. Then the evidence piles up, and pretty soon, they're closing in on the monster.

It puts us in a tough spot, but that's why they pay us the big bucks.

The Secret Agency has about ten ways to kill the monster, but only one or two work, and it's never the same ones. These guys spend all their time working up ways to kill the monster. They've done it again and again. Usually they try to kill the monster three or four ways before they find the right way to kill him, and then they do that. It's always a big show, and we've been in it up close where some of the monster got on us.

When we arrived at the airport the driver went through the secret gate and drove us to the unlighted runway and the Secret Airplane. I was pretty worried about the way I'd packed because I'd been warm all day and I think I put in too many light clothes. Cold rain in the forties would render me ineffective. Sleet would render me ineffective. I'd also forgotten my gloves. I knew Elaine would have gloves, an extra pair, but we'd done that before. They don't fit.

As he stopped at the Secret Plane, the driver said, "What are you going to recommend about the monster?"

Elaine said, "You're just the driver; you don't need to know."

The driver said, "I'm also the pilot and the Director of the Mission. Climb aboard. I'm interested to hear your ideas." He changed hats and led us onto the Secret Plane.

The secret airplanes are small but nice. They have a fridge with all the stuff we don't have at home. We don't keep candy in our fridge. Elaine and I have a policy of never going for the fridge right away, but as we begin our descent, we always enjoy a light snack. The Director of the Mission didn't want a snack. He wanted to know what we were going to recommend about the monster.

"You know our recommendation," Elaine told him.

"You make the same recommendation every time," the Director of our Mission told her. "Do you know the facts of this case?"

"We've studied the dossier and we've seen the papers. This is a textbook monster."

"And we need to destroy it before it does more damage or harm." The Director was firm on this. He spoke into the radio, circled the plane, and landed in a dark place.

"We need to study the monster," Elaine said. How many times had we said this? We said this every monster. "You can't kill it. We need to keep it alive."

"Tell that to the next farmer who loses his family and all his livestock and outbuildings," the Director of the Mission said.

"We've met the people who have suffered harm and damage," I told the Director. We had moved into his command tent now, and we were looking at the big maps taped to the table. Elaine and I had met these people at every monster and their stories made us sick and dizzy. They hated us because we wanted to save the monster. These were terrible moments for us, sitting in the rocks and rubble of someone's house, usually smoke rising around us, while the survivor looked at us as if we were the monster. Well, we weren't the monster! We were trying to save the monster so we could study the monster. Sometimes, the monster was one of a kind, and the Secret Agency only wanted to blow it up or hang it or drown it in acid, trying their various methods until they found the one that worked.

"What if it was your family!" The survivors of the monster attacks shouted at us. "What if it was you or you!"

This is when Elaine would say, "Then we hope somebody else would capture and study the monster." But this didn't get through and sometimes the survivors of the monster attacks would come up and act like they were going to strike us or jump on us, but over all these years, none have.

"Where's the monster now?" Elaine said.

"Right here," one of the secret guys said, pointing at the telegrid screen. We looked at the screen and could see the little blip moving through the quadrants.

"It's a big monster," Elaine said. She looked at me. "It's as tall as you are."

"And fast," the Director of the Mission said. "But we've got ways to kill this big, fast monster."

"More than one way, I bet," Elaine said.

"Ten ways," the Director of the Mission said, holding up all ten fingers.

A gust of chilly wind ripped at the command tent and Elaine looked at me. "Did you bring your khaki jacket?" she asked.

"I've only got a sweater vest and my old school scarf."

"Oh Ron," she said, and though it was a scolding, I loved to hear it. "You're going to catch a real cold this time and flu season is approaching."

"Is summer flu season?" A chill shot through me because if I was sick, I wouldn't get to hold the baby. I wanted to hold Carlisle. I had to get to Union City and hold the baby!

Now we could hear the droning of big motors, and the man running the telegrid said, "Here come the big robotdrones." On the screen we could see the six big robotdrones.

"They'll get the monster," the Director said.

"No they won't," Elaine said. "The Secret Agency has tried robotdrones on every monster for the last thirty years and the robotdrones have never ever worked against a single monster."

"They might this time," the Director said.

We all put our faces closer to the green telegrid screen. We watched the robotdrones approach the monster and then turn in different directions and go off the screen. The blip of the monster still roved freely.

"Shoot!" the Director swore. "Where'd they go?"

"Sir," the telegrid man said. "One of the robotdrones is coming this way."

We all filed into the bunker under the mission control tent. It was warm down there out of the wind, and Elaine sat by me on one of the sandbags. "This happened before with a robotdrone," she said. "It chased us and blew up some things."

"Don't you criticize the robotdrone program," the Director of the Mission said. "They'll work it out." Around the dark room we could see everybody's eyeballs. The robotdrone roar grew louder and louder and then the explosion shook the mission control bunker and loose dirt filtered down on us all. We went up into the tent, which was ripped up mostly. The telegrid machine was in flinders. By now night had passed and it was dawn's early light and dust and smoke and some small fires.

"You can't kill this monster," Elaine said to the Director. "We need to study him."

"Somebody get this person away from me," he said. "Call me a command vehicle."

"You know," she said, "as well as I do that this monster is one of a kind."

"They're all one of a kind," he said. "We know that. If they were all alike, we could kill them without any trouble." A truckload of men in army gear arrived and began cleaning up the robotdrone debris. They called orders back and forth. Every few minutes we could hear the other robotdrones exploding in the distance, over here and then way over there.

The command vehicle arrived, a big Winnebago painted army green with ten antennae sticking out of the top. We followed the Director of the Mission aboard and looked at the portable telegrid they had in the module. There was nothing on the screen now except the wiggly lines where the robotdrones had crashed and burned various parts of the country.

"He's not moving now," the Director of the Mission said.

"He's nocturnal," Elaine said.

"We've seen several nocturnal monsters," I said. "In our studies."

The Director of the Mission looked at me.

"If we could capture him and study him," Elaine said, "we'd know a lot more about nocturnal monsters."

I could tell the Director of the Mission did not like to hear the word *nocturnal*. He had a look on his face that indicated he was going to scream if we said it again.

"Let's drive up to the quadrant where the monster was last marked," he said. "And see what we see. We'll lay out the glowing bags of poison; they sometimes work."

"They've never worked," Elaine said. "They're just another way of inflating your budget. We've never had a monster, even those starved monsters in New Zealand, who fell for the glowing poison bags."

"We'll deploy the glowing bags of poison if I say so," the Director of the Mission said. He opened the storage room where we could see the bags glowing.

The driver of the command Winnebago was a young woman in army clothes. She was one of the best drivers we'd ever had and never took any corners too hard. The refrigerators in the command Winnebagos aren't as interesting as the ones in the Secret Airplanes. They have some bottled water and cold cuts, but no candy and no fresh fruit. I made us all a turkey sandwich with cheddar for the long drive to Quadrant 44.

Quadrant 44 was desolate in a windy, springtime way. The prairie here was barren of trees and only marked here and there by humpy bluffs grown with long grass. We stood on one bluff and surveyed the entire area. A herd of cattle grazed nearby in the rippling waves of grass. We could see a long way and there was nothing but a couple spires of smoke on the horizon.

"He's out here somewhere."

"He's lying in the grass or he's found a hole," Elaine said.

"Deploy the glowing bags of poison," the Director of the Mission said.

"We're here to save the monster and study him," I said. "We can't help you deploy the glowing bags of poison."

"They're heavy," the Director of the Mission said. "We need help."

We watched the driver and the Director of the Mission struggle with a glowing bag of poison.

Elaine stood with her arms folded.

"The bags of poison are not effective," I told her. "They won't kill the monster. We've never seen a monster fall for the glowing bags of poison." We could see the driver sweating as she lifted her end of the bag of poison. They could not lift it out of the Command Winnebago, but they were going to keep trying, bumping it along the floor of the vehicle toward the door. The driver was sweating and the Director of the Mission was huffing and puffing.

"O.K.," Elaine said, taking hold of the first bag, "but the Secret Agency is full of big bad baloney." So, this way we helped them deploy the glowing bags of poison. By the time we'd finished, we were all thirsty and we sat drinking bottled water in the Command Winnebago, listening to the wind blow.

"What'd you do before you joined the Secret Agency, Monster Division," Elaine asked him.

"I was in their motor pool. They've got some stuff in there. It isn't a typical motor pool."

"Do they have that One-Man Radar-deflecting Hovercraft," I asked him. We'd heard the same rumors everyone else had.

"You didn't hear it from me," the Director said. He reached in a small drawer and pulled out a deck of cards. They were shiny black playing cards with the Secret Agency's Insignia in the center. "You want to see some card tricks?" He shuffled the deck and did some good tricks. The Lost Soldier, The Everlasting Three, No Diamonds, and he ended with Big Jack. "Yeah, I was in motor pool, but I had to move up. I didn't make up the Secret Agency's monster policy, but I'm the Director now."

"No family?" Elaine asked him.

"I've got the monster," he said. When he said it, he looked like that one actor, a guy I like.

It was a breezy afternoon on the old prairie. We'd been up all night, the three of us. I didn't know if the driver had been up all night or not. We were all tired in the Command Winnebago out on the empty prairie in the long afternoon. Sleep filled me up like sand in an hourglass and I put my feet up and went out.

The command Winnebago rocked slightly in the wind. It wasn't unpleasant. I dreamed the same old dreams where I was working in the lab. I had something on the burner and something in the sink and I was missing a vial of something. I was stretched out between the two projects trying to keep them from blowing up. We've had a few unplanned explosions, but fewer than most small research facilities. When things blow up in Elaine's lab, we never spend very much time on recrimination and negative energy. We usually clean up and try something else. In my dream both projects were about to blow, when Elaine came in with her arms full of boxes. I had some trouble in the dream getting her attention, but when I did, she turned off the water and then she turned off the burner, and we ate lunch. In the boxes she had Chinese food and we ate in the dream for a long time.

I woke at midnight. The wind had stopped. Everyone else was still asleep, and the Director of the Mission was a noisy sleeper, the way worried people often can be. Elaine and I had done a ton of sleep research over the years. Our conclusion was that sleep knits up the raveled sleeve of care. Lack of sleep is a factor in most crime, and the worst place to try to sleep is prison. It's a terrible cycle that goes on and on. Our article went on and on. I was glad to see the Director of the Mission sleeping, because he was a man who had important decisions to make every minute, and sleep would help with that.

It was a clear night out, stars, but I could see something else outside the windows. Something was glowing and at first I thought it was the bags of poison we had deployed, but then I saw the shape nearby. I knew what it was, and I quietly woke Elaine. We opened the door on the still prairie and we walked out to the glowing object. It was one of the cows laid out dead and glowing. We could see the other cattle where they lay glowing in the night. They were beautiful and terrible, the kind of thing you don't see twice. Elaine called back to the Director of the Mission who stood in the Command Winnebago doorway, "You've killed all these cattle with your stupid glowing bags of poison."

The Director of the Mission called out to us. "Get back here right now. The monster is coming this way!"

"You've poisoned all the cattle!" Elaine cried out.

"Get back here!" the Director screamed. "He is approaching!"

"He is approaching," the driver called.

We looked around in a complete circle. There was nothing in the quiet world except the square box of the Command Winnebago. The sky was bigger than the earth and it was jostling with stars. The poisoned cows glowed like little scattered campfires.

"We should go back," I said.

Elaine was thinking it over. I loved this feature of hers. She was evaluating what to do.

"He's going to think we tried to poison him," I told her.

"Listen," she said.

I'd been listening. There was nothing, except the Director of the Mission calling and calling, get back, come back here now, I order you back here, he's coming, we see him on the screen, come back, etcetera.

"We want to save you!" Elaine called into the night. She was walking further away from the Command Winnebago.

"Did you hear the monster?" I asked her.

"Something," she said.

Behind us I heard the Director of the Mission cry, "I've called in the Space Lasers! Come back here!"

"The Space Lasers don't work!" Elaine said. I knew she was right with this one. The Space Laser was like handing a baby a flashlight; the beams went everywhere. We'd seen the Space Lasers one time in Canada and they wouldn't melt snow.

"Ten seconds!" the Director of the Mission called. Nine, eight, seven, six. . . .

The first big laser beam zipped past us like a flashbulb and then another ran behind us, bright and silent. Pretty soon the whole plain was crisscrossed with great lines of light in a kind of entertainment. The flashes were painful and I had to squint. From time to time in the display, two or three streams of photons would converge and we'd hear the hiss of burning grass. Elaine took my hand and we sat down in the thick prairie grass. She was rapt, and I knew she wanted to know if we might see the rumored Big DeLuxe Lasers. There had been so much talk about these super lasers, the next phase in laser work. The shafts of resonant light hummed back and forth. We'd worked with lasers and we'd had our difficulties. Suddenly, in a flash brighter than a force-four magnesium flare, our shadows were printed on the grassy world in a microsecond, and we saw for a true fact the Big DeLuxe Laser, a rod of light thick as a column in the Supreme Court. It beamed down and then split and fizzled. It hit near the Command Winnebago, and we heard glass break as the windshield exploded and smoke poured out. The Director and the driver stumbled out of the door coughing in the roving lasers. In the flashes the two Secret Agency employees looked like they were doing a jerky puppet dance.

A moment later the Space Lasers abated and the world was dark again and silent, though we couldn't see anything for four of five minutes while our eyes adjusted.

The driver led the Director of the Mission by the elbow over to where we stood in the grass. The Command Winnebago was burning lazily behind us.

"Don't tell me those lasers aren't powerful," the Director of the Mission said.

"We've killed the cattle," Elaine told him. "This happens again and again."

The driver stared in horror at the glowing cow.

The Director was speaking into his phone. "Get me a Gas-Bearing Hovercraft right now," he said. "We're in quadrant 44 near the little fire."

"We saw him on the screen," the woman driver said to us. "He's right here. Did you see him?"

"He's here somewhere," Elaine said. "I could tell, but we had no visual."

The driver went to the Director of the Mission and clenched the front of his khaki shirt in both of her hands. "I'm just a driver," she said, "and I think I'm a good driver, but I'm not a monster person. I'm not a cow killer. What are we doing here? What do I drive now?" She pointed over to the flaming Command Winnebago.

"What's your name, soldier," the Director of the Mission asked her.

The driver let go of the Director of the Mission's shirt and stepped back into a salute, saying, "Corporal Ashton."

The Director of the Mission returned the salute, and he looked into her face like a man reading important news in a letter. "Corporal Ashton, we've been through a lot together on this mission, and now your duty is to get us to Union City." We saw him press a field compass in her palm.

"Hey," I said, "our son is mayor of Union City. They just put his name on the water tower."

"Well, he's going to have his hands full with this guy," the Director said.

"What do you mean?" I asked him.

"Quadrant 44 is right outside Union City. This monster is definitely heading toward Union City. He's on a collision course with Union City. You people," the Director said. "Now how do you feel about save the monster, study the monster?"

Then we heard a humming sound like an old vacuum in the other room of a house, and we spotted the sleek little One-Man Radar-Deflecting Hovercraft sliding over the prairie coming our way. It was as neat as the rumors had it. The craft came up and hovered before us, humming. The pilot was a young guy who peeled off his gas mask and asked the Director, "Did you have lasers? Were the lasers out here?"

"Forget the lasers," the Director said. "Prepare to lay down the Green Gas." We could see the gas tubes on the back of the hovercraft.

"Will do," the young guy said, handing us each a polygold gasmask. He began circling us with the hovercraft in wider and wider circles and then we saw the first plumes of the Green Gas drifting over the ground. It made a pretty layer in the pale night.

"You won't need that gasmask," Elaine told Corporal Ashton, "the gas isn't going to hurt you." The woman had the mask on and looked up from her compass at us. The Director had his mask on.

Elaine dropped her gasmask onto the ground and so did I. She's taken the lead in some of our best work. Now she took my hand and we hurried north toward Union City.

"Be careful of that Green Gas!" the Director said, muffled through his gas mask. "Watch out!"

The Green Gas swirled around our legs as we kicked through it. We'd seen four gases total that the Secret Agency deploys and they haven't had any discernable effect in years. They're all caffeine based, so there's a little stimulation, but it dissipates. We could hear the prairie dogs starting to yip and scramble in the living world. Morning is a blessing everywhere, of course, and I could smell the new day coming for us. The light on the horizon was a pearl crescent prying the edge of the dark firmament.

"I didn't know Quadrant 44 was next to Union City," Elaine said. We stopped and I could just see her worried face in the small light. "It's hard. Everything tests you."

"Life's a real experiment," I said. It was what we always said when we were stymied. We'd been stymied plenty by various stymies.

Behind us I could hear the Director and Corporal Ashton jogging to catch up. The Director had retrieved our gas masks and swung them as he ran. He was in charge of every aspect of this mission.

I turned to Corporal Ashton. "We're going to see our grandson for the first time. We've never even seen him, and finally our work has brought us to this town." Daylight was inventing Union City.

"I loved my grandpa," Corporal Ashton said. The corporal was full of the green gas, and she asked Elaine, "How do you make love last? Is the monster part of it? Do you need a monster?"

This was a discussion Elaine usually took up, but I could see other thoughts on her face. She merely said to the young soldier, "A monster makes falling in love easier, but love can withstand the absence of monsters."

"Don't worry about the monster, Corporal Ashton," the Director of the Mission said. "He's nocturnal."

We came to the railroad trestle and stepped down the gravel bank to the footbridge. We could see the silver water tower on its six tall legs. Then the Director of the Mission said, "After we regroup and get some chow, I'm going to call in the magneto screens."

"Do that," I told him. We both knew too well how stupid the big noisy magneto screens were. They would do nothing but wreck everybody's wristwatch for forty miles.

"His name is Grant?" the Director pointed at the water tower. "Look at those letters." We could see our son's name. We'd all taken a little of the gas and felt stimulated. "They're ten feet tall. You guys sure did something right to raise a mayor like that."

Elaine had let go of my hand now, and I saw her step in front of the Director of the Mission. She had him by the shoulders as if he were a lectern, and she was face to face with him. "Hello," she said. "Listen. What else have you guys got, besides the magnetos? Can you call in the vacuum ray? Come on, look at that tank. This is Union City. There are two thousand people here. You're the Secret Agency; isn't there something you can do?"

A true work of fiction does all of the following things, and does them elegantly, efficiently: it creates a vivid and continuous dream in the reader's mind; it is implicitly philosophical; it fulfills or at least deals with all the expectations it sets up; and it strikes us, in the end, not simply as a thing done but as a shining performance.

—JOHN GARDNER

Cathedral

Raymond Carver

This blind man, an old friend of my wife's, he was on his way to spend the night. His wife had died. So he was visiting the dead wife's relatives in Connecticut. He called my wife from his in-laws'. Arrangements were made. He would come by train, a five-hour trip, and my wife would meet him at the station. She hadn't seen him since she worked for him one summer in Seattle ten years ago. But she and the blind man had kept in touch. They made tapes and mailed them back and forth. I wasn't enthusiastic about his visit. He was no one I knew. And his being blind bothered me. My idea of blindness came from the movies. In the movies, the blind moved slowly and never laughed. Sometimes they were led by seeing-eye dogs. A blind man in my house was not something I looked forward to.

That summer in Seattle she had needed a job. She didn't have any money. The man she was going to marry at the end of the summer was in officers' training school. He didn't have any money, either. But she was in love with the guy, and he was in love with her, etc. She'd seen something in the paper: HELP WANTED—*Reading to Blind Man,* and a telephone number. She phoned and went over, was hired on the spot. She'd worked with this blind man all summer. She read stuff to him, case studies, reports, that sort of thing. She helped him organize his little office in the county social-service department. They'd become good friends, my wife and the blind man. How do I know these things? She told me. And she told me something else. On her last day in the office, the blind man asked if he could touch her face. She agreed to this. She told me he touched his fingers to every part of her face, her nose—even her neck! She never forgot it. She even tried to write a poem about it. She was always trying to write a poem. She wrote a poem or two every year, usually after something really important had happened to her.

When we first started going out together, she showed me the poem. In the poem, she recalled his fingers and the way they had moved around over her face. In the poem, she talked about what she had felt at the time, about what went through her mind when the blind man touched her nose and lips. I can remember I didn't think much of the poem. Of course, I didn't tell her that. Maybe I just don't understand poetry. I admit it's not the first thing I reach for when I pick up something to read.

Anyway, this man who'd first enjoyed her favors, the officer-to-be, he'd been her childhood sweetheart. So okay. I'm saying that at the end of the summer she let the blind man run his hands over her face, said goodbye to him, married her childhood etc., who was now a commissioned officer, and she moved away from Seattle. But they'd kept in touch, she and the blind man. She made the first contact after a year or so. She called him up one night from an Air Force base in Alabama. She wanted to talk. They talked. He asked her to send him a tape and tell him about her life. She did this. She sent the tape. On the tape, she told the blind man about her husband and about their life together in the military. She told the blind man she loved her husband but she didn't like it where they lived and she didn't like it that he was a part of the military-industrial thing. She told the blind man she'd written a poem and he was in it. She told him that she was writing a poem about what it was like to be an Air Force officer's wife. The poem wasn't finished yet. She was still writing it. The blind man made a tape. He sent her the tape. She made a tape. This went on for years. My wife's officer was posted to one base and then another. She sent tapes from Moody AFB, McGuire, McConnell, and finally Travis, near Sacramento, where one night she got to feeling lonely and cut off from people she kept losing in that moving-around life. She got to feeling she couldn't go it another step. She went in and swallowed all the pills and capsules in the medicine chest and washed them down with a bottle of gin. Then she got into a hot bath and passed out.

But instead of dying, she got sick. She threw up. Her officer—why should he have a name? he was the childhood sweetheart, and what more does he want?—came home from somewhere, found her, and called the ambulance. In time, she put it all on a tape and sent the tape to the blind man. Over the years, she put all kinds of stuff on tapes and sent the tapes off lickety-split. Next to writing a poem every year, I think it was her chief means of recreation. On one tape, she told the blind man she'd decided to live away from her officer for a time. On another tape, she told him about her divorce. She and I began going out, and of course she told her blind man about it. She told him everything, or so it seemed to me. Once she asked me if I'd like to hear the latest tape from the blind man. This was a year ago. I was on the tape, she said. So I said okay, I'd listen to it. I got us drinks and we settled down in the living room. We made ready to listen. First she inserted the tape into the player and adjusted a couple of dials. Then she pushed a lever. The tape squeaked and someone began to talk in this loud voice. She lowered the volume. After a few minutes of harmless chitchat, I heard my own name in the mouth of this stranger, this blind man I didn't even know! And then this: "From all you've said about him, I can only conclude—" But we were interrupted, a knock at the door, something, and we didn't ever get back to the tape. Maybe it was just as well. I'd heard all I wanted to.

Now this same blind man was coming to sleep in my house.

"Maybe I could take him bowling," I said to my wife. She was at the draining board doing scalloped potatoes. She put down the knife she was using and turned around.

"If you love me," she said, "you can do this for me. If you don't love me, okay. But if you had a friend, any friend, and the friend came to visit, I'd make him feel comfortable." She wiped her hands with the dish towel.

"I don't have any blind friends," I said.

"You don't have *any* friends," she said. "Period. Besides," she said, "god-damn it, his wife's just died! Don't you understand that? The man's lost his wife!"

I didn't answer. She'd told me a little about the blind man's wife. Her name was Beulah. Beulah! That's a name for a colored woman.

"Was his wife a Negro?" I asked.

"Are you crazy?" my wife said. "Have you just flipped or something?" She picked up a potato. I saw it hit the floor, then roll under the stove. "What's wrong with you?" she said "Are you drunk?"

"I'm just asking," I said.

Right then my wife filled me in with more detail than I cared to know. I made a drink and sat at the kitchen table to listen. Pieces of the story began to fall into place.

Beulah had gone to work for the blind man the summer after my wife had stopped working for him. Pretty soon Beulah and the blind man had themselves a church wedding. It was a little wedding—who'd want to go to such a wedding in the first place?—just the two of them, plus the minister and the minister's wife. But it was a church wedding just the same. It was what Beulah had wanted, he'd said. But even then Beulah must have been carrying the cancer in her glands. After they had been inseparable for eight years—my wife's word, *inseparable*—Beulah's health went into a rapid decline. She died in a Seattle hospital room, the blind man sitting beside the bed and holding on to her hand. They'd married, lived and worked together, slept together—had sex, sure—and then the blind man had to bury her. All this without his having ever seen what the goddamned woman looked like. It was beyond my understanding. Hearing this, I felt sorry for the blind man for a little bit. And then I found myself thinking what a pitiful life this woman must have led. Imagine a woman who could never see herself as she was seen in the eyes of her loved one. A woman who could go on day after day and never receive the smallest compliment from her beloved. A woman whose husband could never read the expression on her face, be it misery or something better. Someone who could wear makeup or not—what difference to him? She could, if she wanted, wear green eye-shadow around one eye, a straight pin in her nostril, yellow slacks and purple shoes, no matter. And then to slip off into death, the blind man's hand on her hand, his blind eyes streaming tears—I'm imagining now—her last thought maybe this: that he never even knew what she looked like, and she on an express to the grave. Robert was left with a small insurance policy and half of a twenty-peso Mexican coin. The other half of the coin went into the box with her. Pathetic.

So when the time rolled around, my wife went to the depot to pick him up. With nothing to do but wait—sure, I blamed him for that—I was having a drink and watching the TV when I heard the car pull into the drive. I got up from the sofa with my drink and went to the window to have a look.

I saw my wife laughing as she parked the car. I saw her get out of the car and shut the door. She was still wearing a smile. Just amazing. She went around to the other side of the car to where the blind man was already starting to get out. This blind man, feature this, he was wearing a full beard! A beard on a blind man! Too much, I say. The blind man reached into the back seat and dragged out a suitcase. My wife took his arm, shut the car door, and, talking all the way, moved him down the drive and then up the steps to the front porch. I turned off the TV. I finished my drink, rinsed the glass, dried my hands. Then I went to the door.

My wife said, "I want you to meet Robert. Robert, this is my husband. I've told you all about him." She was beaming. She had this blind man by his coat sleeve.

The blind man let go of his suitcase and up came his hand.

I took it. He squeezed hard, held my hand, and then he let it go.

"I feel like we've already met," he boomed.

"Likewise," I said. I didn't know what else to say. Then I said, "Welcome. I've heard a lot about you." We began to move then, a little group, from the porch into the living room, my wife guiding him by the arm. The blind man was carrying his suitcase in his other hand. My wife said things like, "To your left here, Robert. That's right. Now watch it, there's a chair. That's it. Sit down right here. This is the sofa. We just bought this sofa two weeks ago."

I started to say something about the old sofa. I'd liked that old sofa. But I didn't say anything. Then I wanted to say something else, small-talk, about the scenic ride along the Hudson. How going *to* New York, you should sit on the right-hand side of the train, and coming *from* New York, the left-hand side.

"Did you have a good train ride?" I said. "Which side of the train did you sit on, by the way?"

"What a question, which side!" my wife said. "What's it matter which side?" she said.

"I just asked," I said.

"Right side," the blind man said. "I hadn't been on a train in nearly forty years. Not since I was a kid. With my folks. That's been a long time. I'd nearly forgotten the sensation. I have winter in my beard now," he said. "So I've been told, anyway. Do I look distinguished, my dear?" the blind man said to my wife.

"You look distinguished, Robert," she said. "Robert," she said. "Robert, it's just so good to see you."

My wife finally took her eyes off the blind man and looked at me. I had the feeling she didn't like what she saw. I shrugged.

I've never met, or personally known, anyone who was blind. This blind man was late forties, a heavy-set, balding man with stooped shoulders, as if he carried a great weight there. He wore brown slacks, brown shoes, a light-brown shirt, a tie, a sports coat. Spiffy. He also had this full beard. But he didn't use a cane and he didn't wear dark glasses. I'd always thought dark glasses were a must for the blind. Fact was, I wished he had a pair. At first glance, his eyes looked like anyone else's eyes. But if you looked close, there was something different about them. Too much white in the iris, for one thing, and the pupils seemed to move around in the sockets without his knowing it or being able to stop it. Creepy. As I stared at his face, I saw the left pupil turn in toward his nose while the other made an effort to keep in one place. But it was only an effort, for that eye was on the roam without his knowing it or wanting it to be.

I said, "Let me get you a drink. What's your pleasure? We have a little of everything. It's one of our pastimes."

"Bub, I'm a Scotch man myself," he said fast enough in this big voice.

"Right," I said. Bub! "Sure you are. I knew it."

He let his fingers touch his suitcase, which was sitting alongside the sofa. He was taking his bearings. I didn't blame him for that.

"I'll move that up to your room," my wife said.

"No, that's fine," the blind man said loudly. "It can go up when I go up."

"A little water with the Scotch?" I said.

"Very little," he said.

"I knew it," I said.

He said, "Just a tad. The Irish actor, Barry Fitzgerald? I'm like that fellow. When I drink water, Fitzgerald said, I drink water. When I drink whiskey, I drink whiskey." My wife laughed. The blind man brought his hand up under his beard. He lifted his beard slowly and let it drop.

I did the drinks, three big glasses of Scotch with a splash of water in each. Then we made ourselves comfortable and talked about Robert's travels. First the long flight from the West Coast to Connecticut, we covered that. Then from Connecticut up here by train. We had another drink concerning that leg of the trip.

I remembered having read somewhere that the blind didn't smoke because, as speculation had it, they couldn't see the smoke they exhaled. I thought I knew that much and that much only about blind people. But this blind man smoked his cigarette down to the nubbin and then lit another one. This blind man filled his ashtray and my wife emptied it.

When we sat down at the table for dinner, we had another drink. My wife heaped Robert's plate with cube steak, scalloped potatoes, green beans. I buttered him up two slices of bread. I said, "Here's bread and butter for you." I swallowed some of my drink. "Now let us pray," I said, and the blind man lowered his head. My wife looked at me, her mouth agape. "Pray the phone won't ring and the food doesn't get cold," I said.

We dug in. We ate everything there was to eat on the table. We ate like there was no tomorrow. We didn't talk. We ate. We scarfed. We grazed that table. We were into serious eating. The blind man had right away located his foods, he knew just where everything was on his plate. I watched with admiration as he used his knife and fork on the meat. He'd cut two pieces of meat, fork the meat into his mouth, and then go all out for the scalloped potatoes, the beans next, and then he'd tear off a hunk of buttered bread and eat that. He'd follow this up with a big drink of milk. It didn't seem to bother him to use his fingers once in a while, either.

We finished everything, including half a strawberry pie. For a few moments, we sat as if stunned. Sweat beaded on our faces. Finally, we got up from the table and left the dirty plates. We didn't look back. We took ourselves into the living room and sank into our places again. Robert and my wife sat on the sofa. I took the big chair. We had us two or three more drinks while they talked about the major things that had come to pass for them in the past ten years. For the most part, I just listened. Now and then I joined in. I didn't want him to think I'd left the room, and I didn't want her to think I was feeling left out. They talked of things that had happened to them—to them!—these past ten years. I waited in vain to hear my name on my wife's sweet lips: "And then my dear husband came into my life"—something like that. But I heard nothing of the sort. More talk of Robert. Robert had done a little of everything, it seemed, a regular blind jack-of-all-trades. But most recently he and his wife had had an Amway distributorship, from which, I gathered, they'd earned their living, such as it was. The blind man was also a ham radio operator. He talked in his loud voice about conversations he'd had with fellow operators in Guam, in the Philippines, in Alaska, and even in Tahiti. He said he'd have a lot of friends there if he ever wanted to go visit those places. From time to time, he'd turn his blind face toward me, put his hand under his beard, ask me something. How long had I been in my present position? (Three years.) Did I like my work? (I didn't.) Was I going to stay with it? (What were the options?) Finally, when I thought he was beginning to run down, I got up and turned on the TV.

My wife looked at me with irritation. She was heading toward a boil. Then she looked at the blind man and said, "Robert, do you have a TV?"

The blind man said, "My dear, I have two TVs. I have a color set and a black-and-white thing, an old relic. It's funny, but if I turn the TV on, and I'm always turning it on, I turn on the color set. It's funny, don't you think?"

I didn't know what to say to that. I had absolutely nothing to say to that. No opinion. So I watched the news program and tried to listen to what the announcer was saying.

"This is a color TV," the blind man said. "Don't ask me how, but I can tell."

"We traded up a while ago," I said.

The blind man had another taste of his drink. He lifted his beard, sniffed it, and let it fall. He leaned forward on the sofa. He positioned his ashtray on the coffee table, then put the lighter to his cigarette. He leaned back on the sofa and crossed his legs at the ankles.

My wife covered her mouth, and then she yawned. She stretched. She said, "I think I'll go upstairs and put on my robe. I think I'll change into something else. Robert, you make yourself comfortable," she said.

"I'm comfortable," the blind man said.

"I want you to feel comfortable in this house," she said.

"I am comfortable," the blind man said.

After she'd left the room, he and I listened to the weather report and then to the sports roundup. By that time, she'd been gone so long I didn't know if she was going to come back. I thought she might have gone to bed. I wished she'd come back downstairs. I didn't want to be left alone with a blind man. I asked him if he wanted another drink, and he said sure. Then I asked if he wanted to smoke some dope with me. I said I'd just rolled a number. I hadn't, but I planned to do so in about two shakes.

"I'll try some with you," he said.

"Damn right," I said. "That's the stuff."

I got our drinks and sat down on the sofa with him. Then I rolled us two fat numbers. I lit one and passed it. I brought it to his fingers. He took it and inhaled.

"Hold it as long as you can," I said. I could tell he didn't know the first thing.

My wife came back downstairs wearing her pink robe and her pink slippers.

"What do I smell?" she said.

"We thought we'd have us some cannabis," I said.

My wife gave me a savage look. Then she looked at the blind man and said, "Robert, I didn't know you smoked."

He said, "I do now, my dear. There's a first time for everything. But I don't feel anything yet."

"This stuff is pretty mellow," I said. "This stuff is mild. It's dope you can reason with," I said. "It doesn't mess you up."

"Not much it doesn't, bub," he said, and laughed.

My wife sat on the sofa between the blind man and me. I passed her the number. She took it and toked and then passed it back to me. "Which way is this going?" she said. Then she said, " I shouldn't be smoking this. I can hardly keep my eyes open as it is. That dinner did me in. I shouldn't have eaten so much."

"It was the strawberry pie," the blind man said. "That's what did it," he said, and he laughed his big laugh. Then he shook his head.

"There's more strawberry pie," I said.

"Do you want some more, Robert?" my wife said.

"Maybe in a little while," he said.

We gave our attention to the TV. My wife yawned again. She said, "Your bed is made up when you feel like going to bed, Robert. I know you must have had a long day. When you're ready to go to bed, say so." She pulled his arm. "Robert?"

He came to and said, "I've had a real nice time. This beats tapes, doesn't it?"

I said, "Coming at you," and I put the number between his fingers. He inhaled, held the smoke, and then let it go. It was like he'd been doing it since he was nine years old.

"Thanks, bub," he said. "But I think this is all for me. I think I'm beginning to feel it," he said. He held the burning roach out for my wife.

"Same here," she said. "Ditto. Me, too." She took the roach and passed it to me. "I may just sit here for a while between you two guys with my eyes closed. But don't let me bother you, okay? Either one of you. If it bothers you, say so. Otherwise, I may just sit here with my eyes closed until you're ready to go to bed," she said. "Your bed's made up, Robert, when you're ready. It's right next to our room at the top of the stairs. We'll show you up when you're ready. You wake me up now, you guys, if I fall asleep." She said that and then she closed her eyes and went to sleep.

The news program ended. I got up and changed the channel. I sat back down on the sofa. I wished my wife hadn't pooped out. Her head lay across the back of the sofa, her mouth open. She'd turned so that her robe had slipped away from her legs, exposing a juicy thigh. I reached to draw her robe back over her, and it was then that I glanced at the blind man. What the hell! I flipped the robe open again.

"You say when you want some strawberry pie," I said.

"I will," he said.

I said, "Are you tired? Do you want me to take you up to your bed? Are you ready to hit the hay?"

"Not yet," he said. "No, I'll stay up with you, bub. If that's all right. I'll stay up until you're ready to turn in. We haven't had a chance to talk. Know what I mean? I feel like me and her monopolized the evening." He lifted his beard and he let it fall. He picked up his cigarettes and his lighter.

"That's all right," I said. Then I said, "I'm glad for the company."

And I guess I was. Every night I smoked dope and stayed up as long as I could before I fell asleep. My wife and I hardly ever went to bed at the same time. When I did go to sleep, I had these dreams. Sometimes I'd wake up from one of them, my heart going crazy.

Something about the church and the Middle Ages was on the TV. Not your run-of-the-mill TV fare. I wanted to watch something else. I turned to the other channels. But there was nothing on them, either. So I turned back to the first channel and apologized.

"Bub, it's all right," the blind man said. "It's fine with me. Whatever you want to watch is okay. I'm always learning something. Learning never ends. It won't hurt me to learn something tonight. I got ears," he said.

We didn't say anything for a time. He was leaning forward with his head turned at me, his right ear aimed in the direction of the set. Very disconcerting. Now and then his eyelids drooped and then they snapped open again. Now and then he put his fingers into his beard and tugged, like he was thinking about something he was hearing on the television.

On the screen, a group of men wearing cowls was being set upon and tormented by men dressed in skeleton costumes and men dressed as devils. The men dressed as devils wore devil masks, horns, and long tails. This pageant was part of a procession. The Englishman who was narrating the thing said it took place in Spain once a year. I tried to explain to the blind man what was happening.

"Skeletons," he said. "I know about skeletons," he said, and he nodded.

The TV showed this one cathedral. Then there was a long, slow look at another one. Finally, the picture switched to the famous one in Paris, with its flying buttresses and its spires reaching up to the clouds. The camera pulled away to show the whole of the cathedral rising above the skyline.

There were times when the Englishman who was telling the thing would shut up, would simply let the camera move around over the cathedrals. Or else the camera would tour the countryside, men in fields walking behind oxen.

I waited as long as I could. Then I felt I had to say something. I said, "They're showing the outside of this cathedral now. Gargoyles. Little statues carved to look like monsters. Now I guess they're in Italy. Yeah, they're in Italy. There's paintings on the walls of this one church."

"Are those fresco paintings, bub?" he asked, and he sipped from his drink.

I reached for my glass. But it was empty. I tried to remember what I could remember. "You're asking me are those frescoes?" I said. "That's a good question. I don't know."

The camera moved to a cathedral outside Lisbon. The differences in the Portuguese cathedral compared with the French and Italian were not that great. But they were there. Mostly the interior stuff. Then something occurred to me, and I said, "Something has occurred to me. Do you have any idea what a cathedral is? What they look like, that is? Do you follow me? If somebody says cathedral to you, do you have any notion what they're talking about? Do you know the difference between that and a Baptist church, say?"

He let the smoke dribble from his mouth. "I know they took hundreds of workers fifty or a hundred years to build," he said. "I just heard the man say that, of course. I know generations of the same families worked on a cathedral. I heard him say that, too. The men who began their life's work on them, they never lived to see the completion of their work. In that wise, bub, they're no different from the rest of us, right?" He laughed. Then his eyelids drooped again. His head nodded. He seemed to be snoozing. Maybe he was imagining himself in Portugal. The TV was showing another cathedral now. This one was in Germany. The Englishman's voice droned on. "Cathedrals," the blind man said. He sat up and rolled his head back and forth. "If you want the truth, bub, that's about all I know. What I just said. What I heard him say. But maybe you could describe one to me? I wish you'd do it. I'd like that. If you want to know, I really don't have a good idea."

I stared hard at the shot of the cathedral on the TV. How could I even begin to describe it? But say my life depended on it. Say my life was being threatened by an insane guy who said I had to do it or else.

I stared some more at the cathedral before the picture flipped off into the countryside. There was no use. I turned to the blind man and said, "To begin with, they're very tall." I was looking around the room for clues. "They reach way up. Up and up. Toward the sky. They're so big, some of them, they have to have these supports. To help hold them up, so to speak. These supports are called buttresses. They remind me of viaducts, for some reason. But maybe you don't know viaducts, either? Sometimes the cathedrals have devils and such carved into the front. Sometimes lords and ladies. Don't ask me why this is," I said.

He was nodding. The whole upper part of his body seemed to be moving back and forth.

"I'm not doing so good, am I?" I said.

He stopped nodding and leaned forward on the edge of the sofa. As he listened to me, he was running his fingers through his beard. I wasn't getting through to him, I could see that. But he waited for me to go on just the same. He nodded, like he was trying to encourage me. I tried to think what else to say. "They're really big," I said. "They're massive. They're built of stone. Marble, too, sometimes. In those olden days, when they built cathedrals, men wanted to be close to God. In those olden days, God was an important part of everyone's life. You could tell this from their cathedral-building. I'm sorry," I said, "but it looks like that's the best I can do for you. I'm just no good at it."

"That's all right, bub," the blind man said. "Hey, listen. I hope you don't mind my asking you. Can I ask you something? Let me ask you a simple question, yes or no. I'm just curious and there's no offense. You're my host. But let me ask if you are in any way religious? You don't mind my asking?"

I shook my head. He couldn't see that, though. A wink is the same as a nod to a blind man. "I guess I don't believe in it. In anything. Sometimes it's hard. You know what I'm saying?"

"Sure, I do," he said.

"Right," I said.

The Englishman was still holding forth. My wife sighed in her sleep. She drew a long breath and went on with her sleeping.

"You'll have to forgive me," I said. "But I can't tell you what a cathedral looks like. It just isn't in me to do it. I can't do any more than I've done."

The blind man sat very still, his head down, as he listened to me.

I said, "The truth is, cathedrals don't mean anything special to me. Nothing. Cathedrals. They're something to look at on late-night TV. That's all they are."

It was then that the blind man cleared his throat. He brought something up. He took a handkerchief from his back pocket. Then he said, "I get it, bub. It's okay. It happens. Don't worry about it," he said. "Hey, listen to me. Will you do me a favor? I got an idea. Why don't you find us some heavy paper? And a pen. We'll do something. We'll draw one together. Get us a pen and some heavy paper. Go on, bub, get the stuff," he said.

So I went upstairs. My legs felt like they didn't have any strength in them. They felt like they did after I'd done some running. In my wife's room, I looked around. I found some ballpoints in a little basket on her table. And then I tried to think where to look for the kind of paper he was talking about.

Downstairs, in the kitchen, I found a shopping bag with onion skins in the bottom of the bag. I emptied the bag and shook it. I brought it into the living room and sat down with it near his legs. I moved some things, smoothed the wrinkles from the bag, spread it out on the coffee table.

The blind man got down from the sofa and sat next to me on the carpet.

He ran his fingers over the paper. He went up and down the sides of the paper. The edges, even the edges. He fingered the corners.

"All right," he said. "All right, let's do her."

He found my hand, the hand with the pen. He closed his hand over my hand. "Go ahead, bub, draw," he said. "Draw. You'll see. I'll follow along with you. It'll be okay. Just begin now like I'm telling you. You'll see. Draw," the blind man said.

So I began. First I drew a box that looked like a house. It could have been the house I lived in. Then I put a roof on it. At either end of the roof, I drew spires. Crazy.

"Swell," he said. "Terrific. You're doing fine," he said. "Never thought anything like this could happen in your lifetime, did you, bub? Well, it's a strange life, we all know that. Go on now. Keep it up."

I put in windows with arches. I drew flying buttresses. I hung great doors. I couldn't stop. The TV station went off the air. I put down the pen and closed and opened my fingers. The blind man felt around over the paper. He moved the tips of his fingers over the paper, all over what I had drawn, and he nodded.

"Doing fine," the blind man said.

I took up the pen again, and he found my hand. I kept at it. I'm no artist. But I kept drawing just the same.

My wife opened up her eyes and gazed at us. She sat up on the sofa, her robe hanging open. She said, "What are you doing? Tell me, I want to know."

I didn't answer her.

The blind man said, "We're drawing a cathedral. Me and him are working on it. Press hard," he said to me. "That's right. That's good," he said. "Sure. You got it, bub. I can tell. You didn't think you could. But you can, can't you? You're cooking with gas now. You know what I'm saying? We're going to really have us something here in a minute. How's the old arm?" he said. "Put some people in there now. What's a cathedral without people?"

My wife said, "What's going on? Robert, what are you doing? What's going on?"

"It's all right," he said to her. "Close your eyes now," the blind man said to me.

I did it. I closed them just like he said.

"Are they closed?" he said. "Don't fudge."

"They're closed," I said.

"Keep them that way," he said. He said, "Don't stop now. Draw."

So we kept on with it. His fingers rode my fingers as my hand went over the paper. It was like nothing else in my life up to now.

Then he said, "I think that's it. I think you got it," he said. "Take a look. What do you think?"

But I had my eyes closed. I thought I'd keep them that way for a little longer. I thought it was something I ought to do.

"Well?" he said. "Are you looking?"

My eyes were still closed. I was in my house. I knew that. But I didn't feel like I was inside anything.

"It's really something," I said.

White Angel

Michael Cunningham

We lived then in Cleveland, in the middle of everything. It was the sixties—our radios sang out love all day long. This of course is history. It was before the city of Cleveland went broke, before its river caught fire. We were four. My mother and father, Carlton, and me. Carlton turned sixteen the year I turned nine. Between us were several brothers and sisters, weak flames quenched in our mother's womb. We are not a fruitful or many-branched line. Our family name is Morrow.

Our father was a high school music teacher. Our mother taught children called "exceptional," which meant that some could name the day Christmas would fall in the year 2000 but couldn't remember to take down their pants when they peed. We lived in a tract called Woodlawn—neat one- and two-story houses painted optimistic colors. The tract bordered a cemetery. Behind our back yard was a gully choked with brush and, beyond that, the field of smooth, polished stones. I grew up with the cemetery and didn't mind it. It could be beautiful. A single stone angel, small-breasted and determined, rose amid the more conservative markers close to our house. Farther away, in a richer section, miniature mosques and Parthenons spoke silently to Cleveland of man's enduring accomplishments. Carlton and I played in the cemetery as children and, with a little more age, smoked joints and drank Southern Comfort there. I was, thanks to Carlton, the most criminally advanced nine-year-old in my fourth-grade class. I was going places. I made no move without his counsel.

Here is Carlton several months before his death, in an hour so alive with snow that earth and sky are identically white. He labors among the markers, and I run after, stung by snow, following the light of his red knitted cap. Carlton's hair is pulled back into a ponytail, neat and economical, a perfect pine cone of hair. He is thrifty, in his way.

We have taken hits of acid with our breakfast juice. Or, rather, Carlton has taken a hit, and I, in consideration of my youth, have been allowed half. This acid is called windowpane. It is for clarity of vision, as Vicks is for decongestion of the nose. Our parents are at work, earning the daily bread. We have come out into the cold so that the house, when we reenter it, will shock us with its warmth and righteousness. Carlton believes in shocks.

"I think I'm coming on to it," I call out. Carlton has on his buckskin jacket, which is worn down to the shine. On the back, across his shoulder blades, his girlfriend has stitched an electric blue eye. As we walk I speak into the eye. "I think I feel something," I say.

"Too soon," Carlton calls back. "Stay loose, Frisco. You'll know when the time comes."

I am excited and terrified. We are into serious stuff. Carlton has done acid half a dozen times before, but I am new at it. We slipped the tabs into our mouths at breakfast, while our mother paused over the bacon. Carlton likes taking risks.

Snow collects in the engraved letters on the headstones. I lean into the wind, trying to decide whether everything around me seems strange because of the drug or just because everything truly is strange. Three weeks earlier, a family across town had been sitting at home, watching television, when a single-engine plane fell on them. Snow swirls around us, seeming to fall up as well as down.

Carlton leads the way to our spot, the pillared entrance to a society tomb. This tomb is a palace. Stone cherubs cluster on the peaked roof, with their stunted, frozen wings and matrons' faces. Under the roof is a veranda, backed by cast-iron doors that lead to the house of the dead proper. In summer this veranda is cool. In winter it blocks the wind. We keep a bottle of Southern Comfort here.

Carlton finds the bottle, unscrews the cap, and takes a good, long draw. He is studded with snowflakes. He hands me the bottle, and I take a more conservative drink. Even in winter, the tomb smells mossy. Dead leaves and a yellow M&M's wrapper, worried by the wind, scrape on the marble floor.

"Are you scared?" Carlton asks me.

I nod. I never think of lying to him.

"Don't be, man," he says. "Fear will screw you right up. Drugs can't hurt you if you feel no fear."

I nod.

We stand sheltered, passing the bottle. I lean into Carlton's certainty as if it gave off heat.

"We can do acid all the time at Woodstock," I say.

"Right on. Woodstock Nation. Yow!"

"Do people really *live* there?" I ask.

"Man, you've got to stop asking that. The concert's over, but people are still there. It's a new nation. Have faith."

I nod again, satisfied. There is a different country for us to live in. I am already a new person, renamed Frisco. My old name was Robert.

"We'll do acid all the time," I say.

"You better believe we will." Carlton's face, surrounded by snow and marble, is lit. His eyes are vivid as neon. Something in them tells me he can see the future, a ghost that hovers over everybody's head. In Carlton's future we all get released from our jobs and schooling. Awaiting us all, and soon, is a bright, perfect simplicity. A life among the trees by the river.

"How are you feeling, man?" he asks me.

"Great," I tell him, and it is purely the truth. Doves clatter up out of a bare tree and turn at the same instant, transforming themselves from steel to silver in snow-blown light. I know then that the drug is working. Everything before me has become suddenly, radiantly itself. How could Carlton have known this was about to happen? "Oh," I whisper. His hand settles on my shoulder.

"Stay loose, Frisco," he says. "There's not a thing in this pretty world to be afraid of. I'm here."

I am not afraid. I am astonished. I had not realized until this moment how real everything is. A twig lies on the marble at my feet, bearing a cluster of hard brown berries. The broken-off end is raw, white, fleshy. Trees are alive.

"I'm here," Carlton says again, and he is.

Hours later, we are sprawled on the sofa in front of the television, ordinary as Wally and the Beav. Our mother makes dinner in the kitchen. A pot lid clangs. We are undercover agents. I am trying to conceal my amazement.

Our father is building a grandfather clock from a kit. He wants to have something to leave us, something for us to pass along. We can hear him in the basement, sawing and pounding. I know what is laid out on his sawhorses—a long, raw wooden box, onto which he glues fancy moldings. A pearl of sweat meanders down his forehead as he works. Tonight I discovered my ability to see every room of the house at once, to know every single thing that goes on. A mouse nibbles inside the wall. Electrical wires curl behind the plaster, hidden and patient as snakes.

"Sh-h-h," I say to Carlton, who has not said anything. He is watching television through his splayed fingers. Gunshots ping. Bullets raise chalk dust on a concrete wall. I have no idea what we are watching.

"Boys?" our mother calls from the kitchen. I can, with my new ears, hear her slap hamburger into patties. "Set the table like good citizens," she calls.

"O.K., Ma," Carlton replies, in a gorgeous imitation of normality. Our father hammers in the basement. I can feel Carlton's heart ticking. He pats my hand, to assure me that everything's perfect.

We set the table, fork knife spoon, paper napkins triangled to one side. We know the moves cold. After we are done I pause to notice the dining room wallpaper: a golden farm, backed by mountains. Cows graze, autumn trees cast golden shade. This scene repeats itelf three times, on three walls. "Zap," Carlton whispers. "Zzzzzoom."

"Did we do it right?" I ask him.

"We did everything perfect, little son. How are you doing in there, anyway?" He raps lightly on my head.

"Perfect, I guess." I am staring at the wallpaper as if I were thinking of stepping into it.

"You guess. You guess? You and I are going to other planets, man. Come over here."

"Where?"

"Here. Come here." He leads me to the window. Outside, snow skitters under the street lamps. Ranch-style houses hoard their warmth but bleed light into the gathering snow.

"You and I are going to fly, man," Carlton whispers, close to my ear. He opens the window. Snow blows in, sparking on the carpet. "Fly," he says, and we do. For a moment we strain up and out, the black night wind blowing in our faces—we raise ourselves up off the cocoa-colored deep-pile wool-and-poly-ester carpet by a sliver of an inch. I swear it to this day. Sweet glory. The secret of flight is this: You have to do it immediately, before your body realizes it is defying the laws.

We both know we have taken momentary leave of the earth. It does not strike either of us as remarkable, any more than does the fact that airplanes some-times fall from the sky, or that we have always lived in Ohio and will soon leave for a new nation. We settle back down. Carlton touches my shoulder.

"You wait, Frisco," he says. "Miracles are happening. Goddam miracles."

I nod. He pulls down the window, which reseals itself with a sucking sound. Our own faces look back at us from the cold, dark glass. Behind us, our mother drops the hamburgers into the skillet. Our father bends to his work under a hooded light bulb, preparing the long box into which he will lay clockwork, pendulum, a face. A plane drones by overhead, invisible in the clouds. I glance nervously at Carlton. He smiles his assurance and squeezes the back of my neck.

March. After the thaw. I am walking through the cemetery, thinking about my endless life. One of the beauties of living in Cleveland is that any direc-tion feels like progress. I've memorized the map. We are by my calculations 350 miles shy of Woodstock, New York. On this raw new day I am walking east, to the place where Carlton and I keep our bottle. I am going to have an early nip, to celebrate my bright future.

When I get to our spot I hear low moans coming from behind the tomb. I freeze, considering my options. The sound is a long, drawn-out agony with a whip at the end, a final high C, something like "ooooooOw." A wolf's cry run backward. What decides me on investigation rather than flight is the need to create a story. In the stories Carlton likes best, people always do the fool-ish, risky thing. I find I can reach decisions this way—by thinking of myself as a character in a story told by Carlton.

I creep around the side of the monument, cautious as a badger, pressed up close to the marble. I peer over a cherub's girlish shoulder. What I find is Carl-ton on the ground with his girlfriend, in a jumble of clothes and bare flesh. Carlton's jacket, the one with the embroidered eye, is draped over the stone, keeping watch.

I hunch behind the statue. I can see the girl's naked arms, and the famil-iar bones of Carlton's spine. The two of them moan together in the brown win-ter grass. Though I can't make out the girl's expression, Carlton's face is twisted and grimacing, the cords of his neck pulled tight. I had never thought the expe-rience might be painful. I watch, trying to learn. I hold on to the cherub's cold wings.

It isn't long before Carlton catches sight of me. His eyes rove briefly, ecsta-tically skyward, and what do they light on but his brother's small head, sticking up next to a cherub's. We lock eyes and spend a moment in mutual decision. The girl keeps on clutching at Carlton's skinny back. He decides to smile at me. He decides to wink.

I am out of there so fast I tear up divots. I dodge among the stones, jump the gully, clear the fence into the swing-set-and-picnic-table sanctity of the back yard. Something about that wink. My heart beats fast as a sparrow's.

I go into the kitchen and find our mother washing fruit. She asks what's going on. I tell her nothing is. Nothing at all.

She sighs over an apple's imperfection. The curtains sport blue teapots. Our mother works the apple with a scrub brush. She believes they come coated with poison.

"Where's Carlton?" she asks.

"Don't know," I tell her.

"Bobby?"

"Huh?"

"What exactly is going on?"

"Nothing," I say. My heart works itself up to a hummingbird's rate, more buzz than beat.

"I think something is. Will you answer a question?"

"O.K."

"Is your brother taking drugs?"

I relax a bit. It's only drugs. I know why she is asking. Lately police cars have been cruising past our house like sharks. They pause, take note, glide on. Some neighborhood crackdown. Carlton is famous in these parts.

"No," I tell her.

She faces me with the brush in one hand, an apple in the other. "You wouldn't lie to me, would you?" She knows something is up. Her nerves run through this house. She can feel dust settling on the tabletops, milk starting to turn in the refrigerator.

"No," I say.

"Something's going on," she sighs. She is a small, efficient woman who looks at things as if they gave off a painful light. She grew up on a farm in Wisconsin and spent her girlhood tying up bean rows, worrying over the sun and rain. She is still trying to overcome her habit of modest expectations.

I leave the kitchen, pretending sudden interest in the cat. Our mother follows, holding her brush. She means to scrub the truth out of me. I follow the cat, his erect black tail and pink anus.

"Don't walk away when I'm talking to you," our mother says.

I keep walking, to see how far I'll get, calling "Kittykittykitty." In the front hall, our father's homemade clock chimes the half hour. I make for the clock. I get as far as the rubber plant before she collars me.

"I told you not to walk away," she says, and cuffs me a good one with the brush. She catches me on the ear and sets it ringing. The cat is out of there quick as a quarter note.

I stand for a minute, to let her know I've received the message. Then I resume walking. She hits me again, this time on the back of the head, hard enough to make me see colors. "Will you *stop?*" she screams. Still, I keep walk-ing. Our house runs west to east. With every step I get closer to Yasgur's farm.

Carlton comes home whistling. Our mother treats him like a guest who's overstayed. He doesn't care. He is lost in optimism. He pats her cheek and calls her "Professor." He treats her as if she were harmless, and so she is.

She never hits Carlton. She suffers him the way farm girls suffer a thiev-ing crow, with a grudge so old it borders on reverence. She gives him a scrubbed apple and tells him what she'll do if he tracks mud on the carpet.

I am waiting in our room. He brings the smell of the cemetery with him— its old snow and wet pine needles. He rolls his eyes at me, takes a crunch of his apple. "What's happening, Frisco?" he says.

I have arranged myself loosely on my bed, trying to pull a Dylan riff out of my harmonica. I have always figured I can bluff my way into wisdom. I offer Carlton a dignified nod.

He drops onto his own bed. I can see a crushed crocus stuck to the black rubber sole of his boot.

"Well, Frisco," he says. "Today you are a man."

I nod again. Is that all there is to it?

"*Yow,*" Carlton says. He laughs, pleased with himself and the world. "That was so perfect."

"I pick out what I can of "Blowin' in the Wind."

Carlton says, "Man, when I saw you out there spying on us I thought to myself, *Yes.* Now *I*'m really here. You know what I'm saying?" He waves his apple core.

"Uh-huh," I say.

"Frisco, that was the first time her and I ever did it. I mean, we'd talked. But when we finally got down to it, there you were. My brother. Like you *knew.*"

I nod, and this time for real. What happened was an adventure we had together. All right. The story is beginning to make sense.

"Aw, Frisco," Carlton says. "I'm gonna find you a girl, too. You're nine. You been a virgin too long."

"Really?" I say.

"*Man.* We'll find you a woman from the sixth grade, somebody with a lit-tle experience. We'll get stoned and all make out under the trees in the bone-yard. I want to be present at your deflowering, man. You're gonna need a brother there."

I am about to ask, as casually as I can manage, about the relationship between love and bodily pain, when our mother's voice cuts into the room. "You did it," she screams. "You tracked mud all over the rug."

A family entanglement follows. Our mother brings our father, who comes and stands in the doorway with her, taking in evidence. He is a formerly hand-some man. His face has been worn down by too much patience. He has lately taken up some sporty touches—a goatee, a pair of calfskin boots.

Our mother points out the trail of muddy half-moons that lead from the door to Carlton's bed. Dangling over the end of the bed are the culprits them-selves, voluptuously muddy, with Carlton's criminal feet still in them.

"You see?" she says. "You see what he thinks of me?"

Our father, a reasonable man, suggests that Carlton clean it up. Our mother finds that too small a gesture. She wants Carlton not to have done it in the first place. "I don't ask for much," she says. "I don't ask where he goes. I don't ask why the police are suddenly so interested in our house. I ask that he not track mud all over the floor. That's all." She squints in the glare of her own outrage.

"Better clean it right up," our father says to Carlton.

"And that's it?" our mother says. "He cleans up the mess and all is forgiven?"

"Well, what do you want him to do? Lick it up?"

"I want some consideration," she says, turning helplessly to me. "That's what I want."

I shrug, at a loss. I sympathize with our mother but am not on her team.

"All right," she says. "I just won't bother cleaning the house anymore. I'll let you men handle it. I'll sit and watch television and throw my candy wrappers on the floor."

She starts out, cutting the air like a blade. On the way she picks up a jar of pencils, looks at it, and tosses the pencils on the floor. They fall like fortune-telling sticks, in pairs and criss-crosses.

Our father goes after her, calling her name. Her name is Isabel. We can hear them making their way across the house, our father calling "Isabel, Isabel, Isabel," while our mother, pleased with the way the pencils looked, dumps more things onto the floor.

"I hope she doesn't break the TV," I say.

"She'll do what she needs to do," Carlton says.

"I hate her," I say. I am not certain about that. I want to test the sound of it, to see if it's true.

"She's got more balls than any of us, Frisco," he says. "Better watch what you say about her."

I keep quiet. Soon I get up and start gathering pencils, because I prefer that to lying around and trying to follow the shifting lines of allegiance. Carlton goes for a sponge and starts in on the mud.

"You get shit on the carpet, you clean it up," he says. "Simple."

The time for all my questions about love has passed, and I am not so unhip as to force a subject. I know it will come up again. I make a neat bouquet of pencils. Our mother rages through the house.

Later, after she has thrown enough and we three have picked it all up, I lie on my bed thinking things over. Carlton is on the phone to his girlfriend, talking low. Our mother, becalmed but still dangerous, cooks dinner. She sings as she cooks, some slow forties number that must have been all over the jukes when her first husband's plane went down in the Pacific. Our father plays his clarinet in the basement. That is where he goes to practice, down among his woodworking tools, the neatly hung hammers and awls that throw oversized shadows in the light of the single bulb. If I put my ear to the floor, I can hear him, pulling a long, low tomcat moan out of that horn. There is some strange comfort in pressing my ear to the carpet and hearing our father's music leaking up through the floorboards. Lying down, with my ear to the floor, I join in on my harmonica.

That spring our parents have a party to celebrate the sun's return. It has been a long, bitter winter, and now the first wild daisies are poking up on the lawns and among the graves.

Our parents' parties are mannerly affairs. Their friends, schoolteachers all, bring wine jugs and guitars. They are Ohio hip. Though they hold jobs and meet mortgages, they think of themselves as independent spirits on a spying mission. They have agreed to impersonate teachers until they write their novels, finish their dissertations, or just save up enough money to set themselves free.

Carlton and I are the lackeys. We take coats, fetch drinks. We have done this at every party since we were small, trading on our precocity, doing a brother act. We know the moves. A big, lipsticked woman who has devoted her maidenhood to ninth-grade math calls me Mr. Right. An assistant vice principal in a Russian fur hat asks us both whether we expect to vote Democratic or Socialist. By sneaking sips I manage to get myself semicrocked.

The reliability of the evening is derailed halfway through, however, by a half dozen of Carlton's friends. They rap on the door and I go for it, anxious as a carnival sharp to see who will step up next and swallow the illusion that I'm a kindly, sober nine-year-old child. I'm expecting callow adults, and what do I find but a pack of young outlaws, big-booted and wild-haired. Carlton's girlfriend stands in front, in an outfit made up almost entirely of fringe.

"Hi, Bobby," she says confidently. She comes from New York, and is more than just locally smart.

"Hi," I say. I let them all in despite a retrograde urge to lock the door and phone the police. Three are girls, four boys. They pass me in a cloud of dope smoke and sly-eyed greeting.

What they do is invade the party. Carlton is standing on the far side of the rumpus room, picking the next album, and his girl cuts straight through the crowd to his side. She has the bones and the loose, liquid moves some people consider beautiful. She walks through that room as if she'd been sent to teach the whole party a lesson.

Carlton's face tips me off that this was planned. Our mother demands to know what's going on here. She is wearing a long, dark red dress that doesn't interfere with her shoulders. When she dresses up, you can see what it is about her, or what it was. She is the source of Carlton's beauty. I have our father's face.

Carlton does some quick talking. Though it is against our mother's better judgment, the invaders are suffered to stay. One of them, an Eddie Haskell for all his leather and hair, tells her she is looking good. She is willing to hear it.

So the outlaws, house-sanctioned, start to mingle. I work my way over to Carlton's side, the side unoccupied by his girlfriend. I would like to say something ironic and wised-up, something that will band Carlton and me against every other person in the room. I can feel the shape of the comment I have in mind, but, being a tipsy nine-year-old, can't get my mouth around it. What I say is "Shit, man."

Carlton's girl laughs. I would like to tell her what I have figured out about her, but I am nine, and three-quarters gone on Tom Collinses. Even sober, I can only imagine a sharp-tongued wit.

"Hang on, Frisco," Carlton tells me. "This could turn into a real party."

I can tell by the light in his eyes what is going down. He has arranged a blind date between our parents' friends and his own. It's a Woodstock move—he is plotting a future in which young and old have business together. I agree to hang on, and go to the kitchen, hoping to sneak a few knocks of gin.

There I find our father leaning up against the refrigerator. A line of butterfly-shaped magnets hovers around his head. "Are you enjoying this party?" he asks, touching his goatee. He is still getting used to being a man with a beard.

"Uh-huh."

"I am, too," he says sadly. He never meant to be a high school music teacher. The money question caught up with him.

"What do you think of this music?" he asks. Carlton has put the Stones on the turntable. Mick Jagger sings "19th Nervous Breakdown." Our father gestures in an openhanded way that takes in the room, the party, the whole house—everything the music touches.

"I like it," I say.

"So do I." He stirs his drink with his finger, and sucks on the finger.

"I *love* it," I say, too loud. Something about our father leads me to raise my voice. I want to grab handfuls of music out of the air and stuff them into my mouth.

"I'm not sure I could say I love it," he says. "I'm not sure if I could say that, no. I would say I'm friendly to its intentions. I would say that if this is the direction music is going in, I won't stand in its way."

"Uh-huh," I say. I am already anxious to get back to the party but don't want to hurt his feelings. If he senses he's being avoided, he can fall into fits of apology more terrifying than our mother's rages.

"I think I may have been too rigid with my students," our father says. "Maybe over the summer you boys could teach me a few things about the music young people are listening to these days."

"Sure," I say loudly. We spend a minute waiting for the next thing to say.

"You boys are happy, aren't you?" he asks. "Are you enjoying this party?"

"We're having a great time," I say.

"I thought you were. I am, too."

I have by this time gotten myself to within jumping distance of the door. I call out, "Well, goodbye," and dive back into the party.

Something has happened in my absence. The party has started to roll. Call it an accident of history and the weather. Carlton's friends are on decent behavior, and our parents' friends have decided to give up some of their wine-and-folksong propriety to see what they can learn. Carlton is dancing with a vice principal's wife. Carlton's friend Frank, with his ancient-child face and I.Q. in the low sixties, dances with our mother. I see that our father has followed me out of the kitchen. He positions himself at the party's edge; I leap into its center. I invite the fuchsia-lipped math teacher to dance. She is only too happy.

She is big and graceful as a parade float, and I steer her effortlessly out into the middle of everything. My mother, who is known around school for Sicilian discipline, dances freely, which is news to everybody. There is no getting around her beauty.

The night rises higher and higher. A wildness sets in. Carlton throws new music on the turntable—Janis Joplin, the Doors, the Dead. The future shines for everyone, rich with the possibility of more nights exactly like this. Even our father is pressed into dancing, which he does like a flightless bird, all flapping arms and potbelly. Still, he dances. Our mother has a kiss for him.

Finally I nod out on the sofa, blissful under the drinks. I am dreaming of flight when our mother comes and touches my shoulder. I smile up into her flushed, smiling face.

"It's hours past your bedtime," she says, all velvet motherliness. I nod. I can't dispute the fact.

She keeps on nudging my shoulder. I am a moment or two apprehending the fact that she actually wants me to leave the party and go to bed. "No," I tell her.

"Yes," she smiles.

"No," I say cordially, experimentally. This new mother can dance, and flirt. Who knows what else she might allow?

"Yes." The velvet motherliness leaves her voice. She means business of the usual kind. I get myself off the sofa and I run to Carlton for protection. He is laughing with his girl, a sweaty question mark of hair plastered to his forehead. I plow into him so hard he nearly goes over.

"Whoa, Frisco," he says. He takes me up under the arms and swings me a half turn. Our mother plucks me out of his hands and sets me down, with a good, farm-style hold on the back of my neck.

"Say good night, Bobby," she says. She adds, for the benefit of Carlton's girl, "He should have been in bed before this party started."

"*No*," I holler. I try to twist loose, but our mother has a grip that could crack walnuts.

Carlton's girl tosses her hair and says, "Good night, baby." She smiles a victor's smile. She smoothes the stray hair off Carlton's forehead.

"*No*," I scream again. Something about the way she touches his hair. Our mother calls our father, who comes and scoops me up and starts out of the room with me, holding me like a live bomb. Before I go, I lock eyes with Carlton. He shrugs and says, "Night, man." Our father hustles me out. I do not take it bravely. I leave flailing, too furious to cry, dribbling a thread of spittle.

Later I lie alone on my narrow bed, feeling the music hum in the coiled springs. Life is cracking open right there in our house. People are changing. By tomorrow, no one will be quite the same. How can they let me miss it? I dream up revenge against our parents, and worse for Carlton. He is the one who could have saved me. He could have banded with me against them. What I can't forgive is his shrug, his mild-eyed "Night, man." He has joined the adults. He has made himself bigger and taken size from me. As the Doors thump "Strange Days," I hope something awful happens to him. I say so to myself.

Around midnight, dim-witted Frank announces he has seen a flying saucer hovering over the back yard. I can hear his deep, excited voice all the way in my room. He says it is like a blinking, luminous cloud. I hear half the party struggling out through the sliding glass door in a disorganized whooping knot. By that time everyone is so delirious a flying saucer would be just what was expected. That much celebration would logically attract an answering happiness from across the stars.

I get out of bed and sneak down the hall. I will not miss alien visitors for anyone, not even at the cost of our mother's wrath or our father's disappointment. I stop at the end of the hallway, though, embarrassed to be in pajamas. If there really are aliens, they will think I am the lowest member of the house. While I hesitate over whether to go back to my room to change, people start coming back inside, talking about a trick of the mist and an airplane. People resume their dancing.

Carlton must have jumped the back fence. He must have wanted to be there alone, singular, in case they decided to take somebody with them. A few nights later I will go out and stand where he could have been standing. On the far side of the gully, now a river swollen with melted snow, the cemetery will gleam like a lost city. The moon will be full. I will hang around just as Carlton must have, hypnotized by the silver light on the stones, the white angel raising her arms across the river.

According to our parents the mystery is why he ran back to the house full tilt. Something in the graveyard may have scared him, he may have needed to break its spell, but I think it's more likely that when he came back to himself he just couldn't wait to return to the music and the people, the noisy disorder of continuing life.

Somebody has shut the sliding glass door. Carlton's girlfriend looks lazily out, touching base with her own reflection. I look, too. Carlton is running toward the house. I hesitate. Then I figure he can bump his nose. It will be a good joke on him. I let him keep coming. His girlfriend sees him through her own reflection, starts to scream a warning just as Carlton hits the glass.

It is an explosion. Triangles of glass fly brightly through the room. I think that for him, it must be more surprising than painful, like hitting water from a great height. He stands blinking for a moment. The whole party stops, stares, getting its bearings. Bob Dylan sings "Just Like a Woman." Carlton reaches up curiously to take out the shard of glass that is stuck in his neck, and that is when the blood starts. It shoots out of him. Our mother screams. Carlton steps forward into his girlfriend's arms and the two of them fall together. Our mother throws herself down on top of him and the girl. People shout their accident wisdom. Don't lift him. Call an ambulance. I watch from the hallway. Carlton's blood spurts, soaking into the carpet, spattering people's clothes. Our mother and father both try to plug the wound with their hands, but the blood just shoots between their fingers. Carlton looks more puzzled than anything, as if he can't quite follow this turn of events. "It's all right," our father tells him, trying to stop the blood. "It's all right, just don't move, it's all right." Carlton nods, and holds our father's hand. His eyes take on an astonished light. Our mother screams, "Is anybody *doing* anything?" What comes out of Carlton grows darker, almost black. I watch. Our father tries to get a hold on Carlton's neck while Carlton keeps trying to take his hand. Our mother's hair is matted with blood. It runs down her face. Carlton's girl holds him to her breasts, touches his hair, whispers in his ear.

He is gone by the time the ambulance gets there. You can see the life drain out of him. When his face goes slack our mother wails. A part of her flies wailing through the house, where it will wail and rage forever. I feel our mother pass through me on her way out. She covers Carlton's body with her own.

He is buried in the cemetery out back. Years have passed—we are living in the future, and it has turned out differently from what we'd planned. Our mother has established her life of separateness behind the guest room door. Our father mutters his greetings to the door as he passes.

One April night, almost a year to the day after Carlton's accident, I hear cautious footsteps shuffling across the living room floor after midnight. I run out eagerly, thinking of ghosts, but find only our father in moth-colored pajamas. He looks unsteadily at the dark air in front of him.

"Hi, Dad," I say from the doorway.

He looks in my direction. "Yes?"

"It's me. Bobby."

"Oh, Bobby," he says. "What are you doing up, young man?"

"Nothing," I tell him. "Dad?"

"Yes, son."

"Maybe you better come back to bed. O.K.?"

"Maybe I had," he says. "I just came out here for a drink of water, but I seem to have gotten turned around in the darkness. Yes, maybe I better had."

I take his hand and lead him down the hall to his room. The grandfather clock chimes the quarter hour.

"Sorry," our father says.

I get him into bed. "There," I say. "O.K.?"

"Perfect. Could not be better."

"O.K. Good night."

"Good night. Bobby?"

"Uh-huh?"

"Why don't you stay a minute?" he says. "We could have ourselves a talk, you and me. How would that be?"

"O.K.," I say. I sit on the edge of his mattress. His bedside clock ticks off the minutes.

I can hear the low rasp of his breathing. Around our house, the Ohio night chirps and buzzes. The small gray finger of Carlton's stone pokes up among the others, within sight of the angel's white eyes. Above us, airplanes and satellites sparkle. People are flying even now toward New York or California, to take up lives of risk and invention.

I stay until our father has worked his way into a muttering sleep.

Carlton's girlfriend moved to Denver with her family a month before. I never learned what it was she'd whispered to him. Though she'd kept her head admirably during the accident, she lost it afterward. She cried so hard at the funeral that she had to be taken away by her mother—an older, redder-haired version of her. She started seeing a psychiatrist three times a week. Everyone, including my parents, talked about how hard it was for her, to have held a dying boy in her arms at that age. I'm grateful to her for holding my brother while he died, but I never once heard her mention the fact that though she had been through something terrible, at least she was still alive and going places. At least she had protected herself by trying to warn him. I can appreciate the intricacies of her pain. But as long as she was in Cleveland, I could never look her straight in the face. I couldn't talk about the wounds she suffered. I can't even write her name.

. . . what is useful is eavesdropping, listening, talking to people in an informal way, sitting around tables swapping stories, listening to kids. I might take notes, too. And I keep huge notebook sketches. I have one that's just physical descriptions: faces postures, walks, the way somebody's elbows point outward, their complexion, the cast of their eyes, any scars, pockmarks, peculiar gaits, accents, odd ways of holding the mouth. So all these things I'll write down at odd moments as I travel . . . And when I approach a new novel, I know the characters I want and will look through to see if I can find a physical description that fits.
—E. ANNIE PROUX

How to Talk
to a Hunter

Pam Houston

When he says "Skins or blankets?" it will take you a moment to realize that he's asking which you want to sleep under. And in your hesitation he'll decide that he wants to see your skin wrapped in the big black moose hide. He carried it, he'll say, soaking wet and heavier than a dead man, across the tundra for two—was it hours or days or weeks? But the payoff, now, will be to see it fall across one of your white breasts. It's December, and your skin is never really warm, so you will pull the bulk of it around you and pose for him, pose for his camera, without having to narrate this moose's death.

You will spend every night in this man's bed without asking yourself why he listens to top-forty country. Why he donated money to the Republican Party. Why he won't play back his messages while you are in the room. You are there so often the messages pile up. Once you noticed the bright green counter reading as high as fifteen.

He will have lured you here out of a careful independence that you spent months cultivating; though it will finally be winter, the dwindling daylight and the threat of Christmas, that makes you give in. Spending nights with this man means suffering the long face of your sheepdog, who likes to sleep on your bed, who worries when you don't come home. But the hunter's house is so much warmer than yours, and he'll give you a key, and just like a woman, you'll think that means something. It will snow hard for thirteen straight days. Then it will really get cold. When it is sixty below there will be no wind and no clouds, just still air and cold sunshine. The sun on the windows will lure you out of bed, but he'll pull you back under. The next two hours he'll devote to your body. With his hands, with his tongue, he'll express what will seem to you like the most eternal of loves. Like the house key, this is just another kind of lie. Even in bed; especially in bed, you and he cannot speak the same language. The machine will answer the incoming calls. From under an ocean of passion and hide and hair you'll hear a woman's muffled voice between the beeps.

Your best female friend will say, "So what did you think? That a man who sleeps under a dead moose is capable of commitment?"

This is what you learned in college: A man desires the satisfaction of his desire; a woman desires the condition of desiring.

The hunter will talk about spring in Hawaii, summer in Alaska. The man who says he was always better at math will form the sentences so carefully it will be impossible to tell if you are included in these plans. When he asks you if you would like to open a small guest ranch way out in the country, understand that this is a rhetorical question. Label these conversations future perfect, but don't expect the present to catch up with them. Spring is an inconceivable distance from the December days that just keep getting shorter and gray.

He'll ask you if you've ever shot anything, if you'd like to, if you ever thought about teaching your dog to retrieve. Your dog will like him too much, will drop the stick at his feet every time, will roll over and let the hunter scratch his belly.

One day he'll leave you sleeping to go split wood or get the mail and his phone will ring again. You'll sit very still while a woman who calls herself something like Janie Coyote leaves a message on his machine: She's leaving work, she'll say, and the last thing she wanted to hear was the sound of his beautiful voice. Maybe she'll talk only in rhyme. Maybe the counter will change to sixteen. You'll look a question at the mule deer on the wall, and the dark spots on either side of his mouth will tell you he shares more with this hunter than you ever will. One night, drunk, the hunter told you he was sorry for taking that deer, that every now and then there's an animal that isn't meant to be taken, and he should have known that deer was one.

Your best male friend will say, "No one who needs to call herself Janie Coyote can hold a candle to you, but why not let him sleep alone a few nights, just to make sure?"

The hunter will fill your freezer with elk burger, venison sausage, organic potatoes, fresh pecans. He'll tell you to wear your seat belt, to dress warmly, to drive safely. He'll say you are always on his mind, that you're the best thing that's ever happened to him, that you make him glad that he's a man.

Tell him it don't come easy, tell him freedom's just another word for nothing left to lose.

These are the things you'll know without asking: The coyote woman wears her hair in braids. She uses words like "howdy." She's man enough to shoot a deer.

A week before Christmas you'll rent *It's a Wonderful Life* and watch it together, curled on your couch, faces touching. Then you'll bring up the word "monogamy." He'll tell you how badly he was hurt by your predecessor. He'll tell you he couldn't be happier spending every night with you. He'll say there's just a few questions he doesn't have the answers for. He'll say he's just scared and confused. Of course this isn't exactly what he means. Tell him you understand. Tell him you are scared too. Tell him to take all the time he needs. Know that you could never shoot an animal; and be glad of it.

Your best female friend will say, "You didn't tell him you loved him, did you?" Don't even tell her the truth. If you do you'll have to tell her that he said this: "I feel exactly the same way."

Your best male friend will say, "Didn't you know what would happen when you said the word 'commitment'?"
But that isn't the word that you said.
He'll say, "Commitment, monogamy, it all means just one thing."
The coyote woman will come from Montana with the heavier snows. The hunter will call you on the day of the solstice to say he has a friend in town and can't see you. He'll leave you hanging your Christmas lights; he'll give new meaning to the phrase "longest night of the year." The man who has said he's not so good with words will manage to say eight things about his friend without using a gender-determining pronoun. Get out of the house quickly. Call the most understanding person you know who will let you sleep in his bed.

Your best female friend will say, "So what did you think? That he was capable of living outside his gender?"

When you get home in the morning there's a candy tin on your pillow. Santa, obese and grotesque, fondles two small children on the lid. The card will say something like "From your not-so-secret admirer." Open it. Examine each carefully made truffle. Feed them, one at a time, to the dog. Call the hunter's machine. Tell him you don't speak chocolate.

Your best female friend will say, "At this point, what is it about him that you could possibly find appealing?"

Your best male friend will say, "Can't you understand that this is a good sign? Can't you understand that this proves how deep he's in with you?" Hug your best male friend. Give him the truffles the dog wouldn't eat.

Of course the weather will cooperate with the coyote woman. The highways will close, she will stay another night. He'll tell her he's going to work so he can come and see you. He'll even leave her your number and write "Me at Work" on the yellow pad of paper by his phone. Although you shouldn't, you'll have to be there. It will be you and your nauseous dog and your half-trimmed tree all waiting for him like a series of questions.

This is what you learned in graduate school: In every assumption is contained the possibility of its opposite.

In your kitchen he'll hug you like you might both die there. Sniff him for coyote. Don't hug him back.
He will say whatever he needs to to win. He'll say it's just an old friend. He'll say the visit was all the friend's idea. He'll say the night away from you has

given him time to think about how much you mean to him. Realize that nothing short of sleeping alone will ever make him realize how much you mean to him. He'll say that if you can just be a little patient, some good will come out of this for the two of you after all. He still won't use a gender-specific pronoun.

Put your head in your hands. Think about what it means to be patient. Think about the beautiful, smart, strong, clever woman you thought he saw when he looked at you. Pull on your hair. Rock your body back and forth. Don't cry.

He'll say that after holding you it doesn't feel right holding anyone else. For "holding," substitute "fucking." Then take it as a compliment.

He will get frustrated and rise to leave. He may or may not be bluffing. Stall for time. Ask a question he can't immediately answer. Tell him you want to make love on the floor. When he tells you your body is beautiful say, "I feel exactly the same way." Don't, under any circumstances, stand in front of the door.

Your best female friend will say, "They lie to us, they cheat on us, and we love them more for it." She'll say, "It's our fault; we raise them to be like that." Tell her it can't be your fault. You've never raised anything but dogs.

The hunter will say it's late and he has to go home to sleep. He'll emphasize the last word in the sentence. Give him one kiss that he'll remember while he's fucking the coyote woman. Give him one kiss that ought to make him cry if he's capable of it, but don't notice when he does. Tell him to have a good night.

Your best male friend will say, "We all do it. We can't help it. We're self-destructive. It's the old bad-boy routine. You have a male dog, don't you?"

The next day the sun will be out and the coyote woman will leave. Think about how easy it must be for a coyote woman and a man who listens to top-forty country. The coyote woman would never use a word like "monogamy"; the coyote woman will stay gentle on his mind.

If you can, let him sleep alone for at least one night. If you can't, invite him over to finish trimming your Christmas tree. When he asks how you are, tell him you think it's a good idea to keep your sense of humor during the holidays.

Plan to be breezy and aloof and full of interesting anecdotes about all the other men you've ever known. Plan to be hotter than ever before in bed, and a little cold out of it. Remember that necessity is the mother of invention. Be flexible.

First, he will find the faulty bulb that's been keeping all the others from lighting. He will explain, in great detail, the most elementary electrical principles. You will take turns placing the ornaments you and other men, he and other women, have spent years carefully choosing. Under the circumstances, try to let this be a comforting thought.

He will thin the clusters of tinsel you put on the tree. He'll say something ambiguous like "Next year you should string popcorn and cranberries." Finally, his arm will stretch just high enough to place the angel on the top of the tree.

Your best female friend will say, "Why can't you ever fall in love with a man who will be your friend?"

Your best male friend will say, "You ought to know this by now: Men always cheat on the best women."

This is what you learned in the pop psychology book: Love means letting go of fear.

Play Willie Nelson's "Pretty Paper." He'll ask you to dance, and before you can answer he'll be spinning you around your wood stove, he'll be humming in your ear. Before the song ends he'll be taking off your clothes, setting you lightly under the tree, hovering above you with tinsel in his hair. Through the spread of the branches the all-white lights you insisted on will shudder and blur, outlining the ornaments he brought: a pheasant, a snow goose, a deer.

The record will end. Above the crackle of the wood stove and the rasp of the hunter's breathing you'll hear one long low howl break the quiet of the frozen night: your dog, chained and lonely and cold. You'll wonder if he knows enough to stay in his doghouse. You'll wonder if he knows that the nights are getting shorter now.

Don't think of biography as a history of accomplishment but as a history of desire.
—BIOGRAPHER ON NPR

Live Life King-Sized

Hester Kaplan

Late in the summer of 1993, a hurricane with the gentle name of Tess smashed everything I had into a million pieces. From a window in the cement cooling house where I waited out the storm, I watched the wind suck all the water from the pool, lift the thatch roof from the tiki hut, and detonate the last of the beach chairs. Square by square, the dining room patio was untiled, and just before Tess changed course, a single wave plucked out the entire length of dock.

Hours earlier, my staff had left for the main island, cramming themselves into four tiny boats that seemed more dangerous than any hurricane. I'd told them to take what food they wanted from the kitchen freezers—we'd lose power and it would all spoil—but they still hid it in their bags and under straw hats. They yelled that I was a crazy yellow-haired man to stare a hurricane in the eye. "She will think you're making fun of death," they warned, shielding themselves from the hot wind that was already blowing up their bright shirts, "and death will make fun back at you." On this island, superstitions and sightings are as plentiful as the joints of coral that cut your feet in the sand, and so I waved them away.

Weeks later, a few of my staff straggled up the trashed beach looking for work, but the rest had been spooked away for good and I never saw them again. During the next exhausting year, there wasn't a time when I wasn't picking up broken glass or scrubbing away the pocks and pecks of seawater and sand. I hammered shingles onto the roofs of twenty cabanas, quarried slabs of bluebitch stone, rebuilt the dock, spent all the money I had and borrowed more. When the repairs were almost finished, I got on the phone and begged every travel agent I'd ever had anything to do with in my fifteen years as owner of this place (at twenty-five I had taken over from my mother, now retired to the heart of Manhattan), to steer clients my way. They promised they'd do what they could.

Finally, at the height of my first season back in business, from behind the rethatched tiki bar, I stood for a moment and looked gratefully out at my guests around the pool. Five women from a book group ordered drinks from Tom, who was stiff and unsure in his khakis and flowered shirt, when he was used to carrying buckets and hammers and wearing nothing but a pair of running shorts bleached gauzy. I expected the women to start reading—the same book, of course—but they gazed at the water instead, hands under their thighs, trying on the unfamiliar work of relaxation. Three men I'd checked in the night before when they arrived from a day of delayed flights and too many mixed drinks were already asleep on chaises, their tight faces to the sun. The Jensen family reunion—thirteen in all—took up more than their share of space with their gear and noise. Scattered couples, including a pair on their honeymoon, filled out the small but adequate crowd. Down at the beach, an awkward man lumbered onto a jet-ski while his wife stood on the sand and shouted cautions at him.

The day was brilliant, the heat tempered by the trade winds, and for a lifting moment I heard the hymn I'd been waiting for since the day Tess tore through. Every host, every cook, every seducer listens for his particular sound, and mine was the simple noise of my existence—people at leisure. But despite the sound, I also knew I was barely hanging on to the place I loved so much. I'd left myself no margin for another disaster, and this might be the final decisive season for me. The possibility that I could fail so easily and lose all this—my life, the only place I knew and wanted to be—made me dizzy enough to crouch down and rest my forehead against iced bottles of beer at the base of the bar.

At a sudden shift in the air, I stood again. When I looked past the pool, I saw a deathly figure moving among the shadows. He took forever on desiccated, sticklike legs to move through the low seagrape trees, some of which were badly deformed from the storm. When he stepped out, the bright glare of the sun seemed to shock him absolutely still. His thin, gray lips pursed, and his eyes receded in sore, watery sockets. The hymn died instantly as eyes fixed on the man's distended belly, which urged itself against a pink shirt, and ears attuned to his labored wheeze. Men pulled their knees up, a child fussed, its mother tensed, I held my breath, stunned. Very soon, the man's wife hurried out of the shade to lead her husband to a chair; in a neon pink bathing suit, she looked obscene with health next to him.

I had checked her in the evening before—they were Cecelia and Henry Blaze, from just outside Boston. Henry, she'd explained while signing the registration slip with her own gold-capped pen, didn't travel well, they would skip dinner. Under the bougainvillea'd portico, I could just make out his bent shape among the bags Jono was piling into the cart that would buzz them to their cabana. They were staying for three weeks, Cecelia reminded me as she slipped her pen back in her purse, and she hoped the weather would hold. She was in her mid-fifties, and I could see that she'd been pretty once, but overefficiency and some sadness had taken it out of her. Distracted by noise in the kitchen at that moment, I didn't think about the Blazes again.

Now as Henry Blaze creaked himself onto one of the pool chairs, I anxiously waited for leisure to return poolside, but I saw from the looks on the faces of the other guests that it wasn't going to come back so easily. No one wants to see reality on vacation, and this was an awful lot of reality on such a bright day. If my first thought about Henry Blaze was get him the hell out of here, my second was, is this death making fun back at me? Tess had nearly wiped me out. After everything, I was not going to let a dead man kill me now.

Before dinner that evening, I searched for my one remaining pair of long white pants and linen shirt. My cabana—bedroom, sitting room, bathroom— was the only place that still looked like the hurricane had just blown through. I had replaced the broken windows, but the roof continued to leak and the floor buckled. My bed was unmade—I didn't allow housekeeping in here—the unused half covered with papers, clothes, music tapes I had ordered through the mail, a plate and coffee cup from breakfast.

Some views might be bigger, but I liked the one from my bedroom best. A blue lozenge of water glimmered at the end of a tunnel of seagrape leaves, a less-is-more equation of beauty, and for a seductive second I was stuck on it. I heard calm among the guests, the routine clink of drinks being served on the dining room patio, the two young men I'd hired the week before joking as they put away beach equipment. I had a startling flash of Blaze among the trees, and the possibility that I might lose all this—and then where would I go?—hit me for the second time that day. The outside world seemed tremulous and without borders.

It was too late to iron my shirt once I found it, so I tried to smooth out the wrinkles as I walked to the dining room where the guests were already attempting to outdo each other with descriptions of the sunset. Relieved that Blaze was not around—I assumed he was eating in his cabana and I was spared for the moment—I entered the room as the perfectly confident proprietor.

The book group, shiny in sundresses, ordered a bottle of wine as I stood by their table, hands behind my back. I inhaled their smells that made me a little forgetful as I leaned over glossy shoulders to pour. One of the women had a wonderful, shocked laugh and a head of spiky hair I liked. At another table, the Jensens already had the waiters in a state of mild panic, which seemed to give Bob Jensen a feeling of great power. I'd seen this type before, entitled not by the having of money, but simply by the spending of it. Still, I couldn't deny that the table exuded a kind of welcome, affluent energy.

"How are you all doing?" I said, placing my hand on Jensen's shoulder. I felt the burn on his thick skin through his shirt—I wasn't surprised he'd flipped the sun the finger. He ordered a beer, while some of the older Jensens looked like they'd slipped gently unnoticed into a fugue state. It is true that this business only survives on repeats and referrals, so I brought maraschino cherries for the kids and a very cold beer for Bob Jensen.

I did the room from table to table, made up for the lags the new cook and dining room staff left. This was the head-filling work I was at ease in, the careful organization of a meal, the murmurs of diners, the matte of the red tile floor which would later be mopped down for the night. I heard tones of teasing waft out from the kitchen, and I stared at the spiky-haired woman from the book group, her dress drooping on her shoulders to reveal a glistening chest. I wondered what it would be like if she came back to my wind-whipped cabana and lay on my bed; I'd done this enough times over the years to pacify myself, but never for love. She reminded me that I hadn't stopped to read a book in a long time, and it had been even longer since I'd slept with a woman.

There was a hiss of rubber on the tile just then, and the sound made me recall riding my tricycle around the dining room in the windy off-season, skirting the tables like street corners and stoplights I'd seen in the picture books my mother gave me. But the hissing was Cecelia Blaze, or rather the portable oxygen tank she pulled behind her on a small dolly as she entered the room, clear tubing and the mask draped on a metal hook. She stopped to watch her husband in a white shirt and a pair of beltless pants step cautiously over the threshold of the dining room. The tufts of hair on his alabaster scalp had been combed into temporary compliance.

I showed the Blazes to the last empty table, between the Jensens and the book club. Cecelia ordered for both of them, and when the bisque came, Blaze sipped his loudly and banged the bowl with a large gold pinkie ring set with a red stone. Cecelia did not look at her husband, but stared at the view as she ate. I wondered what twist had led her to marry this older man—and what crueler twist had led them to plague me now.

Blaze didn't look up when I stood by their table, and I could tell he was accustomed to not responding until he was good and ready, that he'd once been in charge of people and things. Cecelia and I talked about hikes she might take, and when I asked if she were interested in a jet-ski—I was only trying to feel something out about these people, what would stir or startle them—she laughed, grateful, I think, for even this lame bit of flattery.

"How about me?" Blaze said.

It was more than I'd heard him say before, and the strength of his voice was unsettling, when I had expected something closer to a rasp or a whisper. His wife pretended he hadn't spoken at all and went back to her soup.

The book club ordered another bottle of wine, and when Blaze began to wheeze, I hurried to pull the cork and pour, to catch the eye of the spiky-haired woman, to make conversation and offer distraction. Cecelia slowly touched her mouth with a napkin and put it by her plate before she stood. A sense of urgency had gripped me and the room, which was now watching the scene with distaste. She began to fumble with the tubing from the oxygen tank, and small words tumbled from her lips. Blaze's shoulders heaved in an increasingly labored way. A waiter stopped short with his tray of melting ice cream for the Jensens.

"Here, let me help you," I offered, and bent down next to Cecelia, who was now kneeling, her skin pale against the red tiles. Her skirt was unwrapped up the length of a freckled thigh, revealing sad white underpants.

"I have it," she said, but continued to pull uselessly at the tubing.

A nervous odor rose off Blaze. I was now almost cheek to cheek with his wife, and a little desperate. "The goddamn thing's taped up," I said.

Cecelia shot me a look of disapproval. She flipped her skirt shut, sat back, and with what seemed like total, prideful indifference, tossed the problem to me; her husband was going to die in *my* dining room. Blaze shifted to the right then, and with a small, almost dainty cough, threw up his dinner. A moment later he took a full, wheezeless sigh while a splatter slid off his square knees onto the floor.

I stood too fast and motioned for my staff to come clean up; suddenly they were blind to me, and I was dizzy.

"Goddamn it!" Blaze said. For the first time we looked directly at each other, and I saw from his eyes that he wasn't really old at all. I could have felt sorry for him then—all this misery in a man just sixty—I was even less forgiving than earlier that he'd chosen my place for this freak show of his.

After some cleaning up, Cecelia slouched her husband out of the room. I assured the book group that Blaze would be fine, though I could see them rallying as concerned women now and not vacationers. I sent Jensen another beer, which he received with a shrug, and I turned on the ceiling fan to blow the death smell of Henry Blaze out to sea.

Later, the book club played poker and scattered plastic chips on the patio floor, their tone a little off, like people having a good time at a wake. I heard the clatter of bikes and mopeds behind the kitchen as the staff heckled their way home. In the front office, I checked the computer as I did every night now, to see if new reservations had come in since I'd last looked. There was only one, and that not yet confirmed. I put my head in my hands.

"Jesus H., that was some scene with the old man tonight," Bob Jensen said, peering into the office and startling me. "Disturbing you?"

"Disturbing me? No, just shutting up for the night," I said. I wanted to tell him not to stroll where he wasn't welcome, and I knew by the way he was hanging around that I'd have to open the bar and give the guy a drink on the house pretty soon. I turned out the office light.

"So, I thought he was going to die right there," Jensen continued, as we walked outside. He shivered for a second in the heat. "You know that noise he made, like a spoon went down his garbage disposal. Kind of freaked my wife and kids. Let's not even talk about the spewing."

"Let me get you a drink, Mr. Jensen," I said, and led him to the dark tiki bar. He hoisted himself onto a stool and told me what a nice place I had. With his broad back half turned to me, he watched the anoles skitter by the pool lights and sipped his Cuba Libre.

"Okay, what I'm wondering," he said, "is maybe the old guy could eat earlier or later or in his cabana, or something. You don't think I'm being hard, do you?" Jensen said, his voice falsely sappy. "And I'm not saying he shouldn't be here at all because hey, that's his right too. I just think he could be less here, if you see what I mean. I'm sure I speak for the other guests, and I *know* I speak for the Jensens, all fourteen of us."

"Thirteen," I corrected.

There's a set of twins," he said, and his tongue explored the inside of his cheek as though now daring me to charge him for one more person, when I'd sat him next to death at dinner. "The ten-year-olds. You probably missed them, everyone always does. Anyway, I'd like to see what you can do about the problem. This is our one vacation a year, know what I mean? We plan to make it a regular thing too, come back here maybe, if all goes well."

The fat fuck was threatening me. "Can I top you off?" I said, holding up the bottle of rum. But he waved it away, finished the rest of his drink in a final gulp, and said goodnight. I saw him jump back as a tiny emerald lizard crossed his path.

The book club quit around midnight and made their way, loopy with booze and solidarity, through the trees. Finally, I could go to my cabana. This not-going-to-bed-before-the-last-guest was one of my mother's more tenacious policies. She'd also say Blaze should stay, and bring him his meals herself if that's what needed to be done to keep him happy and hidden. It was a win-win situation financially, she'd declare—her own uneasiness inconsequential—her eye always on business and the next season. But I simply wanted Blaze gone, off my island before he ruined it. His ghostliness, his precarious hold on things, felt too much like mine at the moment.

Though it was late and I was exhausted, I walked toward the Blazes' cabana. From the path, I could see the two defiant fist-shaped rock outcroppings that towered over an eddying, unpredictable pool below, shaded violet even in the dark. I know my part of the island is inspired with natural, moody beauty, and that night I noticed how a winking luminescence seemed to rise from the coral reefs. Cecelia was playing cards on the open terrace and listening to a symphony on the only radio station we got on the windward side of the island. Henry, in a white robe, was asleep in the hammock chair, his head lolled to one side. Cecelia looked up suddenly, though I don't think she saw me hidden by the curve of the path. She looked pained, as if she'd lost something. She might have simply caught a flash off the water just then that made her want to go home as desperately as I wanted them to leave. For this, for her, I decided to let them have the night.

It wasn't until I was in the light of the bathroom back in my cabana that I noticed the spattering of spew—as Jensen had put it so eloquently—on the cuffs of my pants. I had to scrub with an old toothbrush and a cracked bar of soap to get them clean.

"You want us to leave," Blaze said the next morning when I showed up on the terrace of his cabana. Alone and in the full sun, he sat in the hammock swing again, an open book on his lap. He seemed transfixed by something out on the water.

I hadn't expected to arrive at the point so quickly, and it took me a moment to catch up. "I'm concerned about you, that's all," I said. "We have no medical facilities here that I'd trust to treat anything more than a moped burn or diarrhea. We're really not equipped to handle an emergency."

"Like death, for instance, which is hardly an emergency, Mr. Thierry. I take it your guests didn't like my performance at dinner," he said. "But now Cecelia has those nice bookish women to talk to because of me. They've adopted her, I think."

"Please, Mr. Blaze." My impatience surprised him only a little—I could tell he enjoyed revving people up and letting them whirl uselessly. "I'm trying to hold onto this place, and I do know I can't afford to have guests pull out now because they're unhappy or decide to go somewhere else next year for whatever reason. I'm not sure this is the best place for you to be."

"You mean I'm not an asset." Blaze countered my ugly lack of sympathy and squinted at the water again. "Your guests are too uptight."

"You have to understand my position." The truth was I could only ask him to leave; I couldn't actually force him out.

"I understand your position well enough, Mr. Thierry. Now look at mine."

Blaze was not wearing a shirt, and I saw how trim and beautiful his body must have been before he got sick, before he became distended, toxic and puffy in some places, deflated in others. A bracelet of thin black leather circled his wrist, a strange touch on such a pale American. I was repulsed by his body, and when I turned away I saw what he'd been looking at so intently while we talked. On the large sandbar not far offshore, the honeymooners from Philadelphia were bare-chested, their faces pressed tightly together. She was lying on top of him, while his hands circled the sides of her breasts and then the rise of her ass. Their bright orange kayaks sat nose-first on the sand, the single palm tree fanning a wasted shade over them.

"Not exactly private, is it?" Blaze laughed, a little wistfully, I thought.

I sat down on the low wall. My eyes adjusted to the darkness of the room behind Blaze, and to the squadrons of pill bottles and inhalers on the wicker bureau. Last night's oxygen dolly stood by the unmade bed. For the first time, it occurred to me that Blaze might have AIDS, with his collection of mis-matched and terrible ravages. Our island is an oil well of pleasure, and I'd seen enough sick people standing in cool and furtive doorways in town to know this particular disease.

"Why did you come here?" I asked.

"You think I singled you out?"

"Seems that way," I said. "There are a million islands, Mr. Blaze. You could have gone to Club Med even—they would have given you your own bikinied nurses round the clock."

"Not my thing, Mr. Thierry." Blaze looked up at the sky. "I can see the hur-ricane did a lot of damage here. This was the most beautiful spot on earth, and I've been to some pretty spectacular places all over the world. I remem-ber you. I remember your mother too."

"You've been here before?" I asked, skeptically.

"Several times actually, last with my first wife, years and years ago. You must have been around thirteen then, miserable and pimply, performing an impressive repertoire of antisocial activities for the guests. You once stood on a rock and peed into the water while we were having dinner in the dining room. Your mother tried to distract us with shrimp cocktail. Jumbo shrimp, she kept saying, look at the size of their tails. All I saw was your skinny ass in the sunset. Still, I always thought it must have been paradise for you, growing up on this island. And now look at you—all business and good interpersonal skills to boot."

There were times I forgot how much I once hated this place, how I couldn't wait to get away. Despairingly fatherless, I had searched among each season's new arrivals for possible candidates. My mother gave me nothing to go on, though. She claimed to know little about who he was. Not because he'd knocked her up and disappeared, or was some married mystery, I was meant to understand, but because that's how she'd wanted it. Mother and child only, the picture of paradise. I was fathered by some resort guest who'd been turned on by my mother's independence and sharp business sense; her long toes, tanned face, and light eyes; the skittery sounds at night; this place so far from his home; the erotic heat in the dark. All she might have had of him was a credit card receipt in her files.

"Why did you come back?" I asked.

"I heard you were hurting for business, I thought I'd help you out a little."

"But I don't think that's what you're doing," I said. "You are definitely not good for business."

"I want to die here, Mr. Thierry," Blaze said, sounding as tired as he looked all of a sudden. "I was hoping you might be sympathetic."

Removed and up in his windy cabana on the bluff, Blaze stayed away from the other guests, and I had Tom bring him his meals. With Blaze out of my sight, I even allowed myself to feel hopeful and hear the hymn bounce off the blue-bitch stone and pool's surface again. The Jensen kids napped by the pool. A man, still laughing, had to be brought back off the water when the breeze died on his windsurfer. The honeymooners slept past lunch; other guests settled into their own muted routines, while I willingly busied myself with work, the supplying of other peoples' pleasure. Cecelia Blaze had been encircled by the book group—they seemed a useful novelty to each other—and her appearance each morning was good news to me and a reminder that three weeks would go by quickly. Blaze would leave, sick but alive, as he had come.

So perhaps it was some blind gratitude finally, or simply curiosity during a hopeful moment, that inspired me to deliver Blaze's lunch myself one noon. Motionless and drained in the shadows indoors, he did not seem surprised to see me, though it had been days. He tentatively examined the tray with his head drawn back, as though the fish might jump up and bite him. I understood then that for someone as sick and weak as he was, the wrong food, wind, breath, dose could easily kill him.

He'd eaten some bad meat in Poona once and had nearly died from it. "My stomach ulcerated. I shit blood," he explained. He took a bite of fruit—he was not starving himself—which he chewed with his front teeth. "You don't know where Poona is, do you, Kip?"

"I haven't done a whole lot of traveling," I said. "Look, I wanted to let you know I appreciate . . ."

"Northern India. That's your geography lesson for today," Blaze interrupted. Did I know he was the largest importer of Indian movies to the United States? The demand was voracious, he explained, not to be believed, and then he pushed away his plate and could barely keep his eyes open long enough to see me leave. When I delivered his dinner, he was in the same place I'd left him, earlier, though this time he didn't talk. His lips were chalky from something Cecelia had administered to him, and the air had a cool, ventilated feel to it.

The next day he was a little more alert, and in painfully slow sentences described for me the time he'd spent in the backs of tiny Indian import shops in Queens, Detroit, and Los Angeles, sitting, on overturned milk crates with his Indian friends, drinking yogurt shakes and nibbling sweetened fennel seeds. He was hazy with fatigue, full of admiration for the exotic, lost in memory. I felt myself being drawn back to these places with Blaze—I had never known the kind of easy friendship he was describing—but still I was anxious to leave his dark sickroom with its sour, clinical odors.

In spite of my aversion, I fell into a routine of bringing Blaze his meals, perhaps to ensure that he'd continue to stay away from the other guests by satisfying his increasing need to talk. One morning at the end of his first week on my island, I found Blaze in bed, his skin a new shade of green. He'd been thinking of some of the many trips to India he'd made alone, he said, as though I'd always been standing there listening. I should imagine him, he urged, sweating with pleasure in a New Delhi hotel, burning his throat on spices in Madurai, lapping at the hot air with his tongue as he hung out a train window. His large house outside of Boston was full of bolts of silk and painted boxes he had brought back from his trips. The closets stank of vegetal sizing and the oil of polished copper. Cecelia and his two grown daughters had no interest in any of it.

"Can you picture it?" he asked. "Tell me, can you see it?"

"I was born on this island, delivered by the cook's grandmother. A lime tree was planted over my placenta. As a child, I'd given names to crabs in the kitchen so they wouldn't be forgotten at dinnertime, I'd followed anoles around trees because I'd been told they led to diamonds. I knew the female pungency of every leaf and the taste of dirt and sun here, but nowhere else."

"Sure," I said, trying appease his growing agitation. "I can picture it."

Blaze was energetically angry all of a sudden, frustrated that he could not describe anything to me with true accuracy anymore: touch, smell, a spinning head, what it felt like to be completely lost. He recalled words these days, he said, only from the practice of having spoken them before. Imagine, he begged, being robbed of everything in the dank of a park underpass in Bombay by a smooth, beautiful Indian boy only moments after sharing pleasure with him. And imagine walking back to the hotel with pockets flapping empty, ribs aching from fear and a few swift kicks, spent and feeling exhilarated beyond belief, as though it was one of the great moments of life.

"I need you to understand," Blaze said.

I understood; he was talking about love. But what did I know about that, or what love would make a person do? "I have to go," I said, and turned away.

There was noise in the bathroom just then that startled us both, the dull thump of Cecelia's wet towel dropped on the floor. Blaze's eyelids fluttered at this sudden reminder of his wife. I sat down on the side of his bed. I wondered then if it was disease itself or the shame of this disease—it was AIDS, I was sure now—that kept submerging so many of his memories, a struggle either way.

Blaze lifted his head from the pillow, moved his hand toward my wrist, and then withdrew. "Do you see why I want to die now?" he said.

Cecelia came out of the bathroom, her fingers inept at the buttons on her shirt, her face pale from what she'd obviously just heard him say. She sat in one of the wicker chairs and crossed her legs.

"Don't be such a priss," Blaze said to her, having regained full breath now. He was unkind; she was long-suffering. They seemed to accept their complicity in the situation.

"He was telling me about some of his trips," I said.

"I'm sure he was." She nodded. "Did he tell you how he once forgot to walk clockwise around a Buddhist shrine?" She began to laugh, and pulled her knees up girlishly. "They nearly arrested him. Oh, I don't know, it just seems like the strangest thing to me."

"Cece," Blaze said, as though he'd been trying to get her to understand forever, "it is so much more than that."

Her face suddenly tightened as she considered him. Was she picturing at that moment her husband bent over another man, thrusting with passion? Was she wondering where his tongue and mouth had been? He must have also slept years of nights in bed with her, the comforter over them with reassuring weight, the dry kiss on the lips as equally reassuring. My husband is not queer, she would tell herself, he does not have sex with men because he is my husband. She wasn't going to indulge or spare him now—dying was killing her too, after all. She fiddled with her hair while her eyes watered; the love of her life was retreating, and he didn't want her to come along.

That evening, still distracted from the morning's scene with the Blazes, I wandered out onto the patio. The book group, having splintered during their week, was back together for a last dinner, looking forced and tired. The spiky-haired woman touched my hand as I walked by—too little, too late, too difficult, I thought—she only wanted me to see something.

"Look," she said, and nodded toward the sandbar where Blaze and I had seen the half-naked honeymooners days earlier. I offered a Deserted Evening package—wine and lobster at sunset on the tiny island—for an extra fee. It had been my mother's idea early on, an appreciation of the romantic streak in others. At most, there had only been a few takers a season. "God, it's wonderful to see them out together," she sighed.

At the edge of the sandbar, one of the beach boys was helping Cecelia step out of the dingy. In the evening light, her turquoise dress was diaphanous and slinked around her ankles. Blaze was hunched and uncertain as he lifted his knobby leg to climb out of the boat, one hand heavy on the boy's shoulder. He had not been farther than the terrace of his own cabana in almost a week, and this vastness must have startled him.

Cecelia smoothed a blanket on the sand as the boy left in the boat and Blaze sat down next to her. What a joke to offer up this sandbar as deserted. When you were on it, it felt alone and tiny and the single palm seemed enormous, but from the height of the patio—and from Blaze's terrace, as I had seen—it was a theater stage on which to act out this peculiar marriage. Cecelia's adjustment of her dress, Blaze's shift to one side as he removed something sharp from under himself, the splash as she clumsily poured wine—these were larger than life, lit up for all to see. Blaze had to know this.

We saw how Cecelia wanted to kiss her husband, so when he offered only a cheek, she forcefully took his face in her hands and pulled him toward her, pressing her mouth against his. No one spoke, and Jensen, with his knee bouncing at top speed, stared alternately at his own wife with her broad, peeling nose and at the Blazes. When I smelled the sizzle of garlic, shrimp, and lime juice, I hustled people in, tripping a little over my own feet.

Alone as I watched again in the almost dark, I saw Cecelia drop the dress off her shoulders to reveal her breasts. She straddled her husband, who was on his back, leaned down so her face was against his. They stayed like this for a long time, past the time I heard dinner brought to the tables and the sunset faded.

"You think they're okay?" Jensen said. He had left his family still eating, and stood next to me on the patio. He smelled of steak and pepper. Jensen had continued to poke his head into my office from time to time, giving me a moronic thumbs-up and looking for something to throw his weight against. I knew he was inflated with a dangerous amount of sun and restlessness.

"I'm sure they're fine," I told him, but I wasn't sure at all, and was immobilized by the idea that Blaze was finally dead and Cecelia, in some love/grief clutch, was frozen too. A freak high tide should suck the corpse out to sea and dump it on some other island.

"Let me help you get them," Jensen offered, nodding toward the sandbar. As we went down to the beach and pulled the dingy out, I wondered if I'd misjudged the guy all along—a man who is idle is sometimes not himself, or too much himself. Jensen easily rowed to the sandbar while I was transfixed by the napkin which bloomed from his pants pockets at each stroke.

"Jesus, her dress," Jensen said to me. "Hey there," he yelled to Cecelia. "Everything okay?" We were eddying in the water, Jensen's oars firm against the night's stronger and deeper current.

Cecelia slid off her husband ungracefully and covered herself as she rose from all fours. "I didn't want to wake him up. I guess I didn't realize how late it is."

"Time to come back." I jumped out of the boat and dragged it up to the sandbar with Jensen still sitting in it, sucking his teeth and showing no intention of getting out.

Cecelia leaned down toward her husband. When he opened his eyes, I could tell how disoriented he was by the water at eye level, the dark.

"I can't move," he said.

"Oh, come on, Henry." Cecelia put her hands on her hips. "It's late. These men are waiting. Try." She touched his leg with her foot.

"What's up?" Jensen yelled from the boat.

"I'm all gripped up, Cece," Blaze said. "I'm sorry."

Cecelia turned so closely to me I thought she was going to collapse against my chest, but it was only so she could whisper. "This happens sometimes when he's still for a long time, so you're going to have to carry him." Then she stepped back and waited, her arms across her chest with that odd indifference again.

I knelt down and lifted Blaze's head off the sand. It was the first time I'd touched him, and I was surprised by his softness. I struggled ineffectively until I called to Jensen. His eyebrows rose as though I'd interrupted him, and then he gestured for me to come close.

"Well, shit, what's wrong with him first, Thierry?" he said. "Cancer, AIDS, something catching? What, before I get my hands all over him."

I hesitated for a second and looked at his unpleasantly red face. "I don't know, Mr. Jensen. I'm not a fucking doctor."

I stared at Jensen with obvious contempt while he considered whether or not to hit me. Finally he jumped out of the boat, brushing his shoulder against mine.

"Can you sit?" he yelled at Blaze, as though he were deaf.

Blaze narrowed his eyes even further. "What do you think?"

Jensen and I managed to haul Blaze into the dinghy and lean him against his wife. A small crowd had gathered on the beach, and then, as we were lifting him from the boat, Blaze slipped away from us like a hooked but determined fish. Cecelia and the others gasped, while I wanted to throw my head back and howl with laughter, fall to my knees while the tears streamed down my cheeks. My hands went weak, my bowels and stomach quivered, and Blaze sank fast and helpless in the shallows. It was where he wanted to be, after all. I should just let him go.

But I grabbed him instead. Jensen was stunned and Blaze was an even more impossible weight now. His eyes were closed, as though he had decided to pass calmly through this humiliation and his failure. Someone had wheeled one of the wooden beach chairs down to the water's edge, and we managed to lay Blaze on it. His dripping clothes hung on the distorted angles of his body, making him look even worse than before. Jensen left, calling to his kids who were gawking over the patio railing as though he hadn't seen them in weeks. People flirted around us for a few seconds, while Cecelia sat on the end of the chair and stared out.

"I need to stay here for a minute," Blaze announced.

"I'm going to get you a blanket, a sweater, something," Cecelia said numbly. She stood and walked away.

"She's weaving—it's the wine." Blaze watched her go, and then pulled a pack of still-dry cigarettes from his shirt pocket. "Have a lighter, Thierry?"

"Jesus Christ," I said, and lit his cigarette. "You're smoking."

"Yes." He took a defiantly deep inhale, and looked pleased with himself. "Live life king-sized."

"What's that supposed to mean?"

"Something I liked in an Indian movie, *The Eighth Moon*. Seen it? A real blockbuster," he said. "Everything's about smoking in that country. The prince has just routed a coup, killed a few hundred ingrates, and so he pulls out a cigarette and lights up. 'Live life king-sized,' he declares. It sounded right."

I sat on the end of the chair where Cecelia had been. Blaze's ankle tapped at my thigh as he dragged on his cigarette.

"This outing tonight was my idea," he said, "so don't blame Cecelia. People say she's too stiff, but that's not really true. I think I didn't give her enough

time when I was living—not dying, that is—but I love her. Your little island"—
he waved his cigarette toward the sandbar—"seemed like it might be the right
way to show her." Blaze laughed and pulled himself higher on the chair. "I have
no energy to explain anything anymore, Thierry, my disease, my life, my unnat-
ural passions, as it were. I want to die. Seems I'm not having much luck, though."

"It's a little hard to drown yourself in less than a foot of water." I turned
around to look at him. "*You* live life king-sized, Blaze. My business is going
under."

"Don't be such a pessimist. It shows a great lack of imagination."

"So what if I lose this place," I said, ignoring him. "I can go somewhere else."

"You don't want to do that. You'd get squashed, Thierry. You're an island
boy with your ponytail and skinny legs. Your sneakers are all wrong too. What
do you know about anything or anyone? Look, when was the last time you
even watched television? Stay, reposition yourself, that's all—change with the
times. Maybe you can call this Euthanasia Island, the getaway of a lifetime.
Hospice Hideaway. Offer sunset pillow smotherings, poolside morphine
drips, the feeding tube extraction. Quick turnover. You haven't been in the
real world, Kip—you have no idea how popular this dying thing is." Blaze
tossed his cigarette into the water. "I could make it worth your while. Repeats
and referrals, the blood of the business. I know everyone, I'd bring them
to you, all my friends I've told you about. You help me on my way, and I'll
save your business in return."

"You're asking me to kill you," I said.

Blaze tapped his foot against my thigh again. His offer was horribly simple—if I believed him at all. I thought about how many times, after Tess tore
through and I was on my knees picking up the endless pieces, I said I'd do anything to save my island. I heard water slide into the sand, heat spiral in the
air, the coral reef shift and settle. All my life this sound had been my idea of
a perfect night, and always would be, no matter where I ended up.

"I won't kill you, Blaze," I said absolutely. "Not even to save all this."
Finally, I was more sure of this than anything else in my life.

"Euthanize is the word, Thierry. It's an act of mercy, not business." He
sighed, defeated. "I've been trying to tell you that, to show you. I've told you
all my stories now."

Their week over, the book club and other guests left the next day, and I was
hardly surprised when Jensen checked out with them, a week early, bullying my
office to accommodate his immediate change in plans, dragging his dopey family with him.

The time before a new group of guests arrived had always been a good
break for me and my staff, and now I fell into it, grateful for the distraction.
The staff talked in full island voices again. Together we ogled over the stuff people forgot under beds and in full view. We ate lunch in the kitchen and sloppy
salad with our hands, whisked our bare feet across the floor. Staffers' children, now bravely out from among the trees, wandered around and bounced
on the empty beds. I had Tom bring Blaze his meals again, so I wouldn't have
to see him. On two evenings, I saw Henry and Cecelia standing on the dirt road

that led to the center of the island. I didn't know where they had been or were headed as they looked up at the canopy of trees that kept the moon from lighting their way.

By the middle of the Blazes' second week, there were several last-minute cancellations and occupancy was at an all-time low. I must have seemed shell-shocked as I wandered around, and I felt I'd slipped into some kind of mindlessness. I wondered if this was how Blaze felt, giddy, knowing what would come next, a true dead end, for it was now pretty clear it was over for me. The few remaining guests began to assume the natural liberties that come with an enormous amount of space. Their irritations became public as they echoed off the bluebitch, and they were careless with their things, which I sometimes saw float away with the tide.

One morning I wandered aimlessly behind the kitchen. Inside, a tape played loudly, and I'd been drawn to the open door by the music to watch the women bent and swaying over counters, sweat on the backs of their thick necks, feet slipped out of shoes. I had known them forever, and so I was still paying them with what little I had left, but there was almost no work to do; they were playing cards, sucking on toothpicks, talking. As I watched, I remembered how once one of the staff had come trembling to me. She swore she'd just seen her long-dead father leaning against the kitchen's back door, smoking and waiting for her to get off work, and she wanted me to shoo him away, which I pretended to do. Now I felt those eyes and a hot breath in the shade and left quickly.

That evening, Tom told me the Blazes were waiting for me on the patio. Cecelia was wearing an alarmingly bright dress, huge yellow daisies with blue centers, an ugly island design my mother used to wear on Saturday nights. Henry, in a chair next to her, wasn't eating that day, she told me. First fasting, then a sunset and an enema before bed.

"Like scrubbing the ring off a bathtub," Blaze said. He looked sicker, but also strangely expectant for someone who couldn't expect much of anything anymore. "Has to be done every once in a while so the water's clean. Give it to him, Cece."

"What's this?" I asked, and took the piece of paper Cecelia held out to me. There were fifteen names on the list, all Indian from what I could tell.

"I've invited my friends, just like I told you I would," Blaze said. "You got a few empty rooms at the moment, am I right?"

"A few," I said, weakly. I needed to sit down but leaned heavily against the patio railing, my back to the water.

"Some of them won't be able to come on such short notice, of course," Cecelia said, energized by her sudden usefulness to her husband, even in this deranged task. I couldn't bring myself to look at her, to see what she might or might not understand. "They're Henry's friends, really. You know he was up late last night trying to arrange this over the phone."

"Not easy," Blaze said. "But believe me, I've arranged much more complicated deals than this one. It didn't take much convincing; I offered something for nothing. Most people are pigs." Cecelia laughed at this, and looked a little surprised at her gaiety. Blaze gave her a puzzled look.

"All these people are coming here," I said to Blaze. "Do I have that right?"

"You didn't think I was serious, did you. I can see it in your face," he said. "But a deal is a deal."

Cecelia ignored her husband, as I'd seen her do so many times before. "He's decided he wants them to be here when he dies. They love him." She slapped her hand over her mouth. The way the lowering sun caught in her eyes, I didn't know if she was horrified, thrilled, or both.

Blaze delivered on his promise, and over the next few days fourteen of his friends came to my island. Each arrival was another weight for me, more evidence of a debt I was expected to pay back. As a group, though, these people brought with them an attractive, buoyant life I'd never seen before, a new hymn that I sometimes found myself swaying to. They enthusiastically loved the place and wandered noisily into the dining room at the last minute and stayed for hours, swam at night, slept most of the morning, talked endlessly to me about the island, the birds, and Blaze.

Sanjiv Bhargava, a large and slickly confident man, was Blaze's closest friend among the group, and often sought me out with earnest questions of natural history and my childhood on the island. Three of the guests brought wives who rubbed oil on their dark skin for hours and melted into each other around the pool. Cecelia looked uncomfortable around them at first, so stiff, with her mouth mimicking the curve of her arching hairline. She startled at their hands resting on her arms, her knees, the way they included her.

Blaze sat king-like in the middle, but shut out the sudden activity that now swirled around him. Watching him from the window in the main house that overlooked the pool, I was the only one who noticed that he was in deeper trouble now, that his face contorted with spasms, and he fell asleep with his mouth open. In the space of only a few days, his chest had collapsed so that a hollow preceded him, sat on his lap, sucked up his words. These friends of his—fully paid-for and loving their mid-winter luck—swam and teased, but they never turned their heads to check on him, as though he should be my responsibility now.

One morning Blaze's friends had left him while they went down to the beach. Squinting uncomfortably, Blaze sat in the direct early heat but appeared not to have the strength to move himself. Finally, when I could no longer stand to see him purpling and swelling in the sun, I came out of the main house and moved his chair into the shade. I was quick to hurry away.

"No, don't go yet," Blaze said, and caught my arm. "Tell me, Thierry, how does my future look these days?" The strength of his voice still surprised me.

"I don't know about your future," I stalled. I saw Cecelia and Blaze's friends circling around a pair of sailboats on the beach, considering their next activity. "What do your doctors say?"

Blaze laughed. "You want to know about my doctors? All right," he said. "They are institutionally optimistic. They should all be forced to wear buttons that say, 'Be hopeful,' and at night they should have to lay the buttons down next to their alarm clocks so it will be the first thing they see when they wake up, even before they take a leak. But enough already with the optimism, don't you think? It doesn't do me any good." He nodded toward the beach, his wife and friends, and his eyes teared. "Anyway, I've arranged everything. My friends will be back next year with their big brown families and business partners and silent, glaring grandmas who don't speak English—all on my nickel. So you'll be okay, Thierry, don't worry. Now put me back in the sun."

My mother called a little later. Cold as hell in New York, she said hoarsely, as though clots of snow were lodged in her throat. She'd just walked back from the museum and was thinking of buying a pair of snow pants like the ones all the kids had. Since my mother had left this island—ambivalent, but more than ready—she gorged herself on choice.

"I hear you're running a leper colony down there, you've got people throwing up in the dining room," she said. Her friend at Columbus Travel (sister of the reservationist who'd booked the Jensen family) had called to report. Several others had apparently done the same.

"Yes, a leper colony. We got body parts all over the place, but we can fit fifteen people in one bed." I wondered what she would make of Blaze, still alone and in the sun, if she would recognize him through his disease as someone from another time in her life.

"You can joke if you want," my mother said. "But if *I've* heard it, imagine how many other people have too. Word of mouth can kill your business in a second, Kip. I'm absolutely serious, it doesn't take much."

"I know."

My mother sighed. "This man, Jensen, claims he's going to report you— to whom and for what, who knows, but he's telling everyone. At the very least, he's looking for a full refund. There's an asshole in every crowd, remember that—you have to give him the Asshole Special, even if that means crawling to do it to save the business." My mother stopped short. Giving me advice made her uncomfortable when she'd never gotten or asked for any herself. I knew she'd moved over to the window and was thinking, with enormous, familiar regret, how slowly the traffic below her was moving. "Are you in trouble, Kip?"

From my window, I saw one of Tom's young nephews creep past Blaze's chair and slip into the pool. My staff and their kids hissed at him excitedly to get out of the pool which was off-limits, but he dunked and came up sputtering, his eyes completely round as he rubbed his hands across his nipples, electrifying himself. Blaze stirred in his chair and smiled. Some muted chaos had taken over.

"I am," I told my mother just before we hung up.

Blaze threw something into the pool then, a shell he'd had in his curled hand as though he'd been waiting for this, and the children dove for it. The commotion and splashes which landed on his hot face pleased him, but his body seized with pain in retaliation. I thought he might die then, he was so close even if he lived for weeks or months. Would it be so bad to simply help along the inevitable now? I wondered for the briefest moment how it might happen. I could slip him an overdose in a glass of papaya juice which he would eagerly accept. In the privacy of his cabana, I could cover his face with a damp towel and look away.

But I'd heard the body struggled violently on its own at the end—a thought that made me sick to my stomach—who was I to hold this man down?

As I drove Sanjiv into town one morning he told me that he owned a chain of twelve shoe stores in New Jersey and had at least one relative working in every shop. Earlier, he had asked if he could use the kitchen that night—a meal for Henry was what he had in mind—if I'd show him where he could buy some of the ingredients he needed.

"Full compliance with your requirements and schedule," he had said formally, meaning this was to take place after the regular dinner for the few other guests, and that he would pay for everything. He'd toured the kitchen, walking regally among the staff with their tilted stares and white aprons, found it missing what he needed, hiked up his perfectly pressed black linen shorts, and had given me a broad smile.

I parked the car off the main street, pointed out a few places he might try—though the town was a tourist rip-off and I didn't think he'd have much luck—and told him I'd meet him in the bar across from the post office. I hadn't been in Sportsman's in months, since before the season began. The place was empty and I sat at the bar. I made conversation with Louis, the owner, whom I'd known for years—a guy who came to the island after college and never left. Occasionally, he'd show up for dinner at my place with one of his girlfriends and drive home drunk, his hand probably already between her legs.

"Hey, I hear you have some weird shit happening over at your place," Louis said, in a conspiratorial whisper, though nothing on the island was secret. "Business sucks and you got all these Indians, for one thing. And a guy died?"

"Not that I know of," I said.

"That's not what I heard." Louis looked up at the planked ceiling, fingered a faded shell necklace around his neck. His face was wrinkled and a little vexed. I wondered if all of us island boys seemed alike, boyish and stunted. We were single and childless and might always be. "He died in the pool or something, right?"

Sanjiv walked in just then and put his heavy plastic bags down by the door as if they contained the most fragile flowers. He removed a thin, honey-colored wallet from his back pocket, placed it on the bar, and sat down next to me. It was unusually hot in town that day, and Sanjiv drank his beer in several gulps. He ordered another one, which he rested between his large hands, tapping the glass with his rings.

"Much better," Sanjiv said. "Now we can talk, Mr. Thierry."

"Find what you were looking for?" I asked.

"Surprisingly, yes. Completely successful." He named a few stores. "And I poked around the video shop here as well, to see what's what in a place like this. Large porno selection, one might be surprised to know."

"It can get pretty quiet around here," I said, and Louis smirked. "Long, hot winters. Long, hot summers, long hot in-betweens."

Sanjiv considered this, sipped his beer slowly, and smiled condescendingly at Louis, who got the hint and backed away. "I will have to tell Henry he is well represented. It will give him great pleasure to know that he has reached even such a place as this."

"Blaze is into porno?"

"Well, he imports it, of course. You have to these days to make any money. It is a small part of his business, in fact, but a most lucrative one. He doesn't approve of the stuff."

"Art films, he told me, epics, that sort of thing," I said. "Blockbusters. *The Eighth Moon.* "

"You know that one? Ah, Henry. He's a dealmaker, an orchestrator. I am aware of all his business dealings." Sanjiv laughed. His accent was subtle and covered his words in silk. "You wouldn't think Mrs. Blaze would approve either, would you? And she doesn't, of course." He turned to face me and winked. "She pretends not to know—that and other things. It is a complicated thing, very sad, all of this, AIDS now. We have been lovers, Henry and I, for many years."

We turned back to our beers for a minute, and I felt an enormous pressure to say something, my own confession. "He wants me to help him die. He said he'd bring you here in return."

"Yes, I know that. Henry keeps a promise." Sanjiv nodded, his eyes tearing. "We're all here now to say good-bye. He doesn't look good, I agree, and I imagine he will die on this island." He took a sip of his beer. "Henry has told me about you, Mr. Thierry, that he has known you since you were a little boy, and now he will save your island for you. You're a fine businessman, a proprietor, and this is a wonderful place. You'll make a good decision about things," he said, knowingly.

"Jesus, killing a man is not a business deal," I said, angrily.

Sanjiv shook his head. "No, of course it isn't. It was never meant to be. I love him very much, and I will be sad to see him go, but sometimes this is right. You know, I will be sadder to have him dead in the end."

That evening, I was drawn to watch Sanjiv at work in the kitchen. Easily frustrated, he was also surprisingly awkward as he cooked, bending from the hips as though his back hurt him. The blade of the knife bit into his skin too often, he squinted unhappily at the chaos of chopped onions. His white shirt was stained, and the heft of the pans turned his wrists. When he rolled up his sleeves, I noticed that he wore a black bracelet like Blaze's that circled tightly against his bone.

I was not used to the thick aromas and yellow scents that rose from the pots, nor were the greengaw birds loitering around the open back door, who stopped their night singing as if another hurricane were whistling toward them. Steam pulsed from the food Sanjiv and I brought out to the dining room where Blaze, his wife, and friends were seated around several tables pushed together. They had lit a dozen candles. The few other guests watched from their tables where they were drinking and bored. The windows fogged up, and someone jumped to turn on the ceiling fan. A tape player stashed under the table hummed softly unfamiliar music.

I hadn't been invited to eat, and I had no appetite, but I saw that a place had been left at the table; they waited for me to sit down. The food was startling, and women piled it on my plate. Sweat collected under my eyes. Blaze forced small forkfuls into his mouth and chewed slowly. Every few minutes a toast would be made to him, stories of his generosity, affection, and humor. He stared at me as these testaments linked us closer together with expectation. A heavy silence fell over this farewell dinner. Some of my staff, usually long gone by that hour, smoked cigarettes on the patio and watched me. Something has happened to Kip Thierry, who sat down to eat with these lighter-dark people, they would report. I was under an island spell that had left me confused and could not be good. Nothing would ever be the same after this.

"Now we should thank our host," Blaze said, speaking for the first time that night and turning to Sanjiv.

"We appreciate your finest hospitality, Mr. Thierry." Sanjiv raised his can of Coke. " And we have made Henry the promise that we will be back next year. We will bring our families, if you will have us."

"What do you think, Sanjiv?" Blaze said. He stared at me, not unkindly. "Is a man in his position going to say no to a deal like that?"

A shadow moved behind Blaze in the darkest part of the room. My throat slammed shut, and the shadow passed behind me like a pressing heat across my shoulders. Blaze extracted something from his mouth. Sanjiv wiped his forehead and watched him with a leftward slide of his eyes. Two women whispered like rustling leaves. Cecelia's eyes darted. They were waiting for me to speak, but I couldn't. I thought I might fall over then, my head cleave like a melon on the table.

"Ah, it's all right," Blaze said sweetly, and raised a thin arm over the table. "Are you looking for someone?"

I thought he might help me now, when I could barely breathe. But he was talking to a little boy who had wandered into the room looking for his father and stood frozen, terrified by the sight of Blaze in the candlelight.

I was up earlier than anyone else the next morning, and wandered my island, drawn finally to the path that led to the Blazes'. At the turn of the bluff, I looked up at their cabana, which had taken a particularly hard beating in the hurricane. I'd rebuilt the pointed roof overhang myself out of aged purple heartwood, which now gleamed with its oily veins. But some angles, I realized that morning, would never be fully realigned, and hints of splinter and tarnish were visible everywhere. Up on the stone terrace, I looked into the cabana and saw the single sleeping, sheeted form of Cecelia, her blond hair fanned youthfully across the pillow. At my back, the wind had picked up slightly and blew the smell of salt and the sound of Sanjiv's liquid voice up the island.

When I looked down to the pool that eddied between the two fist-shaped rock outcroppings, even more perfectly visible from this height, the shaded light was green at that hour. The water was clear down to the sand, the slow moving parrot fish, and Sanjiv, who held Blaze in his arms like a baby just above the surface. Sanjiv said something just before he leaned down. I knew that he would drown Blaze then—and wasn't that right for these lovers?—and I would be spared. I wouldn't stop it. Sanjiv kissed Blaze on the mouth and I waited. The currents rocked them, but still Sanjiv wouldn't let Blaze go. I knew at that moment he couldn't do it; he was waiting for me.

By the time I made it down to the eddying pool, I had no idea how long Blaze had been in the water. His skin was a puckered grayish white, and he looked as bad as a person can look and still be alive. There would be no startling transformation when he died, just the relief of pain and the boredom of this. To end it now would be a mercy. Sanjiv placed Blaze, chilled and practically weightless, in my arms. Blaze didn't open his eyes, and there was no struggle as I lowered him and pulled away my hands. His body darkened the water below the surface and warmed it.

Later I watched the island police prepare to take Blaze's body away. Sanjiv had his arm around Cecelia, who told him she had felt a pinch behind her ear earlier when she was in bed. She wanted to know if he thought it had occurred at the same moment Henry died. Sanjiv said yes, it seemed they were connected that way.

Tell me what happened, an island authority said to me.

What had I seen? Two men swimming in a dangerous spot, so I'd gone to help them. I told the authority, whom I'd known since childhood, that Blaze was sick and weak. Sanjiv watched me as though I understood everything now; I had offered my island, and an act of love is no crime. So I said that Henry had drowned, and he seemed to understand the power of the currents when I showed him the exact spot where it had happened.

The Niece

Margot Livesey

H e had replaced five light bulbs that day, and by late afternoon he couldn't help anticipating the soft ping of the element flying apart whenever he reached for a switch. The third time—the fixture on the landing—the thought zigzagged across his mind that these little explosions were a sign, like the two dogs he had come across in the autumn, greyhound and bulldog, locked together, on the grassy slope of the local park. He had given them a wide berth; still he'd felt responsible on the bus the next day when a man had turned puce and slid to the floor. By the fifth light, though, he had given up on superstition and was blaming London Electricity. Some irregularity in the current, some unexpected surge, was slaughtering the bulbs.

The Barrows were away, at a conference in Latvia, which was why the decorating was being done now, but they were the sort of people who kept spares—he could tell from their orderly supplies of toilet paper and condiments—just not in any place he could find. Meanwhile, he gradually emptied the upstairs rooms, slipping the bulbs from bedside lights and desk lamps. Next time he went to the shops, he'd pick up a pack and add it to his bill under "Miscellaneous."

Later, of course, the little zaps made perfect sense. But when the doorbell rang Zeke set aside the wallpaper steamer without a shard of premonition. Often, if he was up a ladder, he didn't answer the knocks and rings of late afternoon—after all, they were never for him—but now the pallor of the sky, the flashes of light and dark, the weariness of working alone, all conspired to make even the prospect of rebuffing a double-glazing salesman, or a greasy haired collector for Oxfam, a pleasure. Last Friday, in a similar mood, he'd found a chap on the doorstep, thin as a junkie, pretending to be blind. He'd had the dark glasses, the white cane, the fluttery stuff with the hands. "You're a painter," he'd said, sniffing slightly. Zeke had ended up giving him fifty pence.

"But how do you know he was a con man?" his mother had asked that night on the phone. "People compensate."

I was looking out of the window and I saw him in the street, checking the 'A to Z.'"

"Barmy," his mother said, but there was a note of admiration in her voice as if a fake blind man might be closer to her ideal son than a conscientious decorator.

Now the door swung open and a woman, no collecting tin, no clipboard, filled his vision. He hadn't replaced the bulb in the hall yet, and in the dim light her features took a few seconds to assemble. He made out abrupt dark eye-brows above a substantial nose and plump, glistening lips, as if the inside of her mouth had flowed onto the outside.

For a moment, Zeke was baffled. Then he went through the steps he'd learned from the poster at the clinic. Eyes wide, a glimpse of teeth, corners of the mouth turning up rather than down: usually these indicated a smile that could, he knew, mean anger but more often meant friendliness. Yes, she was smiling, although not necessarily at him. Her expression had clearly been prepared in advance, but Zeke admired the way she held her face steady at the sight of him, and of his work clothes. His jeans and shirt were so paint-spattered as to be almost a separate entity.

"Good afternoon." She stretched out her hand and, seeing his, white with Spackle, faltered, neither withdrawing nor completing the gesture.

"Hi," he said, hating the single, stupid syllable. She was tall for a woman, his height save for the doorstep, and dimly familiar, though not as herself. As she began to speak, he realized who she reminded him of: the bust of Beethoven on his father's piano. Something about the expansiveness of her features, the way her tawny hair sprang back from her forehead.

"I'm the niece," she said.

Her breath streamed towards him, a chilly plume, carrying more words, perhaps an entire sentence, which Zeke lost as he blinked away Beethoven. "I'm the decorator," he said. "The Barrows are away."

"But they told you I would be here," she said with no hint of a question.

She stooped to pick up the large black suitcases on either side of her, and as she straightened he saw that she was pregnant. She stepped past him—the word "pushed" came to mind—and set the cases, gently, at the foot of the stairs. "Where are you working?"

He nodded toward the living room. She stood in the empty doorway—the door was at the strippers—surveying the room. Under the influence of her attention, Zeke saw again what his work had revealed: the ragged plaster painted not a single color but in pale bands of blue and brown, gray and yellow, the work of some unknown artist. In the middle of the floor the furniture was piled up and draped in dust sheets, like some ungainly prehistoric animal.

"Groovy," she said. " We should do a mural—hunting and fishing, golfing and shopping."

"I don't think your aunt and uncle . . ." Then he caught himself: humor. That had always been tricky for him. Even a question about the hen crossing the road could make him pause. "I told them it was a big job. You never know what you'll find when you strip off the paper. And Emmanuel, the guy who helps me, did his back in."

"How?" she said.

"What?"

"How"—she patted the small of her back—"did he bugger up his back?"

"Reaching for a corner. Snooker, not painting." In the bare space their voices took on burly undertones. Hers was deep anyway. As for his, Zeke wasn't sure.

He had read that humans hear their own voices through the jaw, not the air; every time a tooth is lost or filled, the timbre changes.

"Aren't they due back this week?" she said.

"The nineteenth, they told me."

Finally she shrugged off her coat, revealing a dark-green dress. The heating was on full blast, not his bill, and the house was snug as a tea cozy. She retreated to sling her coat over the banister and then came back into the room with that greedy, pushing motion. As she turned, he saw again, silhouetted against the window, her belly. Who would have expected the whey-faced Barrows to have a niece like this? And older than he'd thought, he saw now, as the light caught the little line like an exclamation mark between her eyebrows.

"Don't let me stop you," she said, her nose, her lavish mouth, bearing down, "working."

A sentence appeared in Zeke's head: *I'd like to tie you to the bed.* How did that get there, inside his brain, about this woman?

"I was taking a break," he said. "Anyway."

He was no longer certain that she was ugly, only that he wanted to keep looking to make sure. But in the empty room he did not dare. This must be why people had furniture: not just for comfort but, like clothing, for camouflage. And why interrogation and torture were traditionally carried out in sparsely furnished spaces.

"When I was fifteen," she said and her tone was such that he couldn't tell if she was talking to him or herself, "my parents let me paint my room. We were a family—this probably sounds absurd—who never painted anything. First I wrote on the wall the things I wanted to be rid of: hypocrisy, mother, father, brother. Then I slapped on the paint, deep purple."

"Did it work?"

Her head swivelled in his direction and he had the sense of being seen at last. "Not," she exhaled, "entirely. But I did like the feeling of making my mark. Do you ever get the glums?"

"No," he said. And then, the word seemed to leap from his larynx, "Sometimes." To his own stupefaction, he imagined telling her the whole deformed story, the one his mother wanted to wrap in euphemisms, like offal in newspaper, and chuck in the dustbin. "Why 'brother?'" he asked.

"I have one." Her eyebrows dashed together. "In America, maybe." She seized a wallpaper brush and fingered the gluey bristles. "Years ago, when I was hitching near Oxford, and a polystyrene salesman picked me up. The back seat of his car was full of those nice white containers, all different sizes. It started to rain, bucketing down, the windscreen wipers going lickety-split, and he said, 'Do you ever think of killing yourself?' His voice was so casual, I was sure I'd misunderstood, like you just now. I said, 'Sometimes.'"

Zeke blinked again rapidly.

"Then he asked if I'd read *Steppenwolf.* I said yes, though to be honest, I wasn't sure. It's one of those books that was in the ether for a while. I looked over at this porky, red-faced, middle-aged bloke and his eyes were brimming. 'I have,' he said. 'Every day I think of it. There's always the razor and the knife.'"

She set aside the brush and flicked a roll of lining paper. "Are you taking off the paper just to put it on again?"

The Barrows, her aunt and uncle, had asked that too. He explained about the old houses of London, how the walls were held up by wood-chip paper. When you removed it, the best way to get a smooth finish was to put on lining paper and paint over that.

"Cup of tea?" he suggested and, cursing himself, backed out of the room. Once, maybe twice a year, he had something that resembled a conversation, something not about fish fingers or telly or who was effing who. And, idiotically, he bolted. Blind rejection was one thing. To be seen, then dismissed, was quite another. He might hate his mother's mealy-mouthed phrases—Oh, Zeke's just under the weather—but the day, six years earlier, that she turned her shiny blue eyes upon him and said, "You'll end up in the loony-bin if you carry on like this," he had felt as if a pickaxe were aimed at the very center of his forehead.

Afraid to return to the living room, he hovered beside the kettle. Give me another surge, he thought, winging his request to head office. He heard a sound from the hall, one thud followed by another.

"Did I scare you?"

Seeing her stocking feet he understood not only the noises he'd just heard but those that came most nights through his bedroom ceiling: one shoe, two shoe.

"Which side are you on?" he said.

"Roundheads or cavaliers? Arsenal or Chelsea? Flat earth or solar system?"

"Mr. or Mrs. Barrow." He pushed a mug of tea towards her. "Whose niece are you?"

"Mr.'s—can't you tell?" Her eyelids grew wide and her chin rose as if defying him not to notice the similarity. "Maybe I could take Emmanuel's place."

Bewildered, Zeke stared at her feet, not broad like her hands but long and slender in dark purple hose. Was this humor, too?

"He's not around," she said. She sounded so definite that for a moment Zeke wondered if she somehow knew Emmanuel. Then he remembered he was the one who had told her about him, the snooker and the bad back. "Perhaps I could lend a hand."

"You?" His chin prickled as if his beard were pushing through the skin.

She gave a hoot. "I'm not offering to spend twelve hours a day up a ladder, but some things are easier with two people, like folding sheets."

I am, thought Zeke, profoundly boring, a notion not contradicted by her announcement that she was going to check out the sleeping arrangements. Heels striking the floor, she carried her tea upstairs.

Normally he quit at five, but today he kept pressing Spackle into even the smallest cracks until close to six-thirty. Then, in the face of an unbroken silence from above, he admitted defeat. He tidied his tools in the way that his old boss Ferdinand had taught him. The two of them had been united in their meticulous attitude towards objects, and their hesitation toward people. "You know, they say the brain has pathways," Ferdinand had said. "Mine are covered with sand." Zeke washed his hands, and called the news of his departure, wanly, up the stairs.

"Wait." There she was on the landing. "Are you coming tomorrow? When?" Her face was once again indistinguishable.

"I aim for eight," he told her. "Shall I bring up your suitcases?"

"No."

The word hit him with such force that he grabbed the banister. He was still wondering what crime he'd committed when she added at more normal volume, "Thanks. I need the keys." She swam down the stairs, stopping on the last one, hand outstretched. He should have guessed then from the way her eyes fastened on his that something was awry, that she wasn't on good terms with her aunt and uncle or that Ms. F.—weren't all fetuses female at first?—was a problematic guest, but the warmth of her breath, the lilt of her perfume, expunged rational thought. Helpless, he laid the keys in her palm.

"Will you be up to let me in?" he said.

"Up with the lark." She made a flapping motion with one hand. "Up with the milkman."

"Are you all right?" he found himself asking.

"There's always the razor and the knife," she said softly. Then—he pictured all the buses of London rising an inch into the air—she leaned forward and pressed her lips to his cheek.

The next morning Zeke rang the bell, knocked, tried the knob. The door stayed resolutely shut, the windows adamantly blank. He even bent down and called, foolishly, through the letter box, "Hello, it's me. Zeke." By the end of five minutes, he was holding onto himself, like a kite on a gusty day. He fished around in his pockets, his bag, and was rewarded with an unmistakable vision of his mobile phone, lying on the floor beside his bed. As he walked to the corner, he counted the fag ends on the pavement, some crushed, some whole, to keep himself from floating away: seven, eight, eleven. Twice he had to stop and retrace his steps to make sure he hadn't missed one. Look down, he thought, not up. In the forecourt of the underground station, he found a free phone and, trying not to think of all the hands, the mouths, that had passed this way, he picked up the receiver and dialed the Barrows' number. The answering machine clicked on with Mr. Barrow's brief, nasal message. She's popped out for a paper, he told himself, she's taking a bath. Walking back, he forgot the cigarettes and placed his feet, carefully, in the middle of each paving stone.

At the house nothing had changed. He knocked, rang, shouted again, before climbing in through the living-room window. He had opened it the day before while using the steamer and, in the excitement of her arrival, neglected his usual security measures. Now the ease with which the sash slid up made him feel stricken; he had left her at the mercy of any passing lunatic or thief.

Inside he began to tiptoe towards the hall, then, reconsidering, attempted his normal gait. "Hello. Anyone home?"

He turned things on: kettle, radio, lights. No flash and zap today. He made the obligatory cup of tea and set to work. But after ten minutes of sanding, he couldn't bear it. The possibility that she was gone bounded into his head and ricocheted around. And he didn't even know her name. He laid the sandpaper aside and, wiping his powdery hands on his jeans, climbed the stairs.

He had reconnoitered the first day he had the house to himself—he always did—flitting through bedrooms, checking wardrobes and drawers, cupboards and desks. It wasn't what Emmanuel thought—snooping for kinky underwear or helpful pills—but the way he coped with strange houses; he picked out a hiding place. Sometimes, when he felt particularly shaky, he even stored provisions there: a bottle of water, a packet of biscuits. Here at the Barrows, he'd chosen the pedestal desk in the study. With his knees drawn up, he fit almost perfectly into the dark U.

Now he moved from one light-bulbless room to another. In the master bedroom the tattered floral wallpaper made his teeth ache. As did the disorder which seemed, mysteriously, to have worsened since his last visit. The drawers of the dressing table were half-open and several of the framed photographs on top lay face down. In the study, next to the desk, the row of machines—computer, printer, fax, even a photocopier—winked at him with little red or green lights. Mrs. Barrow worked at home, she'd explained, editing textbooks. Last, their son—Sean's? Seth's?—old room. She had mentioned him at their first meeting, only to be cut off by her husband in a tone that suggested the boy was already halfway to hell in a handcart. Zeke knew that his own mother had for several months reacted to his name in similar fashion.

Had he ever been so glad to see a suitcase? The larger of the two lay open at the foot of the bed. Not meaning to snoop, he stared at the contents. Almost half the case was filled with small, multicolored boxes of the kind used for earrings and necklaces; the remainder was occupied by two camera cases, a portable CD player, a clock, and a pair of silver candlesticks. For a moment Zeke was tempted to count the boxes, each so orderly and distinct. Then he stepped over to the bed and knelt to bury his face in the pillow. Here she was, and here.

The scrape of a door hurled him to his feet. "Hello," he called, starting down the stairs.

She was in the hall, levering off her boots, heel to toe. "I went to get us fried egg sandwiches." She flourished a paper bag.

"I broke in," he offered.

"Brilliant," she said, handing him the bag. In the kitchen he set out plates, salt and pepper, sheets of paper towel. He had had his usual bowl of cereal only an hour ago; but now, following her example, he ate ravenously. She was wearing a faded blue sweatshirt, the sleeves rolled up, the hem stretched tight. How far along was she, he wondered, trying to recall Emmanuel's sister's configuration at various stages. Six months, maybe seven. Watching her pepper the egg, he realized he had dreamed about her the night before.

Only a fragment remained; she was winching a metal bucket, brimming with water, out of a well. But before he could tell her, she was talking again, describing her stint as an office cleaner when she'd eaten a fried-egg sandwich every day.

"We were meant to start at six. Instead we'd come in at eight-thirty, spray Lysol around, and sit down to our sannies. When the suits arrived at nine, they assumed we were taking a well-earned break after hours of work." She licked her lips, first lower, then upper in a glistening circle. "So what are we doing today? Putting up paper?"

He began to stammer. He was making good progress. Besides, her aunt and uncle were paying him a fair wage.

"I'm serious," she said. "I need something to take my mind off things."

At the time, he assumed a covert reference to Ms. F. Later, when he scrutinized her every utterance, it became one of those mysterious manhole covers, briefly raised over the sewer of secrecy.

Before he could voice further objections—the dust, the fumes—she had spotted a pair of overalls hanging on the back door and the next thing he knew, she had scrambled into them and was demonstrating how well they fit; her belly split the front like a chestnut its shell. "Come on," she said. "I bet you're paid by the job, not the hour."

At first he was embarrassed telling a woman, older than him by perhaps a decade, what to do, but she turned out to be much more biddable than Emmanuel. As they finished the sanding, he on the ladder, she on foot, she lobbed questions in his direction, and despite her careless manner, he sensed that she was, in fact, listening to his answers. Whereas the doctors, to a man and woman, as soon as he opened his mouth, had focused on pencil sharpeners, radiators, door knobs. They were paid—not enough, not by him—to barely feign attention, scribble a couple of notes and, as quickly as possible, write a prescription that would propel him, thank God, out of their offices. But this woman with her fierce brow, her chapped knuckles, for whatever reason, actually seemed interested.

"So," she said, folding the sandpaper onto the sanding block, "is decorating the family business? Or your heart's desire?"

"Neither." He was longing to ask about her, so he offered up himself, a pound of apples, a fistful of bananas. "My father was a greengrocer in Brighton. Got up at four every day, except Sunday, to buy the fruit and veg. Then he worked until seven at night, hauling sacks of potatoes and chatting up housewives."

"Did you live near the sea?" she asked.

"Not far. If I stood on my bed on tiptoe there was a tiny triangle of water." He had done this precisely once, dismayed at what his maneuver had revealed. Now he climbed down the ladder, moved it four feet, climbed back up, and started on the next stretch of cornice.

"I used to think," she said, "life would make sense if I could see the sea every day."

"Not for me. A street makes sense, a house makes sense, but the sea just goes on and on: wave, wave, wave. I couldn't wait to get away. We were ten when we moved." Even the absent-minded doctors had caught these sorts of slips. "Do you see yourself as two people?" a man with a wedge-shaped head had asked, gleefully. Barely one, he had thought but not said. She tapped her sandpaper and said nothing.

In London, Highbury, his father had a new shop, bigger and busier. "I used to help, evenings, Saturdays. Lovely tomatoes. Nice juicy oranges. Then one day one of our regulars, Mrs. Oma, said 'When you're the boss,' and suddenly I understood why my father was always pounding away about what to order, how to price stuff. I started to pay attention in school, do my homework. It drove him mad. 'Do you want to be a dreamer all your life,' he used to say, 'head stuck in a book?'"

"Careful," she said.

Beneath his savage sanding the ladder swayed like a sapling in the wind. He couldn't tell the story without jumping back into that old, hopeless arena. Over fresh sandpaper, he admitted that he had studied accounting at university. "I wanted to do anthropology—I'd read a book about the rain-forest tribes of Papua, New Guinea—but I didn't have the nerve. I needed to know I was heading towards a job."

She didn't ask the obvious question which, as they began to measure and cut the lining paper, enabled him to answer it. The day after his final exams, he couldn't leave the house.

"The people I shared with had all gone away and I'd been looking forward to having the place to myself. But as soon as I stepped outside I worried that I'd left the gas on or the iron or the lights or I hadn't locked the door or I hadn't locked the window or I hadn't flushed the toilet or the cat's water bowl was empty or my mother was trying to phone. It didn't matter how often I checked, it didn't matter if I wrote down I'd checked, I'd reach the street and have to go back. Remember in *Gulliver's Travels* when the Lilliputians tie him down? It was like that. Hundreds of strands of anxiety tugging me back. Soon it was easier not to try to get away."

He slid the scissors through the paper, enjoying the smooth mutter of the blades. "When I got better, I knew I couldn't be an accountant. I liked numbers, but I couldn't cope with the people on the other end of them. One of our neighbors did odd jobs so I started helping him." A strip of paper released from the roll curled back on itself and fell to the floor; he began on the next. "Ferdinand is—" He stopped, searching for the word that would embody his friend, and gave up. "I felt O.K. with him, and gradually, he wanted to retire, so I took over the business."

"Your Dad must have gone nuts."

A hot, dry wind blew through the room. Zeke dropped the scissors. "Break," he said.

He started to ask questions, the same ones she'd asked him—where she grew up, what her mum and dad did; after all these hours it was too late to ask her name. "You know," she said, "when you reach a certain age people don't ask what your parents do. They ask what you do."

But, without waiting, she went on. "My mother, after years as a bored housewife, runs a glorified junk shop. She invents amazing provenances for her goods: this hot water bottle warmed the feet of Marie Antoinette, Dr. Johnson dipped his pen in this very inkwell. My father used to be a schoolteacher. Now he's a chancer. He'll bet on anything: horses, dogs, which of his children will go to rack and ruin first. He's the kind of person who tells everyone else in the cinema to shut up and then chats away for the rest of the film. I take after both of them."

"Do you mean that?" Zeke said.

She stopped and looked at him, eyes flickering. "Yes and no. You know how it is. You make every effort not to be like your parents and then you catch yourself tying your shoelaces in exactly the fussy way your mother does. Or, even worse, doing something you don't really want to do—leaving a huge tip after a bad meal—just to be different from them."

She didn't mention Ms. F., nor did he. Zeke would catch himself wondering whether she really existed. Then he would turn around—or her mother would—and there she was.

At lunchtime, she opened a tin of tomato soup and he made cheese sandwiches. They worked on through the darkening afternoon. Oughtn't she to take a rest? he asked. They could finish the lining paper tomorrow. While he held the plumb line, she drew the chalk marks on the wall. "The smell of chalk always makes me think of school," she said. The street lights came on, buzzy amber splodges, and in the houses opposite curtains were drawn. He bungled the last piece of paper, an awkward corner, then bungled it again. "If at first you don't succeed," she chanted from the foot of the ladder, "try, try, and try again. That was my English teacher's favorite saying: Robert the Bruce and his stupid spider."

Two years ago, even one, he might have presumed himself the spider, vermin to be trampled underfoot; today he recognized encouragement. He mounted the ladder once again and, while she described the Scottish king, hiding in a cave on some Scottish mountain, drawing inspiration from the arachnid's repeated efforts to anchor its web, he smoothed the top of the paper into place and, slowly descending, pressed the seams together.

Now what, he thought, glancing around the neatly papered room. Dismissal?

"Can you make a fire," she said, "while I forage?"

"A fire?" He saw himself soaking the dustsheets with petrol, the *whoompf* of flame engulfing the mute furniture. But then she pointed at the fireplace, the grate messy with cinders. Investigation proved that the Barrows had supplies. He rolled newspapers, added kindling, fire lighter, and coal, tasks he hadn't performed since leaving drafty Brighton. Meanwhile from the kitchen came various sounds, some recognizable, some not. When he came in, she was at the cooker, stirring a saucepan. "Frozen lasagna," she announced. "Tinned spinach, fresh carrots. There's beer in the cupboard under the stairs."

"Thanks. I think I'll have some Ribena."

"Don't you drink?"

"Not often. It makes me . . ." He hesitated between "weird" and "stupid" and eventually chose the latter.

"Not so stupid you don't know it." She reached for a glass and he saw the froth of beer. Stop, he wanted to say. Ms. F. doesn't deserve to start life with a hangover. But before he could think of a polite way, or indeed any way, to voice his concern she was shouting, "Fuck, fuck."

He watched in amazement as she grabbed the saucepan and banged it against the stove, once, twice. Carrots flew.

And then he was in the hall. He had seen her wet lips stretched wide, her eyes starting out of her head, not gestures that had appeared on the poster but, combined with the shouting, fairly unequivocal. In the living room he bent to tend the fire, fighting the desire to climb out of the window and never come back. The first flare of the kindling had died down and the coals were glowing dully when he heard her footsteps.

"Sorry. I got a little carried away."

He could feel her standing behind him. Don't touch me, he thought. *Do*.

"I take my cooking seriously," she said. "Even when it is just tins. What makes you angry?"

You drinking beer, Emmanuel being a wanker, my life. Using the tongs, he moved a knob of coal an inch to the right, an inch to the left.

"If I promise to be quiet, will you come back and keep me company?"

She walked away, not waiting for an answer, and he thought of all the tiny motions—the vertebrae one after another sliding against each other, the hip joints swivelling in their sockets, the tarsals and metatarsals flexing and straightening—that make up departure. Yet the most mysterious motion, the one that couldn't be named or diagrammed, was what spilled a mood into a room. How he knew, with absolute certainty, that she wasn't taking his answer for granted, in either direction, simply leaving him alone to figure it out.

As he sat back down at the kitchen table, she was peering into the oven. "Is there a reason," she said, "for upstairs to be plunged in Stygian gloom?"

He told her about the five light bulbs of the day before. "Interesting." She turned, cheeks flushed from anger or the oven, to face him. "I'm O.K. with appliances, usually. But I can't wear a watch for more than a day or two before it goes haywire. Apparently, I make my own electricity."

They ate off a card table in front of the fire in the freshly papered room. She had found candles in the cutlery drawer, and in their light the ladder cast a hangman's shadow and the furniture loomed. They talked about computers, and whether a person could ever really disappear and if life was better in Papua, New Guinea. She told a story about her grandfather, who had fought in the First World War. Then, at last, she spoke about herself, but almost, Zeke noticed, as if she were talking about another person. Well, that was something he understood. He often felt as if the events in his life, the things people claimed he'd said and done, were really part of a stranger's story. His biology teacher at school had explained that the cells in the body are replaced every seven years. No wonder we don't always feel like our old selves.

"Once, years ago, I had a friend. She was the opposite of me: tiny, neat, ferociously ironic. We shared an office at my first real job, and three or four nights a week we'd go out for a drink after work. I couldn't get enough of her company."

He watched her lips, her eyes, her cheeks, the muscles of her throat and her forehead, and fewer and fewer of her words reached him. But when her story was done, the candles guttering, the fire dying, her face wore an expression he understood. He took her hand. "You did what you could," he said and squeezed her palm against his own. The effort of consolation made him bold.

Her face changed inexplicably, the light in her eyes leaping and fading. Had he done something wrong? Then, as the candles faltered, he understood. With his free hand, he snuffed the flames.

She rose to her feet, the whole magnificent swell of her, pulled him to his feet and led him up the stairs. "Help me," she said, presenting the overalls. Soon she was naked, ample and unabashed. Beside her Zeke felt pallid, sticklike. Can this be happening? he thought. Then she was pulling back the covers, and he was lost. Ms. F., fully acknowledged, never mentioned, lay happily between them.

Hours, days, weeks later she said, "I have to tell you something." For a moment she was silent and he pictured, in the darkness, her eyebrows drawing together. "I'm no more Mr. Barrow's niece than I'm a cavalier." She made a little rasping sound. "Actually, I've never laid eyes on either of the Barrows. A friend told me the house was empty and I needed somewhere to go."

Even as she spoke, he was counting their contiguous places—thighs, hips, elbows, shoulders, floating ribs, biceps, calves—and wherever they touched he felt the slight tingling of her electricity.

"It's not fair," he had told his mother one day after school, "I can't lie like the other boys."

"Everyone lies," she had said. "You're just a slow learner."

Now he remembered how her face had changed when he asked whose niece she was.

"I knew that," he said slowly.

"And don't you wonder who I am? What I'm doing here? You saw what was in my suitcase, didn't you?"

He searched high and low, the spiral of his right ear, the knotted place behind the left temple, the hollow where his skull met his spine, the airy lattice inside his forehead, but he couldn't find a trace of wondering. The Barrows had insurance. Let her take whatever she needed for her, and for Ms. F. What he did find, regrettable but obdurate, was his old fear of the unfamiliar.

"I have to go home," he said. "I'm sorry. It's not you. I just can't handle strange houses, strange beds."

She touched his cheek.

Next morning Zeke knocked only once before setting aside the fried egg sandwiches—he'd asked for brown bread in an effort to offset last night's beer—and sliding the blade of his penknife under the snib of the side window. He left the bag of sandwiches on the kitchen table and climbed the stairs, hoping to find her still in bed, hoping to slip in beside her and bring as many of his current cells as possible into proximity with hers. And this time, he thought, however stupid, however embarrassing, he would ask her name.

The bed was unmade, empty and cold to the touch, the suitcases gone. At the foot of the bed the rug was rolled up and, spread-eagle on the bare wooden boards, lay the overalls, neatly buttoned, arms and legs wide, like an empty person. She had added a head, a crude profile, drawn in chalk. Gazing down, Zeke understood she was sending him a message: something important happened here. Niece or no-niece, she would return.

Shiloh

Bobbie Ann Mason

Leroy Moffitt's wife, Norma Jean, is working on her pectorals. She lifts three-pound dumbbells to warm up, then progresses to a twenty-pound barbell. Standing with her legs apart, she reminds Leroy of Wonder Woman.

"I'd give anything if I could just get these muscles to where they're real hard," says Norma Jean. "Feel this arm. It's not as hard as the other one."

"That's 'cause you're right-handed," says Leroy, dodging as she swings the barbell in an arc.

"Do you think so?"

"Sure."

Leroy is a truckdriver. He injured his leg in a highway accident four months ago, and his physical therapy, which involves weights and a pulley, prompted Norma Jean to try building herself up. Now she is attending a body-building class. Leroy has been collecting temporary disability since his tractor-trailer jackknifed in Missouri, badly twisting his left leg in its socket. He has a steel pin in his hip. He will probably not be able to drive his rig again. It sits in the backyard, like a gigantic bird that has flown home to roost. Leroy has been home in Kentucky for three months, and his leg is almost healed, but the accident frightened him and he does not want to drive any more long hauls. He is not sure what to do next. In the meantime, he makes things from craft kits. He started by building a miniature log cabin from notched Popsicle sticks. He varnished it and placed it on the TV set, where it remains. It reminds him of a rustic Nativity scene. Then he tried string art (sailing ships on black velvet), a macramé owl kit, a snap-together B-17 Flying Fortress, and a lamp made out of a model truck, with a light fixture screwed in the top of the cab. At first the kits were diversions, something to kill time, but now he is thinking about building a full-scale log house from a kit. It would be considerably cheaper than building a regular house, and besides, Leroy has grown to appreciate how things are put together. He has begun to realize that in all the years he was on the road he never took time to examine anything. He was always flying past scenery.

"They won't let you build a log cabin in any of the new subdivisions," Norma Jean tells him.

"They will if I tell them it's for you," he says, teasing her. Ever since they were married, he has promised Norma Jean he would build her a new home one day. They have always rented, and the house they live in is small and nondescript. It does not even feel like a home, Leroy realizes now.

Norma Jean works at the Rexall drugstore, and she has acquired an amazing amount of information about cosmetics. When she explains to Leroy the three stages of complexion care, involving creams, toners, and moisturizers, he thinks happily of other petroleum products—axle grease, diesel fuel. This is a connection between him and Norma Jean. Since he has been home, he has felt unusually tender about his wife and guilty over his long absences. But he can't tell what she feels about him. Norma Jean has never complained about his traveling; she has never made hurt remarks, like calling his truck a "widow-maker." He is reasonably certain she has been faithful to him, but he wishes she would celebrate his permanent homecoming more happily. Norma Jean is often startled to find Leroy at home, and he thinks she seems a little disappointed about it. Perhaps he reminds her too much of the early days of their marriage, before he went on the road. They had a child who died as an infant, years ago. They never speak about their memories of Randy, which have almost faded, but now that Leroy is home all the time, they sometimes feel awkward around each other, and Leroy wonders if one of them should mention the child. He has the feeling that they are waking up out of a dream together—that they must create a new marriage, start afresh. They are lucky they are still married. Leroy has read that for most people losing a child destroys the marriage—or else he heard this on *Donahue*. He can't always remember where he learns things anymore.

At Christmas, Leroy bought an electric organ for Norma Jean. She used to play the piano when she was in high school. "It don't leave you," she told him once. "It's like riding a bicycle."

The new instrument had so many keys and buttons that she was bewildered by it at first. She touched the keys tentatively, pushed some buttons, then pecked out "Chopsticks." It came out in an amplified fox-trot rhythm, with marimba sounds.

"It's an orchestra!" she cried.

The organ had a pecan-look finish and eighteen preset chords, with optional flute, violin, trumpet, clarinet, and banjo accompaniments. Norma Jean mastered the organ almost immediately. At first she played Christmas songs. Then she bought *The Sixties Songbook* and learned every tune in it, adding variations to each with the rows of brightly colored buttons.

"I didn't like these old songs back then," she said. "But I have this crazy feeling I missed something."

"You didn't miss a thing," said Leroy.

Leroy likes to lie on the couch and smoke a joint and listen to Norma Jean play "Can't Take My Eyes Off You" and "I'll Be Back." He is back again. After fifteen years on the road, he is finally settling down with the woman he loves. She is still pretty. Her skin is flawless. Her frosted curls resemble pencil trimmings.

Now that Leroy has come home to stay, he notices how much the town has changed. Subdivisions are spreading across western Kentucky like an oil slick. The sign at the edge of town says "Pop: 11,500"—only seven hundred more than it said twenty years before. Leroy can't figure out who is living in all the new houses. The farmers who used to gather around the courthouse square on Saturday afternoons to play checkers and spit tobacco juice have gone. It has been years since Leroy has thought about the farmers, and they have disappeared without his noticing.

Leroy meets a kid named Stevie Hamilton in the parking lot at the new shopping center. While they pretend to be strangers meeting over a stalled car, Stevie tosses an ounce of marijuana under the front seat of Leroy's car. Stevie is wearing orange jogging shoes and a T-shirt that says CHATTAHOOCHEE SUPER-RAT. His father is a prominent doctor who lives in one of the expensive subdivisions in a new white-columned brick house that looks like a funeral parlor. In the phone book under his name there is a separate number, with the listing "Teenagers."

"Where do you get this stuff?" asks Leroy. "From your pappy?"

"That's for me to know and you to find out," Stevie says. He is slit-eyed and skinny.

"What else you got?"

"What you interested in?"

"Nothing special. Just wondered."

Leroy used to take speed on the road. Now he has to go slowly. He needs to be mellow. He leans back against the car and says, "I'm aiming to build me a log house, soon as I get time. My wife, though, I don't think she likes the idea."

"Well, let me know when you want me again," Stevie says. He has a cigarette in his cupped palm, as though sheltering it from the wind. He takes a long drag, then stomps it on the asphalt and slouches away.

Stevie's father was two years ahead of Leroy in high school. Leroy is thirty-four. He married Norma Jean when they were both eighteen, and their child Randy was born a few months later, but he died at the age of four months and three days. He would be about Stevie's age now. Norma Jean and Leroy were at the drive-in, watching a double feature (*Dr. Strangelove* and *Lover Come Back*), and the baby was sleeping in the back seat. When the first movie ended, the baby was dead. It was the sudden infant death syndrome. Leroy remembers handing Randy to a nurse at the emergency room, as though he were offering her a large doll as a present. A dead baby feels like a sack of flour. "It just happens sometimes," said the doctor, in what Leroy always recalls as a nonchalant tone. Leroy can hardly remember the child anymore, but he still sees vividly a scene from *Dr. Strangelove* in which the President of the United States was talking in a folksy voice on the hot line to the Soviet premier about the bomber accidentally headed toward Russia. He was in the War Room, and the world map was lit up. Leroy remembers Norma Jean standing catatonically beside him in the hospital and himself thinking: Who is this strange girl? He had forgotten who she was. Now scientists are saying that crib death is caused by a virus. Nobody knows anything, Leroy thinks. The answers are always changing.

When Leroy gets home from the shopping center, Norma Jean's mother, Mabel Beasley, is there. Until this year, Leroy has not realized how much time she spends with Norma Jean. When she visits, she inspects the closets and then the plants, informing Norma Jean when a plant is droopy or yellow. Mabel calls the plants "flowers," although there are never any blooms. She always notices if Norma Jean's laundry is piling up. Mabel is a short, overweight woman whose tight, brown-dyed curls look more like a wig than the actual wig she sometimes wears. Today she has brought Norma Jean an off-white dust ruffle she made for the bed; Mabel works in a custom-upholstery shop.

"This is the tenth one I made this year," Mabel says. "I got started and couldn't stop."

"It's real pretty," says Norma Jean.

"Now we can hide things under the bed," says Leroy, who gets along with his mother-in-law primarily by joking with her. Mabel has never really forgiven him for disgracing her by getting Norma Jean pregnant. When the baby died, she said that fate was mocking her.

"What's that thing?" Mabel says to Leroy in a loud voice, pointing to a tangle of yarn on a piece of canvas.

Leroy holds it up for Mabel to see. "It's my needlepoint," he explains. "This is a *Star Trek* pillow cover."

"That's what a woman would do," says Mabel. "Great day in the morning!"

"All the big football players on TV do it," he says.

"Why, Leroy, you're always trying to fool me. I don't believe you for one minute. You don't know what to do with yourself—that's the whole trouble. Sewing!"

"I'm aiming to build us a log house," says Leroy, "Soon as my plans come."

"Like *heck* you are," says Norma Jean. She takes Leroy's needlepoint and shoves it into a drawer. "You have to find a job first. Nobody can afford to build now anyway."

Mabel straightens her girdle and says, "I still think before you get tied down y'all ought to take a little run to Shiloh."

"One of these days, Mama," Norma Jean says impatiently.

Mabel is talking about Shiloh, Tennessee. For the past few years, she has been urging Leroy and Norma Jean to visit the Civil War battleground there. Mabel went there on her honeymoon—the only real trip she ever took. Her husband died of a perforated ulcer when Norma Jean was ten, but Mabel, who was accepted into the United Daughters of the Confederacy in 1975, is still preoccupied with going back to Shiloh.

"I've been to kingdom come and back in that truck out yonder," Leroy says to Mabel, "but we never yet set foot in that battleground. Ain't that something? How did I miss it?"

"It's not even that far," Mabel says.

After Mabel leaves, Norma Jean reads to Leroy from a list she has made. "Things you could do," she announces. "You could get a job as a guard at Union Carbide, where they'd let you set on a stool. You could get on at the lumberyard. You could do a little carpenter work, if you want to build so bad. You could—"

"I can't do something where I'd have to stand up all day."

"You ought to try standing up all day behind a cosmetics counter. It's amazing that I have strong feet, coming from two parents that never had strong feet at all." At the moment Norma Jean is holding on to the kitchen counter, raising her knees one at a time as she talks. She is wearing two-pound ankle weights.

"Don't worry," says Leroy. "I'll do something."

"You could truck calves to slaughter for somebody. You wouldn't have to drive any big old truck for that."

"I'm going to build you this house," says Leroy. "I want to make you a real home."

"I don't want to live in any log cabin."

"It's not a cabin. It's a house."

"I don't care. It looks like a cabin."

"You and me together could lift those logs. It's just like lifting weights."

Norma Jean doesn't answer. Under her breath, she is counting. Now she is marching through the kitchen. She is doing goose steps.

Before his accident, when Leroy came home he used to stay in the house with Norma Jean, watching TV in bed and playing cards. She would cook fried chicken, picnic ham, chocolate pie—all his favorites. Now he is home alone much of the time. In the mornings, Norma Jean disappears, leaving a cooling place in the bed. She eats a cereal called Body Buddies, and she leaves the bowl on the table, with the soggy tan balls floating in a milk puddle. He sees things about Norma Jean that he never realized before. When she chops onions, she stares off into a corner, as if she can't bear to look. She puts on her house slippers almost precisely at nine o'clock every evening and nudges her jogging shoes under the couch. She saves bread heels for the birds. Leroy watches the birds at the feeder. He notices the peculiar way goldfinches fly past the window. They close their wings, then fall, then spread their wings to catch and lift themselves. He wonders if they close their eyes when they fall. Norma Jean closes her eyes when they are in bed. She wants the lights turned out. Even then, he is sure she closes her eyes.

He goes for long drives around town. He tends to drive a car rather carelessly. Power steering and an automatic shift make a car feel so small and inconsequential that his body is hardly involved in the driving process. His injured leg stretches out comfortably. Once or twice he has almost hit something, but even the prospect of an accident seems minor in a car. He cruises the new subdivisions, feeling like a criminal rehearsing for a robbery. Norma Jean is probably right about a log house being inappropriate here in the new subdivisions. All the houses look grand and complicated. They depress him.

One day when Leroy comes home from a drive he finds Norma Jean in tears. She is in the kitchen making a potato and mushroom-soup casserole, with grated-cheese topping. She is crying because her mother caught her smoking.

"I didn't hear her coming. I was standing here puffing away pretty as you please," Norma Jean says, wiping her eyes.

"I knew it would happen sooner or later," says Leroy, putting his arm around her.

"She don't know the meaning of the word 'knock,'" says Norma Jean. "It's a wonder she hadn't caught me years ago."

"Think of it this way," Leroy says. "What if she caught me with a joint?"

"You better not let her!" Norma Jean shrieks. "I'm warning you, Leroy Moffitt!"

"I'm just kidding. Here, play me a tune. That'll help you relax."

Norma Jean puts the casserole in the oven and sets the timer. Then she plays a ragtime tune, with horns and banjo, as Leroy lights up a joint and lies on the couch, laughing to himself about Mabel's catching him at it. He thinks of Stevie Hamilton—a doctor's son pushing grass. Everything is funny. The whole town seems crazy and small. He is reminded of Virgil Mathis, a boastful policeman Leroy used to shoot pool with. Virgil recently led a drug bust in a back room at a bowling alley, where he seized ten thousand dollars' worth of marijuana. The newspaper had a picture of him holding up the bags of grass and grinning widely. Right now, Leroy can imagine Virgil breaking down the door and arresting him with a lungful of smoke. Virgil would probably have been alerted to the scene because of all the racket Norma Jean is making. Now she sounds like a hard-rock band. Norma Jean is terrific. When she switches to a Latin-rhythm version of "Sunshine Superman," Leroy hums along. Norma Jean's foot goes up and down, up and down.

"Well, what do you think?" Leroy says, when Norma Jean pauses to search through her music.

"What do I think about what?"

His mind has gone blank. Then he says, "I'll sell my rig and build us a house." That wasn't what he wanted to say. He wanted to know what she thought—what she *really* thought—about them.

"Don't start in on that again," says Norma Jean. She begins playing "Who'll Be the Next in Line?"

Leroy used to tell hitchhikers his whole life story—about his travels, his hometown, the baby. He would end with a question: "Well, what do you think?" It was just a rhetorical question. In time, he had the feeling that he'd been telling the same story over and over to the same hitchhikers. He quit talking to hitchhikers when he realized how his voice sounded—whining and self-pitying, like some teenage-tragedy song. Now Leroy has the sudden impulse to tell Norma Jean about himself, as if he had just met her. They have known each other so long they have forgotten a lot about each other. They could become reacquainted. But when the oven timer goes off and she runs to the kitchen, he forgets why he wants to do this.

The next day, Mabel drops by. It is Saturday and Norma Jean is cleaning. Leroy is studying the plans of his log house, which have finally come in the mail. He has them spread out on the table—big sheets of stiff blue paper, with diagrams and numbers printed in white. While Norma Jean runs the vacuum, Mabel drinks coffee. She sets her coffee cup on a blueprint.

"I'm just waiting for time to pass," she says to Leroy, drumming her fingers on the table.

As soon as Norma Jean switches off the vacuum, Mabel says in a loud voice, "Did you hear about the datsun dog that killed the baby?"

Norma Jean says, "The word is 'dachshund.'"

"They put the dog on trial. It chewed the baby's legs off. The mother was in the next room all the time." She raises her voice. "They thought it was neglect."

Norma Jean is holding her ears. Leroy manages to open the refrigerator and get some Diet Pepsi to offer Mabel. Mabel still has some coffee and she waves away the Pepsi.

"Datsuns are like that," Mabel says. "They're jealous dogs. They'll tear a place to pieces if you don't keep an eye on them."

"You better watch out what you're saying, Mabel," says Leroy.

"Well, facts is facts."

Leroy looks out the window at his rig. It is like a huge piece of furniture gathering dust in the backyard. Pretty soon it will be an antique. He hears the vacuum cleaner. Norma Jean seems to be cleaning the living room rug again.

Later, she says to Leroy, "She just said that about the baby because she caught me smoking. She's trying to pay me back."

"What are you talking about?" Leroy says, nervously shuffling blueprints.

"You know good and well," Norma Jean says. She is sitting in a kitchen chair with her feet up and her arms wrapped around her knees. She looks small and helpless. She says, "The very idea, her bringing up a subject like that! Saying it was neglect."

"She didn't mean that," Leroy says.

"She might not have *thought* she meant it. She always says things like that. You don't know how she goes on."

"But she didn't really mean it. She was just talking."

Leroy opens a king-sized bottle of beer and pours it into two glasses, dividing it carefully. He hands a glass to Norma Jean and she takes it from him mechanically. For a long time, they sit by the kitchen window watching the birds at the feeder.

Something is happening. Norma Jean is going to night school. She has graduated from her six-week body-building course and now she is taking an adult-education course in composition at Paducah Community College. She spends her evenings outlining paragraphs.

"First you have a topic sentence," she explains to Leroy. "Then you divide it up. Your secondary topic has to be connected to your primary topic."

To Leroy, this sounds intimidating. "I never was any good in English," he says.

"It makes a lot of sense."

"What are you doing this for, anyhow?"

She shrugs. "It's something to do." She stands up and lifts her dumbbells a few times.

"Driving a rig, nobody cared about my English."

"I'm not criticizing your English."

Norma Jean used to say, "If I lose ten minutes' sleep, I just drag all day." Now she stays up late, writing compositions. She got a B on her first paper—a how-to theme on soup-based casseroles. Recently Norma Jean has been cooking unusual foods—tacos, lasagna, Bombay chicken. She doesn't play the organ anymore, though her second paper was called "Why Music Is Important to Me." She sits at the kitchen table, concentrating on her outlines, while Leroy plays with his log house plans, practicing with a set of Lincoln Logs. The thought of getting a truckload of notched, numbered logs scares him, and he wants to be prepared. As he and Norma Jean work together at the kitchen table, Leroy has the hopeful thought that they are sharing something, but he knows he is a fool to think this. Norma Jean is miles away. He knows he is going to lose her. Like Mabel, he is just waiting for time to pass.

One day, Mabel is there before Norma Jean gets home from work, and Leroy finds himself confiding in her. Mabel, he realizes, must know Norma Jean better than he does.

"I don't know what's got into that girl," Mabel says. "She used to go to bed with the chickens. Now you say she's up all hours. Plus her a-smoking. I like to died."

"I want to make her this beautiful home," Leroy says, indicating the Lincoln Logs. "I don't think she even wants it. Maybe she was happier with me gone."

"She don't know what to make of you, coming home like this."

"Is that it?"

Mabel takes the roof off his Lincoln Log cabin. "You couldn't get *me* in a log cabin," she says: "I was raised in one. It's no picnic, let me tell you."

"They're different now," says Leroy.

"I tell you what," Mabel says, smiling oddly at Leroy.

"What?"

"Take her on down to Shiloh. Y'all need to get out together, stir a little. Her brain's all balled up over them books."

Leroy can see traces of Norma Jean's features in her mother's face. Mabel's worn face has the texture of crinkled cotton, but suddenly she looks pretty. It occurs to Leroy that Mabel has been hinting all along that she wants them to take her with them to Shiloh.

"Let's all go to Shiloh," he says. "You and me and her. Come Sunday."

Mabel throws up her hands in protest. "Oh, no, not me. Young folks want to be by theirselves."

When Norma Jean comes in with groceries, Leroy says excitedly, "Your mama here's been dying to go to Shiloh for thirty-five years. It's about time we went, don't you think?"

"I'm not going to butt in on anybody's second honeymoon," Mabel says.

"Who's going on a honeymoon, for Christ's sake?" Norma Jean says loudly.

"I never raised no daughter of mine to talk that-a-way," Mabel says.

"You ain't seen nothing yet," says Norma Jean. She starts putting away boxes and cans, slamming cabinet doors.

"There's a log cabin at Shiloh," Mabel says. "It was there during the battle. There's bullet holes in it."

"When are you going to *shut up* about Shiloh, Mama?" asks Norma Jean.

"I always thought Shiloh was the prettiest place, so full of history," Mabel goes on. "I just hoped y'all could see it once before I die, so you could tell me about it." Later, she whispers to Leroy, "You do what I said. A little change is what she needs."

"Your name means 'the king,'" Norma Jean says to Leroy that evening. He is trying to get her to go to Shiloh, and she is reading a book about another century.

"Well, I reckon I ought to be right proud."

"I guess so."

"Am I still king around here?"

Norma Jean flexes her biceps and feels them for hardness. "I'm not fooling around with anybody, if that's what you mean," she says.

"Would you tell me if you were?"

"I don't know."

"What does *your* name mean?"

"It was Marilyn Monroe's real name."

"No kidding!"

"Norma comes from the Normans. They were invaders," she says. She closes her book and looks hard at Leroy. "I'll go to Shiloh with you if you'll stop staring at me."

On Sunday, Norma Jean packs a picnic and they go to Shiloh. To Leroy's relief, Mabel says she does not want to come with them. Norma Jean drives, and Leroy, sitting beside her, feels like some boring hitchhiker she has picked up. He tries some conversation, but she answers him in monosyllables. At Shiloh, she drives aimlessly through the park, past bluffs and trails and steep ravines. Shiloh is an immense place, and Leroy cannot see it as a battleground. It is not what he expected. He thought it would look like a golf course. Monuments are everywhere, showing through the thick clusters of trees. Norma Jean passes the log cabin Mabel mentioned. It is surrounded by tourists looking for bullet holes.

"That's not the kind of log house I've got in mind," says Leroy apologetically.

"I know *that.*"

"This is a pretty place. Your mama was right."

"It's O.K.," says Norma Jean. "Well, we've seen it. I hope she's satisfied."

They burst out laughing together.

At the park museum, a movie on Shiloh is shown every half hour, but they decide that they don't want to see it. They buy a souvenir Confederate flag for Mabel, and then they find a picnic spot near the cemetery. Norma Jean has brought a picnic cooler, with pimiento sandwiches, soft drinks, and Yodels. Leroy eats a sandwich and then smokes a joint, hiding it behind the picnic cooler. Norma Jean has quit smoking altogether. She is picking cake crumbs from the cellophane wrapper, like a fussy bird.

Leroy says, "So the boys in gray ended up in Corinth. The Union soldiers zapped 'em finally. April 7, 1862."

They both know that he doesn't know any history. He is just talking about some of the historical plaques they have read. He feels awkward, like a boy on a date with an older girl. They are still just making conversation.

"Corinth is where Mama eloped to," says Norma Jean.

They sit in silence and stare at the cemetery for the Union dead and, beyond, at a tall cluster of trees. Campers are parked nearby, bumper to bumper, and small children in bright clothing are cavorting and squealing. Norma Jean wads up the cake wrapper and squeezes it tightly in her hand. Without looking at Leroy, she says, "I want to leave you."

Leroy takes a bottle of Coke out of the cooler and flips off the cap. He holds the bottle poised near his mouth but cannot remember to take a drink. Finally he says, "No, you don't."

"Yes, I do."

"I won't let you."

"You can't stop me."

"Don't do me that way."

Leroy knows Norma Jean will have her own way. "Didn't I promise to be home from now on?" he says.

"In some ways, a woman prefers a man who wanders," says Norma Jean. "That sounds crazy, I know."

"You're not crazy."

Leroy remembers to drink from his Coke. Then he says, "Yes, you *are* crazy. You and me could start all over again. Right back at the beginning."

"We *have* started all over again," says Norma Jean. "And this is how it turned out."

"What did I do wrong?"

"Nothing."

"Is this one of those women's lib things?" Leroy asks.

"Don't be funny."

The cemetery, a green slope dotted with white markers, looks like a subdivision site. Leroy is trying to comprehend that his marriage is breaking up, but for some reason he is wondering about white slabs in a graveyard.

"Everything was fine till Mama caught me smoking," says Norma Jean, standing up. "That set something off."

"What are you talking about?"

"She won't leave me alone—*you* won't leave me alone." Norma Jean seems to be crying, but she is looking away from him. "I feel eighteen again. I can't face that all over again." She starts walking away. "No, it *wasn't* fine. I don't know what I'm saying. Forget it."

Leroy takes a lungful of smoke and closes his eyes as Norma Jean's words sink in. He tries to focus on the fact that thirty-five hundred soldiers died on the grounds around him. He can only think of that war as a board game with plastic soldiers. Leroy almost smiles, as he compares the Confederates' daring attack on the Union camps and Virgil Mathis's raid on the bowling alley. General Grant, drunk and furious, shoved the Southerners back to Corinth, where Mabel and Jet Beasley were married years later, when Mabel was still thin and good-looking. The next day, Mabel and Jet visited the battleground, and then Norma Jean was born, and then she married Leroy and they had a baby, which they lost, and now Leroy and Norma Jean are here at the same battleground. Leroy knows he is leaving out a lot. He is leaving out the insides of history. History was always just names and dates to him. It occurs to him that building a house out of logs is similarly empty—too simple. And the real inner workings of a marriage, like most of history, have escaped him. Now he sees that building a log house is the dumbest idea he could have had. It was clumsy of him to think Norma Jean would want a log house. It was a crazy idea. He'll have to think of something else, quickly. He will wad the blueprints into tight balls and fling them into the lake. Then he'll get moving again. He opens his eyes. Norma Jean has moved away and is walking through the cemetery, following a serpentine brick path.

Leroy gets up to follow his wife, but his good leg is asleep and his bad leg still hurts him. Norma Jean is far away, walking rapidly toward the bluff by the river, and he tries to hobble toward her. Some children run past him, screaming noisily. Norma Jean has reached the bluff, and she is looking out over the Tennessee River. Now she turns toward Leroy and waves her arms. Is she beckoning to him? She seems to be doing an exercise for her chest muscles. The sky is unusually pale—the color of the dust ruffle Mabel made for their bed.

What I strive for in my writing (and what I tell my students to work for) is not feeling. As a writer, you do not want to write feelings. You want to fabricate understanding so the reader can come into the work and then feel what he feels.
    —SUE MILLER, NEWSLETTER INTERVIEW,
    EMERSON COLLEGE

Sheep

Thomas McNeely

Before the sheriff came to get him, Lloyd found the sheep out by the pond. He'd counted head that morning and come up one short. He did the count over because he was still hazy from the night before. And he'd woken with a foul smell in his nose. So he had gone into Mr. Mac's house—it was early morning; the old man would be dead to the world—and filled his canteen with white lightning. He felt shaky and bad and the spring morning was cold. He shouldn't have gone to town the night before.

The sheep lay on its side in some rushes. A flow of yellowish mucus was coming from its nose, and its eyes were sickly thin slits that looked afraid. Lloyd thought the sheep honorable—it had gone off to die so that it wouldn't infect the rest of the flock. Lloyd knew that the sheep's sickness was his fault and that he couldn't do anything about it, but he squatted down next to the animal and rubbed its underside. In this hour before sunrise, when the night dew was still wet, the warmth and animal smell felt good. Lloyd moved his hands in circles over the sheep's lightly furred pink skin and lines of blue veins, its hard cage of ribs, its slack, soft belly. Across the pond, the sun peeked red through the Panhandle dust over a low line of slate-gray clouds. With his free hand, Lloyd took his canteen from a pocket in his jacket, clamped it between his knees, opened it, and drank. For a moment the liquor stung the sides of his tongue, then dissolved in him like warm water. The sheep's lungs lifted up and down; its heart churned blood like a slowly pounding fist. Soon the sun broke free and the pond, rippled by a slight breeze, ignited in countless tiny candle flames. When Lloyd was a child, Mr. Mac used to tell him that at the Last Judgment the pond would become the Lake of Fire, into which all sinners would be cast. Lloyd could still picture them falling in a dark stream, God pouring them out like a bag of nails. The sheep closed its eyes against the light.

When Sheriff Lynch walked up behind him, Lloyd started. He still caressed the sheep, but it was dead and beginning to stiffen. His canteen felt almost empty; it fell from his fingers. By the sun, Lloyd saw it was almost noon. Big, black vultures wheeled so high above that they looked the size of mockingbirds. Uneasiness creeping on him, Lloyd waited for the sheriff to speak.

Finally the sheriff said, "Son, looks like that sheep's dead."

"Yessir," Lloyd said, and tried to stand, but his legs were stiff and the liquor had taken his balance.

"You look about half-dead yourself." The sheriff picked up Lloyd's canteen from the dry grass, sniffed it, and shook his head. "You want to turn out like Mr. Mac? A pervert?"

Lloyd waggled his head no. He thought how he must look: his long blond hair clumped in uncombed cowlicks, the dark reddish-gray circles around his eyes, his father's dirty herding jacket hanging off his broad, slumped shoulders. Sheriff Lynch stood there, his figure tall and straight. He wore a star-shaped golden badge hitched on a belt finely tooled with wildflowers. His face was burnt the rust color of Dumas County soil, the lines on it deep, like the sudden ravines there into which cattle sometimes fell. His eyes were an odd steely blue, which seemed not to be that color itself but to reflect it. He studied Lloyd.

"That probably doesn't make much of a difference now," he said, lowering his eyes as if embarrassed.

"What?" Lloyd said, though he'd heard him.

"Nothing. We just need to ask you some questions."

Lloyd wondered if Mr. Mac had found out about the sheep somehow. "But I ain't stole nothin'," he said.

"I'm fairly sure of that," the sheriff said. A grin flickered in a corner of his mouth, but it was sad and not meant to mock Lloyd. "Come on. You know the drill. Hand over your knife and shears and anything else you got."

After Lloyd put his tools in a paper bag, the sheriff squatted next to the sheep and ran his hand over its belly. His hand was large and strong and clean, though etched with red-brown creases.

When they got up to the house, Lloyd saw three or four law cars parked at odd angles, as if they'd stopped in a hurry. Their lights whirled around and dispatch radios crackled voices that no one answered. Some policemen busied themselves throwing clothes, bottles and other junk out of Lloyd's shack, which was separated from the house by a tool shed. Others were carrying out cardboard boxes. Lloyd recognized one of the men, name of Gonzales, who'd picked Lloyd up for stealing a ten-speed when he was a kid. Lloyd waved at him and called out, but Gonzales just set his dark eyes on him for a moment and then went back to his business. Mr. Mac stood on the dirt patch in front of the house, his big sloppy body looking like it was about to fall over, talking to a man in a suit.

"If you're gonna drag that pond," he said, his eyes slits in the harsh, clear sunlight, "you're gonna have to pay me for the lost fish. I'm a poor old man. I ain't got nothin' to do with thisayre mess."

The man started to say something to him, but Mr. Mac caught sight of Lloyd. His face spread wide with a fear Lloyd had never seen in him; then his eyes narrowed in disgust. He looked like he did when he saw ewes lamb, or when he punished Lloyd as a child.

"Mr. Mac," Lloyd said, and took a step toward him, but the old man held up his hands as if to shield his face.

"Mr. Mac." Lloyd came closer. "I 'pologize 'bout that 'er sheep. I'll work off the cost to you someway."

Mr. Mac stumbled backwards and pointed at Lloyd; his face was wild and frightened again. He shouted to the man in the suit, "Look at 'im! Look at 'im! A seed of pure evil!"

Lloyd could feel his chest move ahead of his body toward Mr. Mac. He wanted to explain about the sheep, but the old man kept carrying on. The sheriff's hand, firm but kind, gripped his arm and guided him toward a police car.

The sheriff sat bolt upright on the passenger side and looked straight ahead as the rust-colored hills passed by outside. A fingerprint-smudged Plexiglas barrier ran across the top of the front seat and separated him from Lloyd. As always, the hair on the nape of the sheriff's neck looked freshly cut. Lloyd had expected him to take his shears and bowie knife, but why were they tearing up his shack? And what was Mr. Mac going on about? Still drunk, probably. He would ask the sheriff when they got to the jail. His thoughts turned to the sheep. He should've put it out of its misery, slit its throat and then cut its belly for the vultures. Not like at slaughter, when he would've had to root around with his knife and bare hands and clean out its innards. What a Godawful stink sheep's insides had! But this would've been easy. It wouldn't have taken a minute.

In the jail two guards Lloyd didn't know sat him down inside a small white room he'd never seen before. The man in a suit who had been talking to Mr. Mac came in, with Sheriff Lynch following. Lloyd hadn't gotten to ask the sheriff what was going on. The man put what looked like a little transistor radio on the table and pressed a button and began to talk.

"Is it okay if we tape-record this interview?" he asked Lloyd.

Lloyd shrugged and smiled a who's-this-guy? smile at the sheriff. The sheriff gave him a stern, behave-yourself look.

"Sure," Lloyd said. "I ain't never been recorded before."

"Okay," the man said. He said all their names, where they were, what date and time it was. Then he opened a file folder. Lloyd didn't like his looks: he had a smile that hid itself, that laughed at you in secret. Mr. Mac could get one of those. And the man talked in one of those citified accents, maybe from Dallas.

"Okay," the man said. "My name is Thomas Blanchard. I am a special agent with the Federal Bureau of Investigation. I work in the serial-homicide division." He shot his eyes up at Lloyd, as if to catch him at something. "Do you understand what that means?"

"Which part?" Lloyd said.

"Serial homicide—serial murder."

"Nope."

"It means to kill more than once—sometimes many people in a row."

"Okay," Lloyd said.

The man gave him another once-over, and said, "You are being held as a material witness in seventeen murders that have occurred in and around this area. You have not been charged in any of them. Should you be charged, you will have the right to counsel, but at this time you have no such right per se. However, as a witness, should you wish to retain counsel, that is also your right. Do you wish to do so?"

Lloyd tried to put the man's words together. Blanchard bunched up his shoulders, like a squirrel ready to pounce. The sheriff leaned back his chair and studied the ceiling.

After he had drawn out the silence, Lloyd said, "I don't know. I'm still pretty drunk to think about suchlike. Would I have to pay for him?"

Blanchard's hand snaked out to the tape recorder, but the sheriff looked at Lloyd and said, "Lloyd, you think you're too drunk to know what you're sayin'? I mean, to the point of makin' things up or disrememberin'?"

"Oh, no," Lloyd said. The sheriff asked him if he was sure, and he said yes. Then the sheriff told him that to retain a lawyer meant he would have to pay for one. In that case, Lloyd said, he didn't want one.

"Sheriff," he said. "What's thisayre all about?"

The sheriff told him he would find out.

But he didn't, not really. Blanchard asked Lloyd about the night before. He'd gone to Genie's Too, where the old Genie's used to be. He'd brought a canteen of Mr. Mac's stuff with him for set-ups, because they'd lost their liquor license. He saw all the usual people there: Candy, Huff, Wishbone, Firefly. Dwight, Genie's old man, did the colored-baby dance, flopping around this brown rag doll and flashing up its skirt. Everybody seemed to be having a real good time. Big plastic bottles were on nearly every table; people talking—men arguing, women listening. People leaned on each other like scarecrows, dancing slow and close, others just close, doing a little bump-and-grind.

Blanchard asked him if he had met anyone, danced with anyone. Lloyd grinned and blushed and sought out the Sheriff, who smiled this time. Lloyd said, "I always been shy. I guess it's my rearing, out on that old ranch. And they got their own group there at Genie's, everybody always foolin' with every-one else's."

By the end of his answer the sheriff's smile had gone.

Blanchard asked Lloyd the same thing about ten different ways—had he seen anyone new there? The questions got on his nerves. He said, "Sheriff, now what's this about?"

The sheriff told him to have some patience.

Blanchard asked about places in Amarillo, Lubbock, Muleshoe, Longview, Lamesa, Reno, Abilene—bars Lloyd had sneaked away to when he wanted to be alone. The ones he could remember were all about the same as Genie's, each with its own little crowd. Blanchard mentioned places from so long ago that Lloyd began to feel as if he were asking about a different person. He drifted off into thinking about Mr. Mac.

Mr. Mac, when Lloyd would ask him where they were, used to say that all he needed to know was that they were in the United States of America. He used to tell Lloyd that where they were was just like Scotland, and then he'd start laughing to himself until his laughs trailed off into coughs.

The sheriff had never, ever laughed at him like that. He didn't have those kind of jokes inside him.

Blanchard began asking personal questions: Did he have a girlfriend? Had he ever? No. How long had he been out at the ranch? All his life—about thirty years, according to Mr. Mac. Was he a virgin?

"Now, sheriff, have I got to answer that?" In truth, he didn't know what he was because, as he often reflected, he didn't know whether what Mr. Mac had done made him not a virgin.

Perhaps sensing this, the sheriff told him, no, he didn't have to answer any more questions. In fact, it might be better to quit for the day. "I'm afraid though, son, we're gonna have to hold you as a suspect."

"Suspect of what?" said Lloyd, a sweat creeping on him like the cold rain when he herded in winter.

Lloyd woke to the stink of his own sweat, and he seemed wholly that sweat and that stench—the stench was him, his soul. The overhead light had been switched on. It was a bare bulb caged by heavy wire. He glanced at the steel place he was in: steel walls, floor, ceiling, toilet, stool, table. Everything was bolted down. The steel door had a small square high window made of meshed security glass, and a slot near its bottom, with a sliding cover, for passing food. Lloyd hid his face in the crook of his arm and shook and wished he could go to Mr. Mac's for some white lightning.

The door clanked open. Lloyd could tell it was the sheriff even though he kept his face hidden and his eyes shut tight. The sheriff put a plastic plate on the table and said, "I was afraid of this." Then he left.

Maybe the food would help. Lloyd stood up, but his legs felt wobbly and his eyes couldn't focus right. He lurched to the stool, planted himself on it, and held the edge of the table. When he picked up the plastic fork, it vibrated in his fingers. His touch sent a jangling electrical charge through his arm and down his back. The harder he gripped, the more it felt as though he were trying to etch stone with a pencil, yet only this concentration made any steadiness possible. Keeping his face close to the plate, he scooped the watery scrambled eggs into his mouth. He fell to his knees and threw up in the toilet. Curled face-down on the floor, Lloyd felt a prickly, nauseous chill seep into his muscles and begin to paralyze him.

Someone not Sheriff Lynch, who seemed by his step to be burly and ill-tempered, grabbed Lloyd's shoulder and twisted his body so that he faced the ceiling. The floor felt cold and hard against the back of his head. The man spread Lloyd's eyelids, opened his shirt, and put a cold metal disc on his chest. Lloyd had not noticed until now, but his heart was racing—much faster than the sheep's. That seemed so long ago. Mr. Mac was angry with him. The man started to yank down Lloyd's pants. Lloyd moved his lips to say no! No! But his limbs and muscles had turned to cement. His mouth gaped open, but he couldn't catch any air. The chill sweat sprang returned. He was a boy again. Mr. Mac's heaviness pressed the air from his lungs, pinned him from behind, faceless, pushing the dull tearing pain into him; he choked Lloyd's thin gasps with old-man smells of sweat and smoke and liquor and his ragged, grunting breath. The man rubbed something on Lloyd's right buttock and then pricked it with a needle. He left without pulling up Lloyd's pants.

His body softened, and the cement dissolved; a cushiony feeling spread through him, as though his limbs were swaddled in plush, warm blankets. He could breathe. He could not smell himself anymore. "Son," he heard the sheriff say. "Put your pants on."

The two of them sat in the little white room, this time without Blanchard.

"Sheriff." Lloyd's words seemed to float out of his mouth. "Sheriff, what's all thisayre 'bout?"

Sheriff Lynch sat across the table. His face changed faintly as animals and unknown faces, then the spirits of Mr. Mac and Blanchard, passed through it. He popped a peppermint Life Saver, sucked on it hard, and pulled back into focus.

"Let me ask you a question first, son, and then I'll answer yours." He reached down next to his chair and put two Ziplock bags with Lloyd's shears and bowie knife in them on the table. Both the shears and knife were tagged, as if they were in hock. The Sheriff pressed them a few times with the tips of his long rust-colored fingers, lightly, as though to make sure they were there, or to remind them to stay still. "Now," he said. "I think I already know the answer to this question, but I need to know from you." He pressed them again. "Are these your knife and shears?"

How should he answer? The sheriff leaned back, waiting, a look on his face that said he didn't want to hear the answer.

"Maybe," Lloyd said.

"Maybe." The sheriff joined his hands behind his head, pointed his eyes up and away, as though he were considering this as a possible truth.

"Maybe," Lloyd said.

"Lloyd Wayne Dogget," the sheriff said, turning his not-blue eyes on him. "How long have I known you? I knew your daddy and your grandpappy when they were alive. I know more about you than you know about you. And you ain't never been able to lie to me and get clear with it. So I'll ask you again— are these your knife and shears?"

Mr. Mac had given Lloyd the shears when he was sixteen. They were long and silvery. At the end of each day of shearing, after cutting the sheep's coarse, billowy hair, Lloyd would sharpen them on a strop and oil them with a can of S'OK to keep off the rust. The merry old man on the green can, a pipe in his mouth, always reminded him of Mr. Mac.

"What if I say yes?" Lloyd said.

Sheriff Lynch sucked on the Life Saver and blew out a breath. He leaned close to Lloyd and put his elbows on the table. "To tell you the truth," he said, "it doesn't make a whit's difference." He pressed the plastic bags again. "There's blood on these tools matches the type of a young lady people saw you leave Genie's with, a young lady who turned up murdered. And I confiscated these two things from you. So it doesn't make a whit's difference what you say, whether you lie or not. I'm just trying to give you a chance to get right with yourself, to be a man." He sank back and ran his hands through his stubbly, iron-gray hair as he bowed his head and looked at the bags. He massaged his clean-cut neck. "Maybe to get right with the Lord, too. I don't know. I don't believe in that kind of thing, but sometimes it helps people."

To Lloyd, the sheriff seemed embarrassed about something. Lloyd wanted to help him. But he was also afraid; he could not remember any young lady, only smiling dark-red lips, the curve of a bare upper arm, honky-tonk music, Dwight flinging the colored-baby doll around.

"Okay, sheriff," he said. "Since it don't make any difference, you know they're mine."

The sheriff escorted him to the showers, where he took Lloyd's street clothes and gave him an orange inmate's jumpsuit and a pair of regulation flip-flops. After Lloyd had showered and changed, the sheriff told him he was under arrest for capital murder, read him his rights, and handcuffed him. They got in his car, Lloyd riding in the front seat, and drove the two blocks to the courthouse. The judge asked him if he had any money or expected any help, and he said no, which was the truth.

Every morning, Sheriff Lynch came to Lloyd's cell and walked with him down to the little white room, where Lloyd talked with his lawyer. When the sheriff opened the door to the room, Lloyd watched his lawyer and the sheriff volley looks under their pleasantries. He remembered a cartoon he'd seen: Brutus and Popeye have each grabbed one of Olive Oyl's rubbery arms. They were stretching her like taffy. He couldn't remember how it ended.

Raoul Schwartz, the lawyer Lloyd had been assigned, said the judge had granted Lloyd a competency hearing, but not very much money to do it with. He, Schwartz, would have to conduct the tests himself and then send them to a psychiatrist for evaluation. In two months the psychiatrist would testify and the judge would decide whether Lloyd was competent to stand trial. Schwartz said they had a lot of work to do. Schwartz said he was there to help.

Schwartz was everything the sheriff was not. He had short, pale, womanish fingers that fluttered through papers, fiddled with pencils, took off his wire-rimmed granny glasses and rubbed the bridge of his nose. When he got impatient, which was often, his fingers scratched at a bald spot on the top of his forehead. Lloyd thought he might have rubbed his hair off this way.

Schwartz wouldn't let him wriggle out of questions, sometimes asking the same ones many times, like Blanchard. He asked about Lloyd's whole life. Sometimes the glare of the white room and Schwartz's drone were like being in school again, and Lloyd would lay his head down on the slick-topped table between them and put his cheek to its cool surface. "Come on, Lloyd," Schwartz would say. "We've got work to do."

Also unlike the sheriff, Schwartz cussed, which was something Lloyd could never abide, and the little man's Yankee accent raked the words across Lloyd's nerves even worse than usual. When Lloyd told him that Sheriff Lynch had been out to talk to Mr. Mac after a teacher had spotted cigarette burns on his arms, Schwartz murmured, "Excellent, excellent. Fucking bastard."

"Who's the effing bastard?"

"Mr. Mac." Schwartz's head popped up just as Blanchard's had when he'd wanted to catch Lloyd at something, only this time it was Lloyd who had caught Schwartz in a lie.

Schwartz began giving Lloyd tests. Lloyd was worried that he might fail them, but he didn't say anything; he had already gotten the impression this man thought he was stupid. But it was the tests that were stupid. First Schwartz asked him about a million yes-or-no questions. Everything from "Do you think your life isn't worth living?" (no) to "Do you ever see things that aren't there?" (sometimes, in the woods). Then came the pictures. One showed a man and a boy standing in opposite corners of a room. At first Lloyd just said what he saw. But this wasn't good enough; Schwartz said he had to interpret it. "Tell me what you think is going to happen next," he said. When Lloyd looked at it closely, he figured the boy had done something wrong and was about to get a good belt-whipping. Schwartz seemed pleased by this. Finally, and strangest of all, Schwartz showed him some blobs of ink and asked him to make something out of them. If Schwartz hadn't been so serious, Lloyd would have thought it was a joke. But when he studied them (Schwartz had used that word—"interpret"—again), Lloyd could see all different kinds of faces and animals, as he had when he'd talked to Sheriff Lynch about his knife and shears.

It only took one little thing to know what the sheriff thought about this testing.

One morning the sheriff walked Lloyd down the hallway without a word, and when he unlocked the door to the white room, he stepped back, held it open, and swooped out his hand in front of Lloyd like a colored doorman.

"Mr. Dogget," he said, for the first time making fun of Lloyd in some secret way.

The sheriff turned and let the door close without so much as a glance at Schwartz. Lloyd wanted to apologize to the sheriff. He was beginning to understand that it came down to this: the worse the sheriff looked, the better he, Lloyd, looked. He felt he was betraying the sheriff, with the help of this strange, foul-mouthed little man. Schwartz seemed to see everything upside-down. When Lloyd had told him about Mr. Mac, even though Schwartz said it must have been awful, Lloyd could tell that in some way he was pleased. When he had told Schwartz about times when a lot of hours passed without him knowing it, like when he'd sat with that sheep, or about drinking at least a canteen of Mr. Mac's white lightning every day for the past few years, Schwartz began scribbling and shooting questions at him. Same thing with the pills and reefer and acid and speed he'd done in his twenties. Even the gas huffing when he was just a kid. Lloyd felt dirty remembering all of it. Schwartz wanted details. Lloyd could almost see Schwartz making designs out of what he told him, rearranging things to make him look pitiful.

"I don't want to do no testin' today," Lloyd said as soon as the door had shut. He sat and leaned back in his chair, arms dangling, chest out.

"Okay," Schwartz said. "What do you want to do?"

"I been thinkin'," Lloyd said. "It don't make no difference if I was drunk or not. That don't excuse what I did."

"But you don't know what you did."

"That don't make no difference. They got the proof."

"They have evidence, Lloyd, not proof."

Another bunch of upside-down words. "But if I can't remember it, then ain't what they got better than what I can say?"

"Lloyd," Schwartz said, his head in his hands, massaging his bald spot. "We've been over this about every time we've talked. I know that it doesn't make common sense at first. But our criminal-justice system—that misnomer— is predicated upon the idea of volition. It means you have to commit a crime with at least an inkling of intention. You can't be punished in the same way when you don't have any idea what you're doing."

This kind of talk made Lloyd's head ache. "All I know," he said, "is I don't want to go foolin' around with truth. It's like the sheriff says—I got to get right with myself and be a man."

"The sheriff says this?" Schwartz's head popped up.

Lloyd nodded.

"Do you talk to the sheriff often?"

"I been knowing Sheriff Lynch since forever. He's like my daddy."

"But do you talk to him? How often do you talk to him?"

"Every chance I get." Lloyd felt queasy. He knew he'd said something he shouldn't have. But his pride in his friendship with the sheriff, perhaps because it was imperiled, drove him to exaggerate. "When we come from my cell, mostly. But any time I want, really. I can call on him any time."

"I don't think it's a good idea for you to be talking to him about your case," Schwartz said.

"And why not?"

"Because anything—anything—you say to him becomes evidence. As a matter of fact, I don't think it's a good idea for you to talk to him at all."

"So who'm I gonna talk to? Myself? You?"

For the next couple of days the sheriff didn't speak to Lloyd unless Lloyd spoke to him first. Schwartz must have done something. But the sheriff never looked at him hard or seemed angry. He mainly kept his words short and his eyes to the floor, as if he was sad and used to his sadness. Lloyd wanted to tell him how he was trying to get right but it was hard. Eventually Lloyd realized that even if he had said this, the sheriff probably wouldn't believe him. If he were trying to get right, then he wouldn't be letting this Schwartz character make him look pitiful. Each morning Lloyd rose early, dressed, and rubbed his palms to dry them as he sat on the edge of his bunk, waiting. When he walked in front of the sheriff down the hallway to the white room, Lloyd could feel the sheriff's eyes taking him in. He tried to stand up straight and walk with manly strides, but the harder he tried, the smaller and more bent over he felt. He was careful not to wrinkle his prison outfit, pressing it at night between his mattress and a piece of plywood the sheriff had given him for his back. He combed his hair as best he could without a mirror.

At night Lloyd lay on his cot and thought about Schwartz. Of course, Schwartz had tricked him into more tests. Next they were going to take pictures of his brain. Lloyd studied Schwartz's words: "volition," "interpret," "diminished responsibility." They all meant you couldn't be punished for your mistakes. This didn't square with Lloyd; he had been punished for plenty of mistakes. That was what Mr. Mac had punished him for; that was what the sheep died of. When you missed one on a head count and it got lost and fell into a ravine; when you forgot to give one a vaccination and it got sick, like the one that had died before Lloyd was taken away, you were punished. But how could he expect Schwartz, a womanish city boy, to understand this?

On one side were Schwartz and the law, and on the other were the sheep and God and the earth and Sheriff Lynch and Mr. Mac and everything else Lloyd had ever known. Who was he to go against all that—to hide from that terrible, swift sword the Almighty would wield on the Final Day? His fear was weak and mortal; it drove him out of his cell to plot with this fellow sinner to deceive God. Some nights Lloyd moaned in agony at the deceit of his life. For in his pride he had latched onto the notion that since he could not remember his gravest sins (and he believed they were all true, they must be true), that he should not have to pay for them in this life. Oh, he would pay for them in eternity, but he flinched at paying here. What upside-down thinking! What cowardice in the face of sins that were probably darker, cloaked as they were in his drunken forgetting, than any he could have committed when he had "volition," as Schwartz called it. Because Lloyd did not know his sins, he could not accept his punishment; but for the same reason, they seemed to him unspeakably heinous.

Lloyd lay on his bunk in the darkness and thought about the pictures he had seen of his brain. Two officers he didn't know had driven him to a hospital in Lubbock to get them taken. The hearing was in a week. Schwartz had pointed out patches in the pictures' rainbow colors, scratching his bald spot and pacing. He'd said that although parts of Lloyd's brain were damaged so that alcohol could cause longer and more severe blackouts in him than in normal people, such damage might not be enough for the court to recognize him as incompetent. And the rest of the tests had proved that he had a dissociative condition but not multiple-personality disorder. Lloyd had wanted to ask if Schwartz thought he was incompetent, but he figured he wouldn't get a straight answer.

In the darkness of the steel room Lloyd touched his head to try and feel the colored patches of heat and coolness that the pictures showed in his brain. He imagined he could sense some here and there. He had come a long way—not many people knew what their brains looked like. But the thought that he might be incompetent frightened him. What if some day one of those big machines they put over his head was put over his chest and a picture was taken of his soul? What would it look like? He saw a dark-winged creature with tearing claws, cloaked in a gray mist.

The knock came to Lloyd in a half-dream, and at first he thought he had imagined the sheriff's voice. The whole jail was quiet; all the inmates were covered in the same darkness.

"Lloyd? Lloyd? You awake, son?" The voice didn't sound exactly like the sheriff's, but Lloyd knew that's who it was. He rose and went to the door, too sleepy to be nervous. He peered out the square window. The glare of the hallway made him squint. The sheriff stood in silhouette, but his steely eyes glinted. Looking at him through the crosshatches of wire in the security glass, Lloyd thought that he, too, looked caged.

"I'm awake, sheriff."

The door opened, and the sheriff said, "Come on." Lloyd could smell whiskey. He followed the sheriff out past the booking area. Everything was still and deserted in the bare fluorescent light. Gonzales dozed in a chair at the front desk with a porno magazine in his lap. The sheriff opened the door to his office, making the same mocking gesture as before, though this time he seemed to be trying to share his joke with Lloyd. He snapped the door's lock and sat down behind his desk. A single shaded lamp glowed in a corner, casting shadows from the piles of paper on the desk and reflecting golden patches from the plaques on the walls.

The sheriff pointed at a low-backed leather chair and told Lloyd to have a seat. "Excuse me gettin' you out of bed, son. I figured this was the only time we could talk."

"It's no trouble."

"You can prob'ly tell I been drinkin'," the sheriff said. "I don't do it as a habit, but I apologize for that, too. I been doin' it more lately. I do it when I'm sick at heart. At least that's my excuse to myself, which is a Goddamned poor one unbefitting a man, if you ask me. But I am. Sick at heart."

He took a long pull from a coffee mug. Lloyd followed it with his eyes, and the sheriff caught him.

"And no," he said, "you can't have any. One of us got to stay sober, and I want you to remember what I'm gonna tell you." He leaned across the desk. "You know what a vacuum is, son? I mean in a pure sense, not the one you clean with."

Lloyd shook his head.

"Well. A vacuum is a place where there ain't anything, not even air. Every light bulb"—the Sheriff nodded at the lamp behind him—"is a vacuum. Space is mostly vacuum. Vacuum tubes used to be in radios. And so on. A place where there ain't nothin'. Is that signifyin' for you?"

Lloyd nodded.

"Good. So we, because we're on this earth with air to breathe, we are in a place that's not a vacuum that's in the middle of a vacuum, which is space. Think of a bubble floating out in the air." The Sheriff made a big circle above the desk with his fingertips. "That's what the earth is like, floating in space. Are you followin' me?"

"I think so."

"Well, are you or aren't you?" the sheriff said with sudden violence. Not waiting for an answer, he yanked open his desk drawer and took out a large folding map of the world. He tumbled it down the front of his desk, weighted its top corners with a tape dispenser and a stapler, and came around the desk to stand next to Lloyd. He told Lloyd what it was and said, "I study this all the time. Do you know where we are right now?"

To Lloyd, the shapes on the map looked like those inkblots. By reading, he found the United States and then Texas, and then he gave up. He shrugged his shoulders. "I don't know, Sheriff."

"That's okay," the sheriff said gently. He pointed to a dot in the Panhandle which someone had drawn with a ballpoint pen. Cursive letters next to it said "Dumas." "This is where we are. Two specks within that dot, on the dark side of the earth, floating in space. Over here"—he pointed to Hong Kong—"it's lunchtime. Japs eatin' their noodles or whatever. Here"—he pointed to London—"people just risin', eatin' their sausages and egg sandwiches."

He stepped back, behind Lloyd, and put his hands on the chair. The heat of his body and the smell of his breath washed over Lloyd.

"But look, son," the sheriff said, "how many places there are. It's some time everywhere, and everybody is doin' something."

The sheriff stood there for a few moments. Lloyd felt as he had when he was a child and watched TV—he couldn't imagine how all those people got inside that little box. Now he couldn't fathom people inside the little dots. The world was vast and stranger than he had ever imagined.

"We are all here doin' things," the sheriff said, "inside this bubble that is not a vacuum. We all breathe the same air, and everything we do nudges everything else." He stepped over and propped himself on the edge of his desk, next to the map, and crossed his legs. The lamp's soft light cast him in half shadow.

"And this is why I'm sick at heart. Because I thought I knew you. Separation is the most terrible thing there is, especially for a man like me." The sheriff gestured to take in the whole room. "This is what I got. It ain't much. You and I aren't that far apart, son. Both of us solitary. But what you done, son, and I do believe you did all that, that separates a man from the whole world. And that's why I said you need to get right with yourself."

Lloyd bowed his head.

"You don't need to tell me you ain't done that." The sheriff's voice rose and quickened, began to quiver. "You and I both know you ain't. But that itself—a negativity, a vacuum—ain't nothing to breathe in. Things die without air. So what I'm askin' you is, I want to do my own competency exam, for my own self. This is between Lloyd Wayne Dogget and Archibald Alexander Lynch. I need to know what's inside you to know what's inside myself. So you tell that lawyer of yours I'll stipulate to whatever he wants. Remember that word—'stipulate.' Now get out a' here." He turned from Lloyd and began folding the map with shaking hands. The corner weighted by the tape dispenser tore. Lloyd could not move.

"Shit," the sheriff muttered. He wheeled unsteadily on Lloyd, his eyes wide with panic and surprise at what he'd said. Lloyd could tell he was afraid, but not of him, as Mr. Mac had been. The sheriff was afraid he might break out of the bubble in which he lived. "Git!" he yelled. "Go tell Gonzales to take you back! Get outta here before I say somethin' foolish!"

"He wants you to do *what* ?" Schwartz paced in the little white room, looking at the floor.

Lloyd was sitting at the table, turning his head to follow Schwartz. Was Schwartz right with himself? He repeated what the sheriff had told him.

"What does that son of a bitch want?" Schwartz said to himself.

"I wish you'd stop cussing around me."

Schwartz made a distracted noise.

"I mean it," Lloyd said. "It's offensive."

Schwartz made another noise. He had gathered his lips into a pucker with his fingers, and he looked at the floor as he paced.

"Especially cussing on the sheriff." When Schwartz didn't answer, Lloyd said, "Are you hearing me? Don't cuss on the sheriff."

"I don't know what kind of game he's trying to play." Schwartz did not stop or raise his eyes from the floor. "But I would guess he's trying to trick some kind of confession out of you."

"Sheriff don't play no games with me," Lloyd said. "He don't have no tricks. You're the one with all the tricks."

"I'll take that as a compliment."

"Sheriff's the one tryin' to help me get right."

"Sheriff's the one tryin' to help you get dead," Schwartz said, mimicking Lloyd.

"Okay, man." Lloyd stood up and pushed the chair away. It squealed on the floor, and Schwartz stopped. Lloyd saw that his own fists were clenched. He hesitated.

"What are you gonna do, Lloyd? Beat me up? Go ahead. I've been expecting this."

"You think I'm stupid," Lloyd said. "And all them tests is to make me look pitiful and incompetent. What do you think that's done to my trying to get right?"

"What do you think that means, Lloyd—'getting right'?" Schwartz moved close to him. He stared straight at Lloyd as he spoke. "It means giving up."

That night, and for the nights and days to come, Lloyd turned over in his mind all he had seen and heard. What he had known was like some foreign language that now he couldn't understand. The worlds of Schwartz and the sheriff, of man and God, of what was in the law and what was in the fields, began to blur, and yet between them grew a chasm in which he hung suspended. He tried to remember what had happened in the places Blanchard had said he'd been, but he couldn't. He could not make them connect the way the sheriff had said all the people in all those dots on the map did. An indifference grew around him, a thin glass glazing that separated him from the rest of humankind.

The sheriff led him down the hallway to the white room without a word or a look, and left him with Schwartz. The hearing was the next day. Lloyd felt as though he were about to take another test. He had fought with Schwartz tooth and nail over the sheriff's proposal, and in the end had gotten his way by threatening to fire him. After Lloyd sat down across the table from him,

Schwartz explained that he and the sheriff had struck a deal: the sheriff had stipulated not to testify about his "competency exam," as he called it, on the condition that he not have to reveal to Schwartz beforehand what it was going to be about.

"I don't like this," Schwartz said, pacing, clicking the top of a ballpoint pen so that it made a *tick-tick* sound like a clock. He sat down again, his elbows on the table and hands joined as though in prayer, and brought his face close to Lloyd's.

"I want to tell you the truest thing I've ever seen, Lloyd. I've seen a man executed. When you are executed in Texas, you are taken to a powder-blue room. This is the death chamber, where the warden, a physician, and a minister will stand around the gurney. Since executions can only take place in Texas between midnight and dawn, it will have that eerie feeling of a room brightly lit in the middle of the night. Before this, in an anteroom, a guard will tell you to drop your pants. Then he will insert one rubber stopper in your penis and another in your anus, to prevent you from urinating and defecating when your muscles relax after you have died. When you are lying on the gurney, the guard will secure your arms, legs, and chest to it with leather straps. The guard will insert a needle, which is attached to an IV bag, into your left arm. Above you will be fluorescent lighting, and a microphone will hang suspended from the ceiling. The warden—I think it's still Warden Pearson—will ask whether you have any last words. When you're finished, three chemicals will be released into your blood: sodium thiopental, a sedative that is supposed to render you unconscious; pancuronium bromide, a muscle relaxant, to collapse your diaphragm and lungs; potassium chloride, a poison that will stop your heart.

"I could tell that my client could feel the poison entering his veins. I had known him for the last three of his fifteen years on death row; he was old enough to be my father. At his execution, I was separated from him by a piece of meshed security glass. There was nothing I could do when he began writhing and gasping for breath. The poison—later I found out it was the potassium chloride, to stop his heart—had been injected before the thiopental. Imagine a dream in which your body has turned to lead, in which you can't move and are sinking in water. You have the sensations given you by your nerves and understood in your brain, but you can't do anything about them. You struggle against your own body. But really, it is unimaginable—what it is like to try to rouse your own heart.

"What if everything goes as planned? A nice, sleepy feeling—the sedative tricking your nerves—will dissolve your fear. The question is, will you want it taken away, fear being the only thing that binds you to life? Will you want to hold on to that, like the survivor of a shipwreck clinging to a barnacled plank? Will you struggle, in the end, to be afraid?"

Schwartz slumped back in his chair and began again to *tick-tick* the top of his pen, so that it made a sound like a clock. The whiteness and silence of the room seemed to annihilate time, as though the two men could sit there waiting forever. They fell on Lloyd like a thin silting of powdered glass.

"You spend a lot of time thinkin' about that, don't you?" Lloyd said.

"Yes."

"You told me that to scare me, didn't you?"

"Yes."

Lloyd thought that Schwartz may have gotten right with himself, in his own way, by seeing what he had seen and thinking on it. But something still didn't add up.

"How do you know I'd be afraid?" Lloyd said. "How do you know that would be the last thing I'd feel?"

"I don't know that." Schwartz *tick-ticked* the pen. "You can never know. That's what's terrible about death."

"Lots of things you don't know when you're alive. So what's the difference?"

Schwartz's fingers stopped, and he stared at Lloyd as though he had seen him purely and for the first time. A knock at the door broke the brief, still moment, and Sheriff Lynch entered. He carried under his arm a stack of manila folders, which he put down on the table. Schwartz rose, studying Lloyd. He shook the sheriff's hand when it was offered. His eyes, though, were fixed on Lloyd. The sheriff caught this, but smiled pleasantly and told Schwartz it was good to see him again.

"Lloyd," he said, and nodded at him. He lifted a chair from the corner, put it at the head of the table, and sat.

"I think I need a little more time to consult with my client," Schwartz said.

The sheriff pressed his fingers a few times on top of the folders. "Okay. How much time do you think you'll need?"

"We don't need no more time," Lloyd said, rocking back and forth in his chair. "I'm ready."

"I'd like to look at what you've got there first."

"But that wasn't the agreement, Mr. Schwartz."

"Come on," Lloyd said. "I'm ready."

"Why don't you listen to your client?"

Looking from Lloyd to the sheriff, Schwartz paled. He seemed pinned in place for a moment; then took off his glasses and rubbed them on his shirt. He put them on again. Sheriff Lynch stared at the stack of folders, his fingertips resting on them like a pianist's, his expression one of patient indulgence toward a child who was finishing a noisy tantrum. Lloyd clenched his hands between his thighs, wondering what would be revealed to him.

"Do you mind if I stand?" Schwartz said.

"Go right ahead." Sheriff Lynch pressed his fingers again to the top folder, as if for luck or in valediction, took it from the stack and opened it in front of Lloyd. Lloyd did not see what was there at first, because Schwartz had made a sudden movement toward the table, but Sheriff Lynch, with the slightest warning lift of his hand, checked him. He faced Schwartz a moment and then turned to Lloyd.

"Go ahead, son," he said. "Tell me what you see."

When Lloyd looked down, he was disappointed. It was another one of those crazy tests. There were shapes of red and pink and green and black. It was the inkblot test, only in color. He studied it more closely to try and make sense of it. He realized it was a picture of something. He realized what it was.

"I think I got it," he said to the sheriff. The sheriff nodded to help him along. "It's a sheep," Lloyd said.

"Look at it a little more closely, son." Lloyd saw Schwartz again move and the sheriff again check him while keeping his neutral blue eyes on Lloyd. Lloyd went back to the picture. He had missed some details.

"It's a sheep gutted after slaughter," he said.

"Turn the picture over, son," the sheriff said. This time, Schwartz did not move and the sheriff did not hold up his hand. Paper-clipped to the backside of the picture Lloyd found a smaller photo of a young woman. She had straight brown hair, wore blue jeans and a red-and-white checkered blouse, and sat in a lawn chair, smiling to please the person who held the camera.

"Now turn the picture over again," the sheriff said, in his steady, calm voice. "What do you see?"

Lloyd tried to puzzle it out, but he couldn't. There must be something he wasn't seeing. He studied the picture. As he followed the shapes and colors of the sheep's emptied body, a trickle of pity formed in him for all three of them—the woman, the sheep and himself—and dropped somewhere inside him. The glaze over him tightened. He could only tell the sheriff that he saw a sheep.

After the sheriff left, gathering the folders under his arm, the room went back to its silence.

"If I'd known," Schwartz said, "I would've had him testify."

"What?" Lloyd said. "If you'd known what?"

"Never mind." Shielding his face with his pale fingers, Schwartz lay his other hand on Lloyd's shoulder. "Never mind, Lloyd. You're perfect the way you are."

They had sat there a long time, the sheriff opening a folder in front of him, asking him the same questions, and then putting it aside. And in each folder Lloyd had seen the same things: a gutted sheep and a pretty young woman. He knew that the sheriff was trying to do something to help him get right, but as the glaze thickened, that chance seemed ever more remote. Before he left, the sheriff had nodded to Lloyd, to acknowledge that he had found his answer, but his gesture was as distant as that of a receding figure waving a ship out to sea. With each drop of pity Lloyd felt himself borne away yet drowning, so that he knew the heart of the man in the execution chamber, suffocating and unable to move, and he wondered how he would survive in this new and airless world.

Five Points

Alice Munro

While they drink vodka and orange juice in the trailer park on the cliffs above Lake Huron, Neil Bauer tells Brenda a story. It happened a long way away, in Victoria, British Columbia, where Neil grew up. Neil is not much younger than Brenda—less than three years—but it sometimes feels to her like a generation gap, because she grew up here, and stayed here, marrying Cornelius Zendt when she was twenty years old, and Neil grew up on the West Coast, where things were very different, and he left home at sixteen to travel and work all over.

What Brenda has seen of Victoria, in pictures, is flowers and horses. Flowers spilling out of baskets hanging from old-fashioned lampposts, filling grottoes and decorating parks; horses carrying wagonloads of people to look at the sights.

"That's all just tourist shit," Neil says. "About half the place is nothing but tourist shit. That's not where I'm talking about."

He is talking about Five Points, which was—is—a section, or maybe just a corner, of the city, where there was a school and a drugstore and a Chinese grocery and a candy store. When Neil was in public school, the candy store was run by a grouchy old woman with painted-on eyebrows. She used to let her cat sprawl in the sun in the window. After she died, some new people, Europeans, not Poles or Czechs but from some smaller country—Croatia; is that a country?—took over the candy store and changed it. They cleared out all the stale candy and the balloons that wouldn't blow up and the ballpoint pens that wouldn't write and the dead Mexican jumping beans. They painted the place top to bottom and put in a few chairs and tables. They still sold candy—in clean jars now, instead of cat-pissed cardboard boxes—and rulers and erasers. But they also started to operate as a kind of neighborhood café, with coffee and soft drinks and homemade cakes.

The wife, who made the cakes, was very shy and fussy, and if you came up and tried to pay her she would call for her husband in Croatian, or whatever—let's say it was Croatian—in such a startled way you'd think that you'd broken into her house and interrupted her private life. The husband spoke English pretty well. He was a little bald guy, polite and nervous, a chain-smoker, and she was a big, heavy woman with bent shoulders, always wearing an apron and a cardigan sweater. He washed the windows and swept off the sidewalk and took the money, and she baked the buns and cakes and made things that people had never seen before but that quickly became popular, like pierogi and poppy-seed loaf.

Their two daughters spoke English just like Canadians, and went to the convent school. They showed up in their school uniforms in the late afternoon and got right to work. The younger one washed the coffee cups and glasses and wiped the tables, and the older one did everything else. She waited on customers, worked the cash register, filled the trays, and shooed away the little kids who were hanging around not buying anything. When the younger one finished washing up, she would sit in the back room doing her homework, but the older one never sat down. If there was nothing to do at the moment, she just stood by the cash register, watching.

The younger one was called Lisa, the older one Maria. Lisa was small and nice enough looking—just a little kid. But Maria, by the age of maybe thirteen, had big, saggy breasts and a rounded-out stomach and thick legs. She wore glasses, and her hair was done in braids around her head. She looked about fifty years old.

And she acted it, the way she took over the store. Both parents seemed willing to take a back seat to her. The mother retreated to the back room, and the father became a handyman-helper. Maria understood English and money and wasn't fazed by anything. All the little kids said, "Ugh, that Maria—isn't she *gross?*" But they were scared of her. She looked like she already knew all about running a business.

Brenda and her husband also run a business. They bought a farm just south of Logan and filled the barn with used appliances (which Cornelius knows how to fix) and secondhand furniture and all the other things—the dishes, pictures, knives and forks and ornaments and jewelry—that people like to poke through and think they're buying cheap. It's called Zendt's Furniture Barn. Locally, a lot of people refer to it as the Used Furniture on the Highway.

They didn't always do this. Brenda used to teach nursery school, and Cornelius, who is twelve years older than she is, worked in the salt mine at Walley, on the lake. After his accident they had to think of something he could do sitting down most of the time, and they used the money they got to buy a worn-out farm with good buildings. Brenda quit her job, because there was too much for Cornelius to handle by himself. There are hours in the day and sometimes whole days when he has to lie down and watch television, or just lie on the living room floor, coping with the pain.

In the evenings Cornelius likes to drive over to Walley. Brenda never offers—she waits for him to say, "Why don't you drive?" if he doesn't want the movement of his arms or legs to jar his back. The kids used to go along, but now that they're in high school—Lorna in grade eleven and Mark in grade nine—they usually don't want to. Brenda and Cornelius sit in the parked van and look at the sea gulls lining up out on the breakwater, the grain elevators, the great green-lighted shafts and ramps of the mine where Cornelius used to work, the pyramids of coarse gray salt. Sometimes there is a long lake boat in port. Of course, there are pleasure boats in the summer, wind surfers out on the water, people fishing off the pier. The time of the sunset is posted daily on a board on the beach then; people come especially to watch it. Now,

in October, the board is bare and the lights are turned on along the pier—
one or two diehards are still fishing—and the water is choppy and cold-look-
ing, the harbor entirely businesslike.

There is still work going on on the beach. Since early last spring, boul-
ders have been set up in some places, sand has been poured down in others,
a long rocky spit has been constructed, all making a protected curve of beach,
with a rough road along it, on which they drive. Never mind Cornelius's back—
he wants to see. Trucks, earthmovers, bulldozers have been busy all day, and
they are still sitting there, temporarily tame and useless monsters, in the
evening. This is where Neil works. He drives these things—he hauls the rocks
around, clears the space, and makes the road for Brenda and Cornelius to drive
on. He works for the Fordyce Construction Company, from Logan, which
has the contract.

Cornelius looks at everything. He knows what the boats are loading (soft
wheat, salt, corn) and where they're going, he understands how the harbor is
being deepened, and he always wants to get a look at the huge pipe running at
an angle onto the beach and crossing it, finally letting out water and sludge and
rocks from the lake bottom that have never before seen the light of day. He goes
and stands beside this pipe to listen to the commotion inside it, the banging
and groaning of the rocks and water rushing on their way. He asks what a rough
winter will do to all this changing and arranging if the lake just picks up the rocks
and beach and flings them aside and eats away at the clay cliffs, as before.

Brenda listens to Cornelius and thinks about Neil. She derives pleasure
from being in the place where Neil spends his days. She likes to think of the
noise and the steady strength of these machines and of the men in the cabs
bare-armed, easy with this power, as if they knew naturally what all this roar-
ing and chomping up the shore was leading to. Their casual, good-humored
authority. She loves the smell of work on their bodies, the language of it they
speak, their absorption in it, their disregard of her. She loves to get a man
fresh from all that.

When she is down there with Cornelius and hasn't seen Neil for a while,
she can feel uneasy and forlorn, as if this might be a world that could turn its
back on her. Just after she has been with Neil, it's her kingdom—but what isn't,
then? The night before they are to meet—last night, for instance—she should
be feeling happy and expectant, but to tell the truth the last twenty-four hours,
even the last two or three days, seem too full of pitfalls, too momentous, for her
to feel anything much but caution and anxiety. It's a countdown—she actually
counts the hours. She has a tendency to fill them with good deeds—cleaning jobs
around the house that she was putting off, mowing the lawn, doing a reorgani-
zation at the Furniture Barn, even weeding the rock garden. The morning of
the day itself is when the hours pass most laggingly and are full of dangers. She
always has a story about where she's supposed to be going that afternoon, but
her expedition can't be an absolutely necessary one—that would be calling too
much attention to it—so there's the chance, always, that something will come
up to make Cornelius say, "Can't you put that off till later in the week? Can't you
do it some other day?" It's not so much that she wouldn't then be able to get

in touch with Neil that bothers her. Neil would wait an hour or so, then figure out what had happened. It's that she thinks she couldn't bear it. To be so close, then have to do without. Yet she doesn't feel any physical craving during those last torturing hours; even her secret preparations—her washing, shaving, oiling, and perfuming—don't arouse her. She stays numb, harassed by details, lies, arrangements, until the moment when she actually sees Neil's car. The fear that she won't be able to get away is succeeded, during the fifteen-minute drive, by the fear that he won't show up, in that lonely, dead-end spot in the swamp which is their meeting place. What she's looking forward to, during those last hours, gets to be less of a physical thing—so that missing it would be like missing not a meal you're hungry for but a ceremony on which your life or salvation depended.

By the time Neil was an older teenager—but not old enough to get into bars, still hanging around at the Five Points Confectionery (the Croatians kept the old name for it)—the change had arrived, which everybody who was alive then remembers. (That's what Neil thinks, but Brenda says, "I don't know— as far as I was concerned, all that was just sort of going on someplace else.") Nobody knew what to do about it, nobody was prepared. Some schools were strict about long hair (on boys), some thought it best to let that go and concentrate on serious things. Just hold it back with an elastic band was all they asked. And what about clothes? Chains and seed beads, rope sandals, Indian cotton, African patterns, everything all of a sudden soft and loose and bright. In Victoria the change may not have been contained so well as in some other places. It spilled over. Maybe the climate softened people up, not just young people. There was a big burst of paper flowers and marijuana fumes and music (the stuff that seemed so wild then, Neil says, and seems so tame now), and that music rolling out of downtown windows hung with dishonored flags, over the flowers beds in Beacon Hill Park to the yellow broom on the sea cliffs to the happy beaches looking over at the magic peaks of the Olympics. Everybody was in on the act. University professors wandered around with flowers behind their ears, and people's mothers turned up in those outfits. Neil and his friends had contempt for these people, naturally—these hip oldsters, toe-dippers. Neil and his friends took the world of drugs and music seriously.

When they wanted to do drugs, they went outside the Confectionery. Sometimes they went as far as the cemetery and sat on the seawall. Sometimes they sat beside the shed that was in back of the store. They couldn't go in; the shed was locked. Then they went back inside the Confectionery and drank Cokes and ate hamburgers and cheeseburgers and cinnamon buns and cakes, because they got very hungry. They leaned back on their chairs and watched the patterns move on the old pressed-tin ceiling, which the Croatians had painted white. Flowers, towers, birds, and monsters detached themselves, swam overhead.

"What were you taking?" Brenda says.

"Pretty good stuff, unless we got sold something rotten. Hash, acid, mescaline sometimes. Combinations sometimes. Nothing too serious."

"All I ever did was smoke about a third of a joint on the beach when at first I wasn't even sure what it was, and when I got home my father slapped my face."

(That's not the truth. It was Cornelius. Cornelius slapped her face. It was before they were married, when Cornelius was working nights in the mine and she would sit around on the beach after dark with some friends of her own age. Next day she told him, and he slapped her face.)

All they did in the Confectionery was eat, and moon around, happily stoned, and play stupid games, such as racing toy cars along the tabletops. Once, a guy lay down on the floor and they squirted ketchup at him. Nobody cared. The daytime customers—the housewives buying bakery goods and the pensioners killing time with a coffee—never came in at night. The mother and Lisa had gone home on the bus, to wherever they lived. Then even the father started going home, a little after suppertime. Maria was left in charge. She didn't care what they did, as long as they didn't do damage and as long as they paid.

This was the world of drugs that belonged to the older boys, that they kept the younger boys out of. It was a while before they noticed that the younger ones had something, too. They had some secret of their own. They were growing insolent and self-important. Some of them were always pestering the older boys to let them buy drugs. That was how it became evident that they had quite a bit of unexplained money.

Neil had—he has—a younger brother named Jonathan. Very straight now, married, a teacher. Jonathan began dropping hints; other boys did the same thing, they couldn't keep the secret to themselves, and pretty soon it was all out in the open. They were getting their money from Maria. Maria was paying them to have sex with her. They did it in the back shed after she closed the store up at night. She had the key to the shed.

She also had the day-to-day control of the money. She emptied the till at night, she kept the books. Her parents trusted her to do this. Why not? She was good at arithmetic, and she was devoted to the business. She understood the whole operation better than they did. It seemed that they were very uncertain and superstitious about money, and they did not want to put it in the bank. They kept it in a safe or maybe just a strongbox somewhere, and got it as they needed it. They must have felt they couldn't trust anybody, banks or anybody, outside of the family. What a godsend Maria must have seemed to them—steady and smart, not pretty enough to be tempted to put her hopes or energies into anything but the business. A pillar, Maria.

She was a head taller and thirty or forty pounds heavier than those boys she paid.

There are always a few bad moments after Brenda turns off the highway—where she has some excuse to be driving, should anyone see her—and onto the side road. The van is noticeable, unmistakable. But once she has taken the plunge, driving where she shouldn't be, she feels stronger. When she turns onto the dead-end swamp road, there's no excuse possible. Spotted here, she's finished. She has about half a mile to drive out in the open before she gets to the trees. She'd hoped that they would plant corn, which would grow tall and shelter her, but they hadn't, they'd planted beans. At least the roadsides here hadn't been sprayed; the grass and weeds and berry bushes had grown tall, though not tall enough to hide a van. There was goldenrod and milkweed, with the pods burst open, and dangling bunches of bright, poisonous fruit, and wild grapevine flung over everything, even creeping onto the road. And finally she was in, she was into the tunnel of trees. Cedar, hemlock, farther back in the wetter ground the wispy-looking tamarack, lots of soft maples with leaves spotty yellow and brown. No standing water, no black pools, even far back in the trees. They'd had luck, with the dry summer and fall. She and Neil had had luck, not the farmers. If it had been a wet year, they could never have used this place. The hard ruts she eases the van through would have been slick mud and the turnaround spot at the end a soggy sinkhole.

That's about a mile and a half in. There are some tricky spots to drive— a couple of bumpy little hills rising out of the swamp, and a narrow log bridge over a creek where she can't see any water, just choking, yellowy cress and nettles, sucking at dry mud.

Neil drives an old blue Mercury—dark blue that can turn into a pool, a spot of swampy darkness under the trees. She strains to see it. She doesn't mind getting there a few minutes ahead of him, to compose herself, brush out her hair and check her face and spray her throat with purse cologne (sometimes between her legs as well). More than a few minutes makes her nervous. She isn't afraid of wild dogs or rapists or eyes watching her out of thickets—she used to pick berries in here when she was a child; that's how she knew about the place. She is afraid of what may not be there, not what is. The absence of Neil, the possibility of his defection, his sudden denial of her. That can turn any place, any thing, ugly and menacing and stupid. Trees or gardens or parking meters or coffee tables—it wouldn't matter. Once, he didn't come; he was sick: food poisoning or the most incredible hangover of his life—something terrible, he told her on the phone that night—and she had to pretend it was somebody calling to sell them a sofa. She never forgot the wait, the draining of hope, the heat and the bugs—it was in July—and her body oozing sweat, here on the seat of the van, like some sickly admission of defeat.

He is there, he's there first; she can see one eye of the Mercury in the deep cedar shade. It's like hitting water when you're dead of heat and scratched and bitten all over from picking berries in the summer bush—the lapping sweetness of it, the cool kindness soaking up all your troubles in its sudden depths. She gets the van parked and fluffs out her hair and jumps out, tries the door to show it's locked, else he'll send her running back, just like Cornelius—are you sure you locked the van? She walks across the little sunny space, the leaf-scattered ground, seeing herself walk, in her tight white pants and turquoise top and low-slung white belt and high heels, her bag over her shoulder. A shapely woman, with fair, freckled skin and blue eyes rimmed with blue shadow and liner, screwed up appealingly against any light. Her reddish-blond hair— touched up yesterday—catching the sun like a crown of petals. She wears heels just for this walk, just for this moment of crossing the road with his eyes on her, the extra bit of pelvic movement and leg length they give her.

Often, often, they've made love in his car, right here at their meeting place, though they always keep telling each other to wait. Stop; wait till we get to the trailer. "Wait" means the opposite of what it says, after a while. Once, they started as they drove. Brenda slipped off her pants and pulled up her loose summer skirt, not saying a word, looking straight ahead, and they ended up stopping beside the highway, taking a shocking risk. Now when they pass this spot, she always says something like "Don't go off the road here," or "Somebody should put up a warning sign."

"Historical marker," Neil says.

They have a history of passion, the way families have a history, or people who have gone to school together. They don't have much else. They've never eaten a meal with each other, or seen a movie. But they've come through some complicated adventures together, and dangers—not just of the stopping-on-the-highway kind. They've taken risks, surprising each other, always correctly. In dreams you can have the feeling that you've had this dream before, that you have this dream over and over again, and you know that it's really nothing that simple. You know that there's a whole underground system that you call "dreams," having nothing better to call them, and that this system is not like roads or tunnels but more like a live body network, all coiling and stretching, unpredictable but finally familiar—where you are now, where you've always been. That was the way it was with them and sex, going somewhere like that, and they understood the same things about it and trusted each other, so far.

Another time on the highway, Brenda saw a white convertible approaching, an old white Mustang convertible with the top down—this was in the summer—and she slid to the floor.

"Who's in that car?" she said. "Look! Quick! Tell me."

"Girls," Neil said. "Four or five girls. Out looking for guys."

"My daughter," Brenda said, scrambling up again. "Good thing I wasn't wearing my seat belt."

"You got a daughter old enough to drive? You got a daughter owns a convertible?"

"Her friend owns it. Lorna doesn't drive yet. But she could—she's sixteen."

She felt there were things in the air then that he could have said, that she hoped he wouldn't. The things men feel obliged to say about young girls.

"You could have one that age yourself," she said. "Maybe you do and don't know it. Also, she lied to me. She said she was going to play tennis."

Again he didn't say anything she hoped not to hear, any sly reminder about lies. A danger past.

All he said was, "Easy. Take it easy. Nothing happened."

She had no way of knowing how much he understood of her feelings at that moment, or if he understood anything. They almost never mentioned that part of her life. They never mentioned Cornelius, though he was the one Neil talked to the first time he came to the Furniture Barn. He came to look for a bicycle—just a cheap bike to ride on the country roads. They had no bikes around at that time, but he stayed and talked to Cornelius for a while, about the kind he wanted, ways of repairing or improving that kind, how they should watch out for one. He said he would drop by again. He did that, very soon, and only Brenda was there. Cornelius had gone to the house to lie down; it was one of his bad days. Neil and Brenda made everything clear to each other then, without saying anything definite. When he phoned and asked her to have a drink with him, in a tavern on the lakeshore road, she knew what he was asking and she knew what she would answer.

She told him she hadn't done anything like this before. That was a lie in one way and in another way true.

During store hours, Maria didn't let one sort of transaction interfere with another. Everybody paid as usual. She didn't behave any differently; she was still in charge. The boys knew that they had some bargaining power, but they were never sure how much. A dollar. Two dollars. Five. It wasn't as if she had to depend on one or two of them. There were always several friends outside, waiting and willing, when she took one of them into the shed before she caught the bus home. She warned them that she would stop dealing with them if they talked, and for a while they believed her. She didn't hire them regularly at first, or all that often.

That was at first. Over a few months' time, things began to change. Maria's needs increased. The bargaining got to be more open and obstreperous. The news got out. Maria's powers were being chipped, then hammered, away.

Come on, Maria, give me a ten. Me, too. Maria, give me a ten, too. Come on, Maria, you know me.

Twenty, Maria. Give me twenty. Come on. Twenty bucks. You owe me, Maria. Come on, now. You don't want me to tell. Come on, Maria.

A twenty, a twenty, a twenty. Maria is forking over. She is going to the shed every night. And if that isn't bad enough for her, some boys start refusing. They want the money first. They take the money and then they say no. They say she never paid them. She paid them, she paid them in front of witnesses, and all the witnesses deny that she did. They shake their heads, they taunt her. *No. You never paid him. I never saw you. You pay me now and I'll go. I promise I will. I'll go. You pay me twenty, Maria.*

And the older boys, who have learned from their younger brothers what is going on, are coming up to her at the cash register and saying, "How about me, Maria? You know me, too. Come on, Maria, how about a twenty?" Those boys never go to the shed with her, never. Did she think they would? They never even promise, they just ask her for money. *You know me a long time, Maria.* They threaten, they wheedle. *Aren't I your friend, too, Maria?*

Nobody was Maria's friend.

Maria's matronly, watchful calm was gone—she looked wild and sullen and mean. She gave them looks full of hate, but she continued giving them money. She kept handing over the bills. Not even trying to bargain, or to argue or refuse, anymore. In a rage she did it—a silent rage. The more they taunted her, the more readily the twenty-dollar bills flew out of the till. Very little, perhaps nothing, was done to earn them now.

They're stoned all the time, Neil and his friends. All the time, now that they have this money. They see sweet streams of atoms flowing in the Formica tabletops. Their colored souls are shooting out under their fingernails. Maria has gone crazy, the store is bleeding money. How can this go on? How is it going to end? Maria must be into the strongbox now; the till at the end of the day wouldn't have enough for her. And all the time her mother keeps on baking buns and making pierogi, and the father keeps sweeping the sidewalk and greeting the customers. Nobody has told them. They go on just the same.

They had to find out on their own. They found a bill that Maria hadn't paid—something like that, somebody coming in with an unpaid bill—and they went to get the money to pay it, and they found that there was no money. The money wasn't where they kept it, in the safe or strongbox or wherever, and it wasn't anywhere else—the money was gone. That was how they found out.

Maria had succeeded in giving away everything. All they had saved, all their slowly accumulated profits, all the money on which they operated their business. Truly, everything. They could not pay the rent now, they could not pay the electricity bill or their suppliers. They could not keep on running the Confectionery. At least they believed they couldn't. Maybe they simply had not the heart to go on.

The store was locked. A sign went up on the door: "CLOSED UNTIL FURTHER NOTICE." Nearly a year went by before the place was reopened. It had been turned into a laundromat.

People said it was Maria's mother, that big, meek, bentover woman, who insisted on bringing charges against her daughter. She was scared of the English language and the cash register, but she brought Maria into court. Of course, Maria could only be charged as a juvenile, and she could only be sent to a place for young offenders, and nothing could be done about the boys at all. They all lied anyway—they said it wasn't them. Maria's parents must have found jobs, they must have gone on living in Victoria, because Lisa did. She still swam at the Y, and in a few years she was working at Eaton's, in Cosmetics. She was very glamorous and haughty by that time.

Neil always has vodka and orange juice for them to drink. That's Brenda's choice. She read somewhere that orange juice replenishes the vitamin C that the liquor leeches away, and she hopes the vodka really can't be detected on your breath. Neil tidies up the trailer, too—or so she thinks, because of the paper bag full of beer cans leaning against the cupboard, a pile of newspapers pushed together, not really folded, a pair of socks kicked into a corner. Maybe his housemate does it. A man called Gary, whom Brenda has never met or seen a picture of, and wouldn't know if they met on the street. Would he know her? He knows she comes here, he knows when; does he even know her name? Does he recognize her perfume, the smell of her sex, when he comes home in the evening? She likes the trailer, the way nothing in it has been made to look balanced or permanent. Things set down just wherever they will be convenient. No curtains or placemats, not even a pair of salt and pepper shakers—just the salt box and pepper tin, the way they come from the store. She loves the sight of Neil's bed—badly made, with a rough plaid blanket and a flat pillow, not a marriage bed or a bed of illness, comfort, complication. The bed of his lust and sleep, equally strenuous and oblivious. She loves the life of his body, so sure of its rights. She wants commands from him, never requests. She wants to be his territory.

It's only in the bathroom that the dirt bothers her a bit, like anybody else's dirt, and she wishes they'd done a better job of cleaning the toilet and the washbasin.

They sit at the table to drink, looking out through the trailer window at the steely, glittering, choppy water of the lake. Here the trees, exposed to lake winds, are almost bare. Birch bones and poplars stiff and bright as straw frame the water. There may be snow in another month. Certainly in two months. The seaway will close, the lake boats will be tied up for the winter, there'll be a wild landscape of ice thrown up between the shore and the open water. Neil says he doesn't know what he'll do, once the work on the beach is over. Maybe stay on, try to get another job. Maybe go on unemployment insurance for a while, get a snowmobile, enjoy the winter. Or he could go and look for work somewhere else, visit friends. He has friends all over the continent of North America and out of it. He has friends in Peru.

"So what happened?" Brenda says. "Don't you have any idea what happened to Maria?"

Neil says no, he has no idea.

The story won't leave Brenda alone; it stays with her like a coating on the tongue, a taste in the mouth.

"Well, maybe she got married," she says. "After she got out. Lots of people get married who are no beauties. That's for sure. She might've lost weight and be looking good even."

"Sure," says Neil. "Maybe have guys paying her, instead of the other way round."

"Or she might still be just sitting in one of those places. One of those places where they put people."

Now she feels a pain between her legs. Not unusual after one of these sessions. If she were to stand up at this moment, she'd feel a throb there, she'd feel the blood flowing back down through all the little veins and arteries that have been squashed and bruised, she'd feel herself throbbing like a big swollen blister.

She takes a long drink and says, "So how much money did you get out of her?"

"I never got anything," Neil says. "I just knew these other guys who did. It was my brother Jonathan made the money off her. I wonder what he'd say if I reminded him now."

"Older guys, too—you said older guys, too. Don't tell me you just sat back and watched and never got your share."

"That's what I *am* telling you. I never got anything."

Brenda clicks her tongue, tut-tut, and empties her glass and moves it around on the table, looking skeptically at the wet circles.

"Want another?" Neil says. He takes the glass out of her hand.

"I've got to go," she says. "Soon." You can make love in a hurry if you have to, but you need time for a fight. Is that what they're starting on? A fight?

She feels edgy but happy. Her happiness is tight and private, not the sort that flows out from you and fuzzes everything up and makes you good-naturedly careless about what you say. The very opposite. She feels light and sharp and unconnected. When Neil brings her back a full glass, she takes a drink from it at once, to safeguard this feeling.

"You've got the same name as my husband," she says. "It's funny I never thought of that before."

She has thought of it before. She just hasn't mentioned it, knowing it's not something Neil would like to hear.

"Cornelius isn't the same as Neil," he says.

"It's Dutch. Some Dutch people shorten it to Neil."

"Yeah, but I'm not Dutch, and I wasn't named Cornelius, just Neil."

"Still, if his had been shortened you'd be named the same."

"His isn't shortened."

"I never said it was. I said if it had been."

"So why say that if it isn't?"

He must feel the same thing she does—the slow but irresistible rise of a new excitement, the need to say, and hear, dire things. What a sharp, releasing pleasure there is in the first blow, and what a dazzling temptation ahead— destruction. You don't stop to think why you want that destruction. You just do.

"Why do we have to drink every time?" Neil says abruptly. "Do we want to turn ourselves into alcoholics or something?"

Brenda takes a quick sip and pushes her glass away. "Who has to drink?" she says.

She thinks he means they should drink coffee, or Cokes. But he gets up and goes to the dresser where he keeps his clothes, opens a drawer, and says, "Come over here."

"I don't want to look at any of that stuff," she says.

"You don't even know what it is."

"Sure I do."

Of course she doesn't—not specifically.

"You think it's going to bite you?"

Brenda drinks again and keeps looking out the window. The sun is getting down in the sky already, pushing the bright light across the table to warm her hands.

"You don't approve," Neil says.

"I don't approve or disapprove," she says, aware of having lost some control, of not being as happy as she was. "I don't care what you do. That's you."

"I don't approve or disapprove," says Neil, in a mincing voice. "Don't care what you do."

That's the signal, which one or the other had to give. A flash of hate, pure meanness, like the glint of a blade. The signal that the fight can come out into the open. Brenda takes a deep drink, as if she very much deserved it. She feels a desolate satisfaction. She stands up and says, "Time for me to go."

"What if I'm not ready to go yet?" Neil says.

"I said me, not you."

"Oh. You got a car outside?"

"I can walk."

"That's five miles back to where the van is."

"People have walked five miles."

"In shoes like that?" says Neil. They both look at her yellow shoes, which match the appliquéd-satin birds on her turquoise sweater. Both things bought and worn for him!

"You didn't wear those shoes for walking," he says. "You wore them so every step you took would show off your fat arse."

She walks along the lakeshore road, in the gravel, which bruises her feet through the shoes and makes her pay attention to each step, lest she should twist an ankle. The afternoon is now too cold for just a sweater. The wind off the lake blows at her sideways, and every time a vehicle passes, particularly a truck, an eddy of stiff wind whirls around her and grit blows into her face. Some of the trucks slow down, of course, and some cars do, too, and men yell at her out of the windows. One car skids onto the gravel and stops ahead of her. She stands still, she cannot think what else to do, and after a moment he churns back onto the pavement and she starts walking again.

That's all right, she's not in any real danger. She doesn't even worry about being seen by someone she knows. She feels too free to care. She thinks about the first time Neil came to the Furniture Barn, how he put his arm around Samson's neck and said, "Not much of a watchdog you got here, Ma'am." She thought the "Ma'am" was impudent, phony, out of some old Elvis Presley movie. And what he said next was worse. She looked at Samson, and she said, "He's better at night." And Neil said, "So am I." Impudent, swaggering, conceited, she thought. And he's not young enough to get away with it. Her opinion didn't even change so much the second time. What happened was that all that became just something to get past. It was something she could let him know he didn't have to do. It was her job to take his gifts seriously, so that he could be serious, too, and easy and grateful. How was she sure so soon that what she didn't like about him wasn't real?

When she's in the second mile, or maybe just the second half of the first mile, the Mercury catches up to her. It pulls onto the gravel across the road. She goes over and gets in. She doesn't see why not. It doesn't mean that she is going to talk to him, or be with him any longer than the few minutes it will take to drive to the swamp road and the van. His presence doesn't need to weigh on her any more than the grit blowing beside the road.

She winds the window all the way down so that there will be a rush of chilly wind across anything he may have to say.

"I want to beg your pardon for the personal remarks," he says.

"Why?" she says. "It's true. It is fat."

"No."

"It is," she says, in a tone of bored finality that is quite sincere. It shuts him up for a few miles, until they've turned down the swamp road and are driving in under the trees.

"If you thought there was a needle there in the drawer, there wasn't."

"It isn't any of my business what there was," she says.

"All that was in there was some Percs and Quaaludes and a little hash."

She remembers a fight she had with Cornelius, one that almost broke their engagement. It wasn't the time he slapped her for smoking marijuana. They made that up quickly. It wasn't about anything to do with their own lives. They were talking about a man Cornelius worked with at the mine, and his wife, and their retarded child. This child was just a vegetable, Cornelius said; all it did was gibber away in a sort of pen in a corner of the living room and mess its pants. It was about six or seven years old, and that was all it would ever do. Cornelius said he believed that if anybody had a child like that they had a right to get rid of it. He said that was what he would do. No question about it. There were a lot of ways you could do it and never get caught, and he bet that was what a lot of people did. He and Brenda had a terrible fight about this. But all the time they were arguing and fighting Brenda suspected that this was not something Cornelius would really do. It was something he had to say he would do. To her. To her, he had to insist that he would do it. And this actually made her angrier at him than she would have been if she believed he was entirely and brutally sincere. He wanted her to argue with him about this. He wanted her protest, her horror, and why was that? Men wanted you to make a fuss, about disposing of vegetable babies or taking drugs or driving a car like a bat out of hell, and why was that? So they could have your marshmallow sissy goodness to preen against, with their hard showoff badness? So that they finally could give in to you, growling, and not have to be so bad and reckless anymore? Whatever it was, you got sick of it.

In the mine accident, Cornelius could have been crushed to death. He was working the night shift when it happened. In the great walls of rock salt an undercut is made, then there are holes drilled for explosives, and the charges are fitted in; an explosion goes off every night at five minutes to midnight. The huge slice of salt slides loose, to be started on its journey to the surface. Cornelius was lifted up in a cage on the end of the arm of the scaler. He was to break off the loose material on the roof and fix in the bolts that held it for the explosion. Something went wrong with the hydraulic controls he was operating—he stalled, tried for a little power and got a surge that lifted him, so that he saw the rock ceiling closing down on him like a lid. He ducked, the cage halted, a rocky outcrop struck him in the back.

He had worked in the mine for seven years before that and hardly ever spoke to Brenda about what it was like. Now he tells her. It's a world of its own, he says—caverns and pillars, miles out under the lake. If you get in a passage where there are no machines to light the gray walls, the salt-dusty air, and you turn your headlamp off, you can find out what real darkness is like, the darkness people on the surface of the earth never get to see. The machines stay down there forever. Some are assembled down there, taken down in parts; all are repaired there; and finally they're ransacked for usable parts, then piled into a dead-end passage that is sealed up—a tomb for these underground machines. They make a ferocious noise all the time they're working; the noise of the machines and the ventilating fans cuts out any human voice. And now there's a new machine that can do what Cornelius went up in the cage to do. It can do it by itself, without a man.

Brenda doesn't know if he misses being down there. He says he doesn't. He says he just can't look at the surface of the water without seeing all that underneath, which nobody who hasn't seen it could imagine.

Neil and Brenda drive along under the trees, where suddenly you could hardly feel the wind at all.

"Also, I did take some money," Neil says. "I got forty dollars, which, compared to what some guys got, was just nothing. I swear that's all, forty dollars. I never got any more."

She doesn't say anything.

"I wasn't looking to confess it," he says. "I just wanted to talk about it. Then what pisses me off is I lied anyway."

Now that she can hear his voice better, she notices that it's nearly as flat and tired as her own. She sees his hands on the wheel and thinks what a hard time she would have describing what he looks like. At a distance—in the car, waiting for her—he's always been a bright blur, his presence a relief and a promise. Close up, he's been certain separate areas—silky or toughened skin, wiry hair or shaved prickles, smells that are unique or shared with other men. But it's chiefly an energy, a quality of his self that she can see in his blunt, short fingers or the tanned curve of his forehead. And even to call it energy is not exact—it's more like the sap of him, rising from the roots, clear and on the move, filling him to bursting. That's what she has set herself to follow—the sap, the current, under the skin, as if that were the one true thing.

If she turned sideways now, she would see him for what he is—that tanned curved forehead, the receding fringe of curly brown hair, heavy eyebrows with a few gray hairs in them, deep-set light-colored eyes, and a mouth that enjoys itself, rather sulky and proud. A boyish man beginning to age—though he still feels light and wild on top of her, after Cornelius's bulk settling down possessively, like a ton of blankets. A responsibility, Brenda feels then. Is she going to feel the same about this one?

Neil turns the car around, he points it ready to drive back, and it's time for her to get out and go across to the van. He takes his hands off the wheel with the engine running, flexes his fingers, then grabs the wheel hard again—hard enough, you'd think, to squeeze it to pulp. "Christ, don't get out yet!" he says. "Don't get out of the car!"

She hasn't even put a hand on the door, she hasn't made a move to leave. Doesn't he know what's happening? Maybe you need the experience of a lot of married fights to know it. To know that what you think—and, for a while, hope—is the absolute end for you can turn out to be only the start of a new stage, a continuation. That's what's happening, that's what has happened. He has lost some of his sheen for her; he may not get it back. Probably the same goes for her, with him. She feels his heaviness and anger and surprise. She feels that also in herself. She thinks that up till now was easy.

Wolinsky's Resort

Edward L. Schwarzschild

Max Wolinsky sits in his Le Sabre, getting ready to sell space. Recently forty-one, he's back in Philadelphia, passing through to give a little help to his strapped and aging father, Caleb. Max looks again at the information he has jotted on a three-by-five card. There's more than enough to work with. *Gail and David Gould. In their seventies. Talked to agents about selling their house. Already visited Breyer's Run and Chestnut Circle. Love the New Jersey shore and used to summer at the Ventnor Motel.* To them, he'll be Larry Zevin, nephew of a dead, distant friend. He plugs his razor into the cigarette lighter and runs the buzzing blades over his face. Then he slaps on his after-shave. Pushing aside his latest cell phone, he fingers through a folder of well-made documents: map, floor plans, artist's rendering, miniature blueprint, and glossy pamphlets. Large teal letters headline each piece of paper: *Oceanview Gardens—Retirement Resort.*

I carry with me the news they desire, Max tells himself as he walks up the winding flagstone path. *I hold the key to their future.* It's a big front yard and there's more land around back, full of fruit trees, flowers, and green grass. A Honda and a Volvo are parked in the driveway. Max rings the bell. When the door opens, he starts pitching to the elderly couple before him. The only word he wants to hear from them is *Yes.* Get them in the habit.

"My name is Larry Zevin," Max says. "I'm Stuart Fox's nephew. Are you Mr. and Mrs. Gould?"

"Yes," says Gail.

"I understand that you wish someday to move near Atlantic City. You want a retirement community by the ocean. On the Boardwalk. Far from the casinos. Affordable. Also at least partially Jewish. Am I right?"

"Yes," says David.

"I have a few things I'd like to show you," Max says. "May I come in?"

"Yes," they both answer. David opens the front door all the way.

Max steps in, moving at their pace. It's ten-thirty in the morning and Gail looks like she plans to work in her garden; she wears faded blue jeans and a grey sweatshirt that matches the wiry hair she has done up in a red bandana. David, in his white oxford shirt, mustard cardigan, and tan slacks, could be on his way to meet a few friends at the golf course. Max glances around at their nice things and decides where he'd like to sit: on the couch, in front of the large window. Get them on either side of him. Let the sun shine on his back and give him an aura of gold. From where he stands by the piano, Max can see the stately dining room, a crystal chandelier dangling down. The kitchen is back and away to the left. At the far end of the dining room, there's a sliding glass door that opens onto a screened-in porch. "This is a wonderful house," he says. "A real estate agent's dream. Probably sell in a flash."

"We were very sorry to hear about Stuart's passing," David says.

"It took us all by surprise, Mr. Goul—"

"David, please."

"Well, David, it's like this. Age did not come gradually to Uncle Stuart. He woke up one morning and it knocked him down and it kept on knocking."

"I still have some coffee in the pot," Gail says. "Can I get you a cup?"

"No coffee for me, thanks, Mrs. Gould. But I'd take a glass of water, if it's not too much trouble."

"No trouble," she says. "And it's Gail."

Following the Goulds to the kitchen, Max notices the paintings on the walls and the antiques that decorate the dining room—candlesticks, vases, salt and pepper mills, a tea set on a wooden cart. He also notices how closely David watches his wife, as if she were in constant danger of falling.

"Yes," Max says, "Uncle Stuart was thrilled with how things were going and he tried to share that. He was the first salesman in the family. Loved the business and taught me quite a bit over the years."

"What exactly happened to him?" David asks.

"There was one stroke and then there was another. Near the end, he struggled to speak." Max pauses. He rubs one of his eyes with his palm. Exhales. Then he goes on. "The words he said were not the sort you and I could understand. He was deep in conversation with himself. But I didn't come here to depress you. I'm just glad to see the two of you doing so well. I'll tell you this, though. The whole situation led me into this new project. It suddenly made sense to me."

"Let's sit down," David says. "Then you'll show us what you've got."

Gail hands out the drinks and they walk back into the living room. Max takes his place on the couch. He sets the glass on the coffee table, pulls out his folder, and puts the case down at his feet. He rests the folder unopened on his lap.

"Tell me this doesn't happen to you," Max says. "People call you on the phone. They don't even know who you are. You say 'Hello?' three times before they realize there's a voice they can talk to. They want to tell you about a deal, an opportunity. It takes five minutes just to get them to stop talking. It takes another five minutes to end the conversation politely. I get those calls myself. 'I'm busy,' I tell them. They offer to call back at a more convenient hour. 'No, no,' I say. 'There will be no convenient hour.' So, up front, here's what I'm emphasizing: you want me to be quiet, you don't want me to go further, just say so. I'll stop right away and I'll disappear. Your time is too precious."

"The phone companies are the worst," David says. "I like telling them I don't have a phone while I'm talking to them, just to hear what they say."

"I bet they keep right on going, don't they? Not me. I'll listen. That's what I want you to know."

As if on cue, Max's cell phone rings, a muffled beeping from his case. "I should answer it," he says. "Do you mind?"

"Not at all," Gail says. "You can go out onto the porch."

Carrying his case and his folder with him, Max steps through the house.

Max doesn't close the glass door behind him, but he speaks quietly. He walks around the porch as he talks, admiring the view and the furnishings. The floor is made of red cedar, like a giant picnic table.

"How's that for timing?" asks his father.

"Perfect, Dad."

"You getting them?"

"I'm getting them," Max answers.

"Attaboy. Now shout what you need to shout."

In a louder voice, close to the door, Max says, "We don't have many left. Tell them I'll do what I can. I'll look on the list." Then he hangs up and hurries to rejoin the Goulds.

"Sorry about that," he says, sitting between them. "Just the office, checking in. Reminding me that things are busy in my absence. So, let me show you what I've got in this folder. You know the Jersey shore pretty well, right?"

"We used to stay in Ventnor for weeks at a time," David says.

"And we ride a bus to the casinos every now and then," adds Gail.

"Ventnor is where we intend to be. We're closing on the land. We've got the designs together. The zoning hearings are almost finished. And, with what the office just told me, we've already reached eighty-seven percent occupancy. But there's still space available. This is a two-bedroom, third-floor, ocean view unit I thought might interest you. Here's what the building itself will look like."

Max drinks his water and watches the Goulds study the documents. They hunch over to get a good look. They quietly hand the papers back and forth to each other. Max waits for questions, admiring the floor plan as it passes before him. It has small pieces of cutout furniture placed in each room, like a child's pop-up book. Each little chair and table is taped to the page so clients can try their own arrangements. The piece that represents the living room's sofa bed actually unfolds, just to show that there will still be plenty of space when guests stay overnight.

David sits up, leans back into the couch, rests his hands near his cardigan's middle button, and slowly rubs one thumb around the other. "When will you start building?" he asks.

"That's an excellent question," Max says. "We want to break ground this summer. Finish construction by the end of the year. Then be ready to open the doors at the start of spring. A little less than twelve months from now. That's our aggressive timeline."

Max is well prepared for the questions that follow, about facilities, meal plans, and health care. He answers in detail, quoting extremely competitive numbers.

"It seems too good to be true," Gail says.

"Tell me about the down payment," David says.

Max drinks a little more water. He does not speak until he has set the glass back gently on the table. "Look," he says. "People have worries. Uncle

Stuart, for instance, he used to worry about what sort of neighbors he'd have. My father, he didn't want to be trapped in the middle of nowhere. So, instead of rushing to down payments, I'd like you to do this. I'd like you to take some time and make a list of concerns. Write down what you want and what you don't want. Imagine the place of your dreams. Everything that comes to mind. Then we can get together again and see if our retirement resort is the right place for you. How does that sound?"

"Sounds sensible," David says.

"I'll leave you these copies of our materials and one of my cards," Max says. "Just give me a call when you've finished your list and we'll set up an appointment. Maybe I'll be able to bring the director with me. In the meantime, if anything new develops on my end, I'll let you know."

"Thanks for coming by," Gail says.

Max closes his case and stands up. "My pleasure," he says.

After parking near 5th and Cheltenham Avenue, Max walks into the basement apartment where his father and his real uncle, Abraham, have lived together ever since the strokes. The smell in that small space carries more than mere below-ground dampness. Caleb and Abe sit in easy chairs and they look as if they are in the process of becoming moss. They can see fragments of legs move past their sidewalk-level window. Judge the weather by the footwear.

Max enters the living room and Abe says, "Maxie!"

Max turns to his father. "I'm going to need the voice, Dad. A few days and it will be time to make the call."

"The voice is always ready. How we doing?"

"Fine. They wanted to talk about down payments. They're making their list. How are you and Arthur Miller Wolinsky?"

"We should take him out for his stroll."

"Month ago," Max says, "I was doing good business in Florida. People like the Goulds everywhere. Ready and willing."

"I was sorry to bother you," Caleb says. "But with Abe here—"

"No, Dad. I should come home more often. I should send more money than I do."

"One of us here is enough, Max. I like knowing you're out in the world, doing business."

"Plenty of people like Abe out there, too. One look in their eyes is enough to know that they're losing it, moving on to some place easier. Some place all their own."

"My territory was not always so small," Abe says.

Caleb kneels on the carpet like a shoe salesman. He helps his brother change from the slippers to sneakers. "Where is there money to be made?" he asks, loosening the laces.

"Try Singapore," says Abe. "What I hear, there's money to be made all over Asia. Try Seoul. Try Tokyo."

"How about Alaska?" asks Max.

"Alaska never fails," Abe answers. "I knew people there. I kept meaning to go."

Caleb guides Abe out of the chair. Max grabs an arm to ease him up. "We're walking," Caleb says. "Here we go."

"Always be closing," Abe says, as they step out the front door.

In the evenings, after Caleb and Abe are asleep, Max goes out to walk alone. He takes New Second Avenue into the suburbs. There are few street-lights, as if the residents don't fear the darkness. He strolls by quiet parks and he's not certain why the word that passes through his mind is *pure*. It's more than the tennis courts, the fields, the ponds, and the landscaped lawns. *I fit here,* Max thinks. *Here in Melrose Park, in Jenkintown, I'm a well-dressed man, a home-owner, a friend of the family.* He walks for hours.

One night, a police car pulls up by his side. Before any questions can be asked of him, Max speaks: "Good evening, officer. Have you seen a dog run-ning around nearby? A Siberian husky. Her name is Tanya."

"I'll keep an eye out," the officer responds before driving off.

When the houses give way to mini-malls, Max enjoys stopping into open businesses—a bar, a pool hall, a laundromat. He gets a drink, shoots a rack, watches a bundle of whites spin in a dryer. He sits silently and no one minds.

On Monday, he finds himself in Rockledge, walking toward the Ennis Dell Bowling Lanes. The building resembles an airplane hangar, placed at the end of a parking lot, next to a supermarket. It's an old-style alley, where you keep score yourself with paper and pencil. There are no arcade games, no loud music, no crazy late-night red pins. But there are locker rooms for men and women. A pro shop. Fifty-four lanes. Machines that look like ovens from the sixties will wash your ball for a quarter. There's also a small bar at the main counter, where you can buy beer, hot dogs, and potato chips. The hot dogs sizzle as they rotate on metal rollers. They smell fine. Max sits on a stool and decides to start with a beer.

The bartender seems to be the only one working the night shift. He's a round young man, with a body like three stacked bowling balls. His shirt has the name Shelly sewn into it in red. "You need shoes?" he asks Max.

"Just beer for now. Might roll a game later."

"Might be room for you," Shelly says, puffing on a cigarette and looking out over the many darkened lanes.

Max smiles and sips the beer set before him. He watches a couple of teenagers who are not taking their games seriously, just hanging out together. Several lanes down, four large-bellied guys get a little loft on each shot. Two men Max's age have leather wraps for their wrists, one towel to dry their hands, another towel to wipe the oil from the ball. They're on separate lanes, prac-ticing. They follow through and strike often. But Max looks longest at two women he sees as mother and daughter. He's spotted them here on other evenings and he's made eye contact with the daughter.

Shelly steps away from the desk to check on a pin-setting machine and Max wonders how much he could take. Only in the suburbs. Some have their alarm systems or their dogs, but most leave themselves open without thinking.

Eventually, the daughter comes over to buy a beer. Waiting for Shelly to get back behind the counter, she lights a cigarette. Max likes the black hair that hangs halfway down her neck. She is trim. She is a few years younger. "Couldn't help noticing," Max says. "You throw a mean hook."

"Thanks."

"But it looks like your mother's the real bowler in the family."

"How'd you know she was my mother?"

"It's what I saw. Used to go to a place like this with my father. My name's Max."

"Estelle," she says.

They shake hands. She has a strong grip. "Why isn't your father here?" Estelle asks.

"He's too far away. You mind if I tell you something corny?"

"Tell me."

"I hear him bowling when it thunders," Max says. He looks down at his hands and then he looks into her eyes. "Let me get you that beer," he says.

"You waiting for someone?"

"I'm drinking a beer."

"You want to roll a game or two with me and my mother? It would be good for us to slow down a little."

"I wouldn't want to impose."

"No one's asking you to impose. Bowl with us if you want to bowl. You can bring your beer. To even things up, I'll buy your next round."

"Let the buyer beware," Max says, getting up off his stool.

"What?"

"I'll just get some shoes and come over."

It takes Max a few frames to warm up, but it's clear to him from the start that he'll never catch Estelle's mother, Janet. Estelle herself is a different story.

Janet reminds him a bit of Gail Gould, silver-haired and hard working. She has her own tan shoes, a monogrammed ten-pound ball, robin's-egg blue, and a compact three-step approach. No wasted motion. No immediate power, either. She can't bend herself down low, so the ball drops from her hand at the line, plunking hard onto the lane, almost into the right gutter. But she's been at it for years and she has the perfect follow-through. Even as the ball bangs against the shiny wood, her arm rises straight up and extends forward, out toward the head pin, as if she's somehow going to grab that pin with her aged hand. Her thumb leads the way. A follow-through like that guides the ball, and it slowly rolls ahead. About midway up the alley, it starts to break. Obeying Janet's thumb, her arm, and her whole body, the ball hooks left, directly into the pocket.

The loudest part of the shot is the initial drop. When the ball finally rolls into the white pins, it barely makes a sound. If you closed your eyes for a moment and then opened them again, you'd wonder how all the pins had been knocked over. After Janet strikes or spares, she claps her hands together, like a child ready to play paddy-cake. She gives Estelle a soft high-five.

Max finds his mark in the fourth frame. Strikes then and again in the fifth. "You look all right," Janet says to him.

"I wouldn't say that," Max says.

"You don't have to," says Estelle.

At the end of the first game, Max misses a spare on purpose. Janet finishes with 184, Estelle with 161, Max with 153. "Loser buys," he says.

"No," says Estelle. "It's my turn."

Max smiles at her. "Don't worry," he says. "You'll lose the next game."

"We'll see. I'm just getting warmed up."

Janet sits in the scorer's chair and laughs. "Sounds like we've got a little competition now," she says.

Max walks back to the counter. He waits for Shelly to put the hot dogs and the beer onto a tray. "The old woman can bowl," Max says.

"You should have seen her ten years ago," Shelly says. "Back before she broke her hip."

When Shelly hands him the tray, Max takes it carefully and says, "Let me ask you this. Any chance that Estelle's boyfriend or husband is going to come through the front door with a tire iron?"

Shelly says nothing.

"I just wouldn't want any kind of ruckus to break out here."

Shelly looks Max in the eyes. "She got divorced a few years ago," he says. "As far as I know, she only bowls with her mother."

"Thanks," Max says.

The second game takes longer. In between shots, they chat together around the scorer's table, until someone says, "I guess it's my turn."

In the sixth frame, when Janet is at the line, Estelle says to Max, "Tell me about your father."

"You're just trying to distract me. And I am already distracted."

"Tell me."

"He threw a back-up ball," Max says. "Tough on the wrist. He was away too often, driving all over for his job."

"What kind of work?"

"He sold textiles from mills to clothing manufacturers. Slammed into an embankment one night outside of New York City. My father was a salesman killed on the road."

Estelle lights a cigarette. After yet another strike, Janet comes back to the table, clapping. "I guess it's my turn," Max says. As he steps past Estelle, he feels her hand brush his shoulder.

Once again, Janet is far ahead. Once again, Max is neck-and-neck with Estelle. During the eighth frame, the two of them stand side-by-side, and he asks her, "Where's your husband?"

"Now *that's* distracting."

"It's not like I'm telling you how badly you need to strike in the ninth," Max says. "But you don't have to tell me if you don't want to. I can understand your need to concentrate." He reaches up to tuck a strand of her hair behind her ear. He lets his hand briefly touch the side of her face.

Estelle puts her hair back where it was. There's a wince in her smile when she says, "Ask my mother or ask me. We'll tell you about husbands who ran off."

"Ran off or kicked out?"

"A little of both," Estelle says.

Janet picks up her spare.

"Watch me," Max says. "Here comes a big strike."

Janet chuckles. "No taunting," she says.

Janet 191. Estelle 165. Max 172.

"That's enough for me," Janet says. "But it looks like we're going to need a rematch sometime soon."

"Well," Estelle says.

"That could be arranged," says Max.

Max walks them to their car and exchanges phone numbers with Estelle. They make tentative plans for Wednesday night. "I'll drive," he says. "Until then, I'll spend all my time practicing." He watches them laugh. He waves as they drive away.

Max opens the door to the dark basement apartment. He hears the hum of the refrigerator and, above that, the breathing of Caleb and Abe. He quietly steps into the bathroom. Then he gets a sheet from the linen closet to spread over the couch. He used to come home more often. When his mother was alive. When they had a house. When his uncle took trains up and down the east coast. He strips to his underwear and tells himself he is not thinking about the past. He wishes the couch were more comfortable.

Two nights later, after a few more games, Max drives Janet and Estelle back to their apartments. He stops at Janet's first and waits in the car while Estelle walks her inside. Then he drives Estelle the three blocks to her place. When he stops the car, she says, "I think I still owe you a beer."

"What if I've had enough beer?"

"You can come in anyhow," she says, and he turns off the engine.

They stand in the kitchen. Estelle opens a bottle of beer and hands it to him. He doesn't take a drink. She opens one for herself. Then she puts it down, wraps her arms around him, and they kiss. There is some awkwardness with Max's bottle, but he manages to set it on the counter. He begins to remember his last kiss. A thousand miles away. Did they ever do anything in a kitchen? Key Largo. Coral Gables. Palm Beach. But he stops those thoughts. In his wallet, on an old business card, he has written something like a mantra: "I do those things which seem correct to me *moment-by-moment*. I trust myself. If security concerns me, I do that which *today* I think will make me secure. The *true* reserve I have is the strength *to act always without fear.* According to the dictates of my mind."

So Max holds Estelle close and wonders where her bedroom is.

Stretched out on top of the comforter, Max watches Estelle light a cigarette. She's flat on her back and she puts the glass ashtray on her stomach. "Do you have to smoke those?" Max asks.

"It's what comes after," she says. "Can't have the before without the after."

"In that case—"

"That's what I thought. You want one?"

"No, thanks. But I'm hoping you'll need another in a little while."

"I'm glad you're looking ahead," she says.

"Are you?" Max asks. "What do you see in your future?"

"I think about a lot of things," she says. "I think about nursing school. My mother would love that. But the truth is I don't like sick people. You're not sick, are you?"

"Do I look sick?" Max asks, standing up. "Don't feel sick." He walks naked to the bathroom and leaves the door open so he can hear her. But she waits for him to come back. When he does, she returns the ashtray to her night table and rolls up against him, resting her head on his chest. He runs a hand through her hair.

"I figure there are nurses who don't have to deal with sick people," Estelle says. "Some of them work for insurance companies, but they're on the phone all the time, and I wouldn't like that either. Then there are the nurses who put people to sleep. The anesthetists. They don't have to listen to much complaining. That's a scary job, though. What if someone doesn't wake up?"

"If you were a nurse, you could take care of your mother."

"I know," Estelle says. "I like that part of it. But what about you? What do you see ahead?"

"I've been selling," Max says. "Now I'm done with selling and I'm not sure what's next. But I can tell you one thing I think about. You ever hear of James Lake Young?"

"No. Who's he?"

"For me, he's an example. Even his name. Lake Young. Like the fountain of youth."

"What did he do?"

"He was born in 1853 and he had an oysterman for a father. When he was three, his father left. So he was alone with his mother and they lived in what would become Atlantic City. When he was old enough to work, he did, and he took care of his mother until she passed away. Lake Young was a carpenter and he got a job patching up the Boardwalk and the new pavilions. Then one day, while he was pounding nails, he met a baker from Philadelphia. They talked and the subject turned to investments. Are you still awake?"

"I'm awake," she says. "I'm listening. But I'm also thinking about the not-so-distant future." She moves her hand over his chest, over his stomach, up and down the inside of his thigh. "Go on."

"To make a long story short," he says.

"Make it long," she says.

"They opened a roller-skating rink and the money poured in. Then a carousel. And in 1891, they bought a pier. The baker made enough money and went back to Philadelphia, but Lake Young was just getting started."

"Getting started," Estelle says, lifting her head from his chest and pushing his legs apart with her hands.

"And then he lived happily ever after."

"No, no," she says. "Tell me."

"Tell you," Max says. "I'm trying."

"I can stop," she says.

"Don't." He looks up at the ceiling. "1906. He opens Million Dollar Pier. Full of rides, shows, exhibits. Harry Houdini. Teddy Roosevelt. Miss America. The kind of place people dream of. And to top it all off. You listening?"

"Yes," she says, pausing for a moment.

He exhales and then he goes on. "To top it all off, he builds his home right on the pier—his own personal concrete Italian villa. Three stories, twelve rooms, a conservatory, a garden, electric lighting designed by Thomas Edison. Eventually, he owns ten miles of beachfront property, acres of land in Florida. He owns steam yachts, a fleet of sailboats, hotels, cottages. He hosts presidents and stars. The leaders of the world. And he always makes sure that everyone knows his address. Do you know what his address was?"

"No," Estelle says, pausing again. "What was his address?"

Max reaches down and brings her up to him. He kisses her forehead. "Number One, Atlantic Ocean," he says.

"That would be an excellent address," says Estelle.

Max rolls her onto her back. "I agree," he says.

Max leaves Estelle's a few hours before dawn. He doesn't wake her, but he writes her a note and puts it on his pillow: *Let's get together tonight. I'll pick you up at nine. Call if you can't make it. So don't call.*

Max doesn't expect anyone to be awake when he walks into the basement apartment. "Maxie!" he hears, and it startles him. Abe is sitting in his easy chair, wearing his terrycloth bathrobe and his slippers, eyes wide open.

"Shh," Max says. "Dad's sleeping."

"I want you to go through the ins and outs of this thing with me," Abe says. "I've got nobody to talk to."

"That's not true," Max answers, even though he knows what he says doesn't really matter. The lines will come out. Over and over. "You've got your brother," Max adds. "You've got me."

"It's a cowardly thing," Abe says.

"You'd like the woman I met," Max says. "You and Dad both."

Abe says nothing. He puts his index finger in his ear and wiggles it for almost a minute.

To get him to leave his ear alone, Max asks, "Where is there money to be made?"

"The jungle," Abe answers, setting his hands in his lap. "It's full of diamonds."

Max sits in his father's chair, next to Abe. They both lean back and look out into the darkness. "Aren't you glad your brother is with you?" Max asks. "Aren't you glad he doesn't put you somewhere and go away?"

"I'm busy. Don't bother me."

"I wonder if you would have stayed with him," Max says. "I wonder if I would. If I will."

"A man can't go out the way he came in," Abe says. "A man has got to add up to something."

"Let me walk you back to bed," Max says. He stands and puts his hand around Abe's gaunt right bicep. Abe rises slowly to his feet and they shuffle to his bedroom. Max watches his uncle curl up on the mattress, still in the bathrobe. After taking off the slippers and pulling up a blanket, Max stands by the door for a little while. Before Abe falls into sleep, or maybe it's after, Max hears him say, "He was a happy man with a batch of cement."

When the cell phone rings in the morning, Max is stepping out of the shower. He dashes from the bathroom, a towel wrapped around his waist. He's happy to hear David Gould's voice. "Larry? Gail and I have made our list. We'd like to schedule another appointment."

"It's good to hear from you, David," Max says. "I was just thinking about you."

"We've been looking over all the material you left us."

Max paces the living room as he talks. He lifts the sheet off the couch and drops it onto the carpet. "Great," he says. "Things have been moving along here, even in just the last few days. In fact, I may have more information for you tomorrow. I think we should try to meet early next week. But let me have until tomorrow before we set a date."

"So things are progressing?"

"Well," Max answers, "as my father likes to say, 'There's always some kind of good news coming up.'"

Caleb walks into the room in a blue sweat suit. Max puts a finger to his lips and his father gives him a thumbs-up. Then Max says, "Tell me about your list, David."

There is the sound of rustling paper. "Here," David says. "Gail wrote down a top three wish list. I'll read it to you: 'I want to walk on the beach in the mornings. I want to hear the sound of the waves as I fall asleep. I want to live someplace people will love to visit.'"

"That's wonderful, David. You two have been doing some work!"

"For me, just the Boardwalk's enough."

"Excellent," Max says. "I look forward to seeing the whole list in the next couple of days. Please give Gail my best, and we'll hopefully talk again tomorrow."

Max says goodbye and puts the phone down. He begins to get dressed. Caleb smiles at him. Max knows it's his smile, too. "I miss working," Caleb says.

"You're working all the time, Dad. All you do is work. And tomorrow you'll need to make the call."

"I'm going to start the coffee. You want some?"

Max sits on the couch, reaching for his socks and shoes. "I've got to get everything ready for tomorrow. But I have to tell you something."

"What?"

"Sit down for a second," Max says, and Caleb joins him on the couch. "I met a nice woman the other night—"

"That's great, son. Where did you meet her?"

"I met her out bowling. She's pretty. Dark-haired. And while we were talking, I told her you were dead."

"Dead?"

"In a car crash, I said. A salesman killed on the road."

"You said that?"

"I did," Max answers. He sees his father staring at him, but not into his eyes. The stare seems to be focused on the side of his face. Max scratches at his clean-shaven cheek.

"I don't need to know this," Caleb says. "You tell people what you need to tell them. That's your job. It's how you make your money. You must have needed to tell her."

"I didn't need to."

Caleb puts a hand on Max's knee. "Dead. 'My father is dead.' You said that?"

Max covers his father's hand with his own. He feels the bones of the knuckles sharp against his palm. "There was no reason," Max says. "But it's what I said. It's what I told her."

"We don't need to talk about this. This is not something we need to discuss further."

"I don't know why I said it. I think you'd like her."

"I look forward to meeting her. 'I'd like you to meet my dead father. This is the dead dad I told you so much about. Go ahead. Shake his hand.'"

"I didn't mean to."

"Don't worry about it."

Max hears Abe shuffling to the bathroom. He hears his uncle say, "Morning coffee like a meal." He hears his uncle piss.

Caleb takes his hand back and stands up. He uses Max's shoulder to push himself away from the couch. "Go on and get everything ready," he says.

"Let me hear the voice," Max says.

Caleb clears his throat. "I'm calling from Larry Zevin's office," he says. "I have an urgent message for Mr. and Mrs. Gould."

"That's it, Dad," Max says. "Perfect."

Max spends the day making arrangements. He talks with associates in Philadelphia and Atlantic City. He gives out the information he has and he finalizes the percentages.

That night, he picks up Estelle. She's not dressed for bowling. She's wearing black jeans and a cream silk blouse. They kiss at the doorway. She invites him in for a drink. He almost says *yes*, but he catches himself. Something doesn't seem correct. His heart races. "Let's go for a drive," he says.

"There's something I want to tell you."

"We'll talk in the car."

She locks up the house and follows him to the Le Sabre. As he drives, she keeps an open hand on his thigh. "You asked about my husband," she says. "I decided I should tell you."

"You don't have to," Max says. "I don't—"

"It's all right," she says. "We married too young. I was twenty-three, dreaming of being a bride. My mother was already divorced and he was jealous of the time I spent with her. Whenever she came over or whenever I went to visit her, he would go out. Sometimes he wouldn't come back for days. Then he didn't come back."

"I'm sorry," Max says. "I am."

"Were you ever married?"

"No."

They drive in silence through the suburbs. Estelle plays with the hair on the back of his neck. His scalp tingles.

At first he doesn't know where he's going. There isn't much traffic. The windows of the houses they pass flicker with the blue haze of computer and TV screens. *What is it with her?* Max wonders. *What do I fear at this moment?*

"In the end," she says, "I don't think he knew what he wanted. Even when it was just the two of us, he was restless. Are you restless?"

"Well," Max says, "I don't have any trouble sleeping."

"You were up pretty early this morning."

"Last night was really something, but a man's still got to make a living."

"A man and a woman both," she says. "You know, I didn't really believe that whole Boardwalk story. You want yachts? A concrete villa? You seem more practical than that. More level-headed."

Max shrugs. "It's a kind of success," he says.

"What kind of father was that guy? Did he have kids at all?"

"I'm not sure," he says, and suddenly he realizes where he's been driving. Can he trust her? It's the people you trust who most often betray you. People you don't trust you don't give a chance. He's not sure whether he's testing her or trying to scare her off, but he stops the car across the street from the Goulds' house and he points to it. He keeps the motor running. "Let me show you something," he says. "Do you see what that is?"

"It's a nice house."

"It *is* a nice house," he says. "And there are two nice old people who live there. Guess what's going to happen to them?"

"I don't know, Max," Estelle says. "Is this a joke or something?"

"No, no. I'll tell you what's going to happen. Tomorrow night, the owners of this house are going to get a call and, because of what they hear, they're going to rush to Atlantic City where they will pay twenty-five thousand dollars for a piece of paper. After they pay, the wife's purse will be stolen. So they will lose more money. Still, they will be convinced to spend the evening in a very posh hotel room. While they're away, a group of young men will go through that back porch. See it jutting out there on the right? They'll break into the house and they'll take everything they can. Including whichever car is left behind. This is something I have arranged. This is what I do."

Estelle sits quietly and holds her hands in her lap. She looks at the house and looks back at him. "I don't know you," she says. "But I know you better than that."

"It's a terrible thing to do," Max says. "It is. But no one will be hurt. And I'll use my share of the money to help take care of my sick uncle. I'll go south, free and clear, at least for a while. Then I'll be able to do things differently. Then I'll be able to make changes."

Max drives the car back the way they came. "I wanted to tell you the truth," he says. "I'm not running off from you. But you should be glad I'm going."

Estelle rolls down her window. She lights a cigarette. "What was the address of that house?" she asks.

"Why?"

"Seems far from Number One, Atlantic Ocean," she says.

Max smiles. "I guess it is," he says.

"People like you," says Estelle. She shakes her head. She watches the cars that pass. Then she says, "Maybe."

"Maybe what?"

"A lot of things. Maybe you are a sick person. Maybe you'll change. Maybe you already have."

Max drives.

"Maybe I should be glad," Estelle says.

Two days later, driving out of town, Max considers stopping. She might come along. There's enough room. Janet could join them eventually. He wouldn't separate a daughter from her mother.

But he goes right past Estelle's building. After a few miles, he pulls over by an alley. He gets out of the car and walks up to a big green dumpster. It's empty. That doesn't keep it from stinking. He throws the cell phone in as hard as he can. The plastic shatters with a bang that echoes up to him. Small black pieces scatter across the rusted metal bottom.

He climbs into the car and drives south, thinking, *I was hoping not to go this way.* Thinking, *Well, this is the way I'm going.*

From the back seat, Caleb calls out, "Florida, here we come!"

Abe is sitting beside his brother. "Always be closing," he says.

The Appaloosa House

Sharon Sheehe Stark

M y father's girl friend's name was Dolores and my mother went by Dusie because she was one. As in pip, as in pistol, as in humdinger. In those days men waited until after the holidays, so he left us on the second of January while the yabba-dabba-doo cartoons on TV tried, by their jangle of Saturday-morning sameness, to deny it, and just as it was starting to snow.

For three days and three nights Dusie observed an oddly formal time of mourning, in the manner of an Irish wake. She called in her friends; she wept and laughed. There was cake and wine, coffee in the fine Belleek cups that had come from Kilkenny. On the fourth morning she came downstairs and said, "Maybe if I'd kept the trash baskets emptied and got somebody out to paint the house last summer like your daddy asked . . ."

I stopped stirring my Sugar Crisp into whirlpools and rolled my eyes up at her.

"But, oh, no, I have to be Madam Nobody-tells-me-what-to-do, Mrs. Stand-on-my-rights, stubborn Irish smarty pants. Maybe if I'd got rid of all the empty olive jars in the fridge?"

We exchanged rueful looks that answered all her silly questions. We alternated weak, well-meaning chuckles and then she put the coffee on. "Did you know he took both bottles of Lavoris?" she said, like it was something she'd read in Ripley's. It was shortly after that that she kicked off the campaign.

Right after breakfast, in fact, she drove us down to Cherry Street; she parked in the loading zone in front of House of deLuca, which was the cruddy yellow brick building where my dad manufactured his line of budget neckties. I waited in the car while she tramped out her message in the strip of snow between the building and the sidewalk. She was wearing a big orange fur coat nearly the same color as her hair. I watched her face turn splotchy as a washerwoman's hands in the cold air.

She was that other kind of Irish, not dusky-haired and delicate but ruddy, rawboned, and sturdy as a pack mule. In funny little schoolgirl shuffle steps, her stadium boots tramped along in the snow. The letters were twenty feet high. "S," then "O." She came around the bottom belly of the "B" with high marching steps and finished with a flurry of furious double-barreled stomps. S. O. B.

"Ma-ah!" I squeaked when she got back in the car.

"What?" she said. "What's wrong with sob? You know, sob sob, sob. Boohoo, the rooster flew the coop."

Next day she called Western Union and made arrangements to have a singing telegram delivered to Dad at work. "What can you give me in, well, a crumb-bum medley?" she asked in the crisp tones of a suburban matron. As carefully as if she were choosing music for a wedding, she made her selections: "Your Cheatin' Heart," "How Come You Do Me Like You Do?" and "Toot-Toot Tootsie, Good-bye."

She called the printer and had him make up announcements. When they came, I helped her stamp and address them. Very plain, very tasteful, which was a distinct departure in a family partial to purple velvet and plaster lawn statuary. But Dusie had the unerring Irish instinct for effect. The message, too, was simple and painfully to the point: MR. AND MRS. NUNZIO DELUCA RESPECTFULLY SUBMIT THAT NUNZIE IS FAT, FORTY AND FOOLING AROUND. NO GIFTS. SEND MONEY. HE'LL NEED IT.

Once we'd get these projects cooking, it was just a matter of time till they boiled over. We lived to hear the affection lurking in the hells and damns of his false indignation. Dusie would take the call on one phone; I'd hang on the hall extension. Or sometimes he'd come by; it didn't take long after the announcements went out. I remember how he went right to the kitchen and, as we stood by gaping, proceeded to make himself a peanut butter banana. It was hard not to draw a mental circle around that scene, hard not to start feeling cozy. A trick, I decided, and for the first time I saw him not as a father but as a man— somebody's man—a man with a middle like a flour bag and stumpy legs. His over-large face and well-tended moustache, combined with two great symmetrical wings of thick salt-and-pepper hair, gave him the look of expecting to turn handsome at any moment. Unruly eyebrows and wet brown eyes; he was growing more like a Nunzie every day. I couldn't picture him with this Dolores person, who probably ate corn off the cob in rows and carried Pretty Feet around in her purse. I wished him a speedy old age so Dolores would see that the old rattletrap wasn't good enough for anyone but us.

"Listen, Kathleen (he never called her Dusie when she was acting like one), I'm just the poor son of an Italian immigrant. How 'bout giving the old boy a break?"

Talking with his mouth full meant he couldn't have been too mad. He was a sucker for her stunts and Dusie knew it. She'd always been able to butter him up with monkeyshines, romping through the neighborhood in sheets, baying at the moon like an escapee from the state hospital down the road. And dying. She "died" all the time. Strokes before breakfast, poisonings at lunch; I grew up thinking everybody's mother "did" heart attacks but probably not as well as mine. And Dad boasted the way some men crowed about their wives' cooking. "You're not gonna believe it, Herb," he'd say, rushing the start of another Dusie story.

Several weeks later, after the weather had made that indisputable turn into spring, we went down to Cherry Street and picketed my dad's plant. Dusie had hand-printed a huge sign that read NUNZIE DELUCA UNFAIR TO WIFE AND KIDS. For most of that sweet spring afternoon we paraded up and down the walk, Albert on one side of her, I on the other. She carried ten-month-old Teena Jo papoose-style on her back. The soles of Albert's shoes flapped and slapped as he walked. I was eleven and wearing one of her size-fourteen house-dresses cinched at the waist with gold and green Christmas ribbon. Stretched-out bobby sox bunched miserably around my ankles. As an afterthought, she'd tucked the Dr. Denton-ed baby in an onion bag. The worst of it was, Albert and Teena Jo weren't even ours.

"Wait till Mrs. Stefka finds out," I taunted. Dusie was supposed to be keeping an eye on them while their mother went shopping. "You're gonna get it, you're gonna get it," I singsonged softly as we pounded the pavement. I was getting too old to be her loyal sidekick anyhow; I was learning to feel "dumb," especially when a fussing old woman came up and gave Albert and me each an orange and a nickel.

Inside the building, Dad's employees, most of whom knew us very well, kept rapping on the dusty panes. They waved and looked vivified; in due course my dad came out and flagged down the Mister Softee truck. He bought us all frozen yo-yo sticks. Then he whacked my mother once on the behind and went back in.

She packed the next four months with sometimes inspired, sometimes second-rate shenanigans. Nuisance calls to his office in assorted foreign accents. The BEWARE OF THE STUD sign on the factory lawn. She bought us both Orphan Annie wigs that made us look like a pair of dried chestnut burrs. In those and dark glasses we followed Dad and Dolores all the way down to Pimlico in Maryland. They never noticed we were behind them or if they did, didn't let on. Not knowing what to do with ourselves once we got to the track, we ended up going to see *Invasion of the Animal People* at some local movie house. "Lotta good that did us," I said to my mirror image in the theater washroom. Framed in that bonnet of curls, my face lost some of its stronger points. I wanted to think flowerlike. I wanted to think fragile. I had his dark popping eyes and sloped forehead, Dusie's sharp nose. I remember thinking my father left us for all the pretty little girls in Dolores's belly; he would buy them horses like the one he'd promised me. I dreamed I drowned their children by the dozens, as fast as they were born, but sometimes they were my own babies, and, ashamed, I hid them in sandy coves and giant potted plants the likes of which have never been seen in our city.

When it was, exactly, I'm not sure, but there came a point when Dusie's intrigues broke away from the mainland and assumed a shape, a life of their own. Became, in a way, an island of compulsiveness. She plotted on paper, drew diagrams, made greasy jottings while stuffing pork chops or frying the garlic Dad had shown her how to make. She started jobs and never finished them. She called the house painters and then couldn't settle on a color. So the men went away disgusted. All night long the house creaked with her meanderings, the hall light flashing on and off, and in the morning her eyes would be bright as fever, her body pulling in six directions, her hands too shaky and eager to pour coffee. "Now listen," she'd say (and sometimes I'd only pretend to), "this oughta give the old guinea pause."

In late summer, around the time the three of us would normally be taking a place at the shore, we went down to House of deLuca with two men and a U-Haul. Lucky for us, my dad wasn't around. In the space of an hour we had a cutting table and three sewing machines and whatever else she needed to start a business in the basement, a mini-necktie factory in competition with Dad's. One night I awoke to a gentle pressure on my shoulder and two incandescent eyes beaming into mine. "House of Spouse," the voice said, and the night sifted shut again. My dad claimed such apparitions all the time; they told him where to put his money at the track. But in the morning Dusie was at the breakfast table ordering labels. "House of Spouse," she reiterated. Wasn't it scrumptious? We'd blow House of deLuca right out of the water.

Before Dad booted her out of the office, she used to keep the company books. Not well, I understood, but adventurously. He used to say she gave him bottom lines that would knock Jefferson off Mount Rushmore. I suspect she learned the business better than she let on, because hers was off the ground in weeks. She knew just where to call for supplies, hired machine operators, a cutter; she and I tacked on labels, pressed and packed boxes. Profit being the least of her worries, she was able to call Dad's jobbers and offer House of Spouse 20 percent cheaper than House of deDummy, as was her wont to call it. Shameless, she even promoted the idea of a "label with a story behind it."

That brought him around of course. He came up the driveway in his new canary-yellow T-bird. He was wearing a turtleneck shirt, Levi cutoffs, and a wide belt with a chunky gold buckle in some kind of zigzag design.

I kept right on playing "Oliver Twist Can't Do This" against the side of the house and was dying for him to say the ball was leaving marks on the paint so I could crack how his opinion didn't mean beans around here anymore. But he just stood quietly by watching, so I finally said, "A longer line at the waist would make you look taller, you know." I said this in a monotone, without missing a single catch, as if there were no meanness at all behind it.

He noticeably sucked in his stomach. Then Dusie came out and as she strode toward us, he said, "One of these days, sister, you're gonna go too far." Last year he would have boomed this in what she called his hotshot-Italian-husband voice. It occurred to me at that moment that "Italian husband" could be a kind of unstable species, one that outside its element reverted quickly to an original state—soft, sweet, and perfectly defenseless.

"I had that equipment coming to me," she said. "The business is half mine."

"That's true, Duze," he said agreeably. "Mind if I get myself a Coke?"

"Be my guest." Her arm swept a grand gesture toward the house.

"Maybe we can discuss this over a Coke."

"Maybe the sky will rain rhubarb."

"Ah, hell, Duze, always gotta be a wiseacre." He threw up his arms and as he turned to go, I saw that his belt buckle was really three big fat letters spelling YES.

Dad needn't have worried his head about the business. Though we were getting orders and holding our own financially, Dusie soon let things slide out of sheer indifference. There were no major goals in her life, only ways and means to short-term spectacles. She rarely even talked anymore of Dad coming back, but the scheming and stewing went on, a ceaseless scudding across her storm-green eyes. There were days I stood in oblique, reluctant awe of her reckless creativity and could see that all those external events—my dad and Dolores and heaven knows what else might strike her—were often only springboards to her intractable genius.

I owned an antique toy, a rusty tin man my grandmother brought from Ireland when she was ten. He clutched an enormous curved pole in both hands and rocked back and forth on one toe from a high perch the size of a dime. I never learned to stop doubting the rickety principles that brought him back each time from his heart-stopping dip over the edge; neither did I trust whatever it was that got us out of prison. Especially after the business with United flight No. 101. Up until then, whatever she did at least evinced a token respect for limits, a sense of comic proportion, as though she'd struck some sort of grudging bargain with the conventional world. What happened was this: Somebody let it slip that Dad was planning to take Dolores to Cincinnati on the eighth of November for the Eastern Haberdashers' Convention. So Dusie did what any self-respecting spurned American housewife would do: She called United and booked that Cincy flight solid. And I helped. We spent days on the phone. In several different dialects and in the names of every prominent citizen we could think of—Dr. Ferguson, J. T. Bigatel from the bank—we made reservations. At some point, the girl said, "Goodness, such interest in this flight. Is there something big going on in Cincinnati?"

"Oh, my, yes," I explained. "It's the annual running of the pipkins. We never miss it." I heard my voice and it was unmistakably Dusie's: her puckish expression on my face, her face on my neck, her neck patching red my body. Her body standing smart as a new broom in my shoes. My shoes. A pair of dirty white sneakers and a broken shoelace. They were mine and they were still on the ground. "Hey, Ma," I said, finally, "isn't the airline going to freak-out over this?"

She looked at me, recognition spreading like a rash. She curdled her mouth and hunched her shoulders up around her head. "Oh, Mother Machree," she said between her teeth.

United *was* furious and if Dad hadn't convinced them she "wasn't all there," Dusie would have been in a pack of trouble. What's more, as it turned out, Dad and Dolores had reservations weeks in advance and, as the result of our finaglings, had the whole plane to themselves all the way to Ohio. Not exactly what Dusie had in mind.

It was nearly winter again when my father came home. Maybe in those days men could be driven back by the first rush of cold through the alleys, the beseeching bells of street-corner Santas. He came in and set his two-suiter down on the rug, flopped into his old Naugahyde chair. You'd have thought he'd just come home from work. He seemed limp and shapeless. His skin could have been an ill-fitting suit and inside nothing but sawdust and old rags. And something else—in some imprecise way he looked strangely subtracted, bare.

"Just like that, Bart?" Dusie said, and whatever else she wanted to say wouldn't come unstuck, so she said, "Just like that, Marvin?"

He gave her his cow-eyed look and laid his hands on his thighs, and then I noticed it was his moustache that was so oddly gone and how shamelessly he sat there stunning us with the sudden pale-pink of his unprotected mouth, his naked face.

"Well!" she said, rancor and resolve bobbing wildly around in her throat. I watched her swallow and swallow again. With all her stubbornness and punch, she could be sliced like scrapple.

"What can I say, Duze? You're the best and the craziest. You're the screwy broad I married. I missed ya, kid."

And I would be tough and dry enough for the two of us. "Where's your YES belt?" I said with a dispassion that was not in my genes. "Swinger!"

After dinner he went into his den and sat alone in the stiff December darkness. I came in pretending it was just to bedevil the daylights out of him. I spoke very quietly, my voice gritty with malice, the sugary kind I was good at. "What's wrong?" I said, "Did good old whatsername . . ." and I slit my finger across my throat, "skiiiiick!" His dark sad eyes working against mine made me sick and sorry at the same time. He held out his arms and I went to him, sat on his lap, laid my head cautiously on his chest. His smell: It was like no other and I remembered how the day he left I'd buried my face in his old Woolrich shirt and breathed and breathed and breathed. He began to stroke my hair, his hands falling clumsy as bear paws, hands heavy with the contemptible syrup of his melancholy, and though it is also possible that I only dreamed it, I have always believed the next thing I did was bite him, my teeth digging down into his shoulder until I could taste the fat salt root of all the tears I never shed.

Then I went in to say goodnight to Dusie. She sat on her bed stunned and sunless as a widow. Over the past months she'd lost a lot of weight; her face was roundeyed, a crumple of planes and angles. "He's home!" I said. "He's home," acting joyful, acting like a child. And after awhile, in a voice full of the old music—my grandmother's voice, the voice Dusie used only for ominous or solemn high occasions—she said, "The harvest is past, the summer is ended and we are not saved." In the arc of lamplight her hair sparked gold and copper around her lost white face. Katy Keenan, whose mother had come from Kilkenny, and she hung her head and said no more.

And not that night or the next, but soon thereafter, I sat up in my bed knowing exactly what she'd meant by those words: first the loss, then the time of "taking measures"; our mischief had outrun the demons; we were home free and now he was back and now we were at risk again. I was grateful and yet grief made me thin as paper.

Dusie observed a period of mourning much longer than the first. She spoke little and took long solitary walks in the cold evening air. Once I awoke and looked out to see the freshly blanketed lawn already littered with snow angels, each one just her size. She devoured mystery stories and the poetry of Yeats. Calmly, methodically, she performed any chore my father asked. His bereavement, too, went on, over and over again announcing itself in his dragging step, his slow, forgetful speech. It was a sorrow I prayed the Lord to forgive, for I could never. But then on the morning of Saint Patrick's Day my mother got up and made us all green waffles, and later that week she did something with freshly baked brownies rolled between her palms that made my dad think Miss Kitt, our cat, had used his pillow as a litter box. We were like a house settling, aching down to itself. The creaks of cautious laughter, the night whispers, the easing of protocols; all the old angers and tyrannies cracking back, snapping into place.

Under the penitential circumstances, it was inevitable that I would get my horse. A magnificent Appaloosa we named Dandy Orbit, after the space program I suppose. Dusie and I both learned to ride and though I was at "that age," I soon became another age, the one that preferred to hang out after school smoking cigarettes by the ice machine at the superette or doing the circuit with high-school motorheads. So Dandy-O became my mother's horse by default and by destiny: Was there any doubt that they belonged together? Dusie with her healthy limbs and flaming hair; she sat resolute and proud as a Keltic queen. And later she would groom him and croon softly, gently stroking his mane. Our vegetable crisper was always full of carrots and apples.

And when she wasn't on Dandy-O she was riding the crest of a new wave of eccentricity. She "died" more frequently than ever, staging dreadful falls and electrocutions. I learned never to take my excuse forms back to school without reading them first. On the blank designated "reason for absence or tardiness" she'd write bubonic plague or hoof-and-mouth disease. Saint Vitus's dance. I looked triskaidekaphobia up in the dictionary: fear of the number thirteen. I handed it back to her: "Just say I had a cold if ya don't mind." She liked to enter buildings through windows and doors that said DO NOT ENTER but I would not say she was a classic madcap. She did not, for instance, dance naked in hotel fountains or go barefoot to the opera or hire skywriters except that once, to say her name.

By mid-August of that year the house had still not been painted, so Dad said he was going to be in Dallas for two weeks and she'd better have it done by the time he got back. Or else! (The "Italian husband" was starting to shine through.) I remember that as she gave the painters their instructions they argued a little. In the end they shrugged and carried out her orders to the letter.

The evening Dad's plane came in I sat waiting in the yard on the big white rock that said THE DELUCAS in capital letters. Then NUNZIE, KATIE, CONNIE, and MISS KITT in small. I wasn't going to miss this moment for anything. Way down the road already he must have seen because the car started to drift onto the Madsons' grass. Then he continued on up and made the turn into our driveway and the car crept slowly along a short distance before coming to a faltering halt. He got out and stood alongside the car for a long time, just staring. The first section, which included the garage and family room had been done conservatively enough in a nice polite beige. The rest was painted paper-bag tan and mottled with great splotches of brown and black. His face was dumbfounded; then perplexed. Then he bumped his head in the Calabrese way. "An Appaloosa house," his lips said without sound.

I think we both caught sight of her at the same time. On the lower, the garage roof, straddling the peak. Dusie in her western boots and flannel shirt;

Dusie with her riding crop. Dusie astride her house in the deep summer evening; behind her the row of poplars like dark feathers against the green and gold sunset.

My father sat down on the rock beside me. He said nothing, nothing, and then he put his head in his hands and began to cry. "What the heck," I said, tipping my head for a second against his shoulder, meaning to give comfort, "Eloise Bumbaugh's mother still wets the bed." I patted his arm. He wiped his eyes and went in, and minutes later I saw him emerge headfirst from the guestroom window. On his hands and knees he scraped across the sugary shingles. When he reached Dusie he grabbed her belt and untangled his limbs. He sidled in behind her, as if he were setting himself snug in the back of a double saddle. He held on, hugging her close, both of them digging in, clinging to beat the band.

It was the summer of my thirteenth year. My parents will not give each other up; they rage and they cling and six years later my father will die in a late-night accident in the company of a girl named Emma Jean Candy. It was a sad house they rode in the dense August twilight, but it was somehow exultant, inexcusably blessed with the grace of their special madness. These things I began to know as I sat forgotten on that flagrant family rock, and still I knew nothing and dared not move or speak for the mysterious forces suspending the thin moon over the black poplars and all the strange and delicate rhythms holding us all safe in this dusky dream, keeping holy the sacrament of balance.

Under the Roof

Kate Wheeler

Moist, lead-lemon Bangkok dawn: Miss Bi Chin's Chinese alarm clock goes off, a harsh metallic sound, like tiny villagers beating pans to frighten the dragon of sleep. She opens her eyes and sees a big fire ant crawling up her yellow mosquito net; feels how the black earth's chill has penetrated her hipbones. At first she does not know where she is.

Tuk-tuks, taxis and motorbikes already roar behind the high garden wall; but the air is still sweet, yesterday's fumes brought down by the dew. She has slept outside, behind her house, under the sal tree. All around her lie pink, fleshy blossoms, fallen during the night.

She lies still on her side, allowing last night's trip to Dom Muang airport to bloom in her mind, seeing the American monk stalk from the barrier, his brown robe formally wrapped to form a collar and tight scroll down his right arm. Straight out of Burma. It delights her to remember his keen, uncertain look as he scanned the crowd for her unfamiliar face. Then she waved, and he smiled. On the way home, the taxi driver charged them only half price.

She heaves up to sitting; the monk, who is standing now at her screened upstairs window, sees her hips' awkward sideways roll, her hands pressing the small of her back. Both of them have the same thought: the body is a heap of suffering! The monk steps back quickly, lest Miss Bi Chin catch him gazing out the window—worrying about what will become of him out here in the world. As he moves into the shadow, he suddenly realizes that the worry itself is the world's first invasion, and again he is struck with gratitude for his robes. Having to be an example for others protects me, too, he thinks. It works from the outside in, the way forcing yourself to smile can make you feel happy.

Miss Bi Chin rolls up her straw sleeping mat and hurries into the house with it under her arm. Her bones ache, but she takes joy in that. Why should she rent a hotel room when she can sleep for free in her own back yard? It's not the rainy season. She will earn great merit for helping the monk to sleep as the rules require, under a roof where there is no woman. By now he must have completed his morning meditation.

In her mind she sees the Thai monks going for alms food right now all over the city: hundreds of them in bright orange robes, bare feet stepping over broken glass and black street garbage. They shave their heads only on full moon day, they have TVs and they seduce American tourists. They don't care if the tourists are women or men. Thai people crave too much for sense pleasures.

Miss Bi Chin would not donate so much as an orange to Thai monks; she saves her generosity for the good, clean monks trained in Burma.

As she lights the gas under the huge aluminum teakettle, the old man comes shuffling into the dark kitchen. He pulls the light cord, searing the room with jerks of blue fluorescence. "Why do you cook in the dark, Chinese sow," he says in Malay. He is her mother's second husband's brother and lived off the family for years in Penang. Now he has come here to torture her and make her life miserable.

"Shh," she says, motioning with her head. The American monk sits cross-legged at a low table in the next room. His eyes are downcast and a small smile curves his lips. Beautifully white, he resembles the marble Buddhas they sell in Rangoon.

"So what? He doesn't understand me," the old man says. "Why don't you bring in a real man for a change? You'd be a lot less religious if you were satisfied." And I'd be happier living here, he thinks, if she were a normal woman, not lost in pious dreams.

His words roll off her mind like dew from the petals of a white lotus. "You will go to all the hells," she predicts. "First the hot and then the cold."

The old man laughs. "I am Muslim. Will I go to the same hell as you and your rag-wrapped *farang*? I am waiting for my breakfast." He walks in and shows all his teeth to the American monk. "Goo mornin sah!"

"Hey," the monk says. "Thanks for the bed. I slept great."

The old man can only nod. He doesn't understand English. Miss Bi Chin bites her tongue, deciding it is better for the monk's peace of mind not to know it was her bed that he slept in. Of course, she moved it into the sewing room.

This American monk is the favorite of the Rangoon abbot, Miss Bi Chin has heard. He's been in intensive meditation for three years, completing two levels of insight practice and the concentrations of the four heavenly abodes. But the monastery's friend in the Department of Religious Affairs lost his position in November, and the monk's last visa renewal application was rejected. He has come to Thailand to apply for re-entry into Burma; approval will take at least three months, if it comes at all. Conditions in Burma are unstable; the government has had to be very strict to maintain order, and it does not want too many foreign witnesses to its methods. Recently, they changed the country's name to Myanmar, as if this would solve its problems.

If the monk cannot return, the abbot may send him back to America to found a monastery. The monk has not been told. The streams of defilements are strong in the West: all the American monks that the abbot has known disrobe soon after they go home, so they can enjoy sense pleasures. Ideally, the monk should stay in Burma a few more years; but the abbot hasn't worn robes all his life to forget that the world is not ideal. This monk is addicted to pondering, a common Western vice, but he has a devoted heart, and his practice has been good. Pork should fry in its own fat; the American devotees cry out for a monastery. This monk may be the perfect candidate.

The abbot sees no reason to make a decision yet. He's asked Miss Bi Chin, the monastery's great supporter, to report on the monk's behavior: whether living unsupervised in capitalist Bangkok becomes his downfall.

Seeing him wait for his food, so still, Miss Bi Chin has no worries. She's studied his face, too, according to Chinese physiognomy. A broad forehead means calm, the deep lines at each side of the mouth mean kindness.

"Breakfast for you." She kneels at the monk's side, offering the dishes from a cubit's distance, as the Buddha prescribed. The monk touches each plate and she sets it on the table. Wheaties, instant Nescafé with condensed milk, sliced mango, lemon cookies from England, and a bowl of instant ramen noodles.

He hasn't seen such food in three years. He smiles in gratitude at Miss Bi Chin and begins eating.

Miss Bi Chin sits on one side with her feet tucked behind her and her hands in the respectful position. Rapture arises in her mind. She has helped Western monks before, and she knows they do not do well on the diet in Rangoon—too much oil and hot pepper. This monk is bony, his skin rough. She will buy chicken extract, milk powder, and vitamins for him, she will take early lunch hours to come and cook his lunch: monks eat no solid food between noon and dawn.

She stops her ears against the sound of the old man, slurping in the kitchen like a hungry ghost.

The monk wipes his mouth. He has finished everything except the noodles, which remind him too much of Burmese food. Miss Bi Chin notices. She'll reheat them for herself with fish paste; the monk's future breakfasts will be entirely Western.

Because the monk is American, he sometimes feels unworthy of being bowed to and, living on donations, guilty about the extent to which he has learned to enjoy such treatment. Miss Bi Chin, for example, is not rich. She works as a secretary at American Express, and says she refused promotion twice so that she can feel free to neglect her job when monks need help. He'd like to thank her for the food, for everything she is going to do for him, but this is not allowed.

If he were still a carpenter, he'd build her a kitchen countertop; as a monk, example and guidance are the only returns he can offer—they're what she expects, he reminds himself, slipping again into the Asian part of his mind. Her donations bring her merit. She supports what I represent, the possibility of enlightenment: not me specifically.

He clears his throat. "Where did you learn such good English?"

"Oh! My mother sent me to a British school in Penang."

"And you speak Burmese, Thai, and what else?"

"Malay, Cantonese, a little Mandarin."

The monk shakes his head. "Amazing. You're one smart lady."

Miss Bi Chin laughs in embarrassment. "I am Chinese, but my family moved to Malaysia, and we had to learn all the languages on the way. If you had my same *kamma*, you would know them, too."

"Listen." The monk laughs. "The abbot did his best to teach me Burmese." It's hard for him to imagine that this woman is also a foreigner here.

"Better for you," Miss Bi Chin says promptly. "For a monk it is most important to maintain virtue and concentration. Learning languages is only worldly knowledge. The Burmese won't let you alone if they know you can speak. When I go to meditate at Pingyan Monastery, I have to hide in my room." She laughs.

The monk smiles, charmed. Faith makes Miss Bi Chin glow like a smooth golden cat; yet her black eyes sparkle wickedly. He will have to be careful to see her as his older sister, or even as a future corpse.

He'd be surprised to know that Miss Bi Chin thinks of herself as ugly. As a child, her mother would tweak her arm hairs and say, "No one will marry you, Black Dog. Better learn English so you can feed yourself." True, no Asian men want Miss Bi Chin, but the reason may not be her skin—there are plenty of married women as dark. No, she is too well educated, too sharp-tongued, and most of all too religious. From her own side, the only Asian men she is interested in are celibate, monks. She had a long relationship with an American, Douglas, the heir to a toy fortune who does business in Bangkok and Singapore. He smokes Dunhills in a holder, and sponsors the publication of Buddhist texts. Younger than she, he left her a year ago for a glamorous twenty-year-old Thai. She still sees him sometimes at Buddhist meetings, drawling his reactionary opinions. How she ever was involved with him is a mystery to her.

Now she cries, "What is there in this world worth talking about? Everything is only blah, blah, blah. I must go to work now and type meaningless reports so that I can sustain my life and yours. I will come back to cook your lunch. Please use my house as you wish. I have many Buddhist books in English. The old man will not bother you."

She shuffles toward the monk on her knees, to remove the plates. Not to introduce the old man as her uncle is one of her secret acts of revenge.

How terrible my life would be without monks, she thinks.

The monk paces slowly up and down Miss Bi Chin's unfurnished living room. His body feels soft and chaotic among the sharp corners, the too shiny parquet, the plastic flowers under a tinted portrait of his abbot, the most famous teacher in Burma. This photograph shows the abbot's terrifying side, when his eyes, hard and sharp, pierce into each person's heart to lay bare its secret flaws. The monk prefers his tenderness, eyes that make you want to fall over sideways.

This is the first day in three years the monk has not been surrounded by other monks, living the life called "pure and clean as a polished shell": its ten precepts, 227 rules, daily alms round, chanting at dusk. The monastery wall was like a mirror facing inward; beyond it was another barrier, the national boundary of Burma. He often used to speculate on what disasters could be happening in the outside world without his knowing. Meanwhile, cocooned within the walls, the discipline of the robes, and the fierce certainties of his teacher, the monk's mind grew dextrous, plunged into nothingnesses too subtle to remember. He was merely left with a yearning to go back to them; now ordinary happiness feels harsh and coarse.

Outside, traffic roars like storm surf. What a city! He was a different man when he passed through on the way to Rangoon, drank a Singha beer at the airport bar, defiantly toasting his future as a renunciate. Even then he'd been shocked by Bangkok—everything for sale: plastic buckets, counterfeit Rolexes, bootleg software; and of course the women, dressed as primly as third-grade teachers, hoping a client will choose to marry them.

Burma may attack your health, he thinks, but Bangkok will suck you to your doom.

What if his visa is denied?

Will he disrobe? His civilian clothes are even now in a suitcase in the monastery's strong room: they must be eaten up by mildew. He's not ready to go back home as a shaven-headed, toga-wearing freak. No way would the abbot let him stay and practice under a Thai, not down here where they've got monks running around claiming to be reincarnations of Gotama the Buddha. There's a Burmese center in Penang, which Miss Bi Chin supported before she moved up to Bangkok; but she said last night it's near a huge highway and so is unsuitable for the absorption practices; plus, she added confidentially, the head monk in Penang hates Westerners. She ought to know: he's her cousin. If I get sent to Penang, the monk thinks, I'll be able to practice patience for about two weeks and then I'll be out of the robes. I was never a lifer, anyway. Or was I?

I know this is only a form.

For sure, he isn't ready just yet to lose the peace, the certainty of being a monk; nor to be separated from the abbot, his teacher: the only man on earth, he's often told himself, he truly, deeply respects. And loves.

He catches himself planning to sneak across the border at Chiang Rai and run up to Rangoon through the forest with help from Karen insurgents. Bowing three times at the abbot's feet. Here I am. In his mind the abbot laughs at him and says, Peace is not in Burma or in Bangkok. Peace comes from dropping one's preferences. That is why we beg for our food, we take what is given.

The monk stops in front of the abbot's portrait and makes the gesture of respect, palms together.

He feels the world stretching out around him. I'm here, he thinks; suddenly he's in his body again, feeling its heaviness and insubstantiality.

He can even feel the strengthening effect of the milk in the Wheaties he just ate. Conditions in Thailand are good for healing the old bod; he can make it a project. In the States he ran and did yoga fairly regularly; in Burma he never exercised. He was never alone, and people would gossip if they saw him in an undignified posture.

Carefully he spreads his sitting cloth, a maroon-and-orange patchwork square, on the straw mat where he ate breakfast; now he lies flat on it, easing the bunched muscles of his shoulders. Slowly he raises his legs to vertical, letting the small of his back flatten against the cool straw. His sacrum releases with a loud pop.

He tucks the skirt of his robe between his knees and raises his buttocks off the ground, until he is in full shoulder stand, the queen of poses, the great redistributor of psychic energy. His mind flies, faster than light, to Vermont.

He's lived as if he'll never go back to where people know him as Tom Perkins, a carpenter and the more or less unreliable lover of Mary Rose Cassidy, who still lives in Brattleboro, where she's a partner in a cooperative restaurant. She's known he would ordain ever since they came East together in seventy-three. They were both moved by the calm faces of monks they saw; but only he had that realization at the great dome of Borobudur in Java. Tapped it, and said, "Empty. That's it! There's nothing inside." Mary Rose saw in his face that it was a deep moment for him. After coming home, they learned to meditate together at a center in western Mass. She kept saying the tradition was sexist and stifled your *joie de vivre;* Tom wondered if she did it only to keep him from getting too far away.

And she didn't expect him to be gone this long. He's written her four letters saying: my practice is getting deep, it's fascinating, I want to renew my visa.

He should've broken up with her. A year ago he knew: but it seemed cruel to cut her off by mail, and more appropriate as a monk to be vaguely affectionate, vaguely disconnected, than to delve into his past and make a big mess. He halfway hoped she'd lose patience and break up with him herself; but she says she's had no other lover since he left, and she sends a hundred dollars every other month to the monastery treasurer for his support. It's more than enough.

She would have stopped sending money. He would've had to be supported entirely by the Burmese. God knows they have little enough to spare. Think what his plane ticket to Bangkok would have cost in kyat. Four months' salary for the average worker, even at the official rate; at the black market rate, the real value of Burmese money: three years' salary.

He lowers his legs as slowly as he can, feeling unfamiliar pulls in his belly and chest.

He turns to look out the large front window—the old man is staring in at him. He's been sweeping dead leaves off the cement courtyard. He wears ancient blue rubber thongs and a checked sarong; his fine-skinned purplish breasts sag over his ribs. His gaze is clouded and fierce, an old man's rage. The monk has assumed that he is some sort of servant, a trusted retainer of Miss Bi Chin's; he didn't quite take the old man into consideration. Now, this stare rips away all barriers between them.

Lying on the floor, his robes in disarray, he's Tom again, for the first time since he ordained.

With as much dignity as he can muster, he gets to his feet and goes out the back door, into the tiny walled garden where Miss Bi Chin slept. The old man has swept the pink sal flowers into a pile. The fresh ones look like parts of Mary Rose; the decaying ones, black and slimy, remind him of things the abbot says about sensuous desire. He watches one blossom fall, faster than he'd expect. It's heavy, the petals thick as blotting paper. He picks it up, rubs one petal into bruised transparency.

I should call Mary Rose while I've got the Thai phone system, he thinks. I need to tell the truth.

Now he wishes he'd studied the rules, for he doesn't know if using the phone would break the precept against taking what is not given. It's a subtle thing, but how impeccable does he have to be? Miss Bi Chin offered her house, but then steered him into her library. She surely expects to do all his telephoning. Surprising Mary Rose with an overseas collect charge isn't too monkly, except that she still considers him her lover. The irony of this is not lost on him.

Well, it's ten P.M. in Brattleboro. If he waits until Miss Bi Chin comes home it'll be too late, and what's more, she'll overhear everything: the phone is in the kitchen where she'll be cooking lunch. He walks around the corner of the house and asks the old man's permission to use the phone.

The old man waggles his head as if his neck had lost its bones. He says in Malay, "I don't understand you, and you don't understand me!"

The monk decides that this weird movement contains some element of affirmation. In any case, his mind is made up.

As he watches his hand travel toward the phone, he remembers the abbot talking about the gradations of defilement. Desire shakes the mind. The body moves, touches the object, touches it, causing the object to move. When he touches the receiver, he picks it up quickly and dials.

"Tom?" The satellite transmission is so clear, Mary Rose sounds like she's in the next room. "Oh, it's fantastic to hear your voice!"

When he hangs up, an hour later, he feels sick—he can't help imagining her expression when she gets the phone bill. Yet he has to admit, he's intensely alive, too, as if he'd stuck his fingers in a socket, as if someone had handed him a sword.

He thinks: Maybe this will create a vacuum that my visa will rush into.

He goes up to Miss Bi Chin's sewing room and closes the door. Cross-legged on his sitting cloth, he tries to cut off all thoughts of Mary Rose so he can send loving-kindness to the abbot, his benefactor. At first tears come, his body feels bludgeoned by emotion; but then his loving feeling strengthens, the abbot's presence hardens in his mind. Suddenly he and the abbot are welded together, a bond tighter than Krazy Glue. The monk's lips curve up: here there is no grief.

Miss Bi Chin and the old man are eating dinner, chicken and Chinese cabbage in ginger sauce; the monk is upstairs reading a list of the Twenty-Four Mental States Called Beautiful.

"Your monk talked on the phone for two hours," the old man says slyly. "He put his feet above his head and then pointed them at the portrait of Pingyan Sayadaw."

It is not true that the monk pointed his feet at the portrait, but as soon as the old man says so, he begins to believe himself. He's tired of having monks in the house, tired of the prissy, superior way his step-niece behaves when these eunuchs are about. What good do they do? They live off other people, beg for their food, they raise no children. The old man has no children either, but he can call himself a man. He was a policeman for six years in Malaysia, until a bullet lodged near his spine.

Miss Bi Chin pretends he does not exist, but he pinches her bicep, hard.

"Ow!" she cries, and jerks her arm away. "I *told* him he could use the house as he pleased." Too late, she realizes she shouldn't have descended to arguing: it causes the old man to continue.

"Well, he did that. He only waited for you to leave before changing his behavior. I think he's a very loose monk. He wandered up the stairs, down the stairs, examining this and that. Out into the garden to stare at the sky and pick up flowers. Then he got on the phone. He'll be poking in the refrigerator tomorrow, getting his own food."

"You just hate monks."

"Wait and see," the old man says lightly. "Have you noticed his lower lip? Full of lust and weakness."

Miss Bi Chin lowers her face until all she can see is her bowl of soupy cabbage. The old man is her curse for some evil deed in the past. How he abuses her, how he tries to poison her mind! She tells herself that the old man's evil speech is a sign of his own suffering, yet he seems to cause her more pain than he feels himself. Sometimes she enjoys doing battle with him—and she has developed great strength by learning to seal off her mental state so that he cannot infiltrate. This strength she uses on different occasions: on a crowded bus when an open sore is thrust beneath her nose, or when her boss at American Express overloads her with work. At other times the old man defeats her, causes her defilements to arise. Hatred. Fear. A strange sadness, like homesickness, when she thinks of him helpless in the grip of his obsessions.

She could never kick him out. Crippled, too old to learn Thai or get a job, how would he survive in Bangkok? And he does make himself useful, he tends the garden and cleans the floors and bathrooms. Even more important, without him as witness, she and her monks would not be allowed to be in the same house together. The Buddha knew human nature very well when he made those rules, she thinks.

Washing up, she hears that the old man has turned on his TV and is watching his favorite talk show, whose host gained fame after a jealous wife cut off his penis, and he had it sewn on again.

"Why do you have to watch that!" she scolds at his fat, unresponsive back.

She goes up to the sewing room in a fury, which dissipates into shame as soon as she sees the monk reading. The light from the window lies flat and weak on the side of his shaven head. His pallor makes him look as if he has just been peeled; her ex-lover Douglas had a similar look, and it gives her a shiver. She turns on the yellow electric lamp so he will not ruin his eyes and leaves the door wide open, as is necessary when a monk and a woman are together in a room.

"Hello, sister," he says. The edges of his eyelids feel burnt by tears; Miss Bi Chin notices redness, but thinks it is from ill health.

She begins to speak even before she has finished her three bows. "Please instruct me, sir, I am so hateful. I should practice meditation for many years, like you, so I can attain the *anagami* stage where anger is uprooted forever. But I am tied to my six sense doors, I cannot become a nun, I must live in this world full of low people. I think also, if I quit my job, who will support you monks when you come to Bangkok?"

As she speaks he takes the formal posture, and unconsciously sets his mouth in the same line as the abbot's in the portrait downstairs. Usually when someone bows to him, the beauty of the ancient hierarchy springs up like cool water inside him. Today he'd like to run from this woman, bunched up on the floor, getting ready to spill out her hot, messy life.

But he has to serve her, or else why give up Mary Rose?

"I'm not *anagami*. I'm just an American monk." He waggles his head from side to side, trying to look cheerful, maybe even throw her off track.

"You are so humble!" she says, looking up at him with eyes tormented and devoted as a dog's.

Oh my God, he thinks. Mary Rose. He forces himself to go on. "I understand your wish to renounce the world. Look at me, I left behind a very good woman to do this. I don't regret it," he adds quickly.

She thinks, he should not be talking about his woman; and then: who was she? He must have loved her, to look so regretful even after three years.

"Of course not. Monks enjoy a higher happiness," she says.

"But you don't need to be a nun to purify your mind. Greed, hatred, and delusion are the same whether you are in robes or not. Don't be hard on yourself. We all get angry."

"I am hard because hatred is hard." She says something in Pali, the scriptural language. But he can tell she's relieved, she's heard something that has helped her. She goes on more softly, "Sometimes I want to strike out against one person."

Miss Bi Chin feels a great relief as she confesses this, as if a rusty pin had been removed from her flesh.

"You'll also hurt yourself." The monk regrets his occasional cruelties to Mary Rose. Once, feeling perverse, he called her a cow, only because he knew she was sensitive about her big breasts. The word, the moment, the look on her face, have come back to his mind hundreds of times. And today she said that he wasted three years of her life, that he is a coward, that he insulted her by not speaking sooner.

"I know! I know!" Miss Bi Chin falls silent.

The monk tries for a better topic. "Who's the old man you have living with you? He gave me quite a look through the window."

He has the psychic powers, Miss Bi Chin thinks. "You've guessed my enemy. My step-uncle. My mother sent him to me. I cannot get rid of him." She picks like a schoolgirl at the hem of her dress, hearing the old man's mocking voice: "If you don't have the guts to throw me out, you deserve whatever you get."

The monk sees her face go deep red. That horrible old man! He sees him staring in the window again, his rheumy, cruel eyes. I'd better be careful though. Maybe they've slept together. You never know, when two people live in the same house.

"Every personal relationship brings suffering," he says cautiously.

"Better to live alone if one wants to free the mind," Miss Bi Chin quotes from the admonitions of the abbot. "Should I ask Uncle to leave?"

"Um, any reason why you can't?"

"Why not!" She giggles. She is not so much planning to kick out the old man as letting herself fall just a little in love with this monk. He is so breezy and American, like a hero in the movies; yet he has much wisdom. "Well, he has to stay here until you get your visa, because you and I would not be able to be in the house alone."

The monk smiles uncertainly. "I may not get a visa."

"Of course you will. You have good *kamma* from practice."

"Yet we never know when our *kamma* will ripen, do we. Good or bad."

They both nod slowly, looking into each other's eyes.

"What will you do if you can't go back?" She really wants to know; and it gives her a thrill to talk about this, knowing that the monk is ignorant of the abbot's intentions. Perhaps she'll report the answer to Rangoon.

"I'll try to remain in equanimity."

"That's a good answer for the abbot, she thinks, but it's not enough for me. She extends herself: "Would you like to go back to your country and begin a monastery?"

"Oh, no," he says lightly.

"Why?"

"I have no interest in making others follow rules. I'm not a cop, basically."

"Don't you miss your home?"

"Yes, but . . ."

"I should have offered you to use the phone. Maybe you want to call your parents."

"I've already used it. I hope that's all right."

A shock runs down Miss Bi Chin's back. So it's true what the old man says. "You used the phone?"

"It was sort of urgent. I had to make a call. I did it collect, there'll be no charge to you. Maybe I should call Penang and confess?"

"Oh, no, no, no," she says. "I offered you to use my house as you wished. Who did you talk to?"

"Well, my old girlfriend from the States," and he finds himself describing the whole situation to Miss Bi Chin, confessing. Recklessly, he even says he might have postponed breaking up because he was afraid to lose a supporter. Because Miss Bi Chin is a stranger—and because she knows so much more about being a monk than he does—he feels compelled to expose his worst motivations. If forgiving words come out of these quietly smiling lips, he'll be exonerated. If her face turns from gold to brass and she casts him out, that will be right also.

As he speaks, Miss Bi Chin feels she is walking through a huge house, where rooms open up unexpectedly one after another. When she was in the British school, she had to read a poem about the East being East and the West being West, and never the twain shall meet. This is not true: she knows she can follow this monk far into his labyrinth, and maybe get lost. For him it is the simplest thing to say: the old man is bad, ask him to leave. But for himself, it is so complicated. In one room of his mind he is a monk, and using the phone was an error; in another room calling was the right thing to do. First he is too strict with himself, then he lets go of the rules altogether.

Should she tell the abbot? What would there be to tell? That the monk used the telephone after she had already given permission? That he was impatient to perform a wholesome act?

Miss Bi Chin has a water heart: it flows in uncontrollable sympathy toward the monk. She knows he was afraid to be forgotten when he went so far from home. That is the true reason he did not cut off this girlfriend, but he is a man and cannot admit such kind of fears.

She interrupts. "If I were Mary Rose," she tells him, "if Mary Rose were Burmese, or even Thai, as soon as you ordained, her reason for sending money would change. She would donate to earn merit for herself. You would then feel grateful but not indebted. You would feel to strive hard in meditation, to make her sacrifice worthwhile. And I think that your mind is very pure and you are trying to perform your discipline perfectly, but because you were in intensive practice you do not know in precise way what monks should do and not do when they are in ordinary life. Therefore I think you should spend your time here studying the texts in my library and learning what you did not learn."

At the end of this speech she is breathless, shocked to hear herself admonishing a monk.

"Thank you," he says. "That's great." His face is broken up by emotion; he looks as if he might weep.

Now, she thinks, should I tell the abbot that his monk is falling apart?

Not yet. It's only his first day.

Within a week it is obvious to the old man that Miss Bi Chin and the monk are in love.

"I should call Rangoon," he teases Miss Bi Chin. They both know he will never do so, if only because he will not know how to introduce the topic to a person he has never met. But the threat gives him power over her. Miss Bi Chin now ignores it when he fails to sweep or clean the bathrooms. The monk sometimes sweeps away the blossoms under the sal tree; the old man stands at the window of the sewing room, enjoying this spectacle. Miss Bi Chin made loud remarks about the toilet but ended up cleaning it herself. She also serves the old man his meals before going in and prattling with the monk. The old man has never felt so satisfied since he moved in here two years ago.

Miss Bi Chin, too, is happy. These days she feels a strange new kind of freedom. She and the monk are so often in the same room—he sits in the kitchen while she cooks, and otherwise they go to the sewing room and study or meditate—that the old man has fewer opportunities to pinch or slap. In the past she even feared that the old man might kill her, but he seems calmed by the monk's purity of mind.

The monk actually wants to know what she thinks about this and that. When she comes home from work, he asks respectfully how her day was, and they discuss her problems. He sees so clearly people's motivation! Then they go to the texts and try to look behind the surface to see what is the effect on the mind of each instruction, always asking, what did the Buddha intend? When they disagree with each other, they don't let each other off the hook: sometimes their arguments are fierce, exciting.

"Why do Burmese and Thais call each other lax?" he asks one night. "The Thais accuse the Burmese because Burmese monks will take stuff straight out of a woman's hand. Then the Burmese turn around and say Thais drink milk after noon. Can't they see it's all relative?"

"You don't know Thai monks," she replies hotly. "Won't take a pencil from a woman's hand but you don't know what they take from her other parts."

"Yeah, but not all Thai monks are bad. What about those old Ajahns up north? They live under trees."

"Insects also live under trees! Burmese get good results in their meditation, in the city or in the forest. You better listen to your own teacher to know what is right. No one reaches enlightenment by saying 'it is all relative.'"

His lips go tight, but then he nods. "You're right. Pingyan Sayadaw says Western skepticism makes people sour inside. You stay at the crossroads and never go anywhere. 'I don't believe this path, I don't believe that path.' Look at the power of mind he has."

"Such a strong monk," she says joyously.

No man has ever yielded to her thinking; it fills her heart with cold, delicious fire.

"Incredible," the monk replies, his pale eyes shining.

Then they meditate together, and her mind becomes so fresh. She feels she is living in the time of the Buddha with this monk. When the old man accuses her of being in love, she retorts that she's always been in love with the truth.

The monk is getting healthy, eating Wheaties and doing yoga every day. Miss Bi Chin often asks if there's anything he needs, so he can say "A bottle of vitamin C" or "A new pair of rubber thongs" without feeling strange. He feels pleasantly glutted with conversation. In Burma, he never sifted through his thoughts, the idea was simply to take in as much as he could. At Miss Bi Chin's, he can sort, digest, refine. She helps direct his studies, she's almost as good as a monk; and in turn he's helping her figure out how to deal with daily life.

A perfect marriage would be like this, he thinks, except sex would screw it up with expectations. At times his feelings for Miss Bi Chin do grow warm, and he tosses on her bed at night; but there's no question in his mind about these feelings. They'll go away at the third stage of enlightenment. Having left Mary Rose, he feels more like a monk than ever. It's good exercise for him to see Miss Bi Chin's loveliness with detachment, as if she were a flower or a painting in a museum. When she exclaims that she's ugly and dark, he corrects her, saying, "All self-judgment reinforces the ego."

He writes the abbot every week. "Living in the world is not as difficult as I feared, but maybe this is because Miss Bi Chin's house is like a monastery. I am studying in her library. Her support is generous and her behavior is impeccable. She sleeps outside, under a tree. One night it rained and she went straight out to a hotel."

The monk has only two fears during this period. One is that the embassy of Myanmar will not approve his visa. The other is that it will. When he thinks of Pingyan Monastery, he remembers its discomforts: diarrhea in the Rains, in April prickly heat.

I have my head in the sand, he thinks; or, I am asleep between my mother's breasts.

Miss Bi Chin is showing the monk a large bruise on her upper arm. It is the blue-black of an eggplant and has ugly spider's legs spreading in all directions around it. If he were not a monk, he'd touch it gently with his finger.

"I can't believe he does this to you," he says. "Don't you want him to leave? I'll be there when you say it. I'll stand over him while he packs."

"If he left, you'd have to go also. Where? He'd come back the next day. He was in the narcotics squad in Malaysia. I don't know what he would do. I think something. He has his old gun in a sack. It is broken but he could fix it."

Hearing about the gun makes the monk's stomach light with horror. Human beings, what they'll do to each other. Imagine a rapist's mind, a murderer's. Delusion, darkness, separation. How has Miss Bi Chin let this evil being stay in the house? How has she been able to live under the roof with such fear?

"He's got to go. If I'm still here he'd be less likely to bother you," the monk says. "I'm an American, after all. He'd get into big trouble if he pulled anything. Now that I can use the phone"—he laughs a little—"I can get on the horn to the embassy."

"But he is my step-uncle," Miss Bi Chin says weakly. She doesn't really want the monk to be proposing this. He sounds not like a monk, but like any other American boasting about his country's power.

"Look," the monk says. "I'll sleep outside. I'll eat outside. I'll stay outside all day. We can leave the gate open so people in the street can see us. I think this thing with the old man is more serious than you think. We can work out the monk part. The Patimokkha only talks about sleeping under the same roof and sharing a secluded seat, and in the second case a woman follower has to accuse me of seducing you."

"Okay. I'll get you a tent," Miss Bi Chin says.

"No way. You didn't have one," the monk retorts. "Why don't you find him a job instead?"

The old man knows something is wrong: when he comes back from the soda shop at six, the two of them are sitting in the patio chairs side by side, facing the gate, like judges.

"You must leave this house tomorrow," Miss Bi Chin says. The monk's face bears a look the old man knows is dangerous: determination mixed with terror, the look of a young boy about to pull a trigger. In a flash he calculates his chances. The monk is not healthy and probably knows no dirty fighting tricks, but is thirty years younger and much larger. He must have been a laborer once, his arms and chest show signs of former strength; and he's been exercising every day.

The old man makes his hands into claws. "Heugh!" he cries, and fakes a pounce: only six inches forward. Of course, the monk leaps to his feet. The old man laughs. This kind of thing brings vigor in old age.

"So you lovebirds want privacy?" he says. "Watch out I don't take the kitchen knife to you tonight. I'm old but I'm still a man."

"I got you a job guarding the Chinese market," Miss Bi Chin says. "They'll give you a room in back." She was surprised how easy this solution was, once the monk opened her mind to it. Now she owes the monk her happiness. Her house suddenly seems vast; her nostrils fill with the sweet scent of sal flowers, as if the old man were a fire emitting sharp smoke which had been put out.

The next morning she calls a taxi. All of the old man's clothes fit into a vinyl sports bag, but his TV is too big to carry on the bus.

Watching him go, old and crooked, out the gate, Miss Bi Chin feels bad. Her mother will not understand. Loyalty is important in a family. She's been living in this house with the American monk, who tells her about the youth revolution when everyone decided their parents were wrong. This was the beginning of meditation in America; even the monk got interested in spiritual things at first because of drugs.

Now the monk meets her in the garden. He's smiling softly. "Remember the test of loving-kindness?" he asks her. "You're sitting under a tree with a neutral person, a friend, and an enemy, and a robber comes and says you have to choose who he'll kill?"

"I remember," she says dully. "I refuse the decision."

The abbot's letter has taken a month to arrive. He writes through an interpreter: "My son in robes: I hope you get a visa soon. I am glad you keep good morality. Miss Bi Chin says you are suitable to be a teacher and your speeches are refined. I praise her for sleeping outside, but maybe it is your turn. Be careful of desire and pride, and do not think too much."

Miss Bi Chin has sent several glowing reports by aerogram. Now she is not so sure. She hates sleeping in the bed, she feels she has lost her power in some obscure way. She and the monk are trying hard to keep the rules. They avoid being in the house together, but there are too many robbers in Bangkok to leave the street gate open, so they rely on the fact that they're always visible from the second floor of the elementary school across the street. They joke about their debt to one small, distracted boy who's always staring out the window; but this is almost like a lovers' joke. Miss Bi Chin feels disturbed by the monk's presence now. When he looks at her with soft eyes she feels nothing but fear. Perhaps he is in love with her. Perhaps he thinks of her at night. She dreads his quick buzz of the doorbell, announcing he's coming in to use the bathroom.

One morning at work she types an aerogram to the abbot. It makes her happy to see the clarity of the Selectric type on the thin, blue paper. "I worry about the American monk. We're alone together in my compound ever since he asked my uncle to leave my house. We try to keep his precepts, but I want your opinion. He spoke about his personal life. There was a woman in love with him at home. He said the precepts are relative, what is most important is the effect on the mind."

She tosses this in her Out box and watches the office boy take it away with her boss's letters to America. For some reason, she thinks of the gun lying in the bottom of the old man's sports bag as he walked off down the street.

"Don't you want to go home and teach your own people?" Miss Bi Chin asks again.

She's brought up this subject many times, and the monk always says no. But today his answer surprises both of them. With the old man gone, things have fallen into place. He likes sleeping under the sal tree, the same kind of tree under which the Buddha was born and died. Monks did this in ancient times, dwelt at the roots of trees. He loves its glossy green leaves and pink flowers; he imagines it is the tradition, and at night his roots go down with its roots, deep into the black soil. "Maybe I'm in a special position," he says. "Americans are hungry for truth. Our society is so materialistic."

"You don't want to be an abbot though," Miss Bi Chin says. "It is too tiring."

"I don't know," he says. "If my teacher asked me to I guess I'd have to go."

"Well, an abbot wouldn't be staying here alone with me, I can tell you that much," Miss Bi Chin bursts out.

That night he lies awake under the sal tree. Why didn't she tell him sooner, if it wasn't proper for him to stay? Is she in love with him? Or is she teaching him step by step?

He remembers the rules he's studied. Miss Bi Chin herself could be the woman follower who accuses him of seduction. Even though they haven't shared a seat, it's possible that if she brings a charge against him, there'd be no power in his denial, since they've been rather secluded together in her compound.

He understands something new: a monk's life has to be absolutely clear-cut. These rules were made for a reason. Ambiguous situations mean murky feelings, subterranean defilements. Again he can thank Miss Bi Chin for showing him how to go.

Whether he gets his visa or not is unimportant. He must go to Penang and live with other monks and prepare for the responsibilities of the future. If the Penang abbot hates Westerners, it's probably because he's never met one who appreciates the robes. If it's difficult to be there, it will develop his mental strength.

He imagines himself a monk in old age. The stubble on his head will grow out white, he'll laugh at the world like his teacher. Old Burmese monks are so very much alive, he thinks. Their bodies are light, their skin emits a glow. If you can feel free amid restrictions you truly are free.

In the morning he is quiet as Miss Bi Chin serves his breakfast on the front patio.

He is red now, not white: his blood is healthy. He keeps his eyes down as she hands him the plates. Wheaties, mango, cookies, Nescafé. Talk to me, she cries inside herself. She stares at his mouth, seeing its weakness and lust. It shows the part of him she loves, the human part.

She hasn't slept all night, and her mind is wild as an untamed elephant. Maybe the abbot will get her aerogram and make the monk disrobe. He'll stay in her house and live a lay life; they can make love after having their conversations. I could call the embassy and withdraw his visa application, she thinks. What is the worst that could happen? That I am reborn as a nun who'll be seduced by a foreigner?

At last she understands the old man, who said once he didn't care if *kamma* punished him in a future life, as long as he got to do what he wanted to in this life. How can we know who we'll be, or who we were? We can only try to be happy.

Frightened by her thoughts, she watches the monk bite a U shape out of his toast. He's being careful, moving stiffly as a wooden puppet; and he must have shaved his head this morning, it is shiny, hairless, there is a small bloody nick over his ear.

She knows she won't be able to cancel his visa application; and that her aerogram will result, not in the monk's disrobing, but in his being sent to Penang and forbidden to stay with her again. She hasn't accused him of downfall offenses, or disgusting offenses. So he'll go on with his practice and maybe become an abbot, or a fully liberated arhat. At least I was full of wholesome moral dread when I wrote that aerogram, she thinks. When the benefits come, I can enjoy them without guilt. Such as they'll be. Someone will give me a new Buddha image, I'll be offered another promotion and refuse it. She laughs under her breath. Is this what I was looking for when, as a young girl, I began running from temple to temple and lost all my friends?

"What are you laughing about," the monk says.

"I was thinking of something."

"I have to go to Penang," he says. His voice is low and hollow, so neither of them is sure he's actually spoken.

"I am sorry my house is unsuitable for you to stay."

"No, it's been wonderful to be here. But I need to be around other monks. I feel like we've been playing with the rules a little bit. We're in a gray area."

He smiles at her coaxingly, but she refuses the bait. "I'll buy you a ticket to Penang this afternoon."

How can she be so cold suddenly? She's pulling him out, compelling him to make the contact. "I'll miss you. Don't tell the abbot, okay?"

"If there is no lust, a monk may say he will miss."

"I want this to stay between us," he says. "You've been like my sister. And teacher. I'm sorry I have to go."

"Every personal relationship brings suffering," she says, but she's smiling at him, finally, a tiny complicated smile he'd never believe could appear on her golden face. Suddenly he sees her eyes are full of tears, and he knows he'll be lonely in Penang, not only for Miss Bi Chin but for Mary Rose, who also fixed things so he could ask for whatever he wanted.

Nothing changes, the old man thinks. There they are, sitting in the front courtyard, talking about nothing. He's standing at the jalousied window of the third-grade classroom, during the children's first morning recess. He knew this was the time. Bi Chin doesn't go to work until nine-thirty.

He woke up in a rage that drove him to the bus stop, still not knowing what he would do—something: he has his pistol in the sports bag. He had it fixed, and late at night he practices shooting at bottles floating in the *khlong* past the Chinese market. His aim isn't what it was. The pistol is heavier than he remembered, his eyes are bad, his arm shakes.

He knew an idea would come when he was actually standing at the window, and it has. He sees one thing he can succeed at. He can at least hit that plate glass window, shatter it behind their heads. He sees it clearly, bursting, shower of light. They run inside and slam the door. Miss Bi Chin in her terror grabs the monk. Ha! They find themselves embracing. That'll be a good one, if he doesn't miss and blow one of their heads off.

Happy with this solution, the old man begins to hum as he unzips the sports bag. The gun's cold oil smell reaches his nostrils, making him sharp and powerful. He's always wanted to break that window, he doesn't know why. Just to see it smash. I'm an evil old man, he thinks. Good thing I became a cop.

Selected Bibliography

Atchity, Kenneth. 1986. *A Writer's Time*. New York: W. W. Norton.

Bauer, Douglas. 2000. *The Stuff of Fiction: Advice on Craft*. Ann Arbor: The University of Michigan Press.

Booth, Wayne C. 1961. *The Rhetoric of Fiction*. Chicago: University of Chicago Press.

Borges, Jorge Luis. 1973. *Borges on Writing*. Ed. Norman Thomas di Giovanni, Daniel Halpern, and Frank MacShane. New York: E. P. Dutton.

Bowen, Elizabeth. 1950. *Collected Impressions*. New York: Alfred A. Knopf.

Brande, Dorothea. 1981. *On Becoming a Writer*. Los Angeles: Jeremy Tarcher.

Burroway, Janet. 1992. *Writing Fiction*, 3rd ed. New York: HarperCollins

Dillard, Annie. 1989. *The Writing Life*. New York: Harper and Row.

Fitzgerald, F. Scott. 1978. *The Notebooks of F. Scott Fitzgerald*. Ed. Matthew J. Bruccoli. New York: Harcourt Brace Jovanovich.

Forster, E. M. 1954. *Aspects of the Novel*. New York: Harcourt Brace & World.

Gardner, John. 1984. *The Art of Fiction*. New York: Alfred A. Knopf.

Hall, Donald. 1979. *Writing Well*. Boston: Little, Brown.

Hemingway, Ernest. 1984. *Ernest Hemingway on Writing*. Ed. Larry W. Phillips. New York: Charles Scribner's and Sons.

Hills, Rust. 1977. *Writing in General and the Short Story in Particular*. Boston: Houghton Mifflin.

Hughes, Elaine Farris. 1990. *Writing from the Inner Self*. New York: HarperCollins.

Hugo, Richard. 1979. *The Triggering Town*. New York: W. W. Norton.

James, Henry. 1947. *The Art of the Novel*. Oxford: Oxford University Press.

———. 1947. *The Notebooks of Henry James*. Oxford: Oxford University Press.

———. 1948. *The Art of Fiction*. New York: Charles Scribner's and Sons.

Kennedy, Thomas E. 2002. *Realism and Other Illusions: Essays on the Craft of Fiction*. La Grande, OR: Wordcraft of Oregon.

Koch, Steven. 2003. *The Modern Library Writer's Workshop*. New York: Random House.

Lodge, David. 1992. *The Art of Fiction*. New York: Penguin Books.

Macauley, Robie, and George Lanning. 1987. *Technique in Fiction*, 2nd ed. New York: St. Martin's Press.

Madden, David. 1988. *Revising Fiction: A Handbook for Fiction Writers*. New York: New American Library.

Minot, Stephen. 1988. *Three Genres*, 4th ed. Englewood Cliffs, N.J.: Prentice-Hall.

O'Connor, Flannery. 1969. *Mystery and Manners.* New York: Farrar, Straus & Giroux.

O'Connor, Frank. 1963. *The Lonely Voice: A Study of the Short Story.* Cleveland: World Publishing.

Pack, Robert and Jay Parini, eds. 1991. *Writers on Writing.* Hanover, New Hampshire: University Press of New England.

Plimpton, George. 1953–1989. *Writers at Work: The Paris Review Interviews,* 8 vols. New York: Viking Penguin.

———. 1989. *The Writer's Chapbook.* New York: Viking.

Reed, Kit. 1982. *Story First: The Writer as Insider.* Englewood Cliffs, N.J.: Prentice-Hall.

Shelnutt, Eve. 1989. *The Writing Room.* Atlanta, Georgia: Longstreet Press.

Stern, Jerome. 1991. *Making Shapely Fiction.* New York: W. W. Norton.

Strunk, William C., and E. B. White. 1979. *The Elements of Style,* 3rd ed. New York: Macmillan.

Times Books. *Writers on Writing: Collected Essays from the New York Times.* 2001. New York: Henry Holt and Co.

Welty, Eudora. 1977. *The Eye of the Story.* New York: Random House.

West, Paul. 2001. *Master Class: Scenes from a Fiction Workshop.* New York: Harcourt.

Writers on Writing; Collected Essays from The New York Times; Times Books; Henry Holt and Co.; N.Y. 2001.

About the Contributors of Exercises

TONY ARDIZZONE is the author of three novels, *In the Garden of Papa Santuzzu, In the Name of the Father,* and *Heart of the Order,* and three collections of stories, *Taking it Home: Stories from the Neighborhood, The Evening News,* and *Larabi's Ox.* His work has received the Flannery O'Connor Award for Short Fiction and the Milkweed National Fiction Prize. He teaches at Indiana University in Bloomington.

THOMAS FOX AVERILL's novel, *Secrets of the Tsil Café* (New York: Blue Hen/Putnam, 2001), was a finalist in the Literary Food Writing Category of the International Association of Culinary Professionals Cookbook Awards. His short fiction has been included in *Prize Stories 1991: The O'Henry Awards,* and been published in *Best of the West 4* (Norton, 1991). He is a writer-in-residence and professor of English at Washburn University of Topeka.

DOUGLAS BAUER has written three novels, *Dexterity, The Very Air,* and *The Famous Book of Iowans,* and two works of nonfiction, *Prairie City, Iowa,* and *The Stuff of Fiction: Advice on Craft.* His stories and essays have appeared in *The New York Times, Esquire, Agni, Epoch, Harper's,* and many others. He lives in Boston and in Northhampton, Massachusetts, where he's currently writer-in-residence and the Elizabeth Drew Professor of English at Smith College.

FRANÇOIS CAMOIN teaches writing at Vermont College and the University of Utah.

RON CARLSON is the author of eight books of fiction, most recently *A Kind of Flying* (selected stories) from W.W. Norton, and the young adult novel *The Speed of Light* (Harpercollins). He teaches writing at Arizona State University.

LAURENCE DAVIES teaches comparative literature at Dartmouth College and edits the collected letters of Joseph Conrad. His stories have appeared in *New England Review, Natural Bridge, Mystic River Review, StoryQuarterly,* and *The Diagram.* He is finishing a novel, *The Cup of the Dead,* and putting together a collection of his microfictions.

GEORGE GARRETT is the Henry Hoyns Professor of Creative Writing at the University of Virginia and the author of twenty-five books. His most recent are: *The Sorrows of Fat City, Whistling in the Dark,* and *My Silk Purse and Yours.* In 1989 he received the T. S. Eliot Award, and more recently won the PEN/Faulkner Bernard Malamud Award for Short Fiction.

KATHERINE HAAKE is the author of two collection of stories, *No Reason on Earth* and *The Height and Depth of Everything*, and of the novel, *That Water, Those Rocks*. Her book on creative writing is titled *In What Our Speech Disrupts: Feminism and Creative Writing Studies*. She teaches at California State University.

LISE HAINES is the author of the novel *In My Sister's Country*. She has twice been a finalist for the PEN Nelson Algren Fiction Award, and has published a collection of poetry. Her work has appeared in a number of literary journals, including Ploughshares, Agni, Crosscurrents and Post Road. Lise Haines is a writer-in-residence at Emerson College and lives with her daughter in Massachusetts.

HESTER KAPLAN is the author of a collection of stories, *The Edge of Marriage*, which received the Flannery O'Connor Award for Short Fiction, and a novel, *Kinship Theory*. Her fiction has been widely published and twice included in *The Best American Short Stories*. She teaches writing at Rhode Island School of Design.

CHRISTOPHER KEANE's forthcoming novel is titled *Christmas Babies*. He is currently writing a screenplay, *The Venus Coalition*, for actor Anthony Quinn, and he teaches a graduate workshop at Emerson College in Boston.

WILLIAM MELVIN KELLEY has published four novels, including the recently reissued *A Different Drummer*, and a book of stories titled *Dancers on the Shore*. He teaches at Sarah Lawrence.

THOMAS E. KENNEDY is the author of *Realism and Other Illusions: Essays on the Craft of Fiction* (Wordcraft, 2002). His most recent books of fiction include the *Copenhagen Quartet*—*Kerrigan's Copenhagen* (2002), *Bluett's Blue Hours* (2003), *Greene's Summer* (2004)—and currently in progress—*Breathwaite's Fall* (2005), all published by Wynkin de Worde. His stories have won featured O. Henry, Pushcart, Angoff, Gulf Coast, and other awards. He lives in Copenhagen, Denmark.

ROD KESSLER, author of *Off In Zimbabwe*, a collection of stories, is completing work on a novel, *Edelman Unsung*. He teaches writing at Salem State College, where he is also editor of *The Sextant* and an alternating director of the Eastern Writers' Conference.

WILLIAM KITTREDGE is the author of *The Nature of Generosity*, as well as an autobiographical book titled *Hole in the Sky* and two previous books, *Owning It All* and *We Are Not in This Together*. He teaches at the University of Montana.

ELIZABETH LIBBEY has published three volumes of poetry: *The Crowd Inside*, *Songs of a Returning Soul*, and *All That Heat in a Cold Sky*. She teaches writing workshops at Trinity College in Hartford, Connecticut.

MARGOT LIVESEY is the award-winning author of a story collection, *Learning by Heart*, and the novels *Homework*, *Criminals*, and *The Missing*

World. Born in Scotland, she currently lives in the Boston area and teaches at Emerson College.

ALISON LURIE's novels include *Foreign Affairs* and *The Truth About Lorin Jones*. She is also the author of *Girls and Boys Forever: Children's Classics From Cinderella to Harry Potter*. She is the Frederic J. Whiton Professor of American Studies at Cornell.

ROBIE MACAULEY is the author of two novels, a collection of short stories, and two nonfiction books. His *Technique in Fiction* (with George Lanning) has been reissued by St. Martin's Press.

DAVID MADDEN is the author of *Bijou, The Suicide's Wife,* and other novels, short stories, plays, poetry, critical studies, and textbooks. He has conducted workshops in creative writing for over twenty-five years and has taught writing at Louisiana State University since 1968.

CAROL-LYNN MARRAZZO is a teacher and writer who lives in New Hampshire. She received an M.F.A from Vermont College in Montpelier and is currently completing a collection of stories titled *Closing Time*.

ALEXANDRA MARSHALL is a Boston writer whose novels include *Gus in Bronze, Tender Offer, The Brass Bed, Something Borrowed,* and *The Court of Common Pleas*.

CHRISTOPHER NOËL is the author of the novel, *Hazard and the Five Delights*, and the memoir, *In the Unlikely Event of a Water Landing*. He teaches in the Vermont College M.F.A. program.

JOY NOLAN was a Writing Fellow at the Fine Arts Work Center in Provincetown. She holds an M.F.A from Vermont College.

DAVID RAY's most recent books are *Not Far from the River* and *The Maharani's New Wall and Other Poems*. *Sam's Book* won the Maurice English Poetry Award in 1988. He is a professor of English at the University of Missouri–Kansas City where he teaches both fiction and poetry workshops.

FREDERICK REIKEN's first novel *The Odd Sea* won the Hackney Literary Award and was selected by both *Booklist* and *Library Journal* as one of the best first novels of 1998. His second novel, *The Lost Legends of New Jersey,* was a *New York Times* "Notable Book of 2000" and *Los Angeles Times* "Best Book of the Year." His short fiction has been published in *The New Yorker*. He teaches at Emerson College in Boston.

KEN RIVARD recently finished a screenplay about a mother and son coping with the son's learning disability and is currently working on a collection of stories and a novel. He teaches a fiction workshop in the Harvard Extension Program.

LORE SEGAL is the author of *Her First America, Other People's Houses,* and more than twenty books for children. She teaches at Ohio State University.

THALIA SELZ has contributed fiction to many magazines, including *Partisan Review, Antaeus, Chicago,* and *New Letters.* Her stories have been anthologized in *Best American Short Stories* and *O. Henry Prize Stories.* She has won twenty-three literary prizes and fellowships. She teaches at Trinity College in Hartford, Connecticut.

PETER JAY SHIPPY is the author of *Thieves Latin,* published by the University of Iowa Press. His poetry and Fiction have appeared in *Ploughshares, The Boston Review, Denver Quarterly,* bookerangUK.com, and elsewhere. In 2003 he was awarded a creative writing fellowship from the NEA. He teaches at Emerson College.

SHARON SHEEHE STARK has published two books of fiction, *The Dealer's Yard and Other Stories* and *A Wrestling Season.* She is a contributor to the *Atlantic,* a recipient of Guggenheim and National Endowment of the Arts fellowships, and is on the faculty of the Vermont College M.F.A. Program in Montpelier.

JAMES THOMAS is the author of *Pictures, Moving,* a collection of stories, and the coeditor of *Sudden Fiction, Sudden Fiction International,* and *Flash Fiction.* He teaches fiction writing at Wright State University, where he also codirects a summer writing program for public school teachers.

MELANIE RAE THON 's most recent novel is *Sweethearts.* She is also the author of the novels *Meteors in August* and *Iona Moon,* and the story collections *First, Body: Stories* and *The Girls in the Grass.* She teaches at the University of Utah.

Credits

Index